THE SOCIAL AND POLITICAL CONFLICT IN PRUSSIA,

1858-1864

THE SOCIAL AND POLITICAL
CONFLICT IN PRUSSIA,

1858-1864

By

EUGENE N. ANDERSON

1968

OCTAGON BOOKS, INC.

New York

Reprinted 1968
by special arrangement with the University of Nebraska Press
OCTAGON BOOKS, INC.
175 FIFTH AVENUE
NEW YORK, N. Y. 10010

LIBRARY OF CONGRESS CATALOG CARD NUMBER: 68-16772

Printed in U.S.A. by
NOBLE OFFSET PRINTERS, INC.
NEW YORK 3, N. Y.

To the students and faculty
of the University of Nebraska

contents

preface

THE present study developed out of a desire to understand the character of liberalism and conservatism in Prussia on the eve of German unification. Who were the liberals? Who were the Conservatives? What were their ideals and how did they conduct themselves in public? How powerful was each group in the state? In conflict throughout the Nineteenth Century, the opponents reached the peak of their antagonism in the years between 1858 and 1866, the the years of the New Era, the constitutional conflict, and the first two wars of German unification. Fundamental social, economic, and political ideals were at stake. One group would have aligned the country with the West; the other sought to preserve the Old Regime. Since the story of Bismarck's crushing defeat of the liberals by his *Realpolitik* after 1864 is well known, the present analysis concentrates upon the internal crisis of 1858 to 1864 within Prussia; and in keeping with the nature of the subject, the method of treatment is topical rather than chronological.

Analyses of social and institutional forces in conflict in the past century and a half should be made for each of the European countries. The Old Regime survived over much of the continent well into the Twentieth Century, and controversies like the one in Prussia occurred in every state. The present study can be justified not merely as a treatment of a crucial period in German history but as an essential chapter in the history of modern Europe. It should help toward making possible a comparative analysis of society and institutions in the modern world, by means of which we should, for example, be able to explain the remarkable difference between the course of development of Europe and that of the United States.

The preliminary research for the present volume was done in Germany over two decades ago. The long delay in completing the work is to be explained first by the author's study of the Stein-Hardenberg period and then by government service. A Social Science Research Fellowship in 1930-31 and further financial assistance from the Research Council of the University of Nebraska have aided substantially in the writing of this book. In addition, the University has made possible its publication. The author wishes to express his gratitude to both organizations.

The extent to which his wife has participated in making this book will be appreciated only by those who know her.

I

THE ISSUES

1 / How the Conflict Arose

I N 1858 King Frederick William IV of Prussia became mentally deranged and had to relinquish the royal authority to his brother, Prince William. The Regent quickly ousted most of the Conservatives in the ministry and appointed right-wing liberals in their stead. The people of Prussia interpreted the Regent's words and actions as an indication of liberalism. In the elections to the Lower House of the Landtag in the next year they threw out the Conservative majority in favor of the liberals. During the course of the next three years, popularly called the New Era because of the hope for the liberal reform of Prussia and the national unification of Germany, the ruler and the liberal majority learned to their dismay that each wished something different from the other. The former harbored two aims, to reform and strengthen the army and to keep his absolute power, while the latter was equally determined to reform Prussia in a liberal sense and to unify Germany. Both William and the liberals confused reality with desire. The Prince thought that he was governing a Prussia like that of his beloved father, Frederick William III (d. 1840), but actually he faced a state in which society had considerably altered. The liberals believed that the Regent appreciated the needs of the time and could be led or pushed into a movement of reform. Through initial misunderstanding and subsequent refusal to compromise they drifted by 1862 into a constitutional conflict. The ruler, who became King on the death of his brother in January, 1861, dismissed the liberal ministers in the next year, again turned to the Conservatives, and in September, 1862, appointed Bismarck as Minister President. The selection of this Junker statesman signified that the controversy over the meaning of the constitution would be resolved by *Machtpolitik*.

In spite of the fact that the elections to the Lower House in 1861 and in 1862 had almost eliminated the Conservatives, the government, through the exercise of all possible pressure upon the voters, tried in 1863 to replace the overwhelming liberal majority by Conservatives. The attempt failed; but the King and his Conservative ministers continued to rule, and as a result of their successful resistance to the liberals they imparted to the constitution the absolutistic interpretation that they wished. Apparently so promising at the beginning of the New Era, liberalism went down to crushing defeat.

How did the conflict between the liberals on the one hand and the King and the Conservatives on the other come about? An explanation involves, first, a portrayal of the ruler's character, second, a comparison between his aims and those of the liberals, and third, a summary of the economic and social changes that had occurred in Prussia since the formative years of the new ruler's youth.

The Prince Regent in 1858 was already sixty-one years old. He had fought in the War of Liberation against Napoleon with the distinction expected of a royal prince and had spent his life in the army. As a second son he had never been intended for the kingship and had received no preparatory training for that position. The family had expected that Frederick William, the eldest son, would ascend the throne, that in due time he would have a male heir, and that Prince William would remain one of the many minor Hohenzollerns, a younger son on the periphery of power, adept, if he had the energy and ambition, in the military (other professions were scarcely of comparable worth) and adjusted to a life of frustration. With the position of supreme power in the state at stake, too thorough and all-round an education might have made a second son dangerous to the legitimate heir; it might have led to comparisons and aroused troublesome ambitions. A careful restriction of training and, after maturity, of employment offered assurance of family and state harmony. No more efficient school in subordination could have been found in the uneventful years after 1815 than the Prussian army.

By the time he became ruler Prince William was too old to change his fundamental views and ways of doing things. He belonged to the ranks of those Hohenzollerns with modest talents and steadiness of character, for he had the moderate and tenacious personality of his father and he lacked entirely the brilliance of his older brother. He had no relations with the artistic and intellectual life of the period. He was first of all a Hohenzollern and then an officer, but an officer of the ordinary, unimaginative, military type and not one like Boyen with a love of literature and philosophy. His model was not that of Frederick the Great but of Frederick William III, his father, a dull, commonsense, conservative person, who in the Napoleonic period had had to be pushed into taking every decision that made him famous and who had reverted to the commonplace as soon as the pressure of international affairs had been removed. Prince William was content to abide within the spiritual limitations of his character, concentrating his emotions as well as his intellect upon the responsibilities of his office. Possessed of a fine sense of moral uprightness and an aversion to hypocrisy, he lived in accordance with the Prussian tradition of frugality, asceticism and the categorical imperative. In keeping with this tradition he appreciated and expected ability in his advisers and loyally held to men of greater talent than himself. He had no understanding of popular politics and did not acquire any after he became ruler. Indeed, he seems to have disliked politics from an instinctive aversion to any source of competition with Hohenzollern power.

As soon as Prince William became Regent, he formulated a program to which he clung tenaciously. The nature of the entire program, consisting mainly of a set of moral standards, can be judged from the initial sentences. After justifying his change of ministers on grounds of harmony of views, he said that "there should not be at present and there should never be any talk of a break with the past. The careful, improving hand shall be laid upon that which shows itself to be arbitrary or contrary to the needs of the time."

The program reflected the inconsistency of thought in William's mind. During the Manteuffel period the Prince had shown a deep antipathy to the hypocrisy, intrigue and brutality of the Conservatives in power and had expressed himself freely against their activity. He had thereby acquired their enmity, and he knew that they had tried as long as possible to prevent his becoming Regent. His program was aimed to rebuke the Conservatives and encourage the mildest form of liberalism, under the one fundamental condition that the monarch retain his power. Thus he spoke of kingship by divine right but also of abiding loyally by the constitution, of advocating apparently liberal reforms but of keeping within the historical tradition of absolutism. The passages about preserving the ruler's authority were clear and emphatic and were repeated throughout the entire document; the statements about reforms never rose above the general, except on the subjects of the military and of taxation to support it. It is clear that the author of this program leaned far more toward the past than toward the future, that his interest in reform was limited by his determination to preserve his own power by divine right, and that in his conception the process of reform consisted of the Landtag's approving his proposals. His idea of kingship under the constitution of 1850 conformed to that held by Conservatives in about every sphere of life. Just as under pressure from the liberals the Conservatives later proposed to have the survivals of the Old Regime—the patrimonial police power, for example—confirmed to them by law, so William regarded the constitution as a legal support to his absolute authority.

The King's lack of understanding of liberalism was evident in his personnel policy. In revamping the ministry in 1858, he appointed right-wing liberals like Count von Schwerin, a type he called conservative constitutionalist;[1] but at the same time he retained von der Heydt as Minister of Commerce and soon added the reactionary General von Roon as Minister of War. The conception of ministerial unity was alien to him; while the ministry had a Minister President, the latter acted as *primus inter pares* and exercised slight authority over the others. The system assured the King greater power by enabling him to pick whom he wished as advisers without being dependent upon one prime minister or one party for the selection of the other members. In the same way William refused to oust reactionary officials from their positions even when their abuse of power had been notorious. When the liberals urged him to dismiss police president Zedlitz in Berlin, as infamous a reactionary as could be found serving the Manteuffel ministry, the King refused, flatly and angrily. One expected officials to be demigods, he scornfully said.[2] Officials existed, he believed, to carry out his orders; they should take on the qualities required of them. That they might sabotage or misinterpret the King's instructions and continue quietly to play the tyrant without the victim's being able to obtain justice was far beyond William's comprehension. Such a thing smacked of politics. The machine of officials, geared for decades to authoritarianism, remained unchanged by the liberal ministers in organization and personnel and stood ready for Bismarck to set again in motion.

Although the King preferred as advisers and ministers men of authoritarian, aristocratic qualities like his own, he could not always handle them. His honest revulsion against hypocrisy could not and

---

[1] *Aus dem Leben Theodor von Bernhardis*, 1834-71 (Leipzig, 1893-1906), IV, 182, 187; *Kaiser Wilhelms des Grossen Briefe, Reden und Schriften,* edited by Ernst Berner (Berlin, 1906) , II, 22.

[2] *Ibid.,* pp. 106-7, 126-27. Zedlitz later became involved in political scandal and in 1861 had to be ousted.

did not compensate for the effects of his intellectual limitations. Persons like Bismarck could convince him, in case it was in his interest and he wished to be convinced, that black was white. Although usually wrong in the fundamental decisions of his career, as a rule he had the extraordinary capacity for being led back to the right track without loss of face or self-confidence. The constitutional conflict offered rich examples of specious reasoning which he was persuaded to believe as honest fact.

Early in his military career Prince William had concluded that the army needed to be reformed—the size increased, the reserves brought under the direct control of the regular officers, and the term of service lengthened. As long as his father and brother reigned, he had been unable to make headway with his ideas; but as soon as he himself assumed power he set to work to achieve his life's purpose. Of one thing he was sure—that he understood military affairs and knew what reforms the army needed. He asserted flatly that anyone, whether military or civilian, who disagreed with him on this question possessed neither the necessary knowledge nor good judgment. To have the Lower House of the Landtag, for which in any case he had little respect, criticize his military program and refuse the funds for carrying it out angered and personally offended him.

Prince William did not comprehend what a flood of reform demands he caused by his modest proposals. His conception of the kind of society in which he lived may be seen from a statement in his program of 1858 about education. The different classes of the population should be given the "necessary education without raising these classes [he meant social classes] above their proper sphere." All too obviously, he still thought of society as it existed in the Old Regime. Although he had bourgeois acquaintances, the society of industrialism and commerce, of freedom of activity and thought, was unknown to him.

The liberal masses were not aware of the ruler's autocratic beliefs and during the New Era supposed that he was on their side. From the little town of Angerburg in East Prussia came an address to that unregenerate democratic deputy, Waldeck: "The people look with trust to you as its courageous fighter for right and truth. Hail to our Royal House! Twice hail to it when men like you are its advisers! The Royal House stands firmly for eternity; its foundation is the people." The non-Prussian *Weser-Zeitung* stated in January, 1861, that there now "sits on the Prussian throne a man whom the German liberals would confidently like to see march at their head." Early in 1861 the *Kölnische Zeitung* jubilantly remarked about the King's proclamation "To My People": "We do not know what we would add to this masterful address of our King William other than a thousand-fold 'yes'! . . . Not only Prussia but all Germany will listen to the glorious words of King William, whose name recalls the greatness of princes, the constitution, legal freedom, for they know that a man wears Prussia's Crown who is as good as his word."[3]

The liberal enthusiasm about the new ruler was hardly justified. As early as 1859 Prince William was becoming alarmed over the effects of his action. The reappearance in politics of persons like Jacoby and Rodbertus, who had been active in the Revolution of 1848, greatly disturbed him.[4] The liberal ministers were pressing him for more reforms, and specific ones, for they in turn were being urged to act by the majority in the Lower House. One of the two reforms in which the ruler was interested, namely, the military, was intensely disliked by all liberals as a measure preserving those Prussian social and institutional forces which the liberals wished to overcome—militarism, caste and absolutism. The liberal ministers were caught between a ruler increasingly concerned about losing his own power and a Lower House of liberals determined to see Prussia reformed and the constitution become a fact.

By the time of the opening of the Landtag in January, 1860, the ministers had persuaded the Regent to state somewhat specifically the reforms he supported. On the question of national unification he remained vague, but he urged reform of the land tax, and he reported that the conditions of provincial and local government were being investigated and that a bill concerning county government would be introduced into the Landtag. These statements marked an advance over the vague phrases of 1858. He proposed to introduce a bill to fix the election districts, a crying need to prevent the repetition of the scandalous gerrymandering in the Manteuffel era. He promised a bill to legalize civil marriage and one to improve education. He devoted most attention, however, to urging the approval of the military reforms. Nor did he offer anything more at the opening of the Landtag in 1861.[5]

---

[3] *Tagesbericht*, No. 75, March 30, 1861, quoting *Volkszeitung* (Berlin), No. 75; *Tagesbericht*, No. 17, Jan. 21, 1861; *ibid*, No. 7, Jan. 9, 1861. The *Tagesbericht* was a summary of the daily press prepared for the King. A copy was to be found in the Prussian State Archives in Berlin-Dahlem.

[4] Von Bernhardi, *op. cit.*, III, 156-57.

[5] Horst Kohl, *Dreissig Jahre preussisch-deutscher Geschichte 1858–1888 in amtlichen Kundgebungen* (Giessen, 1888), pp. 12-15, 20-23.

One may imagine that the liberals would scarcely be satisfied with such a meager program of reform, especially in view of the sacrifices they were expected to make for the sake of strengthening the army. They noted the absence of any reference to reform of the solidly Conservative Upper House or to the introduction of ministerial responsibility; they noted the absence of action against reactionary officials; they were disturbed by the apathy toward national unification and by the general inability to accomplish anything. Their reaction to the King's opening address to the Landtag in 1861 was, according to one observer, glacial.[6]

The aggressive wing of the liberals began in 1860 to take steps toward organizing a vigorous, active party. The next year the German Progressive party emerged, and it soon became the most powerful of all the liberal groups in the state. The election of 1861 reduced radically the number of right-wing Old Liberals or Constitutionals, who had been the government's main supporters, and returned in their stead the Progressives and the like-minded Left-Center party, the one especially powerful in the East, the other in the West, and both in the Central provinces. Between a stubborn ruler and an aggressive Lower House, the liberal ministers found themselves in a more embarrassing position than ever. They urged the slogan "Do not Press!", which the Lower House was decidedly disinclined to heed.

By 1862 the cleft between the King and the liberals could scarcely have been wider. The more acute the conflict became, the more irascible grew the monarch. Easily roused to anger, he was at times inclined to weep. Accustomed to obedience as an officer, a Hohenzollern and a king, he was distressed by the outcome of the elections and needed reassurance of the devotion of his people.

Angry at the Conservatives in the early part of the period, Prince William had resisted their efforts to intrigue against the liberal ministers. When in 1858 Count Eberhard Stolberg, one of the Conservative leaders, had tried to interest William in the plan to establish a Conservative newspaper, the Regent had opposed it and spoken in a decidedly liberal vein.[7] In 1859 he said to the intriguing Stolberg, "In short, this is my ministry and will remain so as long as I live and reign."[8] The Regent disapproved thoroughly of the Conservatives' resistance to reform of the land tax. Since he needed the extra money to support his military, he forced the tax bill through the

[6] Von Bernhardi, *op. cit.*, IV, 135-36.
[7] *Ibid.*, III, 228.
[8] *Ibid.*, III, 233-34.

Upper House. Thereafter, no basic controversy divided him from the Conservatives, and as he became increasingly involved in difficulty with the liberals, he found the Conservatives, eager to serve him, more and more to his liking.

Throughout the New Era the Conservatives had never lost influence at court. They practically monopolized the positions there and were expert at exerting social pressure through personal channels not subject to public control. By way especially of the royal military attachés and Minister of War von Roon they aroused fear of revolution and encouraged the ruler toward absolutism. In 1862 they utilized the latter's anger at the liberals over the military reforms to return to power in the government. Their embarrassment during the New Era at having to be more royal and more conservative than the King was past; henceforth they crowded behind their lord and their lord's new Minister President, Bismarck, in a fight to the finish against liberalism.

In order to understand the other major side in the constitutional conflict, namely, the liberals, we must analyze the main lines of economic and social change that had occurred in Prussia during the preceding half century. The analysis will reveal why in the elections to the Landtag the opposition proved to be so strong and the Conservatives so weak.

In May, 1862, a liberal newspaper wrote: "The Prussian people are no longer that mass of peasants just freed from serfdom or of servile and powerless town-dwellers that Frederick William III ruled. Just as Berlin has risen in two decades from a wretched town of the royal court with 200,000 population to the leading industrial city of Germany and the second commercial city of North Germany, in the same way Breslau, Cologne, Magdeburg and other provincial towns have also grown to be large commercial centers. The anger of the government can no longer strike the big industrialists and merchants of these cities as long as they observe the law. Despotism is no longer possible; the Prussian people have become too intelligent and wealthy for it. The more the estate-owner has withdrawn from community affairs, the more independent the peasant has become. We use the word 'peasant,' which will soon be only a myth, to refer to persons whom it no longer describes. In many areas the peasant already behaves like a townsman and feels and thinks like one. He no longer stands in his village, isolated and dependent upon his own physical strength; through common interests and contacts he has become a conscious part of the nation."[9]

---

[9] Quoted in *Königsberg Hartungsche Zeitung*, May 8, 1862.

Although somewhat exaggerated, particularly in its description of the peasant, the article correctly estimated the general situation.

Between 1816 and 1858, when Prince William became regent, the population of Prussia had increased from 10,320,000 to 17,673,000. By 1864 it rose to 19,200,000. The increase had been a steady one, with the largest gains registered since 1830. All parts of the country had participated in the growth, the Administrative Districts of Liegnitz, Erfurt, Münster, Minden and Aachen showing least, percentagewise, and Köslin, Oppeln and Bromberg enjoying the largest. Some predominantly agricultural Districts had grown in population as much as those with developing industries. A breakdown of the increase by decades discloses that up to 1849 for the state as a whole the rural population had grown faster than the urban; after that date the reverse was true. By the end of 1858 there were in the rural areas 1,672, and in the towns 1,817 persons for every 1,000 in 1816; in 1840 the comparable figures had been 1,461 and 1,411, and in 1849, they had been 1,575 and 1,590.[10]

While the towns and cities with a population of about a thousand or more had scarcely increased in number (some 994 in 1860) since the close of the Napoleonic wars, they had shared in the general growth. The greatest gain had occurred in the large cities, which were well scattered over the state. (See Appendix A.) The areas of coal mining and iron and steel works attracted people in particularly large numbers, nearly doubling their population between 1819 and 1861.[11] Since the increase cannot be accounted for by natural growth, the towns and cities were manifestly drawing people from the rural districts and from the small towns that as yet lacked the opportunities being made available by industry and transportation.

Industrial production, especially since the 1830s, had begun to assume factory proportions and to show a growth in size of plant, capitalization and number of workers. The textile and clothing industry remained the largest employer in 1861. The iron, steel and machinery industry ranked a poor second but gave promise of speedily overtaking textiles. Commerce and construction occupied the third and fourth places respectively, with very little difference between them. Production had been changing to meet the needs of the increasing population. Since master tailors could not turn out enough clothes at a low price

[10] See the tables in *Jahrbuch für die amtliche Statistik des Preussischen Staates* (Berlin, 1863), pp. 109-10.

[11] See Gustav Neumann, *Das Deutsche Reich in geographischer, statistischer und topographischer Beziehung* (Berlin, 1874), I, 368.

to satisfy the demand, the factory assumed the responsibility. The building industry had to expand to house the people and the new machines. The master builders were giving way to construction companies. Iron and steel production was adjusting to the opportunities made available by the construction of railroads, gas works, factories, and the numerous other creations of modern technology. Steam engines were becoming fairly common. The results of the changes in production were evident in the statistics on employment. The number engaged in industry was rising. In 1846 it had been 1,343,821; in 1861 it was 1,786,145. The number of handworkers, male and female, during the same time had declined from 1,470,091 to 1,087,924.[12]

The expansion of industry and the resulting increase in the turnover of goods afforded the opportunities for a rapid enlargement of the middle class. Local persons and capital were being mobilized, and new resources were moving from outside into promising centers.[13] By 1860 Prussia had produced a crop of entrepreneurs in each town except those remaining largely local in character; even in the latter, individuals were to be found who were eager to participate in the economic growth and were angry over the frustration of their ambitions. The number of persons who, beginning with modest or almost no means, succeeded in a few decades in accumulating a considerable amount of wealth or even, for those times, a fortune was comparable to that in other continental countries. These provided the leaders in the development of industrial society. The process remained in an early stage; but by 1860 the outlines of the future social organization were fairly clear.

The changes in the countryside lacked the sharpness of cultural outline of those in the towns, but they were nonetheless real and important. After the Battle of Jena the effort to aid in the revival of Prussia by emancipating the peasants had aroused the ambitions of the rural people and put land in the category of mobile property along with factories and other urban objects. By 1860 peasant emancipation had produced marked economic results. An area of 56,683,005 Morgen of land with 1,478,022 owners had been freed of manorial restrictions. By April 1, 1859, mortgages to the amount of 78,568,380

[12] In 1846 Prussia possessed 1,139 steam engines with 21,715 horsepower; in 1861, the figures were 6,669 engines with 137,377 horsepower. *Jhb. für die amtliche Statistik des Preuss. Staates* (1863), pp. 460-62.

[13] See, for example, the situation in Stettin described in *Bremer Handelsblatt*, March 19, 1859, pp. 121-23.

Thalers had been issued.[14] When one considers that in every case property ownership and in most cases money transactions had been involved, that in every case legal rights and claims had been at stake, one must conclude that a large percentage of the peasantry was being compelled to cultivate the virtues of private ownership and initiative to keep its property. The peasant was forced to assume some of the characteristics of the urbanite; he had to deal in money, to calculate. The responsibilities accruing from emancipation were pushing him into modern society.

The effects upon the large landowners were more evident than those upon the peasantry. Even in the preceding century large-scale agrarians had begun to buy and sell land in order to take advantage of rising prices. In this way some burghers had been able to purchase noble estates (Rittergüter) and other extensive properties, erasing the sharp social and economic separation between town and country. After the period of the Stein-Hardenberg reforms the process had continued at a speedy pace. Although the evidence about land transactions in the Nineteenth Century is inadequate, some trends are to be discerned. Many persons from the Western provinces, the Rhineland and Westphalia, where land was expensive, had been purchasing estates in the Eastern provinces, where land was considerably cheaper. The 1820s and '30s had been hard on owners in the Eastern provinces, who having bought their land at high prices had suffered greatly from the severe decline in the price of agricultural products. Except in Silesia, where many estate-owners had come through the crisis years primarily by raising sheep and selling the wool in the world market, the turnover in estates had been large. Wealthy burghers had bought land not merely around the larger towns and cities but even in remote areas. Droysen, a contemporary expert, published the following data on the ownership of noble estates in 1859.[15]

[14] As many as 82,855 peasant holdings had been established with 5,497,085 Morgen of land; 1,180,133 other properties had been freed of servile duties, involving the abolition of 6,319,352 days of service by animals and 23,444,396 days of personal service. In compensation the peasants had paid or agreed to pay 34,210,962 Thalers in capital, 5,347,323 Thalers in money rent, 287,972 Scheffels of rye, 10,633 Scheffels of wheat, barley and oats, and 1,630,055 Morgen of land. Dr. Georg von Viebahn, *Statistik des zollvereinten und Nördlichen Deutschlands* (Berlin, 1858-68), II, 584-85. A Scheffel was equal to about 1½ bushels, a Morgen nearly an acre, a Thaler about 3 marks, or 75 cents.

[15] Eduard Pfeifer, "Über die Grundsteuer," *Vierteljahrschrift für Volkswirtschaft und Kulturgeschichte* (1864), IV, 96 note. Johannes Ziekursch, *Ein Hundert Jahre Schlesischer Agrargeschichte* (Breslau, 1927), pp. 328, 386. August Meitzen, *Der Boden und die landwirtschaftlichen Verhältnisse des Preussischen Staates* (Berlin, 1868-71), I, 502-3; III, 116, 411, 430-32, 596-98. Von Viebahn, *op. cit.*, II, 984-93.

Prussia	2,313	Noble estates, of which	788	were in burgher possession, or	34%
Posen	1,440	"	957	"	66
Pomerania	1,654	"	1,046	"	64
Branden-burg	1,798	"	1,116	"	62
Silesia	3,132	"	1,857	"	59
Saxony	1,047	"	563	"	54
Westphalia	425	"	378	"	89
Rhineland	466	"	318	"	68
Total	12,275		7,023		Average 57%

A contemporary writer of an informative work on the province of Prussia stated that in 1859 only fifty-nine estates in the entire province had remained in the possession of the same family for at least a hundred years, whereas in Brandenburg there were 395 such estates. He concluded that "a real landed aristocracy" practically no longer existed in the province of Prussia.[16] All in all, with the exception of a few areas, the writer's conclusion about the province of Prussia seems to have applied to the entire state; land had become a commodity of sale and had in the main lost its prestige as the basis for an aristocratic caste. Too many of the estate-owners, whether of noble or of burgher origin, were paying tribute to the ways of capitalism for them to pass as traditional gentry.

The evidence is augmented by a consideration of the expansion of industry into the rural areas. In the Eighteenth Century noblemen had built on their estates distilleries, saw mills, and other kinds of businesses closely associated with agriculture; but by 1860 both the variety and the number of these industries had greatly increased. It was estimated that 64,445 such enterprises were then in operation and that they employed 229,500 technicians and workers. The list included lime burners, brick kilns, several kinds of mills, factories for preparing foods, tobacco factories, sugar refineries, breweries, and so on. By 1861 there were in use for agricultural purposes 242 steam engines with 4,172 horsepower (in 1846 the figures had been 48 and 504 respectively); the saw mills in 1861 used 230 steam engines of 2,913 horsepower (in 1846 the figures had been 25 and 268 respectively); the flour mills in the same year employed 600 steam engines of 8,101 horsepower (in 1846 the figures had been 71 and 927 respectively). Although flour milling was also being done in the towns, one can perceive that the gentry knew the value of modern machinery and methods. The evidence makes conditions sound dangerously like capitalism,

[16] *Die Provinz Preussen* (Königsberg, 1863), pp. 430, 434.

with all the resulting implications of social mobility and the break-down of the caste-state. When one adds the story of the establishment in the villages and rural districts of many factories by bona fide businessmen of burgher origin,[17] the impression is strengthened that the ways of the middle class, the curse of vulgar materialism, the pursuit of Mammon, had overcome the stronghold of Junker moral purity, and that the difference in standards and objectives between town and country was far less noticeable in 1860 than in 1815 or even 1840. Some aristocrats, like the Prince of Pless, went into business on a large scale at the same time that they tried to remain lords of the Old Regime. This type eventually became the backbone of the Free Conservative party and accepted national unification and the economic legislation put through by Bismarck.

Too little is known about the social history of the nobility in the Nineteenth Century for us to be able to state how many aristocrats remained loyal to the Old Regime, how many took the line of the Prince of Pless, and how many turned liberal. It is clear that in the half century or more prior to the constitutional conflict the material and the social structure of the large landownership had been in a process of rapid transformation. Not merely the emancipation of the peasantry and the legalization of the sale of landed estates had brought about this change; the desire to take advantage of the developing opportunties to make money had seized upon this class and was imparting to it some of the characteristics of the bourgeoisie. Material interests were drawing the rural population, aristocratic and peasant, in the direction of liberalism. Whether the attraction proved to be superior to that of the Old Regime depended upon one's social ideals and one's knowledge and understanding of the forces of the age.

The most striking example of the material facilities for change was offered by the improvement in the means of transportation and communication. During the quarter of a century prior to 1860 Prussia had built a railroad system of 737.9 Prussian miles, of which 231.3 miles were double-tracked.[18] In 1816 Prussia had had 419.8 Prussian miles of all-season roads; by 1862 it had 3,756.2 miles. Likewise the local roads were being improved with state aid. People and goods were moving on a scale unprecedented in history. The rate of awakening to non-local interests can be seen from the four-fold increase in

---

[17] Meitzen, *op. cit.*, I, 336 ff.; *Jhb. für die amtliche Statistik des Preuss. Staates* (1863), pp. 461-62.

[18] A Prussian mile was equal to 7,420.4 meters. Meitzen, *op. cit.*, III, 232, 600.

the number of letters sent through the mail between 1842 and 1860 and in the ten-fold increase in the number of telegrams sent in the 1850s.[19] Speed was becoming valuable.

Higher education exhibited far less change than the economic and social aspects of Prussian life. The universities, which should have acted as intellectual leaders, preserved the standard curriculum of half a century earlier. Except in theoretical and experimental science, they had made few concessions to the needs of the developing industrial society. In the summer semester of 1820 there had been 2,368 students in the Prussian universities; in the summer semester of 1861 there were 4,466 students.[20] In only one area, that of the Humanities and the Social Sciences, had the percentage increase in enrollment exceeded that of the population. In consequence there were, for example, fewer doctors per capita in the state than there had been in 1849 (one doctor to 3,076 people in 1861, one to 2,929 in 1849), and in four Administrative Districts the number in absolute terms had declined. As for technical schools, Prussia possessed only one which might be called a school of engineering and it was of modest proportion (385 students in 1864). Most young men had to study that subject in other states. The presence of a couple of small mining schools and an agricultural institute could scarcely compensate for the absence of other facilities. Official Prussia had not yet become aware of the fact that industrialism was able to raise the general standard of living and greatly enhance the per-capita need for professional services.[21]

In 1860 Prussian society was on the move. The hope and promise of a new culture were found over most of the state, in town and country and among all classes. By the time of the constitutional conflict the psychological adjustments of the population varied from that of the person who still tried to be a grand seigneur of the Old Regime while participating on a large scale in modern industrial activity to that of the individual who saw clearly the implications for the total

[19] *Ibid.*, III, 221, 232, 286, 290.

[20] Of these, 729 had studied Evangelical theology, 153 Catholic theology, 741 law, 398 medicine, 347 humanities and what passed as social science. In the summer session of 1861 there were 4,466 students, among them 1,040 in Evangelical theology, 596 in Catholic theology, 655 in law, 753 in medicine, 1,422 in humanities and social sciences. During that time the population had grown from ten million to eighteen million. *Tabellen und Amtliche Nachrichten über den Preussischen Staat für das Jahr 1849*, Hrsg. vom Statistischen Bureau zu Berlin (Berlin, 1851), II, 573-74; *Preussische Statistik*, Hrsg. vom Kgl. Statistischen Bureau in Berlin (1864), p. 47; von Viebahn, *op. cit.*, III, 1146-49.

[21] On the number of doctors and druggists see *Zeitschrift des Kgl. Preussischen Statistischen Bureaus* (Berlin, 1863), pp. 236-39.

culture of changing from a society of caste and local economy to one of mobility. The economic and social turn toward liberalism did not necessarily entail the introduction of political and governmental freedom, but a trend lay definitely in that direction. Could a state introduce freedom into its economy and social organization while preserving absolutism in its government? While the liberals thought not, the King remained emotionally bound to the Old Regime, even when he paid lip service to constitutionalism. The Conservatives were determined to preserve the past and hated the constitution and all those ideals for which it stood. Out of this opposition of cultural values developed the crisis of the early 1860s, when the institutional organization and distribution of political and social power in Prussia and Germany were decided for the next two generations.

2 / Caste and Privilege

ARTICLE FOUR of the Prussian constitution of 1850 stated: "All Prussians are equal before the law. Caste privileges are invalid. Subject to conditions established by law, all public offices are equally open to all who are competent." In 1856 the Conservative leader in the Lower House had introduced a resolution for the abolition of the first two sentences of this article as "wrong" and "reprehensible." The Conservative Minister of Interior had reassured him as follows:

> The government has found and recognized in Article Four the sense that for equal legal conditions, relations and actions equality of the law with respect to the estate shall obtain. But the government has always regarded it as compatible with this position that . . . the special rights and duties of individual estates, classes and corporations which exist according to special and particular laws and are an essential part of the organism of the state—that these special organizations which have the purpose of preserving an estate or a corporation belonging to the State organism—, are not to be regarded as absolutely abolished by Article Four but are far more to be considered as continuing to exist. This interpretation is further to be recognized as correct because the constitution itself sanctions such special legal rights for individual classes and estates—something which it could not do if this recognition contradicted Article Four. Such are the special rights and legal limitations of the military estate, the special rights of judges, the privileges of deputies according to Article Eighty-four.

The minister concluded that it was not necessary to annul Article Four.[1]

---

[1] Ludwig von Roenne, *Das Staats-Recht der Preussischen Monarchie* (Leipzig, 1864), Vol. I, Part 2, pp. 181-82.

The contrast between the explicit words of the constitution and the interpretation given it characterized the Prussian state as a whole. Article Four contained an assertion of a fundamental principle of social organization formulated in the Revolution of 1848. Upon recovering control of the country the Conservatives, not daring to eliminate it, had chosen to annul it by interpretation. To infer that the stipulations of special qualifications, rights and responsibilities of professional groups like military personnel, judges and representatives in the Lower House of the Landtag meant that privileges of the nobility, guildsmen and other sharply separated social groups were also legal transformed Article Four, said the liberals, into an expression of nonsense.

The interpretation of Article Four harmonized with the social ideals to which the Conservatives adhered. They believed in inequality and wished to preserve the organization of society in estates, with each person legally as well as socially restricted to the rights and responsibilities of his caste. Their eyes were directed toward the past, the estates-state; their objective was simply to preserve as much of that social system as they could, above all to preserve the basic structure even if a few concessions in details or in a formal sense, like Article Four, had to be made. The concept of status predominated in their thinking, a concept that opposed social movement and change. It operated in accordance with the ideal of social relationship expressed in the terms lordship and subjection. The three terms summarized the bases of the Conservative social philosophy, the hard core of Conservative behavior around which was elaborated any further theoretical justification.

To the liberals the basic ideal of social philosophy was clearly expressed in Article Four. They interpreted the article as referring to individual persons, and rejected the Conservative interposition of castes and estates, of feudal orders, between the individual person and the state. They believed in freedom of the single person, not freedom of the estate to which the individual members had to be subordinated. They wished, as the liberal Karl Twesten wrote in 1861, "equality before the law and legal security against aristocratic preference and arbitrary power"; they aimed at "the independence and unobstructed development of all for the benefit of all." "Today the world is liberal," Tweston declared with more optimism than truth.[2]

---

[2] Karl Twesten, *Was Uns Noch Retten Kann* (1861), pp. 24-26.

The liberals were starting with the New Era in 1858 the third large-scale attempt in Nineteenth Century Prussian history to transform the state of the Hohenzollerns and Junkers into a modern, free society. During the first attempt, made in the urgent effort to revive the society to fight against Napoleon, the principle of equality had been accepted in law and to some extent in fact. The decree of October 9, 1807, had created the legal possibility for a burgher or a peasant to purchase a noble estate, for a noble or a peasant to take up a burgher occupation, and for a burgher to turn to agriculture. The class restrictions upon occupation were thereby abolished, and in subsequent decades the legal right became an economic reality.[3]

With the elimination of the Napoleonic menace the Conservatives reestablished themselves in authority and restored as much of the Old Regime as they could. The caste restrictions upon the sale and purchase of property could not be re-introduced, for the noble landowners liked the economic advantages of this freedom. But, as we shall see, the nobility succeeded in preserving most of their other privileges and were well established in power when the Revolution of 1848 endangered them once more. The threat to the aristocratic position which arose from a revolution from within proved to be even more serious than that which a half century earlier had come from without in the form of the French under Napoleon. Again the Conservatives were able to survive and to restore their authority, but only by the official introduction of a potentially liberal constitution. When the New Era began, they still controlled Prussia in all the key positions, for even though the constitution used the language of liberalism it remained in 1858 the façade of a society dominated by caste and privilege.

Liberals of all shades agreed that the crucial struggle in Prussia was between Junkerism and the middle class. In April, 1862, the central election committee of the Constitutional party declared in an election broadsheet that "the Prussian people wish and can no longer forego the conclusion of the conflict between burgher and Junkerism."[4] The *National Zeitung* of June 13, 1861, stated that

> . . . According to the program of the German Progressive Party and . . . according to our own conviction the main task for Prussia in our age is the political elevation of the burgher estate. If the burgher estate is politically to carry any weight and to exercise influence on the entire action of the government

---

[3] Von Roenne, *op. cit.*, (1864), Vol. I, Part 2, p. 179.
[4] *Volkszeitung*, April 5, 1862.

to the degree appropriate to it today, it must be represented in a chamber filled with its spirit and independent of any other power. In any case it has to show itself in the Chamber which according to the constitution is called to represent it not as dependent upon the ministry but as a free and strong political power.

Critics will say, the writer continued, that the realization of this claim would give a preferred position to one class, whereas the constitution belonged to the entire nation. The objection could be met by pointing to the fact that a constitutional state should be one of equality before the law, a position supported only by the burghers since the Prussian nobility was hopelessly feudal.

A correspondent from Pomerania to the *Wochenschrift des National-vereins* (November 7, 1862) elaborated upon the shortcomings of the Junkers. These nobles, he asserted, lacked the wealth, the intelligence and the record of public service to maintain their present position. They lacked everything which would justify their retention of power and significance. "It is doubtful," he continued, "whether this party is at all capable of reorganization. ... Pretentious and boastful it presses forward as if to protect the throne, when in reality it is driven only by the narrowest selfishness to find there a refuge for itself." The writer lived in a Junker stronghold and spoke with the anger of one who had learned from experience. Another author complained in the same journal that the equal right of all citizens to occupy state offices existed only on paper, that army officers, ministers and members of the foreign service were almost always aristocrats, that they seem to grow only on family trees. "The real aristocrat, that is, the upper, independent nobility distinguished by rich land holdings, is," he said, "least represented among those who reach for the high and influential positions in the state." This poor court nobility, the Junkers, found the means for its existence solely at court or in state service and therefore eagerly pressed forward into these positions. This nobility, he declared, was "the cancer in our public life."[5]

Neither social origin nor social environment appears to have been basic in conditioning the individual Prussian's attitude toward privilege. One would rightly expect representatives of the middle class, especially from the larger towns and from the Western provinces, to uphold liberalism against the Junkers; but numerous members of the aristocracy condemned their Conservative colleagues as vehemently

[5] *Wochenschrift des Nationalvereins*, Sept. 12, 1862.

as any urban democrat. Freiherr von Vincke, a member of an old and distinguished Westphalian family, depicted them as follows:

> How can a party claim the name 'Conservative' when in the first instance it conserves only its private interests, I may even say, its unconstitutional privileges, when it does not above all conserve that which is the basis of all private right, the public law of the land! How can a party call itself an aristocracy when, unfaithful to the great precedent of the proudest aristocracy of the world, the English, it does not place on its shield the principle of noblesse oblige and press to the front to protect at all times the constitutional rights of the nation![6]

On another occasion the same speaker remarked in the Lower House that as for the claim of the Conservatives to superior patriotism he had not heard that the noble lords had been especially active as subscribers to the recent government loan. "I believe much more," he continued, "that the patriotism of the towns set an example for them at that time."[7]

Von Vincke's colleagues, Professors von Sybel and Gneist, agreed with him completely. "In internal affairs," stated von Sybel in a speech in 1862, "the great conflict of our time is truly not one between crown and parliament but one between the excessive privileges of the nobility and the free right of merit." Gneist asserted that "the lesser rural nobility, alternating as court official and as aide-de-camp, has remained the reason of state in Prussia as in Strelitz" (a small German state).[8]

Religion exercised no more influence upon an individual's view about the Junkers than social position. The right-wing Catholic political leader, Reichensperger-Geldern, criticized the Prussian nobility in terms almost identical with those of the Protestant von Vincke. Like von Vincke, he emphasized the difference between the ideals and behavior of the English and of the German nobility. In England, he said, sharp conflicts between the different classes in society had not appeared as they had in Germany and France and indeed in all con-

[6] *Stenographische Berichte über die Adress-Debatte des Preussischen Abgeordnetenhauses am 27., 28. und 29. Januar 1863* (Berlin, 1863), pp. 171-72. Henceforth referred to as *Adressdebatte 1863*. The debates were published in book form and within a week 100,000 copies were sold. See *Deutsche Vierteljahrschrift* (Stuttgart, 1863), No. 3, p. 92.

[7] *Preussen Stenographische Berichte des Hauses der Abgeordneten*, March 8, 1861; I, 426. Henceforth this source will be referred to as Abg. H., *St. B.*

[8] Julius Heyderhoff (ed.), *Deutscher Liberalismus im Zeitalter Bismarcks* (Bonn and Leipzig, 1925), I, 88 note, 103.

tinental states. England had been spared "the bloody traces" of these conflicts. "Herein lies the punishment for the fact that the French and the German nobility was not receptive to the same knowledge and unselfishness which has made the English nobility and England itself great and glorious and has founded English freedom."[9]

How well entrenched the ideals and practices of privilege and caste were in Prussia in 1860 can be seen from an analysis of the extent to which they dominated the personnel holding the positions of power. At court, in the central government, in the provincial, county and local governments, in the army, wherever political power was exercised, the old Prussia remained largely in control. It held sway over a society which was rapidly increasing the degree of industrialism and commerce, was expanding the professions, and was developing the economic and occupational interests expressed in liberalism. The contrast in the number adhering to the two ways of life, that of caste and privilege and that of liberalism, was extraordinarily sharp; but the former more than compensated for its inferior numerical strength by its occupancy of the strategic positions of authority.

At the top of the structure of power stood the King, William I, filled with faith in his own divine right as ruler and automatically thinking of all Prussians as his subjects. The King had no inclinations whatever toward tyranny. He proposed to be an absolute monarch in the Hohenzollern sense, that is, a ruler who decided personally all issues after consulting the subjects chosen by him as his advisers. A subject who opposed William's authority on a matter of importance to him felt the impact of his anger, whether that subject was a Conservative noble and official or a liberal. When the liberal von Saucken-Julienfelde, an old acquaintance, sought to explain the liberal position during the constitutional conflict, the King would not grant him an audience. When the aristocratic member of the House of Lords, General von der Groben, refused to vote for the land tax reform, the King rebuked him personally and cut him off from court.[10]

The Conservatives were entitled to claim the King—once the liberal ministers could be eliminated. It is clear why the deputation sent to the King in late 1862 and in 1863 to protest the loyalty of the folk to the absolute sovereign and its repugnance to liberalism should have proved to be so effective. The King was deeply moved by these deputations; they represented the Prussian folk as he knew it—peasants, a

[9] Abg. H., *St. B.*, March 9, 1861; I, 440-41.
[10] Von Bernhardi, *op. cit.*, IV, 123-24.

pastor and a country school teacher or two, and a country nobleman to lead them. The society of the Old Regime was perfectly reflected by them; this reflection, moving the King to tears, hardened his heart against the liberals. The Old Regime was the Prussia he could understand, the Prussia for which he had the sympathy of an absolute monarch.

Among the members of the King's immediate family, his wife, a member of one of the lesser German ruling houses, was a staunch liberal. The King had married her after he had been forced to renounce the lady he loved (her noble rank had been too low for a Hohenzollern), and it is doubtful whether Queen Augusta was able in fundamental matters to exercise much influence on her husband. When the Queen urged her views upon him with the zeal of a reformer, the King referred to her in some admiration and awe as a "hot-head." That he was able to resist even her temperament is clearly seen in his relation to Bismarck. She had regarded Bismarck as a bitter enemy since the days of 1848 when as a vehement Junker he had severely criticized the ruling King to her for making any concessions to the revolution and had even proposed, she claimed, to dethrone him. The enmity between the two persisted during the rest of their lives. How much this hostility counted with William may be judged by the fact that in 1862 he appointed Bismarck as Minister President and kept him in power until the end of the reign.

The Crown Prince, William's son, had married a daughter of Queen Victoria of England and was in many respects a liberal. At the height of the constitutional conflict his wife made it known to liberal leaders not only that she read the London *Times* and the *National Zeitung*, the prominent Progressive Party organ in Berlin, but, further, that she sympathized with them. The Crown Prince was treated kindly and respectfully by his father and given some minor share in government; but he lacked the conviction and the courage to defend liberalism against the authority of the crown, and paternal rebuke drove him into silent acquiescence.

While the King was acquainted with many prominent members of the middle class and occasionally associated with them, his regular entourage was drawn from the nobility. Apart from the Queen's and the Crown Prince's personal aides, the court was the incarnation of feudalism. It remained about what it had been under Frederick William IV, a group of noble men and women to whom liberals were repulsive persons unfit for the company of aristocrats. The noble military adjutants, Count von Alvensleben and Edwin von Manteuffel, had more influence upon the King than most of his ministers of the New Era. This feudal, military personnel was constantly spreading rumors of revolution on the part of liberals, democrats and communists: they scarcely distinguished among these factions, labeling any critic of the Old Regime a 'red' and encouraging in the King a mistrust of liberal advisers. The Minister of War, General von Roon, along with other officers, was to be found far more frequently in the King's company than any liberal, whether aristocrat or burgher, and they fed the royal mind with the same kind of reactionism. "Vulgar Philistines," von Roon called the liberals. The liberals knew about the monopoly held by aristocratic Conservatives at court, and the liberal ministers of the New Era were urged to try to modify the situation. The obstacles proved to be too great for them to overcome; the King remained surrounded by persons of the Old Regime.[11]

The extent to which the nobility ran the state may be seen from statistics which a democrat collected and published at Hamburg in 1860. The higher bureaucratic positions were held predominantly by nobles. In the period from April 1, 1858, to April 1, 1860, that is, in the first years of the New Era, six presidents of the provincial administration were appointed, of whom four, or 66.7 per cent, were nobles; ten divisional heads under the presidents were appointed, of whom four, or 40 per cent, were nobles; of the next lower grade only 16.6 per cent were nobles. The position of Landrat was, as we shall see, the most significant one in local goverment; 65.5 per cent of the appointees were nobles. In general, the author estimated, 42.7 per cent of all the newly appointed administrative officials in these years came from the nobility. He showed that the percentages had remained fairly uniform since 1853; that is, the replacement of the Conservative regime of Manteuffel-Westphalen by the supposedly liberal New Era had made almost no difference in the social origin of the powerful administrative personnel.

The same author compiled similar figures for the judicial officials, where, significantly, he found fewer nobles. The judiciary required hard preparatory training and a strict adherence to law which were usually foreign to noble temperaments. The nobility preferred the influential administrative posts, in which aristocratic qualities of leadership could dispense with rigorous intellectual preparation. In 1860, out of 4,964 justice officials, only 463, or 9.3 per cent, were nobles.

---

[11] Martin Philippson, *Max von Forckenbeck* (Leipzig), p. 56; von Bernhardi, *op. cit., passim.*

The percentage of nobles serving as lawyers and notaries was but 5.7. Of the 667 higher officials in the Ministry of Justice, on the Supreme Court, the appellate courts, the courts of first instance, and the higher state attorneys' office, only 114, or 17 per cent, were nobles, while the lower official positions attracted not quite half of even that low figure. The town and city courts were filled almost entirely by persons of burgher origin, and the county judicial system drew no more nobles than the towns, that is, less than 10 per cent. It is not difficult to imagine what pattern took shape: the administrative official, the county Landrat, was an aristocratic conservative who found himself opposed by a burgher county judge devoted to the ideals of liberalism.[12]

The King's ministers were selected almost entirely from the aristocracy. The Minister Presidents from the beginning of his rule to the appointment of Bismarck mirror by their names alone the King's social philosophy. The first was a relative, Prince Karl Anton von Hohenzollern, a figurehead who bore the title until early 1862. When the Prince was able finally to escape the office on grounds of ill health, he was succeeded by the President of the Upper House, Prince von Hohenlohe-Ingolfingen. Neither Minister President took his duties other than lightly; each avoided the work as thoroughly as possible. Their presence, however, assured the King that a line of continuity with the past was being kept. While the other ministers did not have quite such imposing titles, they also came from the nobility. In the ministry of March, 1862, not a single person of burgher origin was to be found. The Berliners called the new crop the "little silent excellencies." One of Bismarck's first acts upon becoming Minister President was to hunt for a burgher to fill at least one ministry, preferably, of course, that of commerce. On similar grounds, Bismarck chose a Jew as his personal banker.

The fact that most of the ministers from 1858 to early 1862 professed to be liberal does not detract from the predominance of caste standards in the selection of the chief officials. In 1848 burghers of the highest ability had been found who were willing to assume the ministerial positions. They could have been selected in the New Era, and under a genuinely liberal king would no doubt have served; but since the King was appalled even at the mild liberalism of some of his appointments, von Patow and von Bonin, for example, it is clear that in his view Prussia should continue to be governed by its aristocracy.

[12] Freimund Gutsmuth, *Patriotische Untersuchungen bezüglich preussischer Zustände* (Hamburg, 1860), pp. 21-29.

He had no feeling for the kind of life out of which could have come a liberal burgher minister, able, aggressive and creative.

Although according to the constitution of 1850 both the House of Lords and the Chamber of Deputies represented the people, the sense in which they did so reflected two different conceptions of representation, one that of the Old Regime, the other that of modern liberal society. Article 65 of the constitution fixed the membership of the House of Lords as follows: (a) the adult royal princes; (b) the heads of the former imperial families in Prussia and the heads of those families which by royal order were given the hereditary right for the first-born in direct line to have a seat and a vote in the Upper House; (c) such members as the King appointed for life, but their number might not be greater than one-tenth of those listed under (a) and (b); (d) ninety members chosen by those who paid the highest direct state taxes; (e) thirty members chosen by their colleagues from among the councillors in the larger towns and cities of the state.[13]

With fifty per cent of the members holding hereditary seats or life-appointments, and ninety others elected by a small group of the highest taxpayers in the state, the House of Lords could hardly have been other than what the liberals called it, the essence of Junkerdom, the seat of reaction.[14] In it were caste and privilege incarnate, with ideals and standards utterly antithetic to those of liberalism. This body was certain to block reforms in the direction of breaking down the old Prussia and creating a modern free state. Even when the king had been persuaded to accept some mild measure of social change, even when he strongly supported a reform, as in the case of the marriage law and the land tax, the House of Lords resisted. In only one case did the king force it to retreat. He needed to reform the land tax in order, he thought, to pay the increased cost of his beloved military reorganization, but the landowners in the Upper House did not feel sufficiently patriotic to make the necessary financial sacrifice. The King finally had to appoint twenty-nine additional peers to force the acceptance of this reform measure. He was not willing, however, to use such coercion for the sake of any other. The liberals saw one reform bill after the other wrecked in the House of Lords. It soon become abundantly clear to the liberals that the preliminary to the achievement of any program of change was the transformation of the

[13] Von Roenne, *op. cit.* (1881), I, 203-16; Meitzen, *op. cit.*, I, 541-42.
[14] *Berliner Börsen Zeitung*, Dec. 12, 1861.

Upper House.[15] They knew that this House did not represent the country as they did, that it rested mainly upon the feudal principle of representation without election, representation by the lord of his subjects, representation by virtue of the lord's superior social position and knowledge and responsibility for the welfare of his subordinates, in short, representation of a kind antithetic to that of liberalism. They learned from experience that such representation meant irresponsibility to anyone or anything other than one's own interests or one's highly subjective conception of the general interest. When they pressed the issue upon the King, he absolutely refused to sanction any changes in the composition and power of the House of Lords. In fact, he came to regard it as the bulwark of royal authority against the aggressive Chamber of Deputies. His devotion to the old Prussia and his determination to preserve as much of it as possible were most clearly evident in his unremitting defence of this stronghold of aristocratic conservatism.

Below the Landtag were to be found as representative bodies the provincial assembly and the county assembly. Each of them the nobility dominated completely. Privilege had in these assemblies a means not merely to obstruct liberal proposals but to utilize the machinery of government for its own purposes. The reason becomes evident from an analysis of the constitution of these bodies.

The assemblies in the eight provinces had been restored in the 1850s to their pre-revolutionary form. Each consisted of three or four estates, depending on the province, of which normally the first represented the nobility and the owners of aristocratic estates, the second the towns, and the third the peasants and frequently the large landowners of the burgher class. In case the assembly was composed of four estates, the nobility was organized into two units, the higher and the lower.[16] These provincial bodies were assemblies of the Old Regime. The main difference lay in the facts that non-noble owners of aristocratic estates could be elected to the first estate and that the number of members of the first estate did not exceed that of the other two combined. Since the assemblies had been created only in the

---

[15] See as samples the expressions of the *Danziger Zeitung,* the *Neue Stettiner Zeitung,* the *Magdeburger Zeitung,* the *Elberfelder Zeitung* in March, 1861, and the speech by von Sybel in April, 1862. *Tagesbericht,* Nos. 58, 63, 65, 66, March 9-19, 1861; Heyderhoff, *op. cit.,* I, 88.

[16] See von Roenne, *op. cit.* (1864), Vol. I. Part 2, pp. 366-72, 385 ff.

1820s, the Conservative government had thought it wise not to impose the usual numerical preponderance of the nobility.[17]

Since the introduction of the constitution and the creation of the Landtag, the provincial assembly had lost much of its former importance. The same cannot be said of the county assembly, the Kreistag. It continued to be the most significant representative institution of local government and was more expressive of the institutional structure of Prussia than the new Landtag.

Control of county government remained from the Old Regime in the hands of the local landholding nobility. The Kreistag was dominated by this class, and the Landrat, the executive official in the county, held the key powers over the rural community and over all the towns in his county, unless the latter happened to be very large. The county government brought peasants and townsmen under the authority of the nobility at a level of government close enough to the population to be in daily relations with it but sufficiently removed to be able to exercise general control. This government established the nobility as the channel of contact and the agency of authority between the central government and the masses of the people.

The county government in 1860 expressed an adjustment of the machinery prior to the Stein-Hardenberg reforms to the changed conditions since those times. To understand it one must first become acquainted with its functioning in the Eighteenth Century. At that time it had been composed of owners of noble estates and of representatives of spiritual foundations, universities and towns which owned noble estates. Even though by royal consent an occasional burgher had been permitted to purchase a noble or knight's estate, he had been unable to sit in the Kreistag. That privilege had been reserved for noble owners alone. The main functions of the assembly had been financial. Meeting twice a year, it had allocated the taxes and other duties which the county had to bear; it had exercised control over the county finances and participated in the administration of the dike, mortgage, fire insurance, poor relief and agricultural credit associations. It had expressed the local views and wishes about county affairs to the central government. Only the noble knights' estate owners had had the right to select the executive officer, the Landrat, from among their

[17] See the decree establishing the provincial estates for Brandenburg in 1823 in Dr. Wilhelm Altmann, *Ausgewählte Urkunden zur Brandenburgisch-Preussischen Verfassungs-u. Verwaltungsgeschichte* (Berlin, 1897); see figures on the membership of these estates in Meitzen, *op. cit.*, I, 534-36.

midst; the representatives of the towns and other organizations owning knights' estates had not been allowed to participate in this election. The selection had had to be approved by the King, and the new Landrat had devoted most of his time to state administrative affairs, the administration of taxes, the levying of recruits, control of a part of the rural police, and other administrative matters pertaining to the central government.[18]

After the Stein-Hardenberg reforms the Kreistags were re-established, with a few concessions to the peasants and towns. These two groups were also permitted now to send deputies to the assembly, but in such small numbers in the Eastern provinces as to prevent them from exercising any influence. Although burgher owners of noble landed properties could sit in the first estate along with the Junkers, the number of them remained small and they were subject to the temptation of the parvenu of being more feudal in their behavior than the genuine aristocrat. In all other respects the functions of the Kreistag continued to be in 1860 about what they had been prior to the Stein-Hardenberg reform period. If anything, the power of the Landrat, who in the Eighteenth Century had been in the process of being transformed from a county official, *primus inter pares,* into a state official, diminished in the Nineteenth Century in favor of greater responsibility and initiative on the part of the Kreistag. That the nobility remained in control is evident from the continuing restriction of the office of Landrat in most counties to the owners of noble landed property and from the first estate's enormous numerical superiority in all counties over the estates of the towns and the peasants.[19]

The disparity between the size of the first estate and that of the other two estates may be seen from a few figures. In 1859 some eighty Schulzes, or village mayors, and other village officials from fifty-three communities in Schlawe County stated in a petition to the Lower House that their Kreistag was composed of seventy-six owners of noble estates, six representatives of the peasants, and six of the towns. Another petition from ten owners of noble estates in County Deutsch-Krone, all members of the first estate in the Kreistag, brought to the attention of the Lower House their situation. The county contained thirty-nine square miles of territory, 50,000 population, five towns, thirty-three noble estates, six demesne and larger estates held on a hereditary rental basis, ninety-one villages and rural market places, some 1,355 peasant owners with a yoke of oxen, and 1,031 lesser peasant owners. The noble estates contained 91,489 Magdeburger Morgen of land, the peasant possessions, 246,000 Morgen. In the Kreistag the owners of noble estates held thirty-five seats, the towns five, and the rural communities only three or "at present perhaps six."[20]

In Westphalia and the Rhineland the effects of the French Revolution and the temporary incorporation of those areas within France had prevented from occurring any such extreme disparity in the distribution of power. French law had been introduced and most of the large estates broken up. The Prussian government after 1815 had been unable to impose the full institutional organization of the Eastern provinces, since it could not find enough noblemen with noble estates. Instead of establishing the overwhelming predominance in the Kreistag of the big landowners, it had varied the distribution of power according to the county.[21] In some, the first estate predominated, as in Düsseldorf, where the first estate had thirty-one, the second six, and the third eight; in others, one of the other two estates had most votes. The difference marked one of the most significant lines of contrast between the social and economic conditions in the Eastern and Western provinces: in the West, many towns, active commerce and industry, few aristocratic estates, in general a burgher culture reinforced by a vigorous peasantry; in the Eastern provinces, fewer towns, little industry except in special places like Berlin, large landed estates, diverse conditions of the peasantry, in some regions free, in others dependent —a predominantly rural culture.

The existing form of county government received severe criticism from peasants, townsmen and numerous large landholders. From every side except the Conservative came the complaint of unfair representation and unjust distribution of financial burdens. As the eighty Schulzes and village elders from Schlawe County said, the enormous disparity between the number of deputies in the first estate and in the other two was not justified by the size of the landholding of the first estate, by the amount of taxes paid, or by their percentage of the population. The peasants, they asserted, paid more county taxes and bore more county burdens than the other two estates together. The petitioners claimed that they were entitled to request an increase in representation on the basis of population figures and amount of taxes

[20] Abg. H., *Drucksachen*, 1859, Vol. III, No. 108, pp. 5-9.
[21] *Ibid.*, *St. B.*, 1863; Vol. V, No. 129, p. 1069.

paid.[22] As this petition showed, the peasants and townsmen objected especially to the abuse by the first estate of the financial power of the Kreistag. The members of that estate used their control of assessment and collection to shift the burden of both state and local taxes upon the others. Since 1841-45 the county assemblies had had the right to levy taxes for county purposes such as road construction and reclamation; and while some county assemblies had behaved fairly, many had approved local taxes for improvements of primary benefit to the large landowners in the first estate. One of the main complaints in the Revolution of 1848 had been directed against this abuse.[23]

Domination over the county assembly assured the large landowners an additional economic advantage connected with the settlement of the differences between former lord and serf over the allocation of property. Growing out of peasant emancipation in the Stein-Hardenberg period, this problem continued to cause trouble in the 1850s. The peasants were sure that the large landowners as members of the commissions set up in the localities to carry out the work were using their position in their own interest.[24] The existence of over 5,600 contested cases in 1860 attested to peasant discontent[25]

The question of reform resolved itself into one of just representation. The economic complaints would be taken care of, it was thought, if a just distribution of power in the Kreistag could be attained. The liberal Minister of Interior, Count von Schwerin, introduced in 1860 into the Lower House a reform bill for the six Eastern provinces, which after lengthy consideration in commission was approved and sent to the House of Lords for action. The representative of the Minister of Interior declared that the nobility in the Eastern provinces had no legal rights and privileges entitling them to a special position in the Kreistag. Their position had been the natural expression of the conditions of the time when peasants were serfs and towns had stood outside the county organization. In the Old Regime the nobles' rights had been balanced by duties. With the emancipation of the serfs and the creation of a landholding peasantry the conditions had changed, and the peasantry had come to demand its own adequate representation. As the towns had been incorporated in the county system of

[22] *Ibid., Drucksachen*, 1859; Vol. III, No. 108, pp. 8-9.

[23] *Ibid.*, 1860; Vol. VI, No. 265, p. 19.

[24] See on this question von Roenne, *op. cit.* (1864), Vol. II, Part 2, pp. 216-19; *Jhb. für die amtliche Statistik des Preuss. Staates* (1863), p. 168.

[25] See statement by government official to the Commission of the Lower House in 1860. Abg. H., *Drucksachen*, 1860; Vol. VI, No. 265, p. 40.

government, the official spokesman declared, they had likewise claimed their fair share of political authority. The government proposed to make the number of deputies in the first estate equal to the sum of those in the other two estates, to abolish the hereditary vote as contrary to Article Four of the constitution, and to enlarge the numerical basis of the first estate by having it represent not merely the owners of noble estates but those possessing land property producing an income of 2,000 Reichsthalers a year.

In advocating the retention of the existing system of three separate estates, the government expressed the views of almost every liberal. The liberal commission of the Lower House reported in 1860 that with the expansion of education and with the introduction of the freedom of land-sale and occupation since 1807, the old law on county government had lost its social and economic basis. The commission condemned the law as an assertion of caste principle and declared that with the elimination of this principle from the central representative assembly the system of county government should also be freed from this feudal vestige.[26] Nonetheless, scarcely anyone thought of merging the three estates in the Kreistag into one. The disparity between town and country and between large landholdings and small ones remained so great, it was argued in the commission, that such a radical change of the present organization would be contrary to fact and create confusion. Almost as unanimous was the view that the large landowners should serve as the leaders of the peasantry and that the reform was necessary to strengthen the political position of the large landlords to enable them better to act as rural leaders.

The peasants, Minister Schwerin declared with the general assent of the liberal deputies, had not yet reached the degree of independence that would protect them against "the desire for unmotivated innovations on the one hand and from centralized, bureaucratic guardianship on the other. The peasant needs the strong leadership of the large landholders as the natural sources of strength of agricultural interests." The minister proposed to make certain that the landlords retained the role of leaders of the peasantry by giving them the additional right to be chosen as deputies in the third estate and especially by making the first estate as large as the other two combined. He thought that the landlords had a well-founded right to such treatment by virtue of their political, social and economic position. As for the small number of representatives of the towns, the second estate, he declared that "the

[26] *Ibid.*, pp. 6-8.

urban interests to be represented in the Kreistag are more uniform than those of the rural areas and therefore permit a numerically smaller representation."

According to Schwerin, almost 2,000 large landholdings of size and value equal to a noble estate but lacking its legal status, should be given the same right of belonging to the first estate. At the same time, he continued, it would be unjust to the owners of noble estates which did not produce an income of 2,000 Reichsthalers a year to deprive them of that historic right. He rejected as too mechanical the standards of size of landholding, amount of taxes paid, or the number of population as the basis of representation. The present inequality in taxation made it impossible to use the amount of taxes paid as a basis; to use the extent of land owned, the minister said, would be unfair to the towns and cities where value depended on commerce and industry rather than on the size of the area held; and to use population as the basis would benefit the urban centers at the expense of the rural.
rural.

The only major objection from the liberal deputies to the government proposal on representation concerned the relative size of the first estate. They thought that the government was merely retaining the old feudal predominance under a new guise. The government denied the charge, stressing the reduction in relative size of the representation in most cases and the abolition of the hereditary vote attached to a knight's estate. It stressed the necessity for the wisdom and independence of the large landowners to be present in the Kreistag and pointed out that the peasants would come to accept this fact and because of their common interests would elect the large estate-owners as deputies.

> It is feared that in the first years after the promulgation of the law the rural communities will be little inclined to seek their representatives among the owners of large estates, for unfortunately the view is still widespread among the peasants that their interests are specifically different from those of the landlords, an opinion in which they have been strengthened by the experience with redemption and separation [he referred to the division of land after peasant emancipation] in the recent decades and through the preservation of the strict division of estates in the county government. It is therefore not to be expected that in free election of county representatives the landlords in all counties will be assured of sufficient respect to assure their election by the rural communities.

The government feared that if its proposal were weakened the ranks of the large landowners would in many counties be extraordinarily thinned in the Kreistag and that in some counties, for example Erfurt, the landlords would not be represented at all. To allow the small landowners to obtain a predominance in the Kreistag, declared the liberal government spokesman, would endanger the interests of the county.[27]

The liberal commission of the Lower House did not share the opinion of the government that the peasantry in the Eastern provinces needed the leadership of the large landowners. But, it continued in its report, "it did not fail to recognize how important and desirable it was that the peasantry, limited in education and judgment and often thinking only of its nearest interests, should not be personally represented in the Kreistag in too large numbers." The commission wished that the peasant's interests would be looked after together with those of the entire county by "the intelligent, common-sensed landlords." It hoped that the rural communities would elect such men as Kreistag deputies and that thereby

> . . . not only would the relations between the estate owners and the rural communities improve, but the way would be opened to create a county representation which would be really unified in the effort to work for the welfare of the county and which would ignore the petty interests of the different election associations, render these associations superfluous and enable a better system, a general election without differentiation between town and country, between landed estates and rural communities, to be introduced.[28]

The Commission rejected the government's proposal to allow fifty per cent of the votes in the Kreistag to the first estate. It recommended a somewhat complicated arrangement in the following terms:

> The entire number of Kreistag deputies shall be divided into three election associations according to the following principles:
> (1) The number of urban deputies is to be determined according to the ratio of urban to rural population as established at the last general census.
> (2) The number of Kreistag deputies left after deducting the number for the towns is to be divided between the association of the large landed estates and the association of the rural communities according to the amount of land belonging to each of these associations.
> After the promulgation of the land-tax equalization law the number of representatives of large and of small land holdings will be determined by the amount of land tax each pays.

[27] *Ibid.*, pp. 40, 52.
[28] *Ibid.*, p. 52.

The number of deputies of the towns will be allocated to the various towns according to the size of the population.

This system would in most areas definitely have been to the advantage of the towns. Only in the rural counties, particularly in the Eastern provinces, would the rural districts have benefited, especially the large landholders who, though few in number, would have had the same representation as the peasants. Even in this case the proposal called for a sliding scale: the size of the representation in a county would vary with the size of the large landholdings. It certainly would have increased the political power of the towns and of the small landowners at the expense of the landed nobility far more than the government planned to do.

Count Schwerin was manifestly endeavoring to preserve as much of the landowning nobility's power as he could and still introduce a bill that would be considered liberal. His assertion that urban interests were much more uniform than rural ones and therefore did not require such extensive representation had the genuine ring of the pre-industrial regime, of a landed magnate to whom live things like grain and livestock and peasants offered much more diversity of interest and required much more attention than inanimate objects like iron and steel and machinery, factories and commerce. His bill was intended for a rural and small-town society in which the large landowners predominated. It called for the elimination of the aristocratic monopoly by the inclusion of non-noble large owners in the first estate and in control of the county; otherwise it proposed in the name of realism to keep the distribution of political and social power nearly as it was.

The liberals would have given much more authority to the townsmen than would the government; but by and large the two agreed in fundamentals. Many liberals were large landowners, and in portraying the ideal type of local leader and the ideal relations between him and the peasantry they were using themselves as models. They were actually trying to realize that ideal—to transform the peasantry into good citizens with more than local and personal interests. They aimed at preparing the peasantry for political equality and political leadership by abolishing the vestiges of feudal privilege in the Kreistag. They were consistent in their ideals, even though they remained cautiously within the existing institutional framework. To judge from the political behavior of numerous peasants in 1848 and in the period just beginning, the liberals were much too cautious in their estimate of the peasants' ability. Nonetheless, prepared to advance farther than the ministry, they were pressing for additional concessions.[29]

Not merely in the distribution of representation in the Kreistag but also in the selection of the Landrat did the liberals improve upon the plans of the ministry. The latter advocated the preservation of the existing method, whereby in most counties the Kreistag nominated three candidates from the owners of noble landed properties, one of whom the king usually, although not necessarily, chose to fill the office. The liberals regarded this article in the government bill as a retention of feudal privilege, and refused to accept it. Instead, they recommended that the stipulation about the candidate's being an owner of a noble estate be eliminated. They were applying generally the practice existing in a number of counties, pointing to that precedent in support of their proposal; otherwise, they were willing to retain the present system. The amendment meant the elimination of another means of control.

The Conservatives regarded the reform of county government as a profound threat to the social order. Employing their usual argument against it, they approved reform in general and in time but held this particular reform unnecessary; the present system was working well; there were no major complaints against it; individual complaints about such matters as road construction did not justify a complete transformation of the system such as the government proposed. In the Kreistag everyone was content, they maintained; there were no differences among the estates. The existing county estates had done much for the land,

> especially by virtue of the hereditary right of representation of the knights' estates, whose bearers have particularly looked after the poorer and more needy inhabitants of the county. The abolition of this hereditary right is an attack on well-earned rights, which could be justified only by most urgent reasons, and these do not exist. The important and beneficial influence of the large estate-owners, which must be preserved for the sake of the welfare of the state, depends to a large extent upon the fact that they are *hereditary* representatives of the county corporation. Through the introduction of elected representatives in

[29] On the distribution of representation in the three estates in the Kreistag in the Eastern provinces, see the figures according to the existing situation, the government proposal, and the proposal of the commission of the Lower House in 1860. Abg. H., *Drucksachen*, 1860; Vol. VI, No. 265, App. A. See the figures for the two Western provinces according to the existing situation and the proposal of the government in 1863. Abg. H., *St. B.*, 1863, Vol. V, No. 129, pp. 1117 ff. See also Meitzen, *op. cit.*, IV, 477 ff.

place of the hereditary ones this influence would be substantially endangered. Also it is to be feared that these innovations will disturb the harmony in the Kreistag among the estates, and such a disturbance will in difficult times be bitterly rued. There is no definite principle in the new proposed county law, even though the latter is better than expected. Also there should be not one county law for all six provinces, but one for each province, so that the provincial differences could be taken into account.[30]

These stock arguments, resting upon illusions supported by traditional power, bore some similarity to the views of the King. In his program of 1858 the ruler had declared that he favored the reform of local government; but "first," he had added in his wooden style, "we must preserve what has just been re-established in order not to arouse new uncertainty and unrest which would only be a grave matter." When Minister von Schwerin insisted on introducing a bill for the reform of county government, the King manifestly exerted his influence in favor of retaining the power of the large landholders, especially the nobles. How well the Conservatives gauged the King's attitude may be seen in the fact that the House of Lords rejected the bill out of hand. The King took no steps to push it through. A similar bill was submitted to the Lower House in 1862, and again a commission brought in a favorable report, with about the same modifications as its predecessor of 1860. In only one respect did the liberals amend the bill, and this change would no doubt have been acceptable to the Lower House of 1860. The amount of direct state taxes paid by each of the three estates should determine the number of deputies. The proposal was at least an improvement over the existing system and that offered in 1860; for it made financial support of the state the basis of representation and had the advantage of relative simplicity. The bill never received consideration in the Landtag, for the constitutional conflict monopolized attention. When Bismarck was made Minister President he buried the reform by referring it to the provincial Landtags for consideration. The possibility of renovating local government at some future time depended upon the outcome of the battle against militarism and absolutism.

The government of the rural communities in the six Eastern provinces remained in 1860 in the hands of the owners of large estates. These owners might be towns, in which case the magistrate of the town exercised the functions of lord; but in the overwhelming number of

[30] Abg. H., *Drucksachen*, 1860; Vol. VI, No. 265, pp. 3-4.

communities the authority rested with the proprietor of the local estate. After hearing recommendations from the village community, the proprietor selected the village Schulze, or mayor, and his aides, except in cases where the position of Schulze devolved upon the owner of a certain piece of property; he supervised the village financial business; he had general authority over the important decisions of the community; and he exercised the police power and in some respects the judicial power. His authority referred both to communities located on his own property and to those in the district of his estate. The responsibility came to him not as an official specifically appointed to this position but as owner of the estate: he had to assume it whether he wished to or not.

Upon this system of government rested the domination over the peasantry by the noble and other landlords in the Eastern provinces. One may judge from its inclusiveness that is was effective. How far the rights of the landlords had been extended in the two decades prior to the Revolution of 1848 may be seen from the legislation about the patrimonial judicial power. In 1827 the clause in the general legal code for the state asserting that to exercise judicial authority a person must meet the judicial qualifications was declared inapplicable to landowners with patrimonial judicial responsibility. By a law of 1838 the latter were allowed, again as an exception to the general legal code, to judge certain cases in which they themselves were parties. By virtue of regulations of that same year and of 1846 they were permitted to appoint deputies to exercise their judicial and their police functions.[31]

Although the Revolution of 1848 abolished the rights of patrimonial police and judicial power and proposed to reform local government, the reforms either could not be carried out in the short period of liberal and democratic control or were in the main abolished as soon as the Conservative government was restored. A law of 1856 re-established the prerevolutionary situation with a new façade. It stated that the patrimonial police power was "a right derived from the sovereign power of the King but as a rule united with the possession of a knight's or other landed estate." The government denied that this measure violated the existing law according to which all such rights belonged to the King. It asserted that the right still remained with the King but that it had been delegated by him to the estate-owners under the general supervision of the state. The Conservative

[31] Von Roenne, *op. cit.* (1864), Vol. I, Part A, pp. 284-88.

Commission of the Lower House appointed to consider the government bill at the time approved this line of argument, but gave it a twist in the feudal sense and toned down the emphasis on the authority of the soverign. It asserted

> that in the Eastern provinces the lord's power as a rule has been tied to the possession of a knight's or other landed estate, that it should remain so and that except in those cases foreseen in the law it could be acquired by inheritance or purchase. This patri-monial power of the estate-owner is not the result of an official position in the narrower sense which is conferred by the king, but rather the office of police administration as a rule is bound to the possession of an estate and in the first line is derived from the patrimonial position. On the other hand the right is not purely private, but is a minor right transferred from the state.

The Conservative government had difficulty applying its own law. It struggled to preserve the patrimonial power of the landed nobility and the burgher large landowners; but what should it do in case the estate to which the patrimonial power was attached was broken up and sold, or acquired by peasants; or what if the lord did not wish the responsibility or fulfilled it poorly? In such cases the government stipulated in the law of 1856 that the patrimonial authority should be transferred to another landed estate, or preferably, that a large landowner should be selected to conduct the business as a state official; or that if no one would accept this as an honorary unpaid position the government might temporarily appoint an administrator with remuneration. If the person with patrimonial power could not per-sonally carry out his functions, he had to appoint a deputy; and the law took care of cases in which an estate district or community district (Gutsbezirk or Gemeindebezirk) was changed in scope and size or in which a landed property should be given or deprived of the patri-monial power. The law made a valiant attempt to preserve the sys-tem in spite of changing conditions.[32]

When the New Era began in 1858, the liberals in the ministry and in the Lower House set to work to reform the local rural government. They did not succeed in accomplishing their purpose, for the quarrel over the military reorganization and then the constitutional conflict destroyed any prospect of a change. The Minister of Interior, Count von Schwerin, early in 1862 did, however, introduce in the Lower House a bill which was considered in commission and afforded the occasion for liberal criticism of the present system.

[32] *Ibid.*, pp. 298-307.

Fundamental was the question of the responsibility for police power in the rural communities. The law of 1856 had restored this power to the local landlords as it had existed before 1848. The government of the New Era criticized the law in the sharpest terms, asserting that it was bad

> . . . because it maintains an unfortunate crippling split in the state between the local institutions and the constitution of the central organization. The patrimonial police power is contrary to the spirit of the constitution. Resting on no delegation of authority, dependent upon no qualifications, bound by no oath, resulting purely from the possession of certain estates acquired in no matter what way, the patrimonial power over other property and persons is not in agreement with the recognition that the executive power belongs to the King alone. It is not in agreement with the abolition of all caste privileges, with the equal right of all citizens to participate in the legislative authority, and so on. After the legislation of the past half century has severed all other political and economic connections between the former patrimonial estate and its subjects, after the estates have been freed for sale and for division, and finally after the new judicial constitution of 1849 has abolished the remains of the patrimonial judicial power, the source of the patrimonial police power, the retention of the latter has become an anomaly.
>
> In general one must say that the overwhelming majority of the landlords do not bother about their patrimonial position and do not satisfy even the most modest requirements of a local police administration. These requirements will increase with the growth of the population and the spread of culture. Indeed, the government has had to transfer a number of police responsibilities of a local character to the nearest state official, the Landrat. Since the latter is already overburdened, the transfer means the slowing down of work.

The government declared that if a reform was not put through legally it would have to extend its authority into these areas by decree, even at the risk of arousing bitter criticism about bureaucratic arbitrariness. It wished to abolish the patrimonial police power and expand the area of responsibility of the rural communities. In this way alone it believed that the present red tape, indolence and indifference in the rural settlements could be overcome, a view which was fully shared by the liberal commission of the Lower House reporting on this matter.[33]

---

[33] See Abg. H., *St. B.*, 1862; Vol. II, No. 3, pp. 8-11; No. 61, pp. 354-56; No. 62, pp. 355-60. Also, No. 4, pp. 10-18, for a discussion of the need to abolish the institution of hereditary Schulze.

The government refused to introduce a bill creating a uniform system of local rural government throughout the state. Count von Schwerin explained that the actual conditions of local government were at present too varied.[34] He was referring to the basic difference between the situation in the six Eastern and the two Western provinces, a difference described in the Lower House in 1861 by the Westphalian liberal aristocrat, Freiherr von Vincke. In the Rhineland and Westphalia, the latter said, the land in noble estates amounted to only five or six per cent; in some Eastern provinces to sixty per cent. In the West a majority of the communities contained no noble estates at all; in the East this was rarely the case.

> We have never had a relation of the landlord to the corporation as such from which comes, for example, the right of the land-owner to name the Schulze, to supervise the finances of the community, to pass on certain measures. We know only a private relation of the landlord to the individuals. Only in rare instances have we had patrimonial judicial power such as is here almost universally the case. It seems almost impossible to introduce here what is entirely acceptable in Westphalia and the Rhineland—to unite the landlord with the rural community which . . . in many places, in Pomerania for example, is composed solely of persons, of day laborers, dependent upon the landlord. These dependent persons would be in a position to outvote the lord and to regulate all community affairs.

Freiherr von Vincke was entirely correct about the Western provinces. The administration of the rural communities in the West, including police and judicial power, lay in the hands of officials selected by the local residents and confirmed, not by a local aristocrat or large landowner, but by the state officials of higher instance. The Conservative government had tried to create a special position for the nobles and estate-owners, but the number of cases in which it had been possible was small. The government had been more successful in the next larger district, the Samtgemeinde or the Amt of Westphalia or Bürgermeisterei of the Rhineland, approximately the same institutions.

The difference between the organization in the East and in the West requires some elaboration. The Samtgemeinde or Amt was lacking in the Eastern provinces. There were two levels of rural local government below the county, the community which was composed either of one village if sufficiently large or of several villages and

[34] *Ibid.*, No. 15, pp. 102-3.

hamlets, and the estate district, Gutsbezirk, which included the large estate and the communities. The owner of the estate exercised governance over the rural communities and in most matters was placed between it and the county government. In the two Western provinces the organization of the Amt was more complicated and more efficient. The Amt occupied a position comparable to that of the Gutsbezirk, but its composition was entirely different. While a single large rural community might constitute an Amt, it was normal for several communities of peasants and one or more noble estates to be members. In case the estate-owners were entitled to personal membership in the county assembly, they were also entitled to participate in person in the Amt assembly; and the office of Amtmann, or head of the district, was usually conferred upon a large landholder, if one were available and willing to accept it. In many instances the office was held by a paid official. Thus, whereas the lord ran the Gutsbezirk in the East and occupied a superior, authoritarian position above the peasants, in the Western Amt or Bürgermeisterei the large landowners and the peasants cooperated in a common assembly in which the peasant representatives outnumbered the others. The Amt assembly elected its own chairman, and by virtue of the institution of common participation it was able to carry out tasks for the good of the district, like road building, the improvement of schools and of facilities for the poor, which the Gutsbezirk could not perform. It enabled a sense of politics and a capacity for leadership to develop among the peasants; it stimulated initiative; it reduced class hostility and encouraged the maintenance of mutual respect among the social groups. It created a liberal atmosphere instead of the authoritarian one to be found in most of the East. It gave to liberalism an institutional basis which made it no longer dependent upon the political attitude of liberal large estate-owners. It was one of the basic factors in the great difference between the society in most of Eastern Prussia and that of Western Prussia.[35] It was not a democratic body; its members did not think or act in terms of social or political equality. But it was a free cooperative assembly of self-respecting and mutually respecting personalities. It created a vastly different situation from that of a lord's calling together at will an array of dependent peasants.

The Conservatives must have recognized that they were most vulnerable to criticism and aroused most hostility among the peasants

[35] See von Vincke's speech in Abg. H., *St. B.*, 1861; III, 1338-40. On the Landgemeindeordnung see von Roenne, *op. cit.* (1864), Vol. I, Part A, pp. 284-88; Vol. II, Part 1, pp. 236-37, 458-60; von Roenne, *op. cit.* (1881), I, 572 ff.

by retaining the patrimonial police power and control over the selection of the village Schulze and aids. To obviate this criticism their representatives proposed a bill in the Landtag in 1862 which was a model of Conservative thinking. The bill called for a transfer of the existing power to the state which would in turn delegate the responsibility back to the large landowners as state agents. The details of this proposal are worth studying as a revelation of the Conservative conception of reform.

According to the bill the patrimonial power was to be abolished and the exercise of these functions transferred to the government. With respect to the police administration, each county excluding the towns should be divided into police districts. "As a rule each community will constitute a police district; nonetheless, if the situation or other conditions make it seem appropriate, several communities (villages, independent Gutsbezirke) might be united into a police district." In each police district the police would be administered as an honorary office. The police administrator would be chosen by the Kreistag from among the owners, renters or administrators of large estates in the district, and only in case these were lacking would other residents be considered. The appointment would be for life. The Landrat should supervise the entire police administration in the county and decide complaints against the police administrators. The police administrator could punish offenders by a fine of not over five Thalers or by imprisonment of three days. The Schulze should act as his agent in the village.

> In communities which include a peasant village and one or several independent Gutsbezirke, the Schulze functions for the entire community; nonetheless it remains permissible for the owners of independent Gutsbezirke to assume the functions of the Schulze for their Gutsbezirke.
> In communities which consist only of an independent Gutsbezirk, the owner of the same is to appoint a Schulze who has equal rights and duties with the other Schulzes.
> If a community contains several independent Gutsbezirke, the right of appointing the Schulze rotates among the different landlords.

So much for the patrimonial police and judicial power. In Article 25 was stated the proposed change in the relation of the lord to the government of the rural community.

> The authority over communal administration which formed a part of the patrimonial power shall henceforth be exercised by a county committee.

The community heads (Schulze, judge, and so forth), magistrates (court personnel, jurymen), and the representatives of not-qualified hereditary Schulzes shall be elected by the community from the number of resident landowners and after a previous expression of opinion by the police-administrator he shall be confirmed and sworn in by the Landrat.

If the confirmation is refused and a second election is also not approved, the Landrat shall appoint an administrator of the position until the community selects a person who will be approved.

. . . Until a new law on county government is promulgated, the functions imposed above on the county committee shall be transferred to the Landrat.[36]

This piece of sleight-of-hand work would have preserved the status quo. The Gutsbezirk would have been preserved, with the owner now exercising his patrimonial police and judicial authority in the name of the state. The police districts would have been fitted to the existing administrative divisions so that each lord would have continued in his previous function. The selection of the officials for the peasant communities would have been made by the Landrat, a large landowner and usually a noble, after consultation with the police administrator, the owner of the large estate and former head of the Gutsbezirk. In view of the number of peasant communities in which peasants were to be selected as local officials, one can well imagine that the advice of the administrative head of the Gutsbezirk would be followed.

The success of the whole plan from the standpoint of the Conservatives depended upon the preservation of the existing form of county government. If the nobles and big landowners had lost control of the Kreistag and of the office of Landrat, their proposed reform of community government and the patrimonial authority would have been too risky for them. There is no reason to believe that the Conservatives would have accepted any major change in the structure of the Kreistag. They knew too well how important that body was for the preservation of their political and social power.

Did the liberals make a mistake in their strategy? Should they have compromised on the military in return for concessions in the matter of local government? The question is debatable. If they could have won an adequate reform of government in county, town and rural community and achieved the abolition of the manorial police and judicial authority in return for acceptance of the military

<hr>

[36] Abg. H., *St. B.*, 1862; Vol. II, No. 33, pp. 192-95.

reforms, they would have destroyed the institutional basis of Conservatism and Junkerdom in society.[37] They might then in time have been able to shape the army to the liberal ideal as well, in so far as an army can be adapted to liberalism. The great question remains whether they could have achieved this compromise, and the evidence all points to a negative answer. The House of Lords flatly opposed any such measures; the King, being at most lukewarm, would have done nothing to break this opposition; and the liberals would have been left with the burden of a huge military expansion and nothing to show in the way of governmental reforms.[38]

---

[37] On January 8, 1862, the *Berliner Allgemeine Zeitung* stated that the reform of the county government was an absolute necessity for the development of the constitution, for the harmonizing of the social conflicts, for the reconciliation between nobility and burghers. When the county governmental reform was really executed, the present angry party battles would cease. Summarized in *Tagesbericht*, No. 6, Jan. 8, 1862.

[38] On county government reform see Abg. H., *Drucksachen*, 1859; Vol. III, No. 108. *Ibid.*, 1860; Vol. III, No. 149; Vol. VI, No. 265. Abg. H. *St. B.*, 1863; Vol. V, No. 129.

3 / The Police State

A PRUSSIAN correspondent wrote to the *Wiesbadener Zeitung* at the close of the year 1861 as follows: "Whoever lives in Prussia feels at every step that the military and police state encloses him in its net, that he as a burgher has fewer rights than the haughty nobility, that a powerful and truly officious bureaucracy may defy unpunished every right of a burgher. In this state the constitution has been planted like foreign rice."[1]

The term "police state" was used at the time to refer to the all-inclusive authority of a centralized bureaucracy. The police were responsible not merely for security against criminal acts but for the operation of the vast network of controls over civilian life which had survived from the period of mercantilism and absolutism. In practice the two kinds of function coalesced. The spirit of the police officials in charge of civilian affairs tended to be identical with that of the security police, namely, to regard any violator as a wilful criminal. Of the two, the officials responsible for the control of civilian activities exercised far more influence upon Prussian life. Together with the military they were the main instruments for the preservation of the authoritarian state and the habits of mind among the civilian population of civic docility and a passionate regard for detail.

Writing in 1873, the liberal lawyer and politician Eduard Lasker portrayed the process by which after the Reform Era the power of the judiciary in Prussia had been ever more restricted and administrative

---

[1] *Tagesbericht*, No. 3, Jan. 4, 1862.

decisions increasingly favored.[2] The process, he said, culminated in the law of May 11, 1842, the main point of which was that complaints about police measures of any sort, even about whether they were legal, necessary or appropriate, had to be made solely to the superior administrative officials. Only in case the plaintiff could show that a police order had violated a privilege or a contractual right could the case be brought before a judge. Reference to the general law, to personal rights, to property rights was not enough to carry the issue before a court. This, Lasker declared, supplied the legal basis of the police state. The administrative official ruled supreme.

In a wider sense, Lasker stated, the police had under their authority all public relations and the larger and more important aspects of personal rights. If a person wished to move to another town he had to obtain the approval of the police in the proposed seat of domicile. Once he had moved, he required police permission for entering any one of a large number of occupations. The police power determined whether and how he might use his piece of land; it had to pass on plans to improve his dwelling; it decided whether he might build a factory and, if so, where and according to what plan; it passed on the installation of machinery. It could lay paths and roads, dig ditches and canals across his fields. It penetrated his home, checked on the upbringing of his children, their school attendance, their religious instruction. It watched over his activities in private associations. It determined the amount of school and church tax he had to pay. It entered his house as tax official or as security officer and searched the premises.

All these powers of the local police and the Landrat could be exercised without any adequate means of protection for the citizen, whose sole defence was to write a complaint, which could be sent, however, even as far as a minister. The procedure was bureaucratic; the official against whom the complaint was made would be ordered to report; and, except in a few recent cases, Lasker said, the plaintiff would not be again consulted. Everything had to be included in the original statement, even though the plaintiff might not have known the grounds for the objectionable action and the officials were not required to inform him. With few exceptions the hearing of witnesses and experts was not required, no one was put under oath, and public hearings were excluded. The deputies in the parliament could bring the mat-

---

[2] The discussion of this topic is based entirely upon Lasker's brilliant analysis in his book, *Zur Verfassungsgeschichte Preussens* (Leipzig, 1874), Ch. IV, pp. 179-213.

ter to the attention of a minister, but whether he took any action depended on him alone and on the aggressiveness of the deputies—certainly a cumbersome way of bringing complaint against a minor official.

If a citizen had suffered property damage through the action of an official, the plaintiff could bring the case before a judge only if the official's superior called the action "contrary to law" or "improper." Even after the case had gone to court, the central or the provincial administrative agency could intervene and force the transfer of the case to an agency known as the Court for Deciding Conflicts of Competence. In case the appropriate minister approved the transfer, this court, dominated by administrative officials, could determine whether the case should be brought before a judge. If it decided in the negative, the plaintiff had no other course of legal action.

This procedure, wrote Lasker, held for civil cases, but with slight variation it was equally valid for criminal action. The judge could immediately initiate a criminal investigation, but no action could be brought against the official without the approval of the state's attorney, another official. Once the state's attorney did initiate proceedings, the Court for Deciding Conflicts of Competence could intervene as in the case of civil actions. Thus an administrative body decided whether an official could be tried in a regular court for some act which had injured a citizen. The letter of the constitution may have been adhered to, concluded Lasker, but not the spirit. The officials were allowed, as before 1848, to interpret the law as they and their administrative colleagues pleased.

Lasker showed that since the 1820s the important laws and even the constitution revealed the effects of this arbitrary practice. The laws guaranteeing the civil rights of the citizens, he wrote, lacked that which would have made them inviolable. They were vague, incomplete, capable of contrary interpretations, full of reservations; they referred to subsequent supplements which would be contradictory to the original terms. One could hardly tell what was the rule and what were exceptions, for anything might be interpreted as an exception. "In practice," Lasker concluded, "every opinion finds a basis, every interpretation its proof, and irreconcilable opponents simultaneously refer sometimes to the spirit, sometimes to the letter of the law to support contrary opinions. The system of incomplete laws has established itself in Prussia."

With a view to changing this system Lasker called attention to two paragraphs in the law which seemed to him invaluable. In these paragraphs it was asserted "that everyone is entitled to exercise his right within the limits of the law and that the laws allow to everyone to whom it gives a right the means to exercise that right."[3] Lasker regarded this right as the foundation of the legal state, and deplored the fact that it no longer prevailed in Prussia. Whenever a law contradicted a police order, he said, the means to implement that law ceased to exist. He gave numerous examples. The law of December 31, 1842, guaranteed freedom of movement to Prussians but allowed the police to check whether the newcomer into a community possessed the necessary property or the necessary physical strength to support himself and his dependents. In actuality, Lasker said, the police did not limit themselves to considering these conditions. Thousands of strong and well-to-do Prussians were forbidden to move to certain communities without having any means to defend themselves against this prohibition. The industry law of 1845 seemed to establish freedom of occupation, but the police decided whether a person was permitted to carry on a particular occupation in a community. Freedom of property was the foundation of all state order and was so recognized in law. "But the police can prevent the owner's use of a piece of land, the construction of factories of certain kinds, and can destroy thereby the value of my property, even though I have evidence in hand that no other interest, either official or private, would suffer from my proposed activity." "Punishment shall be threatened or imposed only in accordance with the law," stated Article Eight of the constitution. Nonetheless, declared Lasker, a law of March 11, 1850, gave to the police the authority to issue prohibitions and commands within the limits of their official authority and in case of violations to threaten to impose penalties up to the sum of ten Thalers or in case of penury a term of imprisonment up to fourteen days. Only in case the order concerned affairs of the agricultural police was the approval of the community representatives required; otherwise the latter could merely express an opinion. This form of "petty legislation," Lasker stated, could be applied to any action falling in any one of nine categories. The inclusiveness of the list supplies the full flavor of the police state:

(1) Protection of persons and property;
(2) Order, security and ease of traffic on public roads, paths, squares, bridges, banks and waters;
(3) Markets and the public sale of foodstuffs;
(4) Order and legality in the public assembly of a large number of persons;

[3] The quotation is from Lasker, not from the original text of the laws.

(5) The public interest with respect to the reception and housing of strangers; the wine, beer and coffee houses and other establishments for the dispensing of food and drink;

(6) Care for life and health;

(7) Precautions against the danger of fire in construction work as well as against actions, undertakings and events in general which are injurious to and dangerous for the common welfare;

(8) Protection of fields, meadows, forests, orchards, vineyards, and so forth;

(9) Anything else which must be ordered in the special interest of the community and its inhabitants by the police.[4]

It would be difficult, declared Lasker, to think of any action which could not be regarded as falling into at least one of these categories. Nonetheless, he added, two sentences in the Prussian private law gave the police even greater power. Of them Lasker wrote:

> Whoever commits an illegal act is suspected of having caused by his own fault any damage resulting from this act. Whoever ignores or neglects to abide by a police law is responsible for all damages which could have been avoided by the observance of the law, just as if the damage had arisen directly out of his action. The violation of a police order therefore often threatens to entail in addition to the direct punishment a far greater responsibility to compensate for damages. And a single police official almost to the lowest level can be the source of such legal effects.

Lasker drew the manifest conclusion from these conditions.

> The most important laws, which should be the foundation of a good economy and of freedom, are reduced to instructions for administrative officials. The execution or neglect of these laws has become an inner affair of the administrative agencies. How the official handles the law is in last analysis a matter to be answered before his conscience and his superior, and in case he has no superior, before his conscience alone.

This, Lasker stated, was the situation which during the Manteuffel regime in the 1850s had made legality a matter of administrative arbitrariness in the interest of the small but powerful Conservative party. It was a situation which liberals wished to correct.

The exercise of authoritarianism required the existence of a system of state and local government that could be controlled from the center. Since the Prussian bureaucracy had developed in the regime of abso-

---

[4] The list is quoted by Lasker from the police law of March 11, 1850.

lutism, an analysis of the hierarchy of control over the state will show how thoroughly the Hohenzollerns had shaped the instruments of administration in their own mold.

The question of the governmental structure, from the province through the county to the town and the rural community, received more attention from the ministry and Lower House of the New Era than any other single item of reform, except, of course, the military. The ministry submitted bills on each of these governmental units, which the Lower House considered, especially in commission, at great length. The King mistrusted the proposed reforms and the Upper House hated them. In his program of 1858 William had recognized the need for improving local government but had rejected any thought of introducing self-government. He expressed the intention of preserving the existing system in order to prevent a repetition of the troubles of 1848. He had not even mentioned those bulwarks of conservatism, county and provincial governments; apparently he considered them to be satisfactorily organized. In view of the King's attitude, the Conservative Upper House felt entirely free adamantly to oppose the liberal reforms. After the Lower House became engrossed in the conflict with the government over the military reorganization, the entire plan was neglected. Upon becoming Minister President Bismarck likewise introduced bills on the questions; but again the constitutional conflict prevented their being acted upon. The structure of government remained unchanged until several years after the Reich was established. Even then the legislation actually preserved the substance of Conservative power. A thorough reform had to wait until the revolution of 1918.

The chain of command began with the Minister of Interior who with the King's approval appointed the president of the government in each province and the director of each regional office under him. Below this director came (a) the county in which the Landrat, as we have seen, was appointed by the King, that is by the Minister of Interior, in most cases after receiving the recommendation of three candidates from the county assembly, or (b) the cities and towns, in which the election by the city council of the burgomaster and all other officials had to be confirmed by the government. In the Eastern provinces, with certain exceptions in Posen,[5] the next lower official, in charge

---

[5] In the province of Posen with its large Polish population, which the Prussian government did not trust, the rural community police power was administered by district commissioners directly under the Landrat. Von Roenne, *op. cit.* (1864), Vol. II, Part 1, pp. 235-40.

of the district (Gutsbezirk), obtained his office by virtue of his ownership of a piece of property to which this right or responsibility was
attached. In the Western provinces the Amtmann, or burgomaster, in
charge of the district was, after consultation with the regional and
provincial heads, appointed in the King's name by the Minister of
Interior. The head of the rural community, the Schulze, and the other
local officials were recommended by the community assembly and appointed, not necessarily from among those recommended, by the district head. In the Western provinces the appointment was subject
to confirmation by the Landrat. Exceptions occurred where the office
of Schulze was, like that of the head of the district, attached to a
particular piece of property. Apart from these two instances of
hereditary authority, the power of appointment or confirmation of the
administrative officials extended without a break from top to bottom
and provided the central government with full control. Officials were
appointed who were amenable to the government and who, as long as
the latter remained Conservative, would with rare exceptions be Conservative or, as the Conservatives loved to say, non-political.

The kind of personnel chosen for the administrative positions made
the control doubly firm. The lower positions were usually filled by
former noncommissioned officers or persons well drilled in the
bureaucracy, the higher positions by individuals with the same general
civil or military experience at an appropriate higher level. The appointments were not entirely of Conservatives, and many administrative officials believed in liberalism. Nonetheless, the relatively small
number who were publicly active in support of this way of life
shows that the system of control was on the whole effective.[6]

The existence of assemblies at the provincial, county, and district
or local levels did not diminish the concentration of power. In each
instance the decisions of the assemblies on all important matters like
the budget, the criteria for the assessment of taxes and other financial
matters, and often on unimportant questions, had to be approved by
the administrative official at that level and by his superior. If the
administrative official regarded an act of the assembly as going beyond its authority, he had the power to suspend the act and appeal
to his superior for a decision. In some cases matters considered by
the rural community, the town council, or the district assemblies had
to be submitted even to the ministry itself for approval. For example,

[6] See statements by Waldeck, Kaiser and von Vincke in the Lower House, *St. B.*,
1861; III, 1333-40.

if the assembly or council proposed to sell a piece of public property or contract a debt, it had to secure authorization from a higher administrative official. It would be difficult to find any action of consequence which the assemblies at any level were allowed to decide on their own responsibility. In case an assembly refused to pass a budget, the administrative official could impose one to cover necessary expenditures. The assemblies were convened by the administrative official at their level and were usually restricted to the agenda which he proposed. The amount of paper work involved in this meticulous control was enormous. In spite of the existence of the assemblies, anything like self-government was completely eliminated.[7]

With the New Era the reform of county government became an acute issue. Under the existing system the first or noble estate in the county assemblies in the Eastern provinces was entirely Conservative, and the second and third estates were carefully preserved for trustworthy persons of the same inclination. The Conservative government before 1848 had limited the eligibility for election in the second estate, that for towns, to present town officials, members of the magistracy and of the town representative council; and election in the third estate was confined to present incumbents in the community government. The liberal Minister of Interior von Schwerin proposed in 1860 to enlarge eligibility to include past officials; but the liberal commission of the Lower House disapproved such a slight extent and recommended that not merely the officials but anyone eligible to vote in the community or town elections should be eligible. The commission argued in favor of the greatest possible increase in voting power, asserting that thereby public interest in county government would be stimulated. It saw no reason to restrict the eligibility for voting with respect to the county assembly more sharply than that for balloting for deputies to the Lower House of the Landtag, and it expressed confidence in the ability of the voters to select able representatives. It regarded the government's proposal as excluding persons who might make excellent deputies, and it accused the government of wishing to preserve the present system of patriarchalism. Since the magistrates in the towns and the Schulze and other officials in the rural communities had to be confirmed in their positions by the government, it said, the latter would be able to exert pressure upon them to do its bidding in the Kreistag. Count von Schwerin denied any such intention, but

[7] See von Roenne, *op. cit.* (1864), Vol. II. Part 1, pp. 441-50, 458-66; Abg. H., *Drucksachen*, 1860; Vol. VI, No. 265.

the liberals clung to their recommendation for expanding eligibility.

In the commission of the Lower House the question of whether the Landrat should have the right to preside over the county assembly was discussed at some length. A liberal deputy pointed out that in the Western provinces it was not compulsory for the Landrat, or the Amtmann, to preside over the district assembly and that the system worked well. The case in the towns was also brought up in support of this view, as was that of representative bodies under constitutional government. The government spokesman countered these arguments by an analysis of the position of the Landrat which revealed the ministry's concern to maintain the prestige of that official and to change the distribution of power as little as possible. Aiming merely at some minor reforms in the system of county government, the ministry denied that the practices in the Western provinces could be applied in the East. It rejected any parallel between the county administration and the town administration, arguing that the town magistracy and the town council were separate organizations, whereas the Landrat could be a member of the county assembly.

> Even if the Landrats are also state officials and organs of the state administration experience shows that they are not prevented thereby from representing before the state government the interests of their counties with vigor and courage, and it can certainly not be asserted that the Landrats feel themselves to be too dependent upon the central administration. The double position of the Landrat which gives him in his capacity as organ of the county corporation an independent position toward the state government offers an important basis and condition for the successful activity of the Landrat.

The government feared that if the position of presiding officer over the Kreistag were denied him, the Landrat would lose prestige in the county and would be forced increasingly into the role merely of an administrative official of the central authority. Even worse, it argued, would be to subject him to competition by making the position of presiding officer elective; for in that case a failure to elect him would be considered a vote of no confidence and a tense relation would develop between him and the Kreistag which would hurt the entire county governmental system. The minister urged that the present power of the Landrat be preserved and that the parliament not try to introduce parliamentary procedures into local government, where, he said, they did not belong.[8]

[8] Abg. H.. *Drucksachen*, 1860; Vol. II, No. 265, pp. 59-60.

The question scarcely deserved the attention it received; more important was the government's plan to create an executive committee composed of the Landrat and at least six members of the Kreistag to work with him and in some respects to control him. Selected by the county assembly these persons would not merely advise the Landrat as before but would have actual responsibility in assisting him to prepare recommendations for the assembly, in planning the execution of decisions and in supporting him in his work. They would not participate in actual administration but would constitute a check on the Landrat's actions. In this way the government hoped to improve the quality of the preparation of matters laid before the Kreistag. It took its cue from the procedure in the province of Posen, where all proposals were criticised by a committee before being submitted to the full assembly. The Landrat needed the advice of men having the confidence of the assembly, argued the government official, for his duties had greatly expanded in kind and in number. The government would also find it useful at times to check the Landrat's recommendations by consulting the executive committee, and it hoped by this institution to reduce bureaucratic influence.

The liberal deputies in the Lower House showed as little confidence in freedom in county government as the ministry. They proposed that the central government keep its present authority. It was even suggested from the liberal side in the commission of the Lower House that central control be strengthened by empowering the King to appoint all Landrats without prior recommendation from the county assembly. In this way, the argument ran, the government would without introducing a spoils system be able to eliminate Landrats who were politically objectionable. The liberals had in mind the dismissal of the overwhelming majority of Landrats, who were Conservative and completely out of sympathy with the New Era. Others defended the right of recommendation of candidates for the position as an act of local self-government. The commission voted for the present system; but in either case the result would have been to maintain the central authority over the Landrat.

The limitations imposed upon Prussian liberalism by respect for tradition were seen with equal clarity in the reaction to the question of whether the county assembly and the town government should have the power of petition to the King on matters other than those pertaining exclusively to the county. The government proposed to retain the existing restriction. To the accusation in the commission that this stipulation violated Article 32 of the constitution allowing all

Prussians the right of petition, it countered by asserting that the restriction was undoubtedly justified and not unconstitutional. The argument in this instance pertained to the county assembly but expressed the views equally about the town governments. The government spokesman asserted that "the personality of a corporation is based upon and also limited by the purpose for which it was established. The county corporation is thus only in so far a person as it pursues the purposes of its constitution. If it goes beyond that point it exceeds its competence, and this would be the case if the Kreistag should petition about general political affairs not directly concerning the county." The overwhelming majority of the liberal commission of the Lower House agreed with the government's view. It added "that the Kreistag deputies were elected because of their qualifications to represent the interests of the county corporation, that one could not conclude therefrom that they were all equally qualified to judge general political affairs, that, moreover, the basis is lacking on which the Kreistag deputies who were present could commit to their decisions those who were absent and finally that the right of petition in political affairs would cause discord in the Kreistag and that to the disadvantage of county affairs the political parties would become more sharply prominent than ever."[9]

Most complaints about bureaucratic control came to the ministry and the Lower House from the towns. The Rhinelanders were so angry over regulation from above that Minister von Schwerin acknowledged the justice of their argument.[10] Conditions were actually no worse in the Western provinces, however, than they were in the six Eastern ones. In the latter the towns had a tradition of freedom established by Stein's reform law of 1808. The restoration after 1815 had steadily whittled away these free rights, and after the Revolution of 1848 the Conservative government had passed in 1853 a law which imposed upon the towns in the Eastern provinces nearly the same control as over those in the West. As soon as the New Era began, the townsmen became loudly critical and demanded reform. They objected to the power of the government to confirm the selection of the burgomaster and their other paid officials. They disliked having to refer to the regional government for settlement of all disputes between the magistracy and the town council. The towns of 10,000 population or less protested the authority of the Landrat by virtue of his police

[9] *Ibid.*, pp. 64-65.
[10] See also Deputy Contzen's statement, Abg. H., *St. B.*, May 2, 1861; II, 1027.

power to interfere in purely town affairs like street lighting. Even the larger towns, although not large enough for each to constitute a county by itself, disliked the Landrat's exercising the same kind of authority over them. It caused bad relations between the Landrat and the town magistracy, they said, by leading to decisions based on ignorance, to an unnecessary increase in bureaucratic work and to delay. It diminished the prestige of the town and the burgomaster relative to the feudal, landowning, usually aristocratic Landrat. The towns objected to the government's exercising so much police power in their midst, asserting that most of these matters were of a local nature, had nothing to do with security, were mainly economic and social in content, and should be left to the local population to handle.[11] In the Eastern provinces the petitioners were practically unanimous in condemning the introduction of the open ballot and the three-class system of voting and requested the return to the method of voting under the town law of 1808, the equal and secret ballot. The towns in the two Western provinces were accustomed to the three-class system and, not having known the other, were less critical; but they also wished the secret ballot.

Although the Minister of Interior of the New Era and the liberal Lower House differed somewhat in details about the reform of town government, they agreed usually about fundamentals. They all accepted the basic principle "that in all cases where higher interests of the state do not require interference from above, self-government of the towns through their constitutional organs is to be permitted freedom of action."[12] They agreed that town government should be uniform throughout the state. With respect to the government's power to approve the selection by the town council of the local officials they agreed that in spite of abuses under the Manteuffel government this power should be kept. The minister wished it to cover all paid officials;

---

[11] The *Nürnberger Korrespondent* published in January, 1861, the following statement. "Whoever wishes to see how police tutelage makes a large city incapable of self-government needs only to visit the capital and residence of the monarchy, Berlin. Scarcely a large city in Europe is less well paved and lighted, scarcely a city in Germany where in snowy weather passage is more endangered. The Berlin cab and omnibus service, which is controlled by the entirely bureaucratic police administration, is distinguished by foolish regulations. Therefore the cabs are worse, the horses lamer, the drivers lazier than in any other city. The people are arbitrarily ruled and taxed by a pasha and have in their magistracy and town council a representative body which is only forced every two years to bother about the city. If Prussia is to cease to be a police state, Berlin must first be given self-government." *Tagesbericht*, No. 4, Jan. 5, 1861.

[12] Abg. H., *Drucksachen*, 1861; Vol. V, No. 160, p. 2.

the commisson of the Lower House restricted it solely to the burgo-master and his assistants. They agreed that the burgomaster should re-tain a suspensory veto over the acts of the town council and of his col-leagues in the magistracy which he considered illegal or contrary to the welfare of the state, and that the issue should be appealed for settle-ment to the regional official of the bureaucracy. They preferred that in certain cases of disagreement over matters of purely local interest the action not be appealed and that it be postponed until the parties could harmonize their views. They retained the existing practice of requiring governmental approval of the local tax system, the contract-ing of town debts, the disposal of cultural articles of historical im-portance, and other predominantly economic matters. In case of the sale of town property the town government was to have a free hand, but it should notify the regional authority of its intention in time for this bureaucratic agent to interfere and block the sale if he saw fit.[13]

The proposed retention of the burgomaster's veto power in the towns showed that the liberals were caught in a dilemma. Although they believed firmly in living in a state of law, they knew that in the smaller towns especially no one except the legally-trained burgomaster would know what the laws were. For the sake of assuring that the law would obtain, they placed the executive in a position to veto the decisions of the popularly elected representative legislature. They re-tained in the town government the relation of the absolute monarch to the Landtag, with the one exception that the burgomaster's veto was limited by the right of appeal to a higher bureaucratic authority. In the name of the legal state they proposed to preserve a large degree of authoritarianism in town government.

An especially bad situation was to be found in the towns of Western Pomerania and Rügen. In proposing reform in 1862 the Minister of Interior described the conditions as follows: The magistracy co-opted new members and served for life. It was a lordship in its own right, able to dismiss burgher officials at will. The citizen body had either no right to elect officials or the very limited one of selecting them from among a number of candidates presented to it. A codified town law did not exist; and where the commission was endeavoring to collect the recent town ordinances, agreement had not been reached or the work concluded. "As a consequence such uncertainty about the law

---

[13] On the reform of town government see Abg. H., *Drucksachen*, 1859; Vol. III, No. 108. *Ibid.*, 1860; Vol. VI, No. 262. *Ibid.*, 1861, Vol. V, No. 160. Also the lengthy discussion in Abg. H., *St. B.*, 1861; Vol. II. *Ibid.*, 1862; Vol. II, No. 15.

exists in these towns that now and then even today the town council and burgher assembly must first be informed by the commission what according to custom and according to sources accessible only to legal scholars are to be considered norms and rules of town administration."[14] The minister proposed to bring the government of these towns into line with that in the rest of Prussia.

The commission disagreed with the Minister of Interior on one major question, that of the system of voting. The minister strongly recommended the retention of the three-class system of voting and the open ballot. He argued that the three-class system worked well, that it was not to blame for the decline in the number of actual voters, and that a better one had not yet been found. He manifestly liked the division of voters into three classes, with the political power allocated according to wealth, as a means of assuring the rule of the upper social groups. He defended open voting by the usual arguments: it stimulated and required civic courage and prevented corruption and hypocrisy. The liberals replied that the three-class system artificially divided at election time the burghers who otherwise were not aware of any such distinctions among themselves. It publically emphasized differences in wealth, again to the detriment of civic cooperation. They utterly condemned the open voting:

> When it is a question in a town not of political elections but of the representation of town interests, factors are emphasized which in other cases are entirely without influence. It is much easier in political elections, in which profound convictions can be made to have great influence, to keep free from entanglements of kinship, friendship and neighborhood, than in cases where in the main nothing but ability to achieve objectives which are the same for all comes into question. It is much easier to say that neighbor, relative, friend or customer has political views which one does not share than to say: he is a man weak in head and heart. Open voting also often disturbs the relation between community government and the citizen body. Many petitions point to the influence which under the present system of voting the burgomaster and the commissioners of the magistracy are able to exert on the voters, an influence which is the easier to exert because the commissioners face not a united body of voters but each voter singly.[15]

In spite of these arguments, Count von Schwerin held to his view; but by the beginning of the next year, 1862, he had come to agree to the

[14] Abg. H., *St. B.*, 1862; Vol. II, No. 15.
[15] Abg. H., *Drucksachen*, 1861; Vol. V, No. 160, pp. 16-17; *St. B.*, 1861; especially the debates on May 2 and 16.

secret ballot. He accepted the commission's argument as valid, and this time he buttressed his change of attitude by the historical fact that the town laws of 1808, 1831 and 1845 had all required the secret ballot and that the system of open voting owed its present force to the legislation of the Manteuffel era.[16] Further experience with Conservative ability to exert political pressure in case of open voting had won him over.

On one question the liberals found themselves in agreement even with the Conservatives. They all advocated the abolition of the tax on entry into the towns. Under the present law each town levied a fee upon anyone seeking to settle there and carry on an occupation. The restriction was opposed in the Eastern provinces but even more so in the Western. With the rise of industrialism, freedom of movement throughout the state had become urgent.[17] The industrial population of the Rhineland was especially angry about the limitation, and since industry was spreading into the rural districts it wished the entry fee to be completely abolished in these communities as well as in the towns proper. "If the small communities close themselves off from one another by this entry tax," declared Deputy Lette in the Lower House in 1861, "then labor will be more expensive for the factories, and the market for labor will be curtailed." The restriction was so disliked that even the House of Lords favored its repeal.[18]

Although the liberal ideal called for local self-government, the evidence supplied by the discussion of the reform of county, town and rural community government shows that neither the liberal Minister of Interior nor the liberal deputies had any intention of reducing sharply the control exercised by the central government. They lacked confidence in the ability of the peasants and townsmen, except in the largest cities, to run their own affairs, and were so devoted to administrative efficiency that they limited the freedom of the townsmen to learn by making mistakes. They denied to a representative body of the leading persons in the county the right to discuss and pass resolutions on matters of state-wide interest. These should be dealt with by another representative body, the Landtag, possibly composed of many of the same persons and certainly representing the same people. So well drilled had all Prussians been in bureaucratic specialization that the most progressive of them were unable to perceive the inconsistency of this opinion with their belief in liberalism. They did not

[16] Abg. H., *St. B.*, 1862, Vol. II, No. 15, p. 104.
[17] See *Ibid.*, 1861; I, 479.
[18] *Ibid.*, March 12, 1861; I, 478.

comprehend the nature and function of politics as a way of solving public problems whether at the national, state or local level. They thought of politics as reserved only to those high and noble affairs of state interest, at a plane of action far above the local. They did not see that politics should permeate an entire people, that otherwise the political activity at the top had no support down the line. They were inclined toward political snobbishness; they did not perceive how enormously important it was for them in the Landtag to have the organized aid of liberal elements in every popular assembly at every level throughout the state. With such support publicly expressed and aggressively supplied the liberal majority in the Lower House might have forced the king to retreat and might have won the constitutional conflict and established parliamentary government. Without this co-operation it allowed the government to retain ultimate power by means of the army and the bureaucracy. It played into the Conservatives' hands, allowing them to divide and rule, to force major groups to keep silent on public, state-wide issues. The liberals might not have succeeded in any case in putting through the House of Lords their reform plans for county and town government; by their attitude toward the right of petition in the county and town assemblies they betrayed the decided shortcomings of their own conception of self-government and of politics and created the major source of weakness in their combat with absolutism and Conservatism. Their thinking in governmental affairs remained to a large extent patterned after the existing institutions and practices of authoritarian bureaucracy.

Deputy Wagener spoke on behalf of the Conservative party against the liberal proposals. The Conservatives, he said, believed in autonomy and self-government of the corporate bodies, but by corporations they meant the castes of the Old Regime, plus such economic units as guilds. They wished in the name of self-government to restore the conditions prior to the Stein-Hardenberg reforms. They regarded it as an illusion to try to decentralize a bureaucratic state. They disavowed what they called the practice of arbitrarily selecting some member of the state organism, giving it a special constitution different from that of the rest of the organs in the bureaucratic state, and calling it self-government. "What you will achieve thereby," stated Deputy Wagener in the Lower House in 1861, "is not autonomy but disharmony, anarchy and disorder." He advocated the restoration of decentralized government as it had formerly existed, and he predicted that "as long as you do not have this either the upper bureaucratic agency will destroy the so-called autonomy or the so-called autonomy will destroy order and will force an increase in government from above, in other words the application of imperialism." He was thinking of the career of Napleon III.

The Conservatives opposed both the three-class system of voting and equal suffrage. They disliked the arbitrary and materialistic basis of the one, the equalitarianism of the other. In place of these, they proposed that each person receive voting power according to his social and political position. They meant thereby to allocate voting power to the social groups of a fully restored Old Regime. Of course they had no use for the secret ballot, dismissing it with the assertion that "in all which one understands, one is conservative," and implying that open voting was necessary so that the Conservatives could be sure that one did understand, that is, understand to be and vote Conservative or suffer the consequences.

The extraordinary criss-crossing of views of Conservatives and liberals on local self-government came out in the discussion of the government's right of confirmation of town officials and control of town affairs. The Conservatives were ready to support the liberals in restricting this right to the burgomaster and the town councillors, "because we are of the opinion," stated Wagener, "that the government has much vexation and little benefit and even less gratitude from doing so and because we do not wish to have it inferred that authority derives solely from the Crown." The Conservatives were willing to limit the control of the government over town affairs even more than the liberals proposed. "When one stretches the right of approval of the government so far that it has the right not merely to suspend those acts which are contrary to law but also those which are opposed to the welfare of the state and the interests of the community," argued Wagener, "then one takes away with one hand the autonomy that one has given with the other."[19] Although differing fundamentally from the liberals in their conception of local self-government, the Conservatives supported those liberal measures which were consistent with their own ideal. That they had no use at all for most liberal policies on local, county and provincial government may be seen from their intransigent opposition to the passage of the reform bills.

Examples of the kind of laws against which Lasker inveighed were to be found in every field; but some of these had special significance for politics, among them the press law, the law concerning the right

[19] *Ibid.*, 1861; II, 1024-25.

of association and assembly, and the law defining the authority of the state's attorney.

The constitution stipulated in Article 27 that "every Prussian has the right to express his views freely in word, writing, print, and picture. Censorship may not be introduced." Then was added the catch clause of a reactionary government: "Every other restriction upon freedom of the press shall be made only by way of legislation." Which part of the clause should prevail, the part guaranteeing freedom of speech and forbidding censorship, or that allowing the limitations of freedom of press by law? It was a case of double meaning, a device which the Conservatives took as the second best to what had existed prior to the Revolution of 1848, a substitute for conditions which they had not quite dared openly to restore.

The Conservative government had passed a press law, May 12, 1851, which suited their needs. This law remained in force through the New Era and the constitutional conflict; and while the ministers of the New Era either interpreted it in a liberal sense or ignored it, Bismarck used it as the basis for ruthless action. The main terms must be explained. Any person proposing to establish a printing shop, a book or art shop, a lending library, a reading room, a shop to sell newspapers, magazines, pamphlets and pictures had to receive the permission of the regional administration. Booksellers and printers had to pass an examination on their ability to handle those trades. They and all those in the other businesses listed had to be persons of "irreproachable character." What this term meant was disputed. The liberals interpreted it as implying that the individual must merely be in full possession of his rights as citizen. The Manteuffel government and subsequently Bismarck used it to annul the right to carry on the occupation "if the person abused it to undermine the principles of religion and morality as well as the foundations of the state and of society."

The law required editors of newspapers and periodicals to place a security sum with the police to assure good behavior. They had to present a copy of each issue to the police and obtain a receipt. The papers could not be sold or posted or even given away without the vendor's or poster's or donor's having a police permit. Only technical and similar periodical publications which did not discuss political and social issues were excepted from the terms. Suits over the violation of the press law were by a law of 1854 no longer to be tried before a jury, and public solicitation of funds to pay the fine of a violator was forbidden. By these measures the Conservatives in the 1850s

had hoped to preserve the freedom of the press, and the government
of the New Era did not take the time to change the law before it was
forced out of office in favor of Bismarck.[20]

Even more circumstantial than the press law was that of 1850 concerning the right of association and of assembly. The constitution
contained two articles about this right. Article 29 stated that "all
Prussians have the right without previous governmental permission
peacefully and without weapons to assemble in closed buildings. This
provision does not apply to assemblies in the open air, which in respect
to the receipt of previous police permission are also subject to the dis-
position of the law." Article 30 declared that "all Prussians have the
right to organize societies for purposes which do not violate the law.
The law regulates, especially for the preservation of public safety, the
exercise of the right guaranteed in this and in the preceding article.
Political associations may be subjected by legislation to restrictions
and temporary prohibitions." Such were the articles of the constitution. They guaranteed freedom of association and assembly, subject
to the law; and the reactionary government after the Revolution of
1848 immediately set to work legally to destroy the rights which the
constitution supposedly guaranteed. The pertinent law of March 11,
1850, is so revealing of the domination over public life exercised by
the police that it must be analyzed in detail.

The terms of the law of 1850 were as follows: A police permit
had to be obtained at least twenty-four hours in advance for holding
any assembly in which public affairs would be discussed. If the assembly opened an hour late or if it was adjourned for longer than an
hour, the sponsors lost the right to hold it and had to seek a new
permit. The chairmen of an association which aimed to influence
public affairs had to supply to the police within three days after the
founding of the association a copy of the statutes and a list of members and to report within the same length of time any changes subsequently made in either. They had also to supply any other information about the association which the police requested. If an association met regularly at a particular time and place, it required a
police permit only for the first meeting. The police were empowered
to have one or two police officials present in uniform at each assembly.
These officials were to be given suitable places and upon demand were
to be supplied by the chairman with information about the speakers.
The police officials had the authority to close the meeting at any time

[20] Von Roenne, op. cit. (1864), Vol. I, Part 2, pp. 89-112.

if proposals were made which incited or encouraged illegal acts or if armed persons appeared whom the chairman was unable to send away. The meeting had to close upon orders of the police present, even if the orders were without justification; the police could use arms to enforce their command.

Associations which held meetings for political discussion were subject to additional restrictions. Women, children of school age and apprentices could not be members or attend the meetings. The associations could not enter into agreement with other associations for common objectives; they could not form common committees or central organizations or make any similar arrangements or carry on correspondence for that purpose. If the police closed a political association, they had to report the case to the state's attorney, who then decided whether to prosecute it in court.

Outdoor public meetings of all kinds had to receive approval by the police at least forty-eight hours beforehand. A permit could be refused if the police regarded the meeting as dangerous to public safety and order. The same conditions attached to staging a parade.[21]

Each violation of the law was subject to a penalty of fine or imprisonment, and the accused was not entitled to trial by jury.

The law remained in effect during the New Era, when it was enforced in a liberal sense, and during the constitutional conflict. In the latter years it performed valuable service for Bismarck's government and, like the press law, was invoked to an extent that would have aroused the admiration of its creators.[22] It placed all public meetings under the arbitrary authority of the local police, and by its prohibition of common organization among political associations it practically prohibited the rise of well-organized state-wide political parties. Intended as an instrument for preserving the social and political status quo by obstructing public discussion, it well suited the purpose.

As Lasker showed, the state's attorney held a key position in the organization of state control over the Prussian people. According to a law of 1849 this official had the power, with a few exceptions of no consequence in this connection, to decide whether an investigation and legal proceedings should be instituted against a person. The courts could not take action before this official introduced the case.

---

[21] After the Landtag elections in 1862 four workers with large signs were placed in front of the Elberfeld town hall. The signs read: "Hurrah for the Constitution! Hurrah for the Law! Von der Heydt Gloriously Defeated! Long Live the King!" The police immediately arrested the workers. *Volkszeitung*, May 9, 1862.

[22] Von Roenne, *op. cit.* (1864), Vol. I, Part 2, pp. 149-53.

He had the right to decide whether or not a case should be tried; and in an authoritarian regime one can imagine how this power would be used. The political supporters of the government would not be tried for violations of the press law, the assembly law, and so on; the opponents of the government would be tried. The office lent itself to even greater abuse by virtue of the fact that the state's attorney did not belong to the judiciary and enjoy the independence of that body, but was a member of the civil administration, subject to the pressure and disciplinary action which could be applied to that branch of the government. We shall see later how Bismarck exploited this instrument of domination.[23]

The Breslau Chamber of Commerce wrote in its annual report for the year 1863 that "our economy has reached that degree of self-dependence which makes police paternalism no longer necessary. In view of the cultural condition of our people it is sufficient for the state police to restrict its activity to supervision or control in so far as these appear to be absolutely necessary for the general welfare."[24]

The liberals considered the question of freedom of economic activity (Gewerbefreiheit) not necessarily of first importance, but basic. In principle and practice economic freedom had been introduced into Prussia by the Stein-Hardenberg reforms, and in spite of some recession it had since then retained its prestige. The industry law of 1845 had reaffirmed Prussia's acceptance of the principle,[25] which not even the reactionary government in the 1850s had dared to repudiate. Nonetheless, the liberals of the New Era were thoroughly dissatisfied with the law of 1845, as well as with the reactionary amendments introduced after the Revolution of 1848. They demanded reform. Too many exceptions had been made to the general application of the principle; too much authority remained with the government to control business. The liberals wanted freedom of enterprise, with control exercised not by government but through competition. They were doubtful about applying their favorite principle to professions of law, medicine, pharmacy and other medical lines: some favored retaining state authorization, while others wished as complete freedom of practice in these professions as in any other. For all other occupations they agreed with the resolutions expressed in September, 1860, by the Congress of German Economists, in which they were heavily represented:

[23] *Ibid.*, Vol II, Part 1, pp. 264-65.
[24] *Preussisches Handelsarchiv*, 1864 (Berlin, 1865), *Jahresberichte*, p. 423.
[25] Von Roenne, *op. cit.* (1884), IV, 418, 438 ff.

The right to carry on an occupation shall not depend upon proof of personal ability.

The Congress is of the opinion that . . . the existing system of licensing has proved to be incompatible with the fundamentals of a healthy economic life; that concern about endangering and burdening the public in particular businesses makes necessary not the restriction of entry into the occupations but the fulfillment of legal conditions in the exercise of them; that part from the stipulations of criminal law the transgression of mere economic legal directives should merely be punished but should not affect the right to carry on the occupation.[26]

One major source of liberal discontent was to be found in the existing system of government concessions so roundly condemned by the Congress of German Economists. A commission of the Lower House of the Landtag presented a report in 1861 in which the following examples were given.[27] Each proprietor of a shop serving food or drink, of a tobacco shop or of a billiard hall had to renew his license every year. The liberal commission objected to the requirement of annual renewal as a major source of trouble. Under the Manteuffel system it had been used as a political weapon.[28] It was conducive to corruption, to chicanery and to the demoralization of the proprietor trying to earn an honest living. It created an enormous amount of unnecessary bureaucratic business, particularly since in the overwhelming number of cases the licenses were renewed without any question of the proprietor's good character. While not opposed to licensing, the commission recommended that requirement of annual renewal be dropped.

Similar difficulties confronted book publishers, book and art dealers, antiquarians, proprietors of lending libraries and reading rooms, and sellers of newspapers, pamphlets and pictures. In order to open one of these businesses a person had to obtain permission from the regional administration. He had to be of good character, and especially in the case of book publishers and book dealers he had to pass an examination before a commission showing his competence. The liberal commission of the Lower House recommended that these restrictions be abolished in favor of freedom of enterprise. As in the case of the proprietors of restaurants and other public houses, the

---

[26] *Bremer Handelsblatt*, No. 467, Sept. 22, 1860, p. 359.

[27] See also von Roenne, *op. cit.* (1884), IV, 463-65; Lasker, *op. cit.*, pp. 179-213. The chamber of commerce of the counties of Arnsberg, Meschede and Brilon included in their report for 1857 a long indictment of this system. *Preuss. Handelsarchiv* 1858; II, 527-29.

[28] As it was to be again by the Conservative governments of 1862.

governmental control had in the name of morality been the means of so much political and church abuse that the liberals wanted to abolish the entire system.[29]

In some localities where the handworkers remained economically powerful and the influence of factories had not yet been strongly felt, the liberals tended in the New Era to be wary of making the question of freedom of occupation a political issue.[30] The Conservatives had since 1848 attempted to keep the handicraftsmen on their side, forming, as the liberals declared, a coalition of Junkerdom and guildism. The government in 1849 had issued an ordinance restoring some of the former authority of the guilds. In a campaign pamphlet in 1861 issued by the Progressive party, Schulze-Delitzsch described the results of this ordinance as follows:

> According to Paragraph 31 of the industrial law of 1849 any factory owner can employ handicraft journeymen of all kinds for factory purposes, while according to Paragraph 47 a master handicraftsman is restricted to apprentices and journeymen of his own craft. According to Paragraph 30 no industrialist has to pass an examination, and according to Paragraph 32 such an unexamined industrialist may carry on any industry similar in purpose to that of a handicraft with the sole limitation that he employ no journeymen outside his factory, something the owner of a large factory will not do anyway. And other than size, no indication of a factory-organized handicraft exists.[31]

Schulze-Delitzsch concluded that the law of 1849 had imposed restrictions solely upon the small handworkers and not upon the factories; and he scoffed at the Conservatives' claim thereby to have prevented economic anarchy.

Liberal ire had been aroused by the fact that the law of 1849 had restored in part the conditions prevailing prior to the Stein-Hardenberg reforms. The law had created the institute of economic councillors, made it necessary in almost all handicrafts for a handworker to pass an examination and belong to a guild, limited the right to carry on the crafts, re-established the statutes of apprentice and journeyman and set up special financial sources for the aid of guildsmen.[32] It had imposed restrictions even upon marketing the wares, all for the supposed pro-

---

[29] Abg. H.. *Drucksachen*, 1861; Vol. IV, No. 126.
[30] *Bremer Handelsblatt*, No. 534, Dec. 28, 1861.
[31] *Hermann Schulze-Delitzsch, Schriften und Reden,* Hrsg. von F. Thorwart (Berlin, 1910), II, 396-97.
[32] Von Roenne, *op. cit.* (1884), IV, 419, 440.

tection of the craftsmen, and had placed the latter under the special protection of the state.

The conflict between autocratic mercantilism and the rising capitalistic industrialism was equally evident in other and economically more important areas, those of insurance and mining. These two branches of the economy already had a history, for each had contributed a considerable share to the economy of the Old Regime; but their role as molding influences in the entire economy lay in the future. Curbed and dominated by governmental regulations expressing the spirit of mercantilism, they stood at the beginning of their greatness. Their struggle for emancipation can only be understood in the light of the restrictions against which they fought.

A law of 1853 had stated that the establishment of an insurance business of any kind had to receive the approval of the administration of the region in which it was to be domiciled, and that approval should be granted only in case the government was convinced of the reliability and integrity of the entrepreneurs.[33] The way in which the system worked was thoroughly condemned by chambers of commerce over the state as expensive, cumbersome and obstructive of private intitiative.[34] The chambers of commerce of the counties of Arnsberg, Meschede and Brilon complained about the difficulties of starting and conducting an insurance business. The state had extended its control so far, the chamber said, that the establishment of even a small community insurance society for cattle had to receive prior approval. Every agent of an insurance company had to convince the government that he was reliable and honorable. One would think, said the chamber of commerce, that the insurance company could be trusted to employ persons of character. The law did not allow it such responsibility. In consequence, the chamber calculated that even after the criterion of political reliability used in the Manteuffel period was no longer applied, it required at least two weeks' time to go through the formality of clearing the person. If one multiplied two weeks by the 166 agents to be found in Prussia, the chamber stated, one arrived at the sum of seven years of time wasted.[35]

The *Berliner Börsen-Zeitung* in 1861 stated that there were twenty-seven different regulations for insurance companies in Prussia—four for the province of Brandenburg, four for Pomerania, three for Silesia, five for Saxony, eight for the province of Prussia and one each for

[33] *Ibid.*, 476.
[34] See *Bremer Handelsblatt*, Aug. 13, 1859, May 12, 1860.
[35] *Preuss. Handelsarchiv*, 1860; I, 744-45.

Westphalia, the Rhineland, and Posen. It wished them unified for the entire state.[36] The same business journal complained about government restrictions upon the activity of fire insurance companies in provinces where local societies for that purpose had been established under government auspices for the special benefit of the Junkers.[37] The story revealed the conflict between the two Prussias:

> It undeniably belonged to the political program of the Manteuffel-Westphalen system in Prussia, now a thing of the past, to preserve the antiquated feudal Institute of Provincial Fire Insurance Societies and to aid them against the competition of the rapidly expanding private insurance companies. The latter were a thorn in the eye of all enemies of progress because they were independent of feudal paternalism. So it is natural that the regulations of provincial societies issued during the reaction period should bear the marks of the system and that the communal Landtags endeavored to make the private companies dependent upon the control of the feudal societies and by all kinds of handicaps to turn the public away from them.
>
> Since these regulations still remain in force and since the management of the provincial societies in view of the inevitable decline of their irrationally conducted institute has recently sought to increase the inequality of rights and to obtain from the ministry further privileges, it appears advisable . . . to analyze one or another of these regulations. . . .

The writer chose as an example the revised regulation of the fire insurance society for the Mark of Brandenburg, the Margravate Nieder-Lausitz and the districts Jüterbogk and Belzig of January 15, 1855. Although according to Paragraph 2 of this regulation the society was to insure only buildings, under the pressure of its officials it expanded into the field of insuring movable property. The business of the society was administered by county directors under the leadership of a general director and the supervision and control of the communal Landtag. Only Landrats and owners of knights' estates who were members of the society were eligible as county directors; they were elected by the Kreistag, with the Landrat usually being preferred.

The stipulations for insuring immovable property were as follows: Through Paragraphs 14 and 15 of the law of May 8, 1837, and the cabinet order of May 30, 1841, it was forbidden in Prussia for agents and societies to give an insurance policy to a customer before local police had inspected the request for insurance and an official declaration had been made that the police had no objections against the

[36] *Berliner Börsen Zeitung,* May 17, 1861.
[37] *Ibid.,* Jan. 11, Feb. 22, 1861.

transaction. This police control, intended to prevent excessive insurance, was not regarded as sufficient in the case of the insurance of buildings, for Paragraph 27 of the regulation of 1855 stated that the county director of the Society had also to approve the transaction. According to Paragraph 1 of their special instructions the county directors might not grant this permission until they were convinced of the accuracy of the proposed amount of the insurance (seven-eighths of the tax value of the buildings). In case of need they had personally to inspect the buildings or have a building commission do so. If the necessary report on the proposed insurance with a private company was not made to the county director, the insured person had to pay a fine of fifty Reichsthalers to the Society. In case a building which had been insured above seven-eights of its worth burned before the policy had received the approval of the county director, according to Paragraph 29 of the regulation the insured person lost all claim to insurance from the private company and the latter had to pay the insurance sum to the Society.

These stipulations offered convenient means for the officials to curb and reduce the competition offered to the Society by the private companies. The county director learned about any intention to insure with a private company. He had the power to use his official influence as Landrat to persuade the applicant either to remain in or to join the Society. Recent cases were known of attempts of this sort, of one in Westphalia even to revive a defunct society. Without a time limit the county director could at his leisure investigate the policy with a private company. If a person proposed to withdraw from the Society and purchase insurance from a private company, he might find himself not covered by insurance while the county director investigated the validity of the new policy, but in case the person proposed to insure with the Society, the county director had to pass on the policy within eight days. The condition that a new building could be insured up to seven-eights of its tax value held only for insurance taken with a private company. In the case of the provincial Society the building could be insured to the extent of its full tax value.

The author of the article denounced as a scandal the provision that the antiquated and decadent provincial Societies should have such power over the private companies, such government support in defending themselves against competition. He was particularly angry over the stipulation that fines and even in some cases the entire insurance sum would have to be paid to the provincial society, and he believed that no judge in Prussia would allow such abuse of justice.

That the writer expressed the opinions of the private insurance world was evident from the numerous similar complaints of the time.

The government of the New Era with von der Heydt, a holdover from the Manteuffel era, still in power as Minister of Commerce made a few minor reforms between 1859 and 1861, such as that of abolishing the necessity for an insurance company to prove the need for its entry into business and for appointing agents in a district.[38]   In the main the old paternalistic controls were preserved, and in 1863 the Breslau Chamber of Commerce was still complaining about the same government obstructions to the insurance business as before.   The private insurance business remained subject to police control of the sale of each policy, an interference, declared the Breslau Chamber of Commerce, which contradicted the fundamental principles of government and economic teachings.   The private companies still objected to government aid to their competitors, the public insurance companies. Police officials in charge of fire prevention in the towns were still permitted to become members of the boards of directors of the public insurance companies, and Schulzes and other officials in the villages acted as agents of these companies.   The private insurance business considered this preferential treament to be utterly unfair.   It wished a free market in insurance and requested that police supervision be kept at the minimum essential for the general welfare.   It defended insurance as a means of education in individual thinking and action and as a basis of moral self-help.   Its proponents were declared to be fighting not merely for economic profit but for a moral cause.[39]

The business interests denounced Minister of Commerce von der Heydt, himself a businessman, for clinging to autocratic power over the economy and failing to recognize the need for a change in attitude and policy.   They asserted that industrialism, particularly in the field of transportation, was creating problems which could not be handled by a government devoted to a mercantilist policy of paternalism inherited from a purely agrarian Old Regime.   Business demanded help in both a negative and a positive sense.   The government should cease exercising such rigid control over business that it blocked enterprise; but it should also perform for business those essential services of which it alone was capable.   It should reshape its entire policy with respect to the economy and adjust to the conditions of a growing industrial society.

[38] *Preuss. Handelsarchiv*, 1861, *Jahresberichte*, pp. 260-61.
[39] *Ibid.*, 1864, *Jahresberichte*, pp. 425-26, 581.

At the meeting of the Congress of German Economists in 1863 the following statement was made:

> Railroads are transforming entire Europe and in entire Europe the position and significance of individual towns and cities. They organize an entire state in the way that formerly a single town was organized. We still find in the old towns a Tanner street where all the tanners live, a Dyers' street where all the dyers live. In the same way we find today a Sheffield, a Birmingham, a Leeds, a Wolverhampton where this or that branch of industry is alone carried on in the entire state.[40]

Every town and region of Prussia was ardently demanding that a line connect it with the rest of the world. The *Königsberg Hartungsche Zeitung* complained, August 4, 1861, that the Province of Prussia was the most neglected of any in railroad construction and therefore suffered from a severe economic handicap. Citizens of towns in other provinces expressed themselves in even more vigorous terms. Nieder-Lausitz had to have railroad connections, declared a correspondent to the *National Zeitung* in Berlin in 1861, or its industry and trade would be ruined. A railroad along the right bank of the Oder was a matter of life or death for Silesia. Each town or region was fighting to develop with the times. Each saw opportunities for expansion and wealth if it could only obtain transportation facilities. Each realized that without a railroad it was doomed to remain static.[41] These were crucial years in which the fate of a town would be decided for decades by whether or not it received a railroad connection.

The annual report of every chamber of commerce was full of denunciations of the government's policy with respect to railroad construction. Criticism of Minister of Commerce von der Heydt was bitter. The minister was accused of retarding construction. Capital had not been willing to invest in railroads which would not pay for themselves, and the minister was reluctant to provide government subsidies. The *Berliner Börsen Zeitung* complained that whereas between 1844 and 1850 some 263 miles of railroads had been built in Prussia with the participation of private capital, in the years 1850-57 only seventy-four miles were built with the aid of private resources, the first at a cost of 113,000,000 Thalers, the second of 56,000,000.[42] In 1858 only thirteen miles *in toto* were built.

[40] *Vierteljahrschrift für Volkswirtschaft und Kulturgeschichte* (1863), III, 267-68.
[41] See for example *National Zeitung*, Jan. 24, 1861; *Tagesbericht*, No. 64, March 16, 1861, citing article in *Schlesische Zeitung*, No. 125.
[42] *Berliner Börsen Zeitung*, Sept. 13, 1859.

In 1862 Prussia had 745.5 miles of railroads. (See Appendix B.) The critics argued that this amount was too small. The government was accused of devoting money to military purposes which should have been put to economic ends. It was denounced for influencing the capital market to deny private loans for railroad construction. "While it is no secret," wrote the *Berliner Börsen Zeitung* on February 18, 1859, "that the government is firmly determined, partly out of consideration of the bad state of the money market, to be most reserved in the near future about concessioning railroads, the number of requests for concessions increases in the Lower House to a vast degree." With the outbreak of the Italian War in 1859 the government was accused of continuing this policy in order to have funds available for state use in case of Prussia's becoming involved in international difficulty; and as the American Civil War and other international complications followed immediately after, the accusations continued. The liberals were angry over what they called the use of public funds for unproductive purposes instead of for the development of an economy which could support such burdens.

Liberal business interests denounced the government for following a policy of mercantilism with respect to railroads. The *Berliner Börsen Zeitung* for September 10, 1861, drew a significant parallel:

> The efforts to bring the entire railroad system under the rule of the state spring from the same spirit that formerly brought the police administration of the towns in the hands of the state. Just as in the latter case it was intended to destroy communal independence and make the police administration into a machine controlled by one power, the Ministry of Interior, so it is now intended to put lead strings on independent economic activity and give it a nurse maid who will listen to the directions of one power, the Ministry of Commerce.

From Beuthen in Silesia came a dispatch to the *Berliner Börsen Zeitung*[43] rebuking the Ministry of Commerce for being unwilling to discuss and attend to the complaints of the citizens. Especially was this the case with the monopolistic and exploitive policy of the railroads in the province of Silesia. Complaints had reached such a state, the paper said, that in all localities "a feeling of bitterness and open indignation predominates."

The coal and iron industries were especially angry. After the economic crisis of 1857 they had suffered from lack of markets and feared English competition. When the Franco-Prussian commercial treaty

---

[43] *Tagesbericht*, No. 25, Jan. 30, 1862.

of 1862 lowered the duty on these items, the producers intensified their demand for lower costs of distribution and more efficient handling of their products by railroads and waterways. They were thankful for the grant made in 1860 of the one-penny freight rate for coal on the railroads, but they wished the low rate to be applied also to iron. They condemned the railroad companies for many acts of commission and omission and sought aid from the government. Coal and iron, asserted the industrialists, constituted the foundation for the economy and should be given every assistance. When they prospered, the entire economy benefited. Instead of being assisted, said the Conference of the Executive Committee of the Association of Mining Interests in Dortmund, the railroads treated the industry as "a fat cow, which was there to be milked by the railroads with the least possible understanding and the most bureaucratic, Pasha-like satisfaction." Service was wretched, the industrialists said; cars were utterly inadequate in number; trains were too few; service was too irregular; stations were closed at night with consequent lengthening of the time required for service; the different railroad companies would not carry each other's cars; mines had to be shut down for lack of cars to ship away the coal; the number of lines was too small. According to the industrialists the entire service suffered from the fact that the government would not allow competing lines to be built and the canal service to be expanded, and would not press the railroads to keep up with the industrial development. The entire business world was angry and vociferous about the need for reform.[44]

The discussion showed that the rising industrialism was creating difficulties for its general line of economic laissez-faire. It was learning that laissez-faire was beneficial to some interests but not to others. The first big source of trouble came from the railroads. In addition to charging too high freight rates, they were imposing differential rates; that is, they charged less in proportion for carrying goods over long distances than over short stretches. The inland towns which were centers of wholesale trade, the old distribution points, and the smaller towns with hopes of economic progress were especially angry. They wished the government to interfere and either to permit competing lines to be built or to force the railroads to change their methods.[45]

Nor did the requests stop at railroads. All-weather roads were likewise wanted, though they were of secondary importance. The towns,

[44] See as examples *Preuss. Handelsarchiv*, 1861, *Jahresberichte*, p. 259; *Berliner Börsen Zeitung*, Feb. 16, Nov. 20, Dec. 12-13, 1861.
[45] See, for example, *Preuss. Handelsarchiv*, 1861, *Jahresberichte*, pp. 376-77.

particularly those of the Western provinces, asked for more canals and the improvement of existing ones and of the other waterways. The canal system, they stated, had not expanded since the days of Frederick the Great. They wished above all that the Rhine, the Weser and the Elbe should be connected. Thereby iron and steel, as well as other bulk articles such as agricultural products, would greatly benefit from freight rates lower than railroads could charge. The railroads would be subject to competition from another kind of carrier and would have to keep their rates at a minimum. In Silesia the economic interests, except the railroads, urged the government to make the Oder River navigable at all times of the year so that their commerce would have cheap means of reaching the outside world. The Cologne Chamber of Commerce envisaged a unified system of water transport joining the Danube and its tributaries, the Rhine, the Weser, the Elbe, the Oder and the Vistula, a water system covering the whole of Central Europe.[46]

All in all, the liberals had a large program of requests to put before the government for economic assistance in developing the country. They realized that each improvement in the means of transportation and communication meant opening up an area to their liberal ideals and methods.

The retention of the law against usury struck the liberals as a survival of medievalism. Its years if not its days were numbered, they thought, even though as late as 1864 the law was still in force.[47] When the government of the New Era endeavored to repeal the law, the Lower House of the Landtag passed the necessary bill, but the Upper House consistently refused to follow suit. The strength of the Upper House's opposition may be seen from the vote in 1860 of 93 to 8 against the governmental bill.[48] The Upper House was determined to maintain the legal limit upon the interest rate, five per cent for customary loans and six per cent for commercial loans. The members made the issue one of morality, of Christianity, as well as of economics. The liberals considered it equally a moral issue, a touchstone as to whether Prussia would accept the changes occurring in all enterprising coun-

---

[46] *Preuss. Handelarchiv,* 1861; *Jahresberichte,* p. 377. The board of directors of the Upper Silesian Railroad recognized the need of connecting the Oder with the railroad, but refused to agree unconditionally to it for fear of losing the trade in transporting zinc, iron and grain and other ballast materials. *Berliner Börsen Zeitung,* March 1, 1861.

[47] *Preuss. Handelsarchiv,* 1864; *Jahresberichte,* p. 118.

[48] *Ibid.,* 1860; I, 453.

tries or whether it would remain subject to the rigid standards of a historic caste. The Conservatives believed that they were protecting the ability of the landowners and handworkers to borrow money cheaply, indeed to afford to borrow it at all. The liberals denounced their opponents' stand as selfish and economically unsound. While apparantly not greatly hindered in their economy by the presence of the usury law, the liberals condemned it as an embarrassing symbol of the dominant forces in Prussian society.

When the government of the New Era introduced a bill in 1860 to repeal the usury law, it explained in considerable detail its motives. The usury law, it stated, did not accomplish its purpose. Instead of inclining or forcing the capitalists to lend money at low rates, the law actually drove funds out of the lending market into enterprises that offered a larger return. Or, the government stated, the lenders well understood how to circumvent the law and obtain the equivalent of a high rate of interest without running any danger of prosecution. Cases under the law almost never came before the courts; when they did, they usually involved lenders who had not been acquainted with the methods of gaining their ends without penalty.

Far from making loan capital more plentiful, the government argued, the usury law reduced the amount available for personal loans and hurt the small handworker or the landowner who already had a large mortgage on his property and suddenly needed more money. A reliable and honest lender would not take the risk for a return of five or six per cent, whereas he might for a larger one. The borrower was therefore driven into the hands of a real usurer. The law stimulated the growth of those conditions which it was intended to prevent. The situation became even worse in time of economic crisis, the government asserted, when, as conditions in 1857 had already shown, the usury law might have to be suspended.

The government denied flatly that the repeal of the usury law would "shock the sense of justice of the people," but argued that an improvement of a law would hardly hurt the public sense of justice. "The existence or non-existence of a legal prohibition offers no proper measure for judging the morality of an action; rather, it is the duty of the law-maker to adapt the laws to the real significance of the act." The real usurer, the government said, would be subject to punishment by law under any circumstances. Moreover, it was impossible to define numerically what was usury, for under some circumstances charging any interest at all might hurt the borrower much worse than charging him ten per cent at other times. Even the state in case of need paid more than the legal limit for loans. The government concluded that the usury law no longer stood in harmony with the sense of justice of the people and ought to be eliminated.

The ministry countered the expression of fear of high rates on land mortgages and a fall in value of the present mortgages by citing the example of England, Oldenburg and other countries. In the case of good securities, it stated, the interest rate even at the present time did not reach the maximum. It was not the height of the legal interest rate but the actual relation of demand to supply that regulated the price of mortgages, and no usury law would in bad times assure to the landowners cheap money. Nor did the government accept the view that the usury law should remain in operation for non-commercial and non-landowning classes even though it might be abolished for the rest of the population. It denied that such a division was either enforceable or advantageous to the lower classes whom it was intended to protect, and it adhered to the principle that a law should as far as possible have general validity.[49]

In the area of mining law Prussia was entering the period of modern industrialism with legal conditions mainly of the Old Regime. The only region with even the semblance of a modern law was the left bank of the Rhine, where the Napoleonic Code had done away with the mercantile system. The confusion of mining codes in the rest of the state expressed the diverse historic origin of the separate parts. Except for the core of Frederick the Great's Prussia, where that ruler had between 1766 and 1772 reduced the number of mining districts to three, each with its code, the territorial accretions had been allowed to retain their particular mining regulations, with new ordinances passed from time to time with respect to them. After the Napoleonic era the situation was so chaotic that the government in 1825 had begun to work on a common code for the entire state. The leisurely attitude with which the old Prussia approached such problems may be seen from the fact that the new proposal was not worked out and submitted to the interested parties until 1862 and did not become law until three years later.[50]

The response of the Chamber of Commerce of Essen, Werden and Kettwig to the terms of the law proposed by the government in 1862 expressed the opinion of all the parties most interested. The chamber thoroughly approved the government's action in basing the bill upon the following principles: "abolition of the mining royalty, emancipa-

[49] *Preuss. Handelsarchiv*, 1860; I, 49-53.
[50] See von Roenne, *op. cit.* (1884), IV, 399 ff.

tion of mining from state paternalism, placing of mining on an equal basis with all other branches of industry, permitting the free, independent exercise of acquired mining rights, abolition of cumbersome formalities which obstruct freedom of action, above all unification of mining law for the entire state." The chamber missed the application of one major principle, "the granting of the character of a juridical person to the mining companies and the free sale of the mining shares." The reforms cleared away the procedural regulations which had been imposed and enforced by the state mining administration and in general, to the extent that its particular nature would allow, placed mining under the rules of civil law like other business enterprises. The bill, and subsequent law, did not permit the complete freedom which the mining operators wished, but it marked one of the most liberal measures taken by the government. Both liberals and many Conservatives, including the Bismarckian government, participated in putting through the reform.[51]

The first part of the 1850s witnessed the founding of new private banks to provide the financial facilities for the rapid expansion of transportation and industry. The *Disconto-Gesellschaft* in Berlin was the most famous of these, but in every fairly large town which had not developed banks in the 1840s or earlier private interests now established new ones. The government was chary about this movement and curbed the rights of these banks as much as possible. It caused them great trouble by restricting sharply their right to issue bank notes. The credit shortage during the economic crisis of 1857 was prolonged by the international political complications evoked by the Italian War in 1859-60; and often in desperate need of funds during these troubles the business interests besieged the government with complaints. Early in 1859 the *Berliner Börsen Zeitung*[52] declared that the monopoly of the Prussian State Bank to issue bank notes had to cease, that the private banks had to be given this right as well. These private banks, it said, were leading only a sham existence and business was suffering for lack of capital.

The protests of the private banks made no impression upon the Prussian government. The cost of military reforms and the mobilization of the army in 1859, the impact of the international crisis upon

[51] See *Preuss. Handelsarchiv.* 1862; *Jahresberichte,* pp. 457-58; "Die Bergwerks-Hütten- und Salinen-Verwaltung in Preussen während 1849-1863," *Vierteljahrschrift für Volkswirtschaft und Kulturgeschichte* (1865) , I, 90; von Roenne, *op. cit.* (1884), IV, 404.

[52] *Berliner Börsen Zeitung,* Feb. 15, 1859.

the budget and a strong desire to keep state control over credit facilities at all times made certain that the government would not relax its restrictions upon the issuance of bank notes. In August, 1864, the banks were still lamenting. At the meeting of the Congress of German Economists at that time, the banker Sonnemann of Frankfurt am Main reported that in Prussia the monopoly of the state bank continued, that the private banks whose concessions would expire in a short time were seriously debating whether in case of the persistence of the present restrictions they should not close down. The banks earned so little profit on their capital as a result of these restrictions, said Sonnemann, that the returns were out of proportion to the risk. He advised them to seek to obtain from the government the right to take unlimited, interest-bearing deposits, and he thought that they might succeed. If they failed to obtain this right, he recommended to them to close their doors; "for a banking business that in ten years' time cannot pay higher than four to five per cent interest is not worth the trouble."[53] Bankers were as dissatisfied as other business men with the vestiges of absolutistic mercantilism.

Passing from the particular to the general, the chambers of commerce expressed the wish for reform of the system of chartering corporations. The existing procedure had been fixed in a law of April 22, 1845. A request was to be considered as appropriate only when the proposed corporation satisfied three conditions: first, the operations of the corporation had to extend beyond one locality; second, the enterprise should be useful from a general point of view and deserve special favor in the interest of the common welfare; third, it had to be of such a nature that the corporate form was necessary and that no other form of organization would suffice. In all cases, stated the law, it was essential to make certain that in the process of being created the corporation give adequate security against deceiving and harming the public. Each request for the right to establish a corporation had to be individually approved by the government.[54]

Under the terms of the law of 1845 an authoritarian bureaucracy could easily obstruct the economic development of the country. It could grant or withhold permission as it saw fit; it might delay with its answer until the entrepreneurs became disgusted and gave up, or

---

[53] See Joseph Hansen, *Gustav von Mevissen, Ein rheinisches Lebensbild,* 1815-1899 (Berlin, 1906), II, 551-53; *Vierteljahrschrift für Volkswirtschaft und Kulturgeschichte* (1864), IV, 198; also a criticism of the banks in *Bremer Handelsblatt,* Jan. 7, 1860, p. 7.

[54] Richard Passow, *Die Aktiengesellschaft* (Jena, 1922) , pp. 63-64.

until a favorable economic situation had passed. A group of entrepreneurs might see an excellent opportunity, it might have the promise
of the necessary funds, it might have settled all details: if it could not
persuade the government of the value of the project, it would be unable to execute its plan. The government might react with some favor
to projects for the construction of railroads which were also of military
value; but other branches of the economy might not fare so well. One
example may suffice. In 1863 the *National Zeitung* reported that the
Prussian Mortgage Insurance Corporation had had to wait four years
before receiving approval. A main objection of the government against
the mortgage banks, the article stated, had been the fear that their
mortgages would offer powerful competition on the market to the
Prussian state bonds. This was a strange view, the article added, "for
the credit of the state rests on the labor of the people."[55]

What the businessmen desired was the introduction of the English
system, the free right to incorporate a business in accordance with
certain legal forms,[56] a right open to anyone and exercisable with a
minimum of bureaucratic circumstance in an objective, normal way.
They did not gain that right until 1870.

The existing, unreformed procedure indicated mistrust and even
disapproval of these growing corporations on the part of autocracy, a
jealous fear that the government might in time be unable to direct the
economy of the state and might have to concede increased power to
private organizations. A reactionary government run by Junkers and
mercantilists disliked the whole conception of a modern corporation,
for its implied the shift from the old forms of wealth which constituted
the basis of their power to new forms conducive to the capitalistic
bourgeoisie and to liberalism. The Conservatives thought that they
could control an economy of agriculture and handicrafts; they knew
that they would not be able to control one of industry. They claimed
that they represented the ideals of morality and justice, that their way
of life alone was advantageous to the state. They accused the liberals
of seeking to further selfish economic interests. One of their members,
Deputy Hahn, declared in 1861 to the Lower House: "The big industrialists wish nothing else than for their capital . . . and their economic knowledge to prevail. They wish to expand the market for
capital and industry by elevating the handicrafts to factories or by
absorbing them." Another, the indispensable Deputy Wagener, asserted to the same body: "We are entirely accustomed to being ac-

[55] *National Zeitung*, Berlin, March 7, 1863.
[56] *Preuss. Handelsarchiv*, 1860; I, 743-44.

cused of pursuing special interests when something is advocated from our side, but when something is originated by the representatives of industrialism and capital these gentlemen naturally never have any other objective in mind than the welfare of their fellow-men and especially of the poorest class."[57] The assertions of these Conservative leaders showed a total lack of understanding of liberalism, a total aversion to a society of freedom which could expand the economy and create opportuntities for new achievements along all lines. The Conservatives were struggling to use the full power of an authoritarian government, a police state, to prevent a change from the society of the Old Regime to that of modern industrialism. The conflict over the form of government involved that over the nature of the society.

Unfortunately the government even of the New Era was not very responsive to economic needs. The key Ministry of Commerce remained in the hands of von der Heydt, a businessman, but a holdover from the Manteuffel ministry, with a definitely mercantilist point of view. Back of him stood the King, whose understanding of economics may be judged from the statement in his program of 1858. "Trade, industry and the closely related means of communication have expanded to an unimagined extent," he had written; "nonetheless we must here also be moderate in the objective so that the spirit of fraud does not wound us. Significant funds must continue to be placed at the disposal of the means of communications; but they must be measured in consideration of all state needs, and we must keep within the budget." The King manifested little enthusiasm for the progress of trade and commerce. The two points of emphasis in his remarks had to do with preventing "the spirit of fraud" from "wounding us" and with assuring that public funds were not devoted to the construction of roads and railroads to such an extent that, for example, his army would suffer from lack of nourishment. He did not mention the fact that commerce and industry were making his state more powerful than ever before, and he failed to perceive that even though the construction of modern means of communication required a large initial outlay of money, the advantages to the state and society would be immediate and out of all proportion to the cost. He sacrificed economic aid for business to the financial needs of his program of military reforms; and both von der Heydt, although in the end under protest, and Bismarck acquiesced in his policy. The economic expansion of these years occurred in spite of the government's indifference.

[57] Abg. H., *St. B.*, May 6, 1861; II, 1096-97. *Ibid.*, May 7, 1861; II, 1107-08.

4 / Militarism

I N his reform program of November, 1858, the Prince Regent included a paragraph about the conditions of the military service which was so veiled in meaning as to be scarcely noticed.

> The army created Prussia's greatness and battled success-fully for its growth. The neglect of the army brought about a catastrophe for it and the state, which was gloriously effaced by the appropriate reorganization of the army, as the victories of War of Liberation revealed. Forty years' experience and two short wars have now made us note that much which has not proved satisfactory needs to be changed. For that work we need calm, peaceful conditions and money, and it would be a criminal mistake if one should display a cheap army organization which for this reason in a decisive moment did not live up to expecta-tions. Prussia's army must be powerful and respected in order when necessary to be a grave political weight in the scales.[1]

The implementation of the idea in this paragraph led to the appoint-ment of General von Roon as Minister of War and of Bismarck as Minister President; it brought about the constitutional conflict, the crushing defeat of liberalism and the victory of militarism and Con-servatism in Prussia and Germany.

The plans for military reform were completed in the next year, 1859, and their execution was initiated with the mobilization for the Italian war that year. In 1860 the government proposed a bill to the Landtag to legalize the entire reform, justifying the action by the fact that the army should be adapted to the changes in population and society which had occurred since the passage of the basic military law

---

[1] Horst Kohl, *op. cit.*, p. 5.

of 1814. The government called attention to the fact that the size of the army remained the same as in 1814, in spite of the fact that the population had increased from ten million to eighteen million and that the stipulation for compulsory universal military service in the law of 1814 was not being carried out. It proposed to increase the number actually called for military service from twenty-six per cent to forty per cent of those subject to military duty. The number of annual recruits would be increased from 40,000 to 63,000 men. The bill aimed to require military service of three years in the regular army for the infantry and four years for the cavalry. The three-year term had been stipulated in the law of 1814, but had actually not been enforced from 1833 to 1853, when the two-year term had been substituted. Since 1853 the longer term had been restored and the bill proposed to make it permanent. The Landwehr or reserve was to be reorganized, with the three youngest year groups incorporated in the regular army and the older ones used merely within the country for garrison and similar duties. The term of service in the army would last from the twentieth to the thirty-sixth year, that is, three years less than at present. Of these sixteen years, seven were to be spent in the regular army, three in active service and four in the reserve. The rest of the term, from the twenty-eighth to the thirty-sixth year, would be served in the Landwehr. The reform made it possible to leave the older men, usually fathers of families, at home in case of mobilization of the troops of the line; previously those who were in the first Land-wehr (Erstes Angebot) had to be called at every mobilization for the army to have enough men. An appropriate number of new regiments was created to take care of the increased size of the standing army. With the levying of more recruits and the alignment of the younger years of the reserve with the standing army, the government expected to keep the size of the army about the same as before but to have much younger regular troops and to bring them under the efficient control of regular army officers.

The Prince Regent regarded the military reform as his own special task. He was from the start determined to stand or fall with it. He declared many times that he would renounce the throne rather than accept any modifications in fundamentals. He believed firmly that an improvement in the military efficiency and strength of the state required increased conscription with intensive training of recruits for a period of three years by regular army officers and the subordination of the Landwehr for the first three years to the authority of the regular officers. The integral combination in his thinking of military, social and political arguments becomes clear from his numerous memoranda and speeches in the military commission. He constantly declared that one could teach a peasant the necessary drills in a few months, but that "to produce the soldierly character in its totality" three years' service was too little. "For two years the recruit will be completely over-powered by drill and instruction; only in the third year will he learn to feel himself a soldier and acquire respect for the uniform, for the seriousness of his profession; and then he will be filled with the spirit of the caste without which an army cannot exist." The Prince nursed a deep distrust of the Landwehr, which von Roon and many regular army officers shared. The Prince related how, when a Landwehr troop had acted so badly in a review before the late Czar Nicholas I, he had been sent ahead by the King to the next review place to prevent a similar disgrace. In the streets one heard at that time the remark, "There goes the dirty Landwehr man." The Prince had been particu-larly impressed by the fact that in the Baden campaign of 1849 the Landwehr troops had had to be driven back into battle by a regiment of the line. When the Landwehr troops hastened to the colors in the mobilization of 1859, he remarked dryly that since then their over estimation of themselves had given way to a healthy humility. Con-sequently, he regarded three years of training as indispensable, argu-ing in 1859 as follows:

> Why did all Landwehr battalions of the Guard hold loyally to their oath of service? [He was referring to the events of 1848-49.] Because the three-year period of service remained in force in the Guard corps without interruption. Infantry regiments of the line wavered. . . . But of all the cavalry regiments of the line not a single one for even a moment became uncertain in its loyalty! Why? Because they also had preserved the three-year period of service.

With such quantitative explanations was his simple military mind content.[2]

Minister of War von Roon concurred in the Prince's low opinion of the Landwehr. He regarded it as "a false and weak military in-stitution," lacking the "genuine, correct, firm soldier's spirit and the secure disciplinary control." He objected that the Landwehr man felt not like a professional soldier but like a civilian, that all this think-ing was directed toward civilian ends, that although he knew some-thing about handling weapons "his soul clung to his farm, his chisel,

---

[2] See the Prince Regent's memorandum of December, 1859, in *Briefe, Reden und Schriften*, I, 461-78; Egmont Zechlin, *Bismarck und die Grundlegung der deutschen Grossmacht* (Stuttgart und Berlin, 1930), pp. 176-77.

his work at his home, not to the flag." One had to appeal to his good will and at times even to his "supposed patriotic sentiment." To clinch his point, von Roon related the incident in 1849 of a despairing commander who had had to buy beer for his Landwehr men to entice them on. A preferable inducement, von Roon thought, was "the restorative of the iron screws of military discipline." He believed that times of general popular enthusiasm would come again, but he thought it foolish to rely upon such means to accomplish indispensable results. He preferred to depend upon "a good and sound organization" to use and augment the enthusiasm if present, or to achieve objectives if absent. Corps spirit, love of honor, loyalty to the warlord were, he said, moral forces which were found in all great armies; the basis of this spirit was to be had in the common deeds, dangers and suffering of military discipline. This foundation, he declared, was lacking in the Prussian Landwehr. He regarded the present Landwehr as a bad political institution, for with it the government could not be master in its own house and had constantly to think of the effect of its action in both internal and foreign affairs upon the armed part of its people, the Landwehr. This was especially the case, he said, since the introduction of constitutional government, for now each Landwehr man could use not only his arm but his tongue. To a certain extent he could check the government. This influence made the government weak where in the interest of the country it should be strong, indecisive and hesitant where it should be positive and swift. Von Roon emphasized the value of the principle "The armed force does not deliberate, it executes."[3]

This frank statement of Prussian militarism could scarcely have been improved upon. The country existed to support the army; the constitution had unfortunately weakened the morale of the army; that weakness caused by the soldier's being also a voter could be overcome solely by exposing him to three years of intensive drill in the military spirit by professional army officers; a civilian as soldier was not to be trusted since he thought too much about those things which he was defending; every eligible male in the state should be forced to undergo this training so that he would be a loyal and obedient subject. One may judge from von Roon's remarks that the military reforms were the means by which the ruler and his Conservative army officers of the nobility hoped to block the constitution's implications

[3] Zechlin, *op. cit.*, pp. 177-79; *Denkwürdigkeiten aus dem Leben des General-Feldmarschalls Kriegsminister Grafen von Roon.* (Breslau, 1892). I, 322-24.

for freedom and a new society and to preserve the old order of caste and absolutism under a constitutional cover.

The liberals understood the significance of the military reforms from the start. They were appalled at the cost. The central committee of the German Progressive Party issued a broadsheet in which it roundly denounced the reforms.[4] The peacetime army for 1862, it said, called for a minimum of 205,000 men, a maximum of 215,000. If one chose the median figure of 210,000, it would mean that Prussia would have twelve soldiers to every 1,000 inhabitants. This figure should be compared with that of ten per 1,000 in Austria, eight in Russia and ten in France. Military expenses crippled Austrian and Russian power to such an extent, the committee argued, that when war finally came the two countries had plenty of soldiers but lacked the means to use them successfully. Even France, which was much richer than Prussia, had had to curtail its military expenditures.

In 1850, the broadsheet continued, Prussia had had an army of 131,000 men and now it was adding 80,000 more. In 1850 the army had cost 26,000,000 Thalers; at present it cost 40,000,000, or 14,000,000 more. This meant that with 3,500,000 taxpayers in the state, the army cost each taxpayer annually four Thalers more. In addition, the country was deprived of the labor power of these 80,000 men, or if one reckoned the value of the work of each at one hundred Thalers a year, the country lost a sum of 8,000,000 Thalers' worth of productive work every year. Thus the army cost the country 22,000,000 Thalers more than in 1850. This was not all, declared the committee of liberals. One must add 3,000,000 Thalers to cover cost of new construction and maintenance of fortifications, barracks and hospitals, of construction of railroads for purely military purposes, of horses, munitions and so on. Moreover, the soldier lived on the meagerest possible terms. His pay of two and a half silver Groschen and one and a half pounds of bread daily was not enough to maintain him. His family, already deprived of his productive services, had to send him food and money. The amount paid by the state for quartering troops was utterly inadequate to cover costs and the burden was unfairly distributed. Nor was the reorganization of the army as yet completed. One could expect fairly soon that the sum of 7,000,000 Thalers would have to be added to the 22,000,000 or 23,000,000. And the navy had not even been mentioned; it needed much more money than it had

---

[4] *Spart im Frieden, dass Ihr Stark im Kriege Seid.* See also *National Zeitung,* Jan. 26, 1861, and the debates in Abg. H., *St. B.,* May 27-28, 1861; III, 1399 ff.

been receiving. The broadsheet estimated that sooner or later the army reform would cost the country some 32,000,000 Thalers more than in 1850, or nine Thalers for each head of a family.

In calculating the size of the force available for immediate mobilization, the liberal broadsheet stated that the reorganization provided only 353,000 men, whereas the army prior to 1860 could muster 344,000 men for immediate service. It concluded that the reform was not worth the effort.

The liberals on the one side and the ruler and his military advisers on the other had entirely different conceptions of defence. The former believed that a country was strong in defence if it was economically prosperous. They feared that the military reforms would wreck the economy and expose the country in time of war to extreme danger. They believed in the intelligent loyalty of each citizen to the country and his willingness and ability to fight in a crisis. They disliked intensely the sense of social inequality which was preserved in the army. The King and his military entourage emphasized the necessity of drill and more drill for the inculcation of social and political obedience, not to say docility. They stressed the organizational aspects of defence and tended to belittle the spiritual; and they had little or no understanding for the economic factors. Two different views of life were here opposed to each other, that of the growing industrial, liberal society and that of the Old Regime.

Numerous complaints, especially in the Western provinces but also in the Eastern, were levelled against the cost of quartering the troops. Since the old system of requiring the locality to pay the cost still prevailed, those towns that had the misfortune to be selected for either temporary or permanent quartering found themselves burdened with excessive expenses, and they petitioned the Lower House to change the system and relieve them of this load. Düsseldorf, for example, had in former years paid 6,000 Reichsthalers, but in 1859 it had had to pay out 50,000. The compensation provided by the government was regarded as much too low; the unfortunate towns had to make up the difference to enable the soldiers to live. From Thorn came the criticism that quartering cost one and a half to two Thalers, whereas the government in summer paid for quarters only eight silver Groschen and five Pfennig and in winter fourteen silver Groschen and one Pfennig. (One Thaler = 30 Groschen; 1 Groschen = 8 Pfennig.) The presence of the troops benefited only the tavern and the shopkeeper, ran the criticism, and was a disadvantage to everyone else because of the increased price of the usual necessities of life and increased wages.

In the West a lively town did not want a garrison to be stationed in its midst. In the Eastern provinces, however, the degree of economic and cultural activity in many towns may be judged from the fact that some of them actually petitioned for garrisons. The presence of soldiers meant to them the stir of life. Nonetheless there was general approval of the recommendation made in June, 1861, by the Commercial and Industrial Association of the Rhineland and Westphalia that the cost of quartering troops be regarded as a state and not a local expense and that it be absorbed by the state budget.[5]

Strenuous objection was raised to increasing the size of the army. The shortage of labor due to mobilization, it was said, would become chronic. Manpower would be wasted; all those months of military service would be devoted to non-productive purposes. Trades could not be learned; idleness and ignorance would result. From Trier came reports in 1862 that persons were emigrating to escape higher taxes and the long military service. At Stettin Doctor Wolff, a leading liberal, stated in August, 1864, that young men in the Baltic towns were prevented by military duty from visiting foreign commercial centers and establishing connections, and that commerce was hurt more by military conscription than any other branch of the economy.[6] Representatives of the other branches raised similar objections. Except among the few Conservatives military service was universally disliked.

The government argued that even with the increase in the size of the standing army the percentage of the population in service remained less than that in any year between 1816 and 1822. In 1816 Prussia had had a population of 10,349,031 and an army of 130,000 men, or 1.25 per cent. The percentage had steadily declined until in 1857 it had reached 0.80 per cent of a population of 17,560,886. The new organization of the army in 1861 put some 205,000 men in the army out of a population of 18,246,760 (1.12 per cent). The government compared these figures, which included both land and sea power, with those for Great Britain (0.75 per cent), France (1.13 per cent), Austria (1.25 per cent), and Russia (1.33 per cent)—to the manifest advantage

---

[5] *Berliner Börsen Zeitung*, Dec. 28, 1859, June 12, 1861. Abg. H., *St. B.*, May 29, 1861; III, 1500. *Ibid.*, Feb. 11, 1861; I, 197-200. *Ibid.*, May 28-29, 1861; III, 1438, 1503. *Kölnische Zeitung*, March 9, 1862.

[6] See chamber of commerce reports of 1860-62; *Kölnische Zeitung*, April 27, 1862; *Vierteljahrschrift für Volkswirtschaft und Kulturgeschichte* (1864), III, 230.

of the government's claim for more manpower to keep up with the others.[7]

The liberals replied with other figures, which included the number not merely of the standing army but of all the troops in service, and came to the conclusion that Prussia had an army of 430,000 men, or almost 2.5 per cent of its population, and that if garrison troops and Landwehr were considered the percentage would reach about four.[8]

The views about the period of service necessary were equally opposed. Claiming that three years were essential to train a soldier, the government contrasted the short term of service in Prussia with the length of it elsewhere. In Russia, it stated, the soldier served from the ages of twenty to thirty-two, in Austria from twenty to twenty-eight, in France from twenty-one to twenty-seven, in Prussia from twenty to twenty-three. If one added the service in the reserve the terms were: in Russia from the age of twenty to that of thirty-five, in Austria from twenty to thirty, in France from twenty-one to twenty-eight, in Prussia from twenty to twenty-seven. The government pointed out that all military obligation in Prussia ceased with the thirty-sixth year, whereas it continued in Bavaria to the sixtieth year and in Russia to the fifty-fifth. It added that it would not be necessary to call to service even in time of war the personnel above thirty-two years of age and concluded that in Prussia the admitted burdens of compulsory military service were held to a minimum.[9]

Severe protests were registered against the government for spending so little for cultural or productive purposes. The *Zeitung für Norddeutschland* remarked in January, 1861, that the present Prussian government was "not all too human" in its support of literature and art, that it was employing no artist of significance. It compared this attitude with that in Bavaria, where recently the King had again given large commissions to German artists. It reported that the artists in Berlin feared the cessation of architectural and other artistic work already in progress there.[10] The *Volkszeitung* (June 14, 1862) reported that newspapers were again expressing the need for a new parliament building. "They forget," this liberal paper commented, "that we still need so and so many barracks for the new regiments. First

---

[7] *Die Innere Politik der Preussischen Regierung von 1862 bis 1866. Sammlung der amtlichen Kundgebungen und halbamtlichen Äusserungen* (Berlin, 1866), pp. 35, 55-56.

[8] *Bremer Handelsblatt,* July 6, 1861.

[9] *Die Innere Politik,* pp. 75-76.

[10] *Tagesbericht,* No. 4, Jan. 5, 1861.

business and then pleasure. Barracks come first." The *Kölnische Zeitung* (March 31, 1862) stated that "the world-famous University of Berlin has no chemical laboratory!" and that apart from the Industrial Institute in Berlin, Prussia had no polytechnic institute. Prussian students had to go to Hanover, Karlsruhe or elsewhere to study engineering. Prussia had money only for the army. Most complaints, as we have seen, were registered about the failure of the government to devote larger sums to the construction of railroads and good roads and to the improvement of canals. The papers and the reports of chambers of commerce were full of such expressions. At the Berlin meeting of the Prussian Commercial Association in March, 1860, the chairman, David Hansemann, an ultra right-wing liberal, declared:

> In *one* sense the convention has expressd itself with unanimity; in several votes it has given to understand with absolute clarity that the state has great cause to devote more public funds to productive purposes (navigable waterways, and so forth). It has been stated that in this respect our fatherland has remained behind other countries. If the same system of saving and devoting state money to other than productive purposes continues in the present degree, as appears likely, Prussia will in the progress of its welfare remain significantly behind other countries. I believe that these unanimous opinions should carry some weight, for they are expressed by an assembly which is composed largely of people who pay no small amount of taxes and who have a great interest in the preservation of state credit and of a good rate for state bonds.[11]

The government tried to refute the charges of excessive burden. In the Lower House Finance Minister von Patow admitted on May 28, 1861, that military costs had cut into expenditures for other purposes but added that the budget for that year contained about the same amount for productive expenditures that it had allotted for the past decade.[12] The semi-official *Stern-Zeitung* in a series of articles in 1862 argued that Prussia had borne similar burdens before and could do so again. It declared that the present high cost was necessary because of failure to keep up the army in past years and that even with the reform Prussia had scarcely attained its former military strength with respect to other countries.[13]

The government claimed that the cost of the military after the reorganization constituted a lower percentage of the total public ex-

[11] *Bremer Handelsblatt*, March 10, 1860, p. 93.
[12] Abg. H., *St. B.*, May 28, 1861; III, 1446-47.
[13] *Die Innere Politik*, p. 33.

penditure than at any time between 1820 and 1849. It offered the following figures as evidence: In 1820 the total public expenditure had been 72,818,848 Thalers, of which the sum of 27,472,223 Thalers, or 37.73 per cent, had been devoted to the army. In 1847, the figures had been 89,563,361 Thalers, 28,305,615 Thalers, and 31.6 per cent. In 1859 they had been 131,137,859 Thalers, 32,315,877 Thalers, and 24.64 per cent. And in 1861 they were 138,585,051 Thalers, 40,361,104 Thalers, and 29.12 per cent. The government further argued, with statistics, that the cost of the army was less in proportion to size of population and army than that in any of the large European states except Russia.[14]

The government's defence did not convince the liberals, who objected to the military budget not so much on grounds of the money's being used wastefully but rather because so much was allocated to the army at all. The justice of the liberals' criticism was acknowledged even within the ministry. In March, 1862, Minister von der Heydt wrote to his colleague von Roon a confidential letter which through some slip appeared in the press. In it he urged a reduction in taxes and in expenses.

> That the larger part [of the reduction in revenue] can occur only in case of a reduction in military expenditures . . . hardly needs to be shown further, for it is sufficiently known to you that expenditures in all other administrative branches have been curtailed for years in order to reduce the deficit caused by the increased needs of the military administration while maintaining the appearance of fulfilling repeated governmental promises. The result has been that the needs postponed from year to year because of lack of funds have become increasingly apparent. It will no longer be possible without disadvantage to the country further to ignore these and to decline those many requests for increased expenditures made in the Landtag during consideration of the budget by pointing to the lack of funds.[15]

In the Lower House Deputy von Ammon, who had served in the War of Liberation against Napoleon, attacked the preferential financial and social position of the military officers. He denounced the amount of their salaries as proposed in the budget as "enormous" and "out of all proportion to those of civil officials." The five hundred majors, for example, he said, had far larger salaries than any civilian councillor

---

[14] *Ibid.*, pp. 39-40, 48-74.
[15] The letter is to be found in the *Volkszeitung*, April 6, 1862. It was reprinted in other papers, but was given a modest summary in Bergengrün, *Staatsminister August Freiherr von der Heydt* (Leipzig, 1908), pp. 288-89.

of comparable rank could hope to obtain. In addition the officers received extra assistance, service, and rations, which augmented their income. While subaltern officers' salaries were not large, these young men were rapidly promoted.

> Compare the long and expensive theoretical and practical preparation which every other state official has to go through. When one considers that, for example, our assessors must wait ten to twelve years for fees or a fixed salary and become gray, while the subaltern officer who entered service at an earlier year will have already in this period of time become a captain, you will find in that situation no similarity.
> When a position is to be filled in the civil bureaucracy there is often no money available. The pension which a retiring official is to receive can mostly be paid only out of the salary of the position become vacant. In the case of the military, on the other hand, everything is richly provided. Every position that becomes vacant is immediately filled. Pensions are easily obtained, and in most cases are larger than those that can be claimed by civil officials of comparable rank.

Von Ammon objected to the military as an "exclusive special caste, the first estate in the country."

> This prejudice is furthered . . . by the undeniable preference for nobles, by the autonomy of regiments [in selecting their own officer personnel] which do not even accept what the highest war lord gives them, . . . by a policy, which, in spite of the view that the soldier should not engage in politics, is characterized by opposition to all liberal progress.[16]

Von Ammon's criticism was approved by Freiherr von Hoverbeck, who expressed the conviction that at the present scale of pay the common soldier was starving, unless he had the good fortune to receive outside support or was able to work on the side.[17] The Berlin correspondent of the *Deutsche Allgemeine Zeitung* contrasted the scale of financial support of the army with that of teachers, which was notoriously low.[18]

The main objection which the liberals had against the military reform grew out of social conditions. Deputy Brämer did not criticize "the corps spirit" as an evil but he denounced "the caste spirit which is formed."[19] Aristocratic caste and privilege dominated the army, he

[16] Abg. H., *St. B.*, May 27, 1861; III, 1398-99.
[17] *Ibid.*, May 27, 1861; III, 1399-1400. Also Ludolf Parisius, *Leopold Freiherr von Hoverbeck* (Berlin, 1897-98), I, 196; II, 200 ff.
[18] *Tagesberichte*, No. 16, Jan. 20, 1862.
[19] Abg. H., *St. B.*, 1861; III, 1468.

said, and served as the basic support for the Old Regime throughout the state. The nobility enjoyed almost a monopoly of the higher officers' posts in the army and by far a majority of all the positions. The only branch in which the nobles did not like to serve was the artillery, where the necessarily strict training in mathematics did not appeal to them.[20] A contemporary stated in 1860 that ninety per cent of the officers in the cavalry were nobles, about seventy per cent in the infantry, and around thirty per cent in the artillery. The higher in rank one went, the larger became the percentage of nobles; over ninety per cent of all generals in all branches of service were nobles. A continuing supply of noble officers was assured by the fact that over seventy per cent of the students in the cadet schools, the military training centers for officers, belonged to the aristocracy.[21]

The guard regiments and others of special social prestige were exclusively officered by nobles. The cadet schools served as training centers of indigent young sons of the numerous military nobility, whose only inheritance, said Minister von Roon, was their sword. While a fourth or a third of the pupils were of bourgeois origin, the schools succeeded in excluding bourgeois influence and in training the authoritarian officer, acutely aware of his superiority over everyone else in the state. General von Roon offered in his own person an example of what the schools produced. He had found in one of them about the only home he had ever known.[22] Their reputation was shown in a secret police report in Breslau, June 25, 1860. An actor in a local theater had asked on the stage: "What is a Cadet house?" He had answered, "A school in which it is made certain that not even by mistake a burgher will become a general." Shouts of laughter and enthusiastic approval, continued the police report, greeted this statement. The police officer added that he had taken steps to investigate, and he was later able to report that the actor had been punished.[23]

The most startling evidence of the caste spirit among the military was offered by the duel in 1861 between General von Manteuffel, the King's military adjutant, and the liberal deputy, Karl Twesten. The

[20] See also speeches of Deputies Hermann, Immermann and Brämer, in Abg. H., *St. B.,* 1861; III, 1465-68. Also von Bernhardi, *op. cit.,* III, 284.

[21] Gutsmuth, *op. cit.,* I, 11-17. Minister von Roon in general gave similar figures for the percentage of noble officers. See his speech in Abg. H., *St. B.,* May 29, 1861; III, 1459, 1462.

[22] On the cadet schools see the remarks by Deputies Fliegel and Brämer in Abg. H., *St. B.,* 1861; III, 1461-62, 1468. Also by von Roon, *Ibid.,* III, 1459, 1462.

[23] *Polizei-Bericht,* Breslau, June 25, 1860. These police reports were used in the Prussian State Archives in Berlin-Dahlem.

latter had published a pamphlet entitled *What Can Still Save Us,* in which he had discussed the condition of Prussia and Germany and had proposed solutions to essential problems. In the course of the analysis he had called General von Manteuffel "a harmful man in a harmful position."[24] The general took personal offence at the remark and challenged the author to a duel. The latter replied that he had not meant to question Manteuffel's personal honor, but as the general insisted on a duel Twesten accepted. The fight took place, ending with Manteuffel unhurt and Twesten wounded in the arm. "Even after Twesten shot, Manteuffel is said to have demanded that he take back his words," wrote Deputy von Ammon to Heinrich Kruse of the *Kölnische Zeitung,* "whereupon Twesten is said to have answered that he could not understand how one could make such a demand of him. Moreover, it is said that Manteuffel did not immediately fire but calmly aimed."[25]

The liberals unanimously condemned the duel. To Twesten it meant that no one of any consequence could attack the military. The *National Zeitung* added that the duel made perfectly clear the military nobility's claim to be an unapproachable caste. The liberal journal saw in this fact the existence of a "disastrous split" in the nation. Deputy von Ammon expressed to his friend Kruse the expectation that the *Kölnische Zeitung* would do its share "for the eradication of this barbaric vestige of a medieval ordeal."[26]

The King reacted in a personal way. "To have to do without Manteuffel's service at this time," he wrote von Roon somewhat incoherently, "the triumph of democracy in having driven him out of my presence, the scandal which this event must make in my closest circle, these are matters which almost rob me of my senses because it puts upon my government another unfortunate stigma!! What will Heaven do with me?"[27] Not a word about Twesten, not a word about the illegality of the event, nothing except concern for his military, his nobility, his government, his own prestige!

The official handling of the duel proved equally revealing. Twesten, the burgher, was suspended from office during the investigation. He was hauled before the court; the three judges found him guilty of having insulted Manteuffel but regarded his acceptance of the challenge as necessary in order not to lose the respect of his peers. Man-

---

[24] The actual word used was "unheilvoll." Heyderhoff, *op. cit.,* I, 63.
[25] *Ibid.,* I, 65.
[26] *Ibid.,* I, 64, 65.
[27] *Briefe, Reden und Schriften,* II, 15.

teuffel continued to confer daily with the King, who could not bear to part with him. In commenting on the disparity of treatment Deputy von Ammon called it "injustice," an example of prejudice, and wished the *Kölnische Zeitung* to emphasize that "truth cannot be refuted by a pistol." The *National Zeitung* remarked: "It is already a scandal that a preferred caste can in violation of the law force its duelling code upon the great majority of citizens which in our century is too enlightened to defend itself with weapons against words; but what if the state measures the illegal action of the parties by different standards because they belong to different occupational classes?"

The reaction of the general public may be gauged from the response to a speech which Twesten made in Berlin in April of the next year as candidate for re-election to the Lower House. He closed his address by asserting: "As for me I hope that I am worthy of the belief that I do not spare my person and that I shall risk more than office and salary before I retreat from political activity so long as I may believe myself able in any way to serve my country." The entire audience of 1,500 people rose and responded by "long-continuing stormy applause."[28]

The difference between the liberal and the Conservative mentality may be seen in the subsequent behavior of the two participants in the duel. Twesten continued to be a courageous and independent political leader. Within a few months of the speech cited above he came to the conclusion that the military reforms had been actually executed to such an extent that the Lower House could not block or fundamentally change them. He held no grudge against the military because of the duel; he served not his hatred but his country. Upon defending his changed opinion, he was thrown out of the Progressive party and in the next year he failed to be re-elected from Berlin; but he clung to his beliefs. Manteuffel remained an egotist, a reactionary, an intriguer. Both von Roon and Bismarck had trouble with him. His were personal characteristics, not necessarily those of Conservatism; but the rigidity of Manteuffel's thinking and acting exemplified the traits of the society in which he moved, and that society included the King. Within the course of the next two years von Roon and Bismarck were both to challenge liberal critics in the Lower House to duels. The affairs were never carried out; but they indicated that the Conservative technique of employing physical force to subdue an opponent was to invade even the legislative chamber of a culturally advanced society.

[28] Heyderhoff, *op. cit.*, I, 66, 87.

The liberals were divided in their conception of what the military force should be. A few favored a militia like that in Switzerland; some, especially in the Western provinces, advocated the right of persons called to service to supply substitutes; some varied this proposal with one in favor of having mercenaries; some wished a nucleus of a professional army, supplemented by a youth trained in sports, gymnastics and shooting. The vast majority of liberals, however, favored the military system erected by General von Boyen in 1814, the system which the King was determined to change. They favored at most a two-year term of active military service for all, and the retention of the Landwehr in its old form.[29]

General von Boyen had organized the Landwehr in two reserves: the second was composed of older men on call in emergency; the first consisted of the personnel which had served its term in the army of the line. The Landwehr was sharply separated from the latter and had its own officers, usually persons who had volunteered for one year, received the necessary training and passed the necessary examinations. The Landwehr battalions of the first reserve formed part of the army of the line; on mobilization they were called to duty, but they preserved their own identity from the regular troops. In this way von Boyen had hoped to associate the people with the regular army, to make the army a people's army, and to prevent a caste feeling from developing among the regular officers, which would once more, as in the Eighteenth Century, weaken the military strength of the state by dividing the civilian and the military population. Von Boyen had drawn these lessons from the experience of the Prussian army since its collapse in 1806 at Jena. Above all, the army should remain a popular force, and the Landwehr was contituted with this intention. Even though by the 1850s the nobility had acquired major control of the higher positions in the Landwehr, the officers of the reserve continued to come in the main from the middle class.[30]

The retention of the Landwehr in the form created by von Boyen meant to the liberals the preservation of the military system that had defeated Napoleon. It signified the system in which militarism had been checked by associating the army with the popular forces of the

---

[29] For the report of the discussion at the Seventh Congress of German Economists, see *Kölnische Zeitung*, May 6, 1862; *Tagesbericht*, No. 18, Jan. 22, 1862, citing the *Allgemeine Zeitung*, No. 20, Jan. 20; *Vierteljahrschrift für Volkswirtschaft und Kulturgeschichte* (1864), III, 220-224.

[30] Gutsmuth, *op. cit.*, I, 18. In 1853 some 64 per cent of the staff officers of the Landwehr were nobles, but only 37 per cent of the first lieutenants and 23 per cent of the second lieutenants.

people. It institutionalized the ideals of the great period of social and political reform and of military devotion to the fatherland. The liberals accused the regular army officers of having deliberately weakened the Landwehr since 1814 by neglecting to train the officers and by failing to assist it in maintaining efficiency.[31] They believed that the regular army sought to create an excuse to destroy the Landwehr as a separate organization and to bring the reserve troops directly under its control. The King's reform program meant to the liberals the culmination of this strategy; and they opposed it as an expression of Junker militarism certain to cause once again a split between the army and the people and to weaken the defences of the state. Only if the Landwehr were rejuvenated and treated as an equal, they thought, would defence be strengthened. The liberals were not opposd to expanding the numbers called to military service. In fact, they favored it, but they did object on military, social and political grounds to the destruction of the Boyen type of army. They felt that the King intended thereby to preserve his absolutism, that the conflict over the military summed up the conflict along the entire front between liberalism and absolutism. "We have only one conflict and only one question of life or death," wrote Deputy von Hoverbeck in January 1862, "upon which everything is concentrated, the military question." Deputy Fischel had already stated in private in April, 1860, that if the Lower House should approve the military bill proposed by the government, "the liberal party would be ruined in the country."[32]

In the course of the conflict over the military reorganization the difference of views about the position of the Landwehr became less important than that concerning the length of the term of service. Should it be three years, or should it be restricted to two? The liberals concentrated on this issue as their major means of blocking the drive for control by Junker militarism. They did not even make an issue of the fact that the army took an oath of allegiance not to the constitution but to the King. Although this question would undoubtedly have come up in time, the liberals had for the present enough difficulty in trying to win on the simplest and clearest of issues, two years' service or three.

In January, 1862, the semi-official *Stern-Zeitung* issued the following warning: "The alternative that confronts us is absolutely clear: if the

[31] See, among others, Parisius, *von Hoverbeck*, I, 173.
[32] See Parisius, *von Hoverbeck*, II. 5. Abg. H., *St. B.*, 1861; III, 1405-06. Von Bernhardi, *op. cit.*, III, 318.

Landtag passes the military budget, our constitutional system triumphs; if the opposite occurs it is lost."[33] The liberals paid little heed to this warning. They maintained that the King should follow the will of the nation as expressed in the reaction of the representatives in the Lower House of the Landtag. The state of mind of the vast majority of the liberals was reflected in an article in the *Wochenschrift des National Vereins* published soon after Bismarck took office.[34]

> The three-year term of service is apparently a dogma to the King and in consequence the orthodox and sanctimonious spiritual fathers call any opposition to the reorganization and the three-year service "a rebellion against the order of God," preach the immaculate sanctity of the new battalions and the new officers' positions and proclaim amidst hosannas the satisfaction of the heavenly armies with the constant increase of the earthly ones. Out of the dogma about the three-year service and out of the horrible picture of revolution this party [the Conservative] has woven the threads with which it knows cleverly and brazenly how to guide the King.
>
> In another address originating among pastors it even says: "the Prussian people will ever more clearly respect and feel under Your Royal scepter that God sits in the regiment and guides all to the best." Thus instead of the usual view of absolutism about divine inspiration God now sits in person in the government, and the rule of the King by means of the Bismarck ministry is frankly identified with God and rule of the universe! Servility was assuredly not pushed farther even under Domitian, and such blasphemy is reported as "heartwarming exaggeration" and causes no offense at all.

The question of military reorganization led to complete antagonism in the relations between the King and his government on the one hand and the Lower House of the Landtag on the other. Faulty handling of the problem on both sides accentuated a fundamental difference and brought the issue to a head. After the King had used the mobilization of 1859 caused by the Austro-Italian war as the occasion for beginning the military reform, his ministry submitted a budget the next year for continuing the work and promised that a bill on the military organization would be placed before the Lower House. In 1860 a bill to that effect was introduced, but consideration of it required so much time that the Lower House did not complete its investigation and once more passed a provisional military budget while making clear that it had not yet decided pro or con about the military re-

[33] *Tagesbericht*, No. 13, Jan. 16, 1862.
[34] Nov. 28, 1862, pp. 1132-33.

forms as such. The King and his Minister of War continued the reorganization as if it were to be permanent. Having seen the hostility of the Lower House to the military proposal, the government in 1861 changed its tactics and stated that a new law on military reorganization was unnecessary, claiming authority under the law of 1814.[35] Nonetheless, the disinclination to oppose the liberals in the ministry caused the Lower House to approve the funds in the extraordinary budget by a very small majority obtained by the votes of all the ministers. Once more the House made clear that the approval of funds was provisional and should not be interpreted as final acceptance of the reorganization. Early in 1862 the ministry was again ready to submit a military bill, but as soon as the liberal ministers were ousted von Roon declared that a change in the law of 1814 was not necessary.

The ministry was certainly not straightforward in its dealings with the Lower House. It knew that the King was determined to reorganize the army and to maintain the reform once it had been accomplished; but instead of saying so and taking at the beginning a legal stand one way or the other and adhering consistently to it, the Minister of War tried first one way of assuring the permanence of the reforms and then another. He proposed a new law; but when he saw that he could not put it through, he declared the reforms enacted on the basis of a law of 1814 to be legal anyway. The Lower House reacted with equal lack of courage and consistency. Twice to grant funds on a provisional basis for a reform which was becoming permanent under its own eyes and about which it knew the King's intentions, and then suddenly to deny those funds and demand reform on its own terms, was hardly good politics or even, for that matter, quite fair to the King. The two sides muddled into the conflict.

Early in 1862 the government once more asked for funds in the regular budget but without a bill on the military reorganization. By this time the House was suspicious and angry, and as the government again declared that the law of 1814 gave the King the power to reorganize and expand the army and that a new law was unnecessary, the liberals accused the ministry of violating its promise to submit legisla-

---

[35] The law of 1814 stated in Paragraph Fifteen that "in war time troops may be attached to or severed from the parts of the army according to need and all units called to service may be enlarged from the ones that remained at home or from those growing up." *Die Innere Politik*, p. 91. The government also referred to the third paragraph of that law which stated that "the size of the standing army and of the Landwehr will be determined by the situation of the state at the time." Rudolf von Gneist, *Die Militärvorlage von 1892 und der preussische Verfassungskonflikt von 1862 bis 1866* (Berlin, 1893) , p. 34.

tion on the question and of trying to deprive the Landtag of its share of control of military affairs. They planned to refuse to grant the extra funds for the military reform and by breaking the budget down into smaller units than at present to tighten the legislative control over military expenditures. They thereby sought to prevent the government from being able to retain the reforms by covering the cost from concealed items in the budget or from funds transferred from one category to another. They aimed to use their constitutional right to pass the budget each year as a means of controlling the size of the army. This action led the King to dissolve the Lower House and call for new elections, the results of which were even more liberal than before.

The liberals were aware of the fact that they were opposing the King on the military question, for the latter had made widely known his determination to stand or fall by the military reorganization. They knew that he regarded the reorganization as entirely within his competence. For a time during the regency the liberal deputy Gneist had been a member of a small group which the Regent had invited each week to the palace. Later he wrote:

> I gained the impression that the Regent recognized without any doubt that personal military duty could be introduced only by a formal law, that namely a three-year term of service could be changed into a four-year term (as was proposed for a time for the cavalry) by a law. But he understood the word *organization* in the sense that had become firmly established among the administrative officials, as compassing any change within the framework of an administrative branch, thus for example the increase in the number of army cadres. In view of Paragraph Three of the law of September 3, 1814, he had no doubt about his authority to determine annually the peace-time strength of the army.[36]

To many people, including liberals, the ruler had asserted that he would abdicate rather than recede on this question. He openly expressed his anger at the Lower House for holding up the final approval of the reforms. As early as 1860 he was accusing the deputies in the Lower House of lack of patriotism because they would not accept his military program. On learning in March of that year that the Lower House was still debating over the length of the term of military service, William "raised his hands in unwilling amazement" and exclaimed, ". . . if only the people would not talk about matters which

[36] Von Gneist, *op. cit.*, pp. 83-84.

they do not understand." A month later he said to some officers that "as long as I live I will never agree to the two-year service," and he was already threatening to abdicate. By June, 1860, he regarded all who opposed the military reforms as "enemies or revolutionaries, . . . because they were seeking to limit the highest attribute of royalty, the war command."[37] And in June, 1861, Deputy von Ammon wrote his friend Kruse of the *Kölnische Zeitung*, "The King thinks and dreams of nothing but soldiers and the day before yesterday said to some deputies that the approval of funds for the military in the extraordinary budget is entirely unacceptable. 'What is, remains; the army organization should become definitive; that is what I wish and it must be done, otherwise I go!' "[38]

The liberals knew that personages at court, especially the King's reactionary brother, Prince Friedrich Karl, and the military adjutants, were stirring the royal anger by conjuring the threat of revolution. In March, 1862, detailed reports were published in liberal newspapers about the military precautions taken during the winter against the possibility of revolution. The liberals had also read the King's statement to the generals of the army at the coronation in the autumn of 1861.

> The crown has descended upon me from God's hands, and when I take it from His holy altar and place it upon my head, I receive His blessing that it be preserved for me! The army has the duty to defend it, and Prussia's kings have never seen the army waver in its loyalty. It has been that which has recently saved the King and the Fatherland in most calamitous storms and has made him secure. I also count on this loyalty and devotion if I have to call upon it against enemies from whatever side they may come.

The implication for the liberals was clear: "from whatever side they may come" included internal as well as external enemies of both the crown and the fatherland.[39]

The conflict over the military reorganization reached a crisis in September, 1862. A commission of the Lower House had for several months been deliberating upon the budget for the military and in September brought in its report. It recommended striking all funds for the reorganization and restoring the budget for the pre-reformed army. The House debated the report extensively. A handful of

[37] Von Bernhardi, *op. cit.*, III, 272-317 *passim;* IV, 5.
[38] Heyderhoff, *op. cit.*, I, 66.
[39] Horst Kohl, *op. cit.*, p. 29. On the liberals' knowledge of the King's attitude, see Parisius, *von Hoverbeck*, I, 176, II, 8, 65 ff; Philippson, *op. cit.*, pp. 52, 57, 59, 87.

liberals, among them Twesten, von Sybel and von Stavenhagen, expressed concern over the fact that the conflict about the military reorganization was involving the person of the King. These liberals argued that the military had actually been reorganized, the new regiments had been created, new officers appointed, the Landwehr broken up. They concluded that the work could not be undone. They stated further that the King had personally committed himself completely to these reforms and that the Landtag could not afford to affront him by forcing the government to restore the *status quo ante*. They wished to reach a compromise with the government by which in return for approval of the reorganization the two-year term of service would be restored. Von Roon intimated that the compromise might be accepted; but the King remained adamant and once more threatened to abdicate. Since the ministers were always susceptible to pressure by this kind of emotional outburst, von Roon rejected the proposed compromise. In consequence, the House passed by an overwhelming vote the recommendation of the commission, refusing funds for the reorganization. If abided by, that resolution would have forced the King to restore the army to its earlier form.[40]

The Lower House would undoubtedly have accepted a compromise on the terms proposed by Twesten and his few colleagues. The actual fact was that the funds for 1862 about which the House was voting at this late date had in the main already been spent. To have been forced to undo the military reform would have weakened Prussia and been an affront to the King. The liberals knew that the King had blocked the acceptance of the compromise, just as they knew that he had been mainly responsible all along for the military program. They were determined to defend the rights of the Lower House even at the risk, or the certainty, of a break with the crown.[41]

The liberals could not comprehend why anyone should be so adamant on the question of the three-year term of service when the evidence was so largely in favor of the two-year period. They cited the fact that from 1833 to 1853 the shorter period had obtained, that two kings plus their generals had regarded it as satisfactory. Even if that had not been the case, they argued,

> We know very well that of the brave soldiers with whom our generals so thoroughly defeated in 1813, 1814 and 1815 a general

[40] On this crisis see Zechlin, pp. 277 ff, and the literature which he cites.
[41] "It is said that not merely von der Heydt but also von Roon is willing to give in, but that yesterday the King rejected evrything." Twesten to Lipke, Sept. 18, 1862. Heyderhoff, *op. cit.*, I, 116; see also Parisius, *von Hoverbeck*, II, 8, 47, 78.

like Napoleon and an army like the French scarcely a single one had served in peace time longer than a year. The Landwehr men had at most been drilled a couple of months and many only a couple of weeks. Now we have no more generals who have actually served in war; nonetheless they think themselves much wiser than Scharnhorst and Blücher ever were. So wise are these gentlemen that they do not doubt for a moment that a seventeen-year-old cadet can enter the line as officer and that the former junior in high school can easily be trained to be a reserve and Landwehr officer in one year's time. All other young people are so awkward and stupid that they must be drilled and maneuvered and must stand watch at least three years before they can be used as soldiers in the field. Let anyone understand that who can![42]

Neither von Roon nor Bismarck had any particular conviction about the term of service. As early as 1859 von Roon had been willing to accept the shorter period, and in the September crisis of 1862 he proposed to accede on this point in return for liberal concessions on others. As for Bismarck, as soon as he became Minister President he frankly told liberal leaders that in time he would win the King to accept the two-year term of service, that with a corresponding number of re-enlisted soldiers he thought it militarily preferable. The attitude of both, however, can be summed up in Bismarck's assertion that he would support the King even if the latter wished a ten-year term of service.[43] They were frankly carrying out the King's orders, no matter what, until they were able to win him to their way of thinking.

As for the Conservatives, they were jubilant over the proposals for military reform. Early in 1860 their leaders handed the ruler a memorandum expressing their loyalty, approving the military reforms and offering to put them through for him, and saying that one could not govern with liberals. They saw an opportunity to regain power, and they were undoubtedly growing in influence. By January, 1861, a Berlin correspondent to the *Zeitung für Norddeutschland* noted that "the military party has won such overwhelming influence at court that retreat is out of the question."[44]

Under the circumstances, prospects of cooling off the King and persuading him to accept anything short of a fight to the finish seemed remote. The height of his temperature may be gauged by a letter which he wrote in August, 1862, to an old liberal acquaintance, von

[42] *Spart im Frieden.* See also Gneist, *op. cit.,* pp. 40-41; Parisius, *von Hoverbeck,* II, 61.
[43] Zechlin, pp. 278-80, 291, 325, 334, 354.
[44] Von Bernhardi, *op. cit.,* III, 281-82, 310; *Tagesbericht,* No. 25, Jan. 30, 1861.

Saucken-Julienfelde, who tried to bring him to comprehend the position of the Lower House on the military question. The King refused to listen to him and replied with the following letter, in which one can still hear the pen stab the paper and the ink explode.

> Who started the conflict? Have I not laid the reorganization of the army before the Landtag with the completest possible frankness, a reorganization which has occurred in an entirely legal and constitutional way? Does the constitution prescribe the number of battalions and the number of annual recruits and horses? Does it prescribe the number of officers and under-officers? No! What does it prescribe? The term of service and the division of the recruits into the line and the reserve. For this division the legal change has already been laid before the Landtag in the session of 1859-60, and in addition the constitutional approval of the money for the reorganization was requested. What has the Second Chamber done? It has attacked and changed the reorganization through persons who understood nothing of the matter; and when the House ran into a *cul de sac* it only granted the funds for the reorganization provisionally. In the following year the House took a similar course and again finally approved the funds in an extraordinary budget. During two years the revolutionary and democratic press has not ceased to scatter lie after lie about the reorganization and the financial situation until the people at last believed that we were on the point of bankruptcy and had an unbearable budget. This had to precede the new plan of operations of the democrats, namely to deny the funds. In order to meet a justified complaint I cancelled almost four millions [Thalers], the excess tax, a concession which very harmfully affected the army even if it was only to be temporary and only on this account acceptable. But even though this concession threw the opposition forces off the track for a moment, it only spurred them on to be ever more shameless and unreasonable in their action against me and my creation, so that we have now reached a turning point.

Then, continued the King, since the ministry was in full agreement with him, since the reorganization was approved "by all thinking military, by all unprejudiced thinking men," and since the funds were available without any undue burden on the land, why did the opposition continue? Why did it demand concessions?

> For absolutely no other reasons than that the desired concessions had to extend to objects which are intended to *destroy* the striking power, the military spirit and the training of the army. War to the death against the monarch and his standing army has been vowed, and in order to reach that goal the Progressivists and democrats and ultra liberals scorn no means, and indeed with rare consequence and deep conviction. . . . The shortening of the term of service is demanded so that firm, well

disciplined military training, the effects of which will hold during the long period of leave, shall not be given the soldier. The under-officers shall become officers, not as everyone could in Prussia since 1808 by passing one and the same examination, but without proving this equality of cultural level, so that a schism will develop in the officers' corps and dissatisfaction will slowly creep into them and the democrats will be able to develop an officers' caste of their own which because they are neither trained nor steeled in their views to stand loyally by the throne are to be won for the revolution. Since loyalty and self-sacrifice for King and throne are to be expected from the present officers and through them to be transferred to the troops, *therefore* the officers' class is slandered in every possible way, and then one wonders that the officers are angry? And even censures them for this!!

"A peoples' army back of Parliament." That is the solution revealed since Frankfurt am Main [he referred to a speech by Schulze-Delitzsch] to which I counter with the watchword:

"A disciplined army that is also the people in arms, back of the King and war lord."

Between these two watchwords no agreement is possible.

The Lower House opposition had burned its bridges in refusing the military funds, the King said, and he had done likewise; he would make no more concessions. They would be beneath the dignity of the crown. He warned von Saucken-Julienfelde and his friends to keep watch or they would be drawn in tow by the revolution.[45]

The King was convinced that in fighting for his military reforms he was defending his position as monarch. He identified the maintenance of his military authority with the welfare of his country. He put the struggle on a moral and a patriotic plane: he and persons who agreed with him were right, all others were revolutionaries. He misinterpreted a speech by Schulze-Delitzsch out of all reason, finding in it convincing evidence that the Lower House planned to take the army away from him, ruin it, and transform it into an instrument of parliament. He had such strange conceptions of how the conflict over the military arose and of who had made concessions that one cannot imagine the possibility of straightening him out on facts. He claimed the dropping of the extra tax as a concession from him; actually, the tax expired and the Landtag did not renew it. The military budget was somewhat reduced in 1862, but the fact was that the Lower House had not passed any budget at all. The King assumed that the military reorganization was legal; the Lower House

[45] Parisius, *von Hoverbeck*, II, 65-68; see a letter of similar content to Vincke-Olbendorf in January, 1863, in *Briefe, Reden und Schriften*, II, 43-45.

disputed the point. The King assumed that the military reform was permanent; the Lower House denied the statement. The King regarded the existing organization of society as a model and the army as the expression of that society; the liberals denounced the feudal caste structure and wished to transform it into a free society. The King thought of a people's army as one commanded by an absolute monarch, with officers chosen from the upper classes, especially the nobility, and trained to be a military caste. The liberals wanted a people's army devoid of caste and representative of a free society. The King had a feeling, not unwarranted, that this liberalism was endangering his authority, and he clung to the old-style army as his main support. Behind the conflict over the military reforms was a social conflict between two different sets of cultural values. The liberals tried, as we shall see in a subsequent chapter, to gloss over this fact, and the King undoubtedly misinterpreted events and exaggerated the danger; but, in last analysis, being sensitive to the threat to his position, he correctly recognized the ultimate danger to absolutism from parliamentary control over military affairs. The issues were all to come to a head in the course of the constitutional conflict.

Agreement about the military reforms could well have been reached even on the King's terms if the government had offered an adequate *quid pro quo*. The liberals were particularly angry because the military sacrifices demanded by the government were not counter-balanced by liberal reforms. "Not even the communal and the county governments have been reformed," declared Deputy Waldeck, "and as long as we have the feudal vestiges in these regions I shall never be able to reconcile it with my conscience to help strengthen these feudal remains by strengthening the caste of officers in the standing army without Landwehr and Landwehr officers." The *Königsberg Hartungsche Zeitung* and the *National Zeitung* reacted in the same way. If the government wanted military reform, let it assure the public that it was not aiming thereby merely to strengthen the Old Regime; let it prove by deeds that it was interested also in developing the economic and social resources of the land and in developing the constitution in a liberal sense. Let it reform the House of Lords so that liberal legislation could be passed. "If a thorough reform of the House of Lords is not allowed, or if some prospect for a quick forward action in the German question is not initiated, the Lower House will not impose this burden [the military reform] upon the country," wrote a Berlin correspondent to the *Grenzboten*; and Deputy von Carlowitz in May, 1861, openly stated in the Lower House that if the Prussian government would take the initiative expected of it in unifying Germany, he would vote in favor of the item in the military budget which he was the opposing. Indeed he would vote for other items; indeed "I would approve still more." For the present policy, he declared, our present army is sufficient.[46] The liberals could have been won to support the military reforms if the King had been willing to initiate action and achieve results. With the King's slow and cautious approach to things, postponing action to some time in the future, and with liberal ministers urging upon their supporters, "Do not press," the liberal representatives of a people eager for state and national reforms could hardly be expected to add the huge burden of what seemed to them useless military expense. Bismarck was to try the other method in the question of national unification, that of action; and he was ultimately to succeed.

To the Prince Regent the problem of financing the military reorganization seemed simple. "In a monarchy like ours," he wrote to Minister von Bonin on November 24, 1859, "the military point of view should never be curtailed by financial or political-economic ones; for the *European position* of the state upon which so much else depends is based upon it."[47] An increase of nearly 8,000,000 Thalers in the military budget seemed to him a matter about which there should be no controversy. The phrase "the European position of the state" justified any sacrifice. William's ideal of civic virtue remained that of the War of Liberation, when every person and every interest in Prussia was subordinated to the purpose of military defence.

The government took the position that the increase in military funds could be supplied without undue sacrifice and pointed to the excellent condition of Prussian state finances as evidence. It claimed that the state had a smaller tax burden than Austria and Spain and a decidedly smaller one than Great Britain, France, Netherlands, and Belgium. It showed that the total state expenditures per head were lower than in any of the other countries except Russia and Portugal and that Prussia covered these expenditures by its income, whereas the majority of the other states did so in part by loans. It claimed that the cost of raising the state funds was lower, that the percentage of funds for other genuine state administration was higher than in the other states, and that even after the reorganization the military cost absorbed

[46] Abg. H., *St. B.*, May 27, 1861; III, 1405-06. *Königsberg Hartungsche Zeitung*, Dec. 4, 1861, Sept. 11, 1862. *National Zeitung*, Feb. 1, 1861. *Berliner Börsen Zeitung*, Jan. 28, 1861. *Tagesbericht*, No. 5, Jan. 7, 1862. Abg., H., *St. B.*, 1861, III, 1476.
[47] Erich Marcks, *Kaiser Wilhelm I.* (Munich and Leipzig, 1918), p. 179.

a smaller part of the net funds than in any of the other great powers.[48] Therefore, the government concluded, Prussia could well afford the reform of the army.

The ministry recognized that some tax reform would be necessary to cover the additional military costs, and it concentrated attention upon the land tax.[49] It justified the reform of the tax with arguments which showed a better historic than prophetic sense.

> The land tax has been proposed especially as a source of income for war needs, for in case of war the burden must be overwhelmingly laid on the landowner. The indirect taxes, out of which the state at present derives a large share of its income, dry up in war, the industrial activity declines, capital is cautious, and there remains finally the return from the land which can be tapped. This was, alas, clearly revealed in the unfortunate year 1807, when the losses which had to be made up by deliveries in transport livestock, grain and other war needs solely in the province of Prussia amounted to 150,000,000 Thalers. In order to avoid such calamities and to establish a military organization which can prevent similar unfortunate events it is desirable to do what is necessary in time and for that purpose to draw especially upon the land in order to prevent the landowners from being exposed in the future to similar spoliation.

To regard a land tax as the main financial reliance for military purposes in a country which was rapidly becoming industrialized may seem out of focus; but the King wholeheartedly supported the tax reform, and solely through his pressure it became law. He needed for his military reforms the 10,000,000 Thalers a year which it was to bring in. While the bill passed the Lower House, with opposition from some liberals as well as from the Conservatives, it was overwhelmingly rejected by the Conservative Upper House. In order to put it through that body in 1861, the King had to use his personal pressure. Because of the necessity for new assessments the tax could not be levied before 1865.

In 1860, that is, before the reform, the land tax preserved the characteristics of its historic past. It was unevenly assessed among the provinces as well as within a single province. Many large estates and peasant holdings were exempt from it or paid only a small sum, whereas others were taxed in varying amounts. The difference in treatment depended upon whether the piece of land preserved a historic legal

---

[48] *Die Innere Politik*, p. 71. See also statements in the Lower House by Finance Minister von Patow. Abg. H., *St. B.*, Jan. 21, May 27, 1861; I, 26, III, 1409.

[49] *Die Innere Politik*, pp. 81-82.

right to exemption from this tax, often also upon whether the owner had succeeded in having his property dropped from the tax records. The state administered some twenty main systems of land taxation, more than one hundred forms of land tax, and so many kinds of buildings tax that one could scarcely count them. The provincial differences were evident from the fact that of the net tax return the land tax produced the following percentages: province of Prussia, 6.14; Posen, 4.93; Pomerania, 6.21; Silesia, 10.53; Brandenburg, 7.75; Saxony, 8.97; Westphalia, 10.0; and the Rhineland, 8.69. The provinces of Silesia, Saxony, Westphalia and the Rhineland had to make up for the low returns from the others. If one added the taxation of the towns, the disparity would have been even more pronounced. Differences among counties were extreme, for many of them had been exempt from the land tax. Thus the county of Lauenburg paid in land and buildings taxes after the reform 403.2 per cent more, the county of Landeshut 41.2 per cent less, than before. Fifty-five counties had to pay 100 per cent more after the reform, whereas ninety had to return less.[50]

The principle of equalization of the land tax throughout the state had been included in the financial edict of October 27, 1810, under pressure of the military defeat by Napoleon. As soon as Prussia had recovered after 1815, the land-owning nobility had made certain that the principle was ignored. It was reasserted in the revolutionary period of 1849-49 but again succumbed to Conservative domination in the 1850s. Military need, this time during peace, once more brought up the question in 1859; and a half century after the principle had first been legally established, it became a reality. The difference in outcome lay solely in the fact that the King needed the money for military reforms. The Conservatives could not enjoy both the expansion of the military and low, privileged taxation. Universal military service entailed the elimination of tax privilege in favor of equalization of financial responsibility to support the state. Those with a historic legal claim to tax privilege should be compensated, according to the bill of 1859, for the abolition of this right; but they should henceforth pay their due shares of taxes like everyone else.

The Conservatives condemned the land tax from the standpoint of national economy as the worst tax one could have. It measured movable and immovable capital and land property, they said, by the same standard; it taxed a single object of property; it imposed a

[50] Meitzen, *op. cit.*, I, 20.

special burden upon a single class for the support of a general need; it used in the present the resources of land property which should be regarded as the real state treasury, the reserve for cases of state calamity; it amounted to a tax on capital, and could be called a form of confiscation. The tax would cripple many peasants, always an object of special concern for the Conservatives, and ruin many landowners. The Conservatives feared that administrative difficulties would be insurmountable. The difficulties of assessment particularly alarmed them, for they apprehended that this work might become subject to politics and might arouse much bad feeling among the natives in the Eastern provinces, above all between peasants and large estate owners. The old and favored argument of "Let well enough alone" was once more advanced.[51]

The government bill contained a proposal to indemnify the large landowners, but not the peasants, who would bear a major loss from the new tax. The Conservative leader Wagener opposed this clause as unfair to the peasants and likely or even sure to cause hostility between peasants and large estate-owners. Nonetheless, as the commission reporter in the Lower House correctly stated, the House of Lords would not accept the bill without the clause. The gentlemen preferred cash to preserving the appearance of equality of treatment. They did not believe in equality anyway, certainly not at the expense of their pocket books. The liberal deputy Schulze-Delitzsch used the opportunity to state that the approval of compensation by the Conservatives was no way to preserve the moral position in society of the nobility. "A political party" (like the Conservative), he said, "which has always participated in the development of our institutions solely in order to defend its caste privileges and prejudices at the expense of the common welfare is naturally inclined to attribute similar motives to other parties because it itself is not aware of any others."[52]

That the criticism made by Schulze-Delitzsch was felt by others to be justified was evident from the argument given by the very right-wing member of the Constitutional party, Bethmann-Hollweg. "Higher political considerations cause me," he said in the Lower House in March, 1861, "to overlook in this matter special doubts which I have raised against the land tax bill. The higher political consideration is that I regard the land tax legislation as the first prerequisite for restoring to the large landowners their position in the country, particularly

[51] *Tagesbericht*, No. 70, March 23, 1861. Abg. H., *St. B.*, March 5, 6, 9, 1861; I, 335-37, 357, 443.

[52] *Ibid.*, March 5, 9, 1861; I, 335-37, 439, 443. *Ibid.*, May 28, 1861; III, 1425.

with respect to the small landowners [the peasantry]. I regard this restoration as necessary so that the large landowners will in the future be equal to the political responsibility without which I regard a satisfactory development of our municipal and county constitutions, and with these the entire political life of our nation, as impossible."[53] The remarks had the stately dignity of a true aristocrat. They continued the finest ideal of true nonpartisan conservatism, the desire to be a leader not for the defence of egoistic interests but for the general good.

While the Conservatives were totally against the land tax reform, the liberals were somewhat divided between those in the heavily taxed provinces favoring reform and those in the lightly taxed ones disliking or even openly opposing the government proposal. Deputy Behrend wished the matter settled once and for all so that the liberals could join forces wholeheartedly and one of the provincial differences between East and West could be overcome.[54] Actually the question did not cause as much trouble between the two main branches of the liberal movement as Behrend implied. The land tax differential was merely symptomatic of the wider range of cultural distinctions between Eastern and Western Prussia, and some of the areas of strongest support of the reform lay in the East. The argument put forth by Deputy Gneist in favor of the measure had more weight with the liberals.

> It is a question of giving our state, which still shows traces of being a conglomerate of former pieces, the character of a definitely unified state. This will be achieved first by means of the unified land tax. In a time in which an incompletely implemented constitution has loosened so much in the state, it is a question of establishing our unity on a firm material foundation, in order now to give Prussia a consistent position in Germany around which new forces can crystallize without danger.[55]

The issue of tax reform showed the interdependence of the parts of the liberal program. The government bill stipulated that the assessment commissions for the new land and buildings tax should be chosen by the provincial and county assemblies. Since these assemblies were at present overwhelmingly dominated by owners of large landed estates, espcially of noble estates, the liberals had to be assured beforehand that the government intended to introduce a bill to reform these assemblies.[56]

---

[53] *Ibid.*, March 9, 1861; I, 439.
[54] Abg. H., *St. B.*, March 6, 1861; I, 355-56.
[55] *Ibid.*, March 8, 1861; I, 423-24.
[56] See *Ibid.*, March 6, 1861; I, 355. *Ibid.*, March 9, 1861; I, 435-36.

The fact that the Conservatives were enthusiastic about military reforms, more military discipline, more officers' positions for the nobility, but decidedly averse to paying taxes for the support of these services aroused deep resentment among the liberals. The latter realized that in this attitude the Conservatives were manifesting scorn for the so-called vulgarity of commercial life. The liberals knew that they were paying largely for the maintenance of a social and political regime which blocked freedom and progress. In the last half century taxes had increased heavily on townsmen but not on the land. As Deputy Riedel asserted in the Lower House in 1861,

> Since the introduction of the land tax over the course of centuries the entire weight of the public burden has gradually been shifted more and more from landowners to the other classes of the people. In recent times not a decade has passed in which new taxes and increases of the old taxes have not been imposed on the non-landowning elements of the people. Most of these taxes are so well laid out that they have enjoyed a natural increase in returns with the increase in population, economic activity, income and property, and have become even more productive for the government. The land tax alone has not been changed in fifty years, in other regions in one hundred, in still others in one hundred and fifty and in many regions in two hundred years and longer, and it has been left so untouched that the gentlemen have the illusion that it is not even a tax but merely a rent.

Deputy Riedel regarded tax reform not as primarily an economic but as a moral issue.[57] He and other liberals showed anger especially over the existing discrimination. A writer in the *Frankfurter Journal* in 1861 asserted that in Hagen a poor laborer who formerly paid one Thaler in tax now had to pay three. The refusal of the nobility in the old provinces to pay taxes, the writer said, sounded to him like scorn and offered no proof of patriotism and no sense of justice.[58]

The heavy tax burden weighed particularly on the supporters of liberalism. Angry protests came to the Landtag from all parts of Prussia and from all groups of the population, except those still enjoying the privileged position of the Old Regime. Chamber of commerce reports loudly denounced the tax burden and prophesied ruin. Salaried employees and the lower middle-class blamed the tax pressure for depriving them of the opportunity to save for their old age or for investment which might improve their economic situation. Industry

[57] *Ibid.*, March 5, 1861; I, 343.
[58] *Tagesbericht*, No. 64, March 16, 1861.

wanted tax reduction to lower costs of production and to improve its competitive position. These were all well-known arguments against taxation at any time. The significant fact was the unanimity and the intensity of feeling.[59]

What added insult to injury for the liberals was the way in which the Conservative Junkers were able to avoid paying the share of the taxes for which they were already responsible. In the first place the Prussians paid nearly twice as much in indirect as in direct taxes, a fact that imposed a major burden upon the poor.[60] In the second place, the class and income taxes were so allocated as to strike the lower income groups, and the government kept raising the percentage paid. In the third place, and above all, the method of assessment enabled the Conservatives to transfer much of the tax burden to others. The system showed again the advantage to the Junkers of controlling the Kreistag and the office of Landrat.

A tax commission was created annually in each county and in each town not belonging to a county for the purpose of assessing the class and income taxes. The commission was presided over by the Landrat or by a commissioner specially appointed by the regional administration. In the counties the commission was composed of representatives of the Kreistag. In the towns not belonging to a county it was made up of representatives of the citizens; but, since most of the towns were incorporated within the county government, the system of assessment in the counties was by far the more important. The Junkers used their power in the Kreistag to select a tax-assessment commission which shifted the burden to peasants and townsmen. One can understand why the issue of reform of county government was regarded as crucial.[61]

The results of the assessment were evident from a circular issued in 1860 by the Minister of Finance. The rural areas paid relatively less tax than the townspeople. For the current year, of an income tax of 3,645,000 Thalers the rural districts paid one-third, although they had more than two-thirds of the population. One person in 157 in the rural areas paid income tax, whereas one in thirty-one did so in the towns. (Income tax began on incomes of 1,000 Thalers). The circular stated that the greater number of wealthy persons in the towns was in part

---

[59] References are so numerous in contemporary newspapers, chamber of commerce reports, Landtag speeches, etc., that it is superfluous to document them here.

[60] See *Berliner Börsen Zeitung*, July 27, 1861. It was estimated in that paper that the Prussians paid 9 florins, 25 kronen per capita, of which 3 florins, 2 kronen came from direct taxes and 5 florins, 12 kronen from indirect.

[61] See the petition from Cologne as reported in the *Kölnische Zeitung*, April 4, 1861.

responsible for this difference; but it added that many peasants were
put under the class tax who should be placed in the lower brackets of
the income tax, and that the big landowners "by and large are assessed
relatively and in part considerably lower . . . than the peasant
proprietors in the higher brackets of the class tax." The circular
further asserted

> . . . that in the estimation of the taxable income of the large
> landowners that which the owners use from their own economy
> for their families, as well as the value of free dwelling, and that
> which is applied from the estate to permanent improvements and
> therefore to increasing its capital value have not been considered
> at all or at only their partial value. How unjust such a pro-
> cedure is becomes clearest by a comparison with town dwellers
> who pay income tax. They have to cover all expenses of living,
> including house rent, out of their income; but although they
> cannot use a part of their income for these purposes and have to
> save capital, they are not allowed to deduct these sums in esti-
> mating their income tax. In some assessment districts for the
> current year the assessment for income tax has declined in com-
> parison with that of last year, and the reason is to be found not
> in the removal or death of payers of large taxes, but in a
> thorough going tax reduction especially for the landowners for
> which the highly unfavorable crop is given as justification.[62]

The criticism was equally applicable to any country in which agriculture paid an income, or,at the lower level, a class tax; but in Prussia
the inequality was particularly felt. When in 1868 Hamburg came to
consider joining the North German Confederation, a commission was
appointed by the Senate and the Citizens Assembly to consider economic and financial questions in connection therewith. It reported
that in comparison with Hamburg in Prussia the higher income
classes were by virtue of the assessment procedure less burdened, that
the middle and lower income classes were much more burdened and
that far wider circles were made to pay taxes. Prussia retained the
class system of taxation of an autocratic government just emerging
from the Old Regime.[63]

The government proposed in 1861 to increase the business tax in
certain instances and to change it in others. The details do not need
to be described; the effect, as stated by government officials in defending the proposal, was to increase the tax burden on commercial under-

---

[62] See C. J. Bergius, "Die Personal —, Vermögens—, und Einkommensteuer in
Preussen," *Vierteljahrschrift für Volkswirtschaft und Kulturgeschichte* (1870), pp.
62-73; Meitzen, *op. cit.*, III, 39.

[63] Bergius, *op. cit.*, pp. 72-73.

takings. The plan caused an outburst of lamentation. The proper title for this law, declared Deputy Schöller, should have been "Authority for the Finance Minister to Raise Several Millions more than Previously according to Need or according to Arbitrary Wish." The bill passed by a vote of 153 to 104, with many prominent liberals voting against it. The Conservatives enjoyed the show. Deputy Wagener remarked: "I believe that we must help you obtain this law; because you so kindly helped us gain the land tax my friends and I will vote for this law."[64]

Objections were raised, although not to the same extent, against the twenty-five per cent increase imposed in 1859 on the milling and slaughter tax. This tax was levied in those towns which were not subject to the income tax, and while the number of towns falling in that category had declined from 132 in 1820 when the tax was imposed to seventy-seven in 1862, the list of those still paying it included almost all the large cities. The tax was unpopular under any circumstances and was retained solely because of the difficulty of finding an alternative. It obstructed commerce, placed an especially heavy burden upon the poorer classes, and was conducive to smuggling and other forms of illegality.[65] That unpopular military reforms should require a twenty-five per cent increase in an unpopular tax just as the depression of 1857 was ebbing did not make either of them attractive to the liberal public.

The government made a few concessions with respect to taxes. After three years, in 1862, it agreed to abolish as no longer needed the twenty-five per cent increase in the milling and slaughter tax. In 1861, 1862 and 1863 it put through legislation, readily accepted by the liberals, reducing and rendering uniform throughout the state the taxes on mining, removing iron mining from a special tax and placing it under the terms of the general business tax. These changes brought financial relief to the mine owners and equalized the competitive tax position of mining in the various parts of the state. While the mining interests expressed great pleasure over each law, the relief came so slowly that they continued to be hostile to the government.[66] None-

[64] See the discussion in Abg. H., *St. B.*, April 9, 10, 11, 1861, Vol. III. For a summary of the business tax system see von Roenne, *op. cit.* (1884), IV, 812 ff., and Meitzen, *op. cit.*, III, 30-33.

[65] Meitzen, *op. cit.*, III, 34-35.

[66] Von Roenne, *op. cit.* (1884), IV, 818 ff.; see the discussion, especially by von Beughem, in the Lower House on March 18, 1861, *St. B.*, Vol. I; on the tax situation see also articles in *Berliner Börsen Zeitung*, Feb. 12, Feb. 20, March 5, 1861, and in *Bremer Handelsblatt*, March 9, 1861.

theless, the trend in taxation was definitely upward. The reductions were of minor significance, except in the case of mining. With land taxes increased, even though more equitably levied, with business taxes higher for many lines, with class and income taxes increased, the liberals were angry at the cost of government and blamed it on the military.

How much weight should be given the complaints is difficult to say. The liberal Minister of Finance von Patow denied that the tax burden was excessive.[67] Certainly the extraordinary economic development of the years after the crisis of 1857 cast doubt on the validity of the complaints. The economy was so flourishing that in the constitutional conflict the liberals defeated themselves. By making so much money and turning in so much revenue to the state, they enabled the government to carry on in spite of the resistance of the Lower House and to cover even the excessive expenditures entailed by two highly unpopular wars.

The irony of the situation arose from the fact that the liberal deputies were being asked for increased taxes while being unable to put through any reforms to counter balance the effect. Certainly it was an anomalous position for deputies enthusiastically elected for the purpose of liberalizing the entire state to have to face the public again without having accomplished a single popular constructive reform, with having to their credit the dubious achievement of approving, even though provisionally, an unpopular military reform directed by its sponsors against liberalism, and with having sanctioned increased taxes to pay for his military reform. One can understand the mood with which the deputies returned to their constituencies. One can perceive why the voters in the elections of 1861 and 1862 eliminated the right-wing conciliatory liberals in favor of more aggressive and determined leaders.

[67] Abg. H., *St. B.*, May 27, 1861; III, 1409.

5 / National Unification

Iₙ 1860 the problem of national unification was, in its modern phase, over a half-century old. In 1848 it had been subjected to a serious attempt at solution. The beginning of the New Era aroused the Prussian liberals to renewed hope for the achievement of the goal, and the Italian unification in 1859-60 revived their belief that within the foreseeable future a similar success should be possible for their own nation. The liberals took the initiative in pressing this issue upon their own state and joined forces with colleagues in the other German states for the struggle. They made the issue an integral part of their program of remaking Prussian and German culture in the pattern of freedom and compelled the indifferent, lukewarm, theoretically interested and hostile elements to respond in one way or another. Four separate social forces interested in the question need to be considered: the King, the liberals, the Conservatives and Bismarck. The reaction of each will be considered in this chapter.

The Political Interest

In theory the King approved of German unity at some time in the future, but he never expected to live long enough to see it. In his program of November, 1858, he had written:

> Prussia must stand in friendly relations with all great powers without giving itself over to foreign influences and without binding its hands too early by treaties. Friendly relations with all other powers are equally offered. In Germany Prussia must make moral conquests by wise legislation of its own, by elevating all moral elements and by adopting elements of unification like the Zollverein, which nevertheless must be subjected to reform. The world must know that Prussia is ready everywhere to protect right. A firm, consequent, and, when it must be, energetic

demeanor in politics combined with wisdom and circumspection must create for Prussia the political prestige and the position of power which it is unable to attain by its material power alone.

In the formulation of that statement the King seemed to approve the general idea of moral conquest in Germany. That he comprehended the import of his assertion appears in the light of subsequent events extremely doubtful. His promise that "Prussia is ready to defend right everywhere" is rather inclusive; but since he also called for coupling "energetic demeanor," when it was necessary, with "wisdom and circumspection" and since he refused to bind his hands by treaty too early, one could anticipate that in the German question very little if anything would be accomplished on his initiative.

During the entire New Era vague statements and timid action continued to characterize the King's policy toward German unity. At the opening of the Landtag in 1860 the ruler declared that "the wish for reform of the Constitution of the German Confederation has recently been expressed again. Prussia will always regard itself as the natural exponent of the objective to raise and bind together the glories of the nation by appropriate institutions and in general effectively to further the totality of German interests by measures of truly practical significance." Such self-satisfied assertions committed him to nothing more than "measures of truly practical significance"; and since each of the three words, "truly," "practical," and "significance" is capable of diverse interpretation, an ardent advocate of national unification could derive from this speech the assurance of nothing.

At the beginning of the Landtag session in January, 1861, the King announced that he had been endeavoring to bring about a revision of the military organization of the German confederation and expressed confidence in the outcome, "since all German governments and all German tribes recognize unanimous cooperation as the most urgent need of our entire fatherland." When the Landtag opened in January, 1862, the King was still talking in generalities, of greater vagueness even than those of his predecessors. He reported "to my regret" that his proposals for reform of the military organization of the Confederation had not reached "a satisfactory conclusion." He was therefore trying to improve conditions by agreements among the separate states for "a greater similarity in military matters" and announced that an agreement had been made with the little state of Saxony-Coburg-Gotha. The King added,

> The need of a general reform of the German constitution has recently been expressly recognized in circles of the German governments. True to the national traditions of Prussia my

government will endeavor constantly to work in favor of such reforms which by corresponding to the real power relations will unite more energetically the forces of the German people and place Prussia in the position to further with increased pressure the interests of the entire fatherland.[1]

The King did not compose these addresses himself, but they had to suit him. It can be assumed that the assertions expressed his own thinking, especially on the vital question of national unity. From the statement of 1862, again one must have inferred, and correctly so, that the King would do nothing. His reference to Prussia as a nation must have implied indifference to the hopes of the German nation. Derived from the Eighteenth Century or earlier, it showed complete ignorance of the ideals and aspirations of German nationalism. To speak of his country's traditional policy of working for reform of the German confederation promised even less, when one recalled the names of the ancestors to whom he was most devoted, Frederick the Great and that arch-particularist and conservative, Frederick William III. When he posed "the real power relations" as the standard for reorganization among the German states, he opened the way either to endless negotiations or to the exercise of superior authority by Prussia; and since the second policy could be ruled out, one could assume that the first would be followed. The King's wish to set Prussia in a position to "further the interests of the entire fatherland with increased emphasis" can scarcely have evoked an enthusistic response from those states that had refused to make any agreement even for improving the Confederation's military defence.

The statement by Foreign Minister von Bernstorff in the Lower House in February, 1862, may be taken as confirmation of the inactive attitude. The Foreign Minister spoke of the desirability of forming a smaller union of German states (by "smaller" he meant the exclusion of Austria), with an executive which would exercise the supreme military command, would conduct foreign affairs, and would have a parliament composed of representatives from the individual states. These reforms were considered desirable. The minister ignored the need for economic unity and for a central authority to further national economic interests. Nor did he offer any assurance of a popular national parliament representing not merely the German states but the German people. The lack of precision about the way in which the representatives were to be selected left doubt as to whether they should be diplomatic representatives, as was the case

---

[1] For the ruler's statements see Horst Kohl, *op. cit.*, pp. 5-6, 12, 22, 33-34.

already with the despised Bundestag of the Confederation, or should be selected from the state parliaments by the deputies themselves in co-operation with the governments, or should be specially elected by the people of the separate states. The minister's remarks left matter once more in the air, a condition for which the King had a special affinity.

In one respect William was prepared to act. He was willing at any favorable opportunity to continue one of the traditions of his house, that of absorbing small German states. In speaking to the liberal von Bernhardi in 1860, the ruler was decidedly of the view that "the small German states must be absorbed in Prussia; he scorned the petty rulers," so von Bernhardi reported, "and thought that they would gain in their personal position by becoming subordinate to a big state."[2] He would have treated them in the same manner that his father and brother had treated those who had been fortunate enough to be absorbed into Prussia in 1815. The princes would have been given a privileged place in the governmental assemblies and allowed to serve in the Hohenzollern army and bureaucracy.

The King particularly despised one of his princely colleagues, the ruler of Kurhesse. This ruler had violated the constitution of 1831 and restored absolute rule. His mistreatment of his subjects was notorious; Kurhesse compared favorably in that respect with the Manteuffel regime in Prussia which in 1858 the King had ousted. William fumed at this colleague, negotiated with and about him, tried to stir the Diet of the Confederation to action against him, and accomplished nothing. The indignity of having to back down before the adamant ruler of Kurhesse was augmented by the fact that the little state separated the Eastern and the Western parts of Prussia at the narrowest place. A Hohenzollern was eager to absorbe this petty principality.

When the King become involved in conflict over military reform with the liberals in his own Lower House, he turned against not merely their domestic program for Prussia but their hope and plan of national unification. The debates in the first informal and unofficial meeting of deputies from the parliaments of the various German states in September, 1862, aroused his ire. The assembly of deputies did not mention Prussia's mission to unify Germany, though liberals were accustomed to stress this point. Instead it demanded the creation of a national parliament composed of deputies elected by the people without interference by the states. The King, who was visiting the Grand Duke of Baden at the time of this assembly, broke into such a storm

[2] Von Bernhardi, *op. cit.*, III, 300; also Parisius, *von Hoverbeck*, II, 8.

of anger "that one could even hear his immoderate words in the street," wrote the Grand Duke to an acquaintance. He became so hostile to the movement for unification that he subsequently caused Bismarck great difficulty.[3] In January, 1871, he was still averse to accepting the title of emperor, and declared, "My son is with his entire soul in the new state of affairs, while it means nothing at all to me. I hold only to Prussia."[4] He tolerated national unification, but he would never have personally pushed it through to completion. That honor belonged to the liberals and especially to Bismarck.

When the liberals spoke of the need for German unification, their justification was based upon the belief that the German people required a larger area of activity than was theirs at present in the separate states. The question of size bore significance in respect both to the German people's role among the nations and to the character of life within the German nation. These formed two facets of an identical problem, the international and the internal; each conditioned the other and could not be understood in isolation.

The German Diet was composed of diplomats representing the practically independent German states, which treated each other as foreign powers. With the possible exception of Prussia and Austria no one of these thirty-three states possessed the necessary resources in land mass, population and wealth to protect itself against foreign aggressors. The medium-sized and small states maintained armies and other services which they could not well afford and which absorbed funds needed for other purposes. They preserved their independence solely under the protection of the principle of the balance of power: the large states of Europe would object to any foreign state seizing one or more of them.

The Prussian liberals recognized that even their own state suffered from the same handicap. In addition to being much smaller in size, population and resources than the other great powers, Prussia was separated into two geographic areas by several German states. It had tried to overcome this fundamental weakness by devoting a larger amount of its energy to the military than did other great powers and by maintaining in absolutism the form of leadership regarded as most efficient and economical for quick action. As the liberal deputy von Forckenbeck said, Prussia could not be liberalized without German

[3] Zechlin, *op. cit.*, pp. 338-39.
[4] Quoted in Parisius, *von Hoverbeck*, I, 218.

unity.[5] The greater resources of a unified Germany would relieve Prussia of the excessive burden of her military power and render absolutism no longer justifiable on military grounds. Bigness would enable the new German state to be an authentic great power, self-confident because of its reserve force without the necessity of constant military tension.

The size of a unified Germany, ran the nationalist argument, would assure the German people independence and security. No great power would then dare attack the country with intentions of conquest. Germans could feel self-respect among the peoples of the world and command respect from them. Like other nations long since politically unified, they would achieve the form enabling them to fulfill their historic destiny. German honor required that the people win the national unity, independence and security which other nations had gained.

Honor, self-respect and the respect of others, the liberal nationalists believed, had to be acquired at home, within Germany. This cardinal point among the advocates of national unification involved the relationship of liberalism and nationalism. By honor and self-respect the liberals referred not merely to relations with other countries; they were speaking not merely of the German nation; they were speaking of the relations of German individuals and social groups with other Germans. They were concerned with the attitude of the nobility toward the middle class and the peasantry, of the military Junkers toward everyone else. They were upholding the liberal principles of social freedom and the dignity of man against caste and privilege. They wanted their own governments to honor and respect not merely those of the upper class but all citizens, and for that purpose they wished a life freed from the tyranny of German rulers, petty or otherwise. They maintained that a nation had the right to develop the forms of public life which it needed and wished, that irrespective of existing legality it had the right to replace the legal and institutional structure of particularism by that of national unity. The ideals of liberalism were employed to justify a people in asserting the right of self-determination within the limits of its own nation.

The major enemy of both liberalism and national unity was particularism, the independent existence of each German state ruled by its own sovereign, usually still in fact an absolute monarch. These

---

[5] Parisius, *von Hoverbeck*, I, 164-65; Philippson, *op. cit.*, p. 43; von Saucken in the *Königsberg Hartungsche Zeitung*, Aug. 2, 1862.

rulers were, like King William I of Prussia, intent upon maintaining their position as autocratic sovereigns of independent states. They had no more inclination to become mediatized than to become figure-heads over parliamentary governments. The liberals were actually aware of the fact that the princes would never give up enough of their power to unify Germany unless they were compelled to do so. The liberals firmly believed that the cabinets, as they called the governments of these rulers, would not unify Germany, that if the German people did not perform that work it would never be executed.

To the liberals particularism meant moral, intellectual and ma-terial stagnation. It deprived the people of the opportunities to realize their potentialities. It prevented "German character in its universality" from realizing itself. Especially in the small states the people found themselves dependent upon the will of the petty ruler. Restricted within the narrow boundary of one of these states, they had too few opportunities to try to accomplish what they wished to do. The ruler was able to keep them under control; the current of life in the large states and in the outside world passed these people by, leaving them frustrated, listless, devoid of the sense of honor and self-respect that comes from personal initiative and achievement. In a small par-ticularistic state, the liberals maintained, man tended to vegetate; the horizon was so close that he was scarcely aware of opportunities be-yond his reach. Occupations were few in number because of the small size of the population and tended to serve almost entirely the local court or the local people. Society was in-bred. Cultural facilities depended in the main upon the will of the ruler as the only per-son with wealth. Political activity and understanding were confined to the small items of local significance and were too concerned with the interests of the ruler to be other than trivial. International affairs and problems of constitutional governance scarcely aroused interest; they lacked reality.

Although the criticism of the effects of particularism was directed mainly at the small or medium-sized states rather than at the large ones, the Prussian liberals recognized that in some respects it applied to their own country as well. Their ruler still thought about his sub-jects in much the same way as his fellow-sovereigns in the lesser states; the people were subjects, therefore with limited comprehension of affairs; the constitution should be interpreted according to the theory of the divine right of kings; military affairs and foreign relations should be the exclusive province of the ruler; the social structure should remain essentially that of the Old Regime, with the nobility at the top helping the King rule the state; the particular state, not the nation, should be the first object of the subject's devotion. Economically, the state also continued to restrict private activities too much for the liberals. Mercantilist control was comparable to that in the other states. It prevented Prussian economic organizations, insurance companies, banks, industries, tradesmen, craftsmen, from freely carrying on business in the other states, and vice versa. Because of particularism modern means of transportation and communication were not being developed quickly or widely enough. The market, even in Prussia, was too small to satisfy the needs of the big corporations and industrial facilities being created. Prussians suffered not to the same extent but in the same way as businessmen in the lesser states. They wanted freedom of movement and domicile and occupation on a national scale. No German state was sufficiently large to provide the necessary area for the exercise of these rights. The German working man, the German industrialist, any German should have the right to earn a living in his nation wherever he chose. Questions of personal honor and self-respect were involved, questions of the dignity of a member of the German nation. Each German was or should be concerned, for the issues affected the life of each individual. Over against his status as a subject of a small state were set his rights as a member of the German nation.

The *klein-deutsch* liberals of north and central Germany, among them the Prussians, worked out a plan for the unification of the country.[6] The essence of it was incorporated in the program of the German Progressive party, a wholly Prussian party whose title indicated its objective. The plan, published in 1861, read as follows:

> The existence and greatness of Prussia depend upon a firm unification of Germany, which cannot be conceived without a strong central power in the hands of Prussia and without a representation of its people. . . .
> Thus we believe that Prussia has the right and the duty to support with pressure the endeavor of the German people to achieve unity within and power without and wherever the rights of the people are violated as in Kurhesse and in Schleswig-Holstein to restore them again by active aid.
> Prussia should never lose from sight its task of winning the approval of the other German tribes for its domestic organization and work. Strict and consistent achievement of the constitutional, legal state, stimulation of all the forces of the peo-

---

[6] By *klein-deutsch* is meant the plan for unifying Germany with the exclusion of Austria. The *gross-deutsch* proponents wished to include Austria.

ple to useful activity, careful treatment and preservation of these forces by wise economy in state expenditures are therefore the indispensable bases of our political objective.[7]

The program was accepted by all *klein-deutsch* liberals, irrespective of party affiliation. They all believed in Prussia's taking the lead, in the moral conquest of the rest of Germany by liberal reforms within Prussia, in having a national government composed of an executive and a popularly elected representative assembly of the nation with authority over military and commercial affairs and foreign relations.[8]

The left-wing and the right-wing liberals differed only over questions of strategy in timing and over distribution of emphasis on the various points of the national program. The Progressive party wished to advance quickly to action. The other liberal groups advised a slower pace; the farther to the right they were the more slowly they were inclined to proceed. The groups differed somewhat in the proposed treatment of the rulers. The Progressive party held most of these rulers in such contempt that it wished to force reforms upon them. The liberals of the right wing advocated respecting the authority of the princes. They stood close to William's own vague idea of unification at some distant time, unification with and by the rulers in such a way as to satisfy everyone. They wished to preserve "the inner independence of the individual states, with Prussian leadership in national, military, diplomatic and commercial affairs."[9] It would have been possible to preserve this inner independence and at the same time unify Germany, depending on one's understanding of these phrases; but the mental reservation behind the statement becomes clear when it is contrasted with ones by the Progessivist Schulze-Delitzsch or his colleague Freiherr von Hoverbeck. At the conference of riflemen in Frankfurt am Main in July, 1862, von Hoverbeck made a speech in which he extended greetings from the majority in the Prussian Lower House and declared "that this majority recognizes no other than the German interests, and that if in some way the so-called Prussian interests should conflict with the German interests, we prefer the German interests!" Schulze-Delitzsch was even blunter. "We work for no one dynasty in Germany, neither for the Hohenzollern nor for

[7] Quoted from Ludolph Parisius, *Deutschlands politische Parteien und das Ministerium Bismarck* (Berlin, 1878), pp. 33 ff.

[8] See the joint resolution of the liberals in the Lower House early in 1862. Parisius, *von Hoverbeck*, II, 13-14.

[9] Parisius, *Politische Parteien*, p. 55.

the Hapsburg, when we wish to establish German unity. We work for ourselves, for the German people!"[10]

The difference between the right-wing or Old Liberals (Constitutionals, as they were called) and the Progressives was one of degree rather than of kind. Each recognized the need for instruments making national unity a reality; but the former preferred federalism with the central government having just sufficient authority to function as the head of the national state. Since the Old Liberals were few in number in Prussia and lost out almost completely as a political force in favor of the Progressive party and the almost equally aggressive Left-Center liberal party, one may assume that on questions of national unity all Prussian liberals, apart from a small handful of *Gross-Deutsche,* shared common objectives.

The plan of the liberals for unifying the nation conformed with their own social and political ideals. Since they had no confidence in the ability or the willingness of the princes to unify the country, they had to devise means for achieving the objective in spite of these persons. The plan called for the progressive transfer of authority from the rulers to the representatives of the people in each state—not all authority, not parliamentary control of government, but enough to push the rulers into national unity. Liberal reforms were essential in each state so that the people would perceive the value of unification for them. The more economic and social progress, the more freedom and cultural reform, the more awake and active the population would be in furthering its own interests. The stronghold of particularism lay in the King and his bureaucracy: liberalism aimed to reduce the authority of both these powers. The freedom for action achieved thereby would benefit economic and other kinds of activity, which would expand the area of life and the range of problems requiring political and economic attention and administrative machinery on a national scale. The liberals saw that there must be real interests of a national scope or there would be no institutional force behind the movement of unification. Each factory builder, each large-scale merchant, each free organization of the professions or other occupational and social groups, each victory for freedom of movement, domicile and occupation, each victory for freedom of speech, press, and assembly, each gain of political power by the representatives of the people meant an increased concern with public affairs and aggressiveness in pushing these interests. Each one meant a greater sense of all Germans

[10] Parisius, *von Hoverbeck,* II. 56; Schulze-Delitzsch, *op. cit.,* III, 191-92.

belonging in one country and a greater confidence in one's ability to work for this goal. When, if he wished, the Prussian could freely live and work in Bavaria, when he could run his own government, when he could manage his own business of German-wide range, when he could read in the papers about conditions in every German state and plans for improving them, then he would be serving and expressing both liberalism and the desire for national unification.

Some machinery was necessary for organizing the liberal-sponsored activity on a national scale, some legal method for focusing the disparate action within each state upon the national objective. The liberals worked out a plan for solving this most complicated problem. In 1859 they organized the National Verein, a kind of holding company for liberal and national activity in each state. It was directed by leading liberals from all over Germany and published a weekly journal. In each state a German progressive party was to be organized to represent and further the interests of liberal and national reform. The choice of name did not matter, although that of German Progessive party was recommended. More important was the unity of purpose among the patries. In each state the liberal party would press its program and at the same time keep in close touch with its colleagues in other states. As these parties grew in influence, they would bring their state governments actively to strive for national unity. The liberal deputies from the various states would work out common policies not merely in the National Verein but in national conferences of parliamentary deputies. The necessary coordination and cooperation would be assured for the pursuit of a common goal. Simultaneous pressure would be applied on all German governments to realize a common plan for national unity.

Prussia was to assume the lead because it was the largest state and could withstand Austria. If it set an example, the lesser states would fall into line, for Prussia had so many political and economic means of pressure upon the lesser states that they would have to follow suit. The closing of the Prussian market, the refusal of a loan, the breaking of diplomatic relations, the release of a press campaign of criticism, these and many other instruments of influence were at Prussia's disposal, not to speak of the sheer power of its army. Prussia held the key to the entire plan. If it became liberal, so would Germany; if it did not, the liberal plan for national unification would fail.

The liberals expected their method of unification to succeed without international intervention and a foreign war. Not even France, the enemy, would dare interfere in a country where the people were wholeheartedly supporting the national movement. Unification would be carried on so calmly, so peacefully, with such devotion and harmony, apart from the objections of a few rulers and aristocrats, that France would have no occasion to interfere. Unity would be achieved so gradually that France would scarcely realize what was occurring before it was too late to act. Enormous expenditures for a Prussian army and vast military reforms would not be necessary. In fact they were a detriment, said the liberals, for they made the non-Prussians think that Prussian militarism was on the aggressive and that the Junkers might be able to destroy liberalism. The King's reform program for the army had to be opposed as a danger to the liberal plan of unification. The funds resulting from the economy of the liberal method, the saving on military expenditure, would be devoted to constructive activity, schools, railroads, and the like, which would further Prussia's moral conquest of the rest of Germany. If an army were needed, Schulze-Delitzsch said in July, 1862, it should be a people's army supporting a people's parliament, not, he inferred, a standing army of an absolute sovereign led by Junkers. The liberals encouraged the activity of the riflemen's clubs, gymnastic societies and other associations building up the defensive power, they said, of the German people; but they placed most emphasis on maintaining the popular character of the Prussian army as established in 1814. To keep the army popular, to hold down expenses, to abolish Junker militarism, all were parts of the plan to unify Germany by peaceful means.

The liberals realized that the execution of their program would take time. They believed that the course of history law with them and that they were sure to win. Even though they knew that they had to be active and to labor for their cause, they derived great assurance from their belief that time worked, not for absolutism, Junkers, and particularism, but for liberalism and national unity.

The liberals could not readily be extreme nationalists, like the National Socialists of a later date, when the main obstacle to the popular conception of national unification lay in the rivalry of two German powers, one, Prussia, which was almost entirely German in population and certainly German in leadership, the other, Austria, which was dominated by the German elements of the population. The situation did not lend itself to extreme nationalist agitation. *Gross-deutsch* and *klein-deutsch* advocates were equally in favor of German unity, even though they differed over their conception of unity. The *klein-deutsch* advocates aimed to exclude Austria from the German state, mainly on two counts: it contained too many non-German peoples, and it was too big either to be absorbed as it was into a unified Germany or to be broken up and the German population incorporated in the new national state. The liberals wished to tie Austria to the new state by an alliance of an especially close character, different from the ordinary foreign alliance in that it rested upon not merely political interest but common nationality. They emphasized the practical and feasible aspects of the *klein-deutsch* solution and did not overemphasize German nationality. They were actually not concerned with the entire German nation, but with only a part of it. A few were *gross-deutsch*, but certainly in Prussia the liberals adhered overwhelmingly to the *klein-deutsch* solution. The reasonable and practical character of it appealed to these liberals in the same way that constitutional government, freedom of occupation, freedom of press and assembly, and other liberal ideals appealed to them.

Extreme nationalism did not seize hold of the Prussians, for Germany was not endangered from abroad and was prospering within. The only possible danger would come from France, which in 1859 became involved in the Italian affair. While many Germans, especially liberals, feared a French attack at the time, their fears soon proved to be unjustified. The movement for national unity owed its drive not to outside threats but to the process of internal transformation under way in Germany society with the development of industrialism and the middle class. It was not merely economic in character; it was cultural; it involved the change from the Old Regime to the free society of modern industrialism. Under these conditions nationalism had little in common with the emotionalism of Fichte and Arndt suffering from the humiliation of the Prussian collapse and the Napoleonic control of Germany. It had nothing in common with Hitlerism. It intended to provide a solid basis of adequate size for the new industrial culture, which should operate in a world still employing power politics but which was essentially peaceful in its international relations. The fact that the liberal movement for national unity coincided with the liberal movement for free trade made this attitude doubly evident. The Fichtean closed commercial state had no significance for these liberals. They rejected economic autarchy and urged expansion of international trade, just as they pressed for trade among the German people within a unified Germany. They sought to consolidate Germany without war either among the Germans or against foreign powers. They chose the nation as the object of their desires because it provided the next largest body for which they could find a justification for political unity.

The liberals hated no one abroad. Their special enemies were German particularists and conservatives who opposed freedom and national unification. They mistrusted France, but not to any excessive degree. Their criteria of behavior were not the amount of physical power but the degree of moral and rational justification one had, the number of persons supporting one's views and the efficiency and character of those persons as shown, not in the accident of their social position obtained by birth, but in their intellectual and material accomplishment and in their moral standards. On these grounds they disliked the exclusiveness of castes, the sense of superiority of the aristocracy, and monopolistic absolutism more than they did the French or any other foreign people. Their feeling of middle-class solidarity made them akin to the French, English and any other middle class. They were very much aware of the greatness of the German people, who they thought were striding toward the achievement of a free culture; but they also recognized that the English in particular were ahead of them, not merely in the fact of national unity but in the fact of the achievement of a progressive economy and a free society and government. They did not envy or hate the French, English or anyone else on that account, for they were too busy and optimistic to succumb to that attitude. The Germans were doing well; they had hopes; they were progressing; they saw the possibility of achieving all their objectives by themselves. Why should they envy or hate anyone else and compensate for their own backwardness by exalting the German nation into a messianic role? They did not believe that they were especially backward any more than that they were in the vanguard. They knew that their nation contained backward forces; but they thought that they could overcome these and accomplish their objectives by themselves.[11]

As on all other questions, with respect to national unification the Conservatives were forced to action by the initiative of the liberals. When they organized for fighting the election campaign in 1861, they called their instrument the Prussian Volksverein, in deliberate opposition to the liberals' National Verein, and stated that it should be the center of Conservative action in Prussia and "offer its hand to colleagues of like mind in the rest of the German fatherland." The first point of the program of this Prussian Union laid down the position on national unity. "Unity of our German fatherland, not in the manner of the Italian kingdom by blood and fire but in the unity of its princes and peoples and in the firm preservation of authority and law. No

---

[11] The position of the liberals on national unification is to be found in so many well-known publications that bibliographical data are superfluous. The Landtag debates and the contemporary newspapers and magazines are particularly valuable.

repudiation of our Prussian fatherland and its glorious history; no perishing in the filth of a German republic; no robbery of the crown and nationality swindle."[12]

Although the Conservatives were still reacting to the Revolution of 1848, not to the existing situation, they showed complete hostility to the liberal conception of national unity. They did so because it was liberal and because it was national. To Wagener, the nationality theory of the liberals was not merely "false" but of such weak character that "you [the liberals] appear to recognize a German as a fellow countryman only in his party uniform." Deputy von Blanckenburg expressed the same thought in blunter form, "Gentlemen, for us national union is ridiculous."[13]

The degree of clarity in the proposal of the Conservatives for achieving national unity may be gathered from an election appeal of October, 1863. The statement revealed that they were much more concerned about preserving the King's power and through it the present structure of social and political power than they were about unifying the Germans. The latter objective was used as a sort of extra argument in favor of the former. The government, the Conservatives declared in this call for popular support, had given two reasons for dissolving the Lower House and asking for new elections: the question of the role of the monarchy in Prussia and the question of the role of Prussia in Germany. The Conservatives accepted these as the main issues in the election:

> The monarchy alone is able to bring our domestic confusion to a healthy conclusion; a strong monarchy alone is able also to preserve and to strengthen Prussia's position in Germany. Let us hold firmly to all which His Majesty the King has guarded and held to firmly as his hereditary and constitutional prerogatives, especially his position as supreme war lord of his people. Let us hold firmly to Prussia's position of power in Germany.... Let us hold firmly to the strength and prestige of our army, which is Germany's sword and Prussia's iron wall. Let us hold firmly to right within and without, and let us enter the election campaign with the slogan to prove to friends and to foes that we have recently celebrated the memory of the great deeds of our ancestors not merely in appearance alone. Since the days of Frederick the Great Prussia can never more be the second but always one of the two first powers in Germany.[14]

[12] Parisius, *Politische Parteien*, p. 42; see also the statement by the Conservative Committee in Königsberg in *Königsberg Hartungsche Zeitung*, Nov. 3, 1861.

[13] Abg. H., *St. B.*, March 2, 1861; I, 308. *Ibid.*, March 28, 1861; III, 1432.

[14] Hugo Müller, *Der Preussische Volks-Verein* (Berlin, 1914), pp. 130-31; also in *Kreuzzeitung*, Oct. 18, 1863.

Wagener worked out a plan for national unification for the Volks-verein which, in so far as the Conservatives had any idea of how to accomplish that objective, may be considered as the party's proposal. Its import may be quickly judged from the details. "The Volksverein demands not plans of fantastic alliance and conquest but the energetic and conscious initiative of the Prussian government in all critical questions of our time, an independent political action on the basis of which one can claim to be recognized and respected as the protection and shield of right and of the legitimacy of the princes and the peoples." The plan recommended not the abolition but the development of the Confederation constitution "by clear and energetic initiative on the part of Prussia" in order finally to bring about "the necessary and desirable reform" of the Confederation by means of "serious negotiations with the German princes and in cooperation with the conservative elements of the individual states." Wagener spoke of the general mistrust of Prussia as a main obstacle to its position in Germany and to its action in the Confederation and deplored the absence of a German prince who would be regarded with confidence from all sides as the true shield of right and legitimacy. It would not be long, he declared, before all peoples would readily place in such a prince the faith which he needed in order to be their shield and defence. If a state would simply fulfill its duty and administer justice, influence would come to it automatically. As for the Diet of the Confederation, Wagener declared that when, instead of ministers, princes placed themselves personally at the head of the German nation, that body would lose its unpopularity. "If the princes wish to remain what they are," Wagener declared, "or if they wish to remain at all, it is high time they came to the front in person."[15]

The election appeal showed that the Conservatives really had no policy for unifying Germany. They wished to maintain the status quo, with power left in the hands of the ruling princes and with the Prussian and Austrian monarchs cooperating as equals to keep out foreign enemies and to keep down internal liberalism. In so far as any changes were to be made in the existing constitution for Germany, they had to be achieved by common agreement among all the rulers; otherwise legal rights and therefore morality would be violated, the door opened to further inroads upon the status quo, to liberalism and nationalism. Conservatism revived its policy of the Metternich era of using international relations as a justification for not reforming at home and as a means of preventing any reform. Just how the German nation would come out of its existing impasse did not bother the Conservatives. Many of them preferred to concentrate merely upon Prussia, as one election propoganda sheet put out by the Königsberg election committee said, "With God for King and Fatherland,"[16] and by Fatherland they meant Prussia.

The Conservatives were necessarily opposed to change. Their emotional response toward opponents varied from indifference to hate, depending upon the degree of danger to them from these forces. They hated the liberals within Germany and they hated Louis Napoleon and the French. They regarded these two forces alike as their greatest enemies. They condemned Louis Napoleon for having established the kind of absolutistic, bureaucratic, centralized government which, they thought, was as contrary to their views and interests as liberalism. For the latter they felt scorn; for Louis Napoleon and his accomplishments they felt fear—fear of imitation in Prussia, fear of Louis Napoleon's using the military power gained by his absolutism to attack Prussia. They maintained the standards of power politics of the Old Regime in international as well as internal relations, and attributing the same standards to Louis Napoleon, they mistrusted him deeply and freely vented their antagonism in words of intense aversion. They were far from being nationalists; but believing in the game of international politics as played by Frederick the Great, they were constantly on the lookout for foreign enemies. Rather ignorant of conditions in other countries, they were not aware of any community of interest with the nobility and other conservatives in other European countries. They were not conservative internationalists; they were conservative Prussians. The extent of their interest in conservatism abroad was limited to Germany and German-speaking Austria. While they were theoretically willing to cooperate with these German and Austrian-German conservatives against the liberal advocates of national unity, they did not bestir themselves to do more than put the idea into words, and they left the initiative and responsibility for action to the conservative governments. They concentrated on preserving their position in Prussia, and for that purpose they supported the King's power. The institutional structure of their society was restricted to Prussia; they had no interest in or occasion for exploiting German nationalism for their own gain as they had after Germany became unified. The new Reich created new institutions of control which they could use

[16] *Königsberg Hartungsche Zeitung,* Nov. 16, 1861.

for the preservation of conservatism and gave a new set of institutions to conserve. After the radical act of national unification the Conservatives could and did accustom themselves to maintaining the conservative character of these institutions; and since the institutions were on a national basis, the Conservatives became nationalists for the sake of their way of life. In the period under consideration, however, the area of their interest remained Prussia, their major enemy not France or any foreign power so much as the liberals and democrats who wished to reform Prussia and to unify Germany. They associated nationalism with liberalism and both with revolutionary destruction of the Old Regime.

When Bismarck became Minister President in September, 1862, he had already cast aside his stock Prussianism of 1849 and recognized the necessity for German unity. He had clarified in his own mind the outlines of the desired organization of a unified Germany and a plan for accomplishing the objective. He had weighed the forces which would oppose unification and those which would support it, and he arrived at a policy which incorporated elements from the liberal program and from the Hohenzollern tradition of power politics. He was to be unable to execute *in toto* the plan which he had worked out; nonetheless, he returned to it after the war of 1866 and built the essentials into the structure of a unified Germany.

Bismarck approached the problem of national unification from the standpoint of Prussian state interests. Whatever accrued to Prussia's advantage should be furthered. He learned from experience as representative at the Diet in Frankfurt am Main in the 1850s that Prussia lacked the resources of the other great powers and needed German support. He recognized that Prussia's position in the geographic center of Europe would force it to become involved in every European affair, that it could not remain passive and in peace, that it must be either hammer or anvil. "We shall appear relatively weak in every connection with other great powers," he wrote in 1857, "as long as we are not stronger than we now are." In the next year he added, "There is nothing more German than the development of properly understood Prussian particularist interests."[17] Bismarck discovered the German nation in his search for means of strengthening Prussia as an international power.

[17] Hans Rothfels (ed.), *Otto von Bismarck. Deutscher Staat. Ausgewählte Dokumente* (Munich, 1925), pp. 129, 127, 192.

Under the existing constitution of the German confederation Prussia would be unable to improve upon its position. Bismarck's criticism of that organization, based on his own experience, had much in common with the condemnatory views of the liberals, but it was put in terms of power rather than in expressions of cultural ideals for the German people. He had concluded that the exercise of the veto by each of the thirty-three or so members of the Diet prevented anything from being accomplished. He expressed to Prince William in March, 1858, his belief that the particularism of the majority of the smaller German governments and the tendencies of the Austrian policies were both un-German, that the Confederation was being exploited to preserve the domestic and foreign security of its members and that it would in time break apart. He condemned Prussian policy for being enthusiastic about "the small state sovereignty created by Napoleon and sanctioned by Metternich," and called this policy one of "blindness toward all dangers with which Prussia and Germany's independence are threatened in the future as long as the nonsense of the present Confederation constitution exists, which is nothing more than a hothouse and conservatory of dangerous and revolutionary particularist activities."[18]

From his experience at the German Diet Bismarck had acquired a profound mistrust of Austria. Again his comments resembled those of the liberals, but again with the difference that they were based on standards of power politics. Austria would act as an independent great power, he said, and exploit its German connections for selfish purposes. The twenty per cent German population in Austria, Bismarck declared, offered no assurance whatever that Austria would follow a policy of advantage to Germany or cooperate with Prussia to that effect. On the contrary, he wrote Prince William, in its relations with Prussia Austria would pursue its own interests, "to combat and reduce Prussia's prestige and influence in Germany as much as possible, but in case of war and against the manifold dangers surrounding Austria to seek to be able to count on the support of Prussia's complete power."[19] Like most of his liberal opponents Bismarck was *klein-deutsch*; in his thinking, the presence of two great powers, Austria and Prussia, created a situation of dualism and rivalry which would have to be eliminated.

The disadvantage and danger of the dualism to Prussia became clear to Bismarck from the behavior of the so-called middle states, the larger

[18] *Ibid.*, pp. 192, 204-05.
[19] *Ibid.*, pp. 131, 193-94.

of the German states, especially Saxony, Bavaria and Württemberg. These, he said, were too small to act like international powers and too large to be conscious of their own intrinsic weakness. Bismarck diagnosed their policy as one of maintaining themselves by playing between Prussia and Austria.

> The belief in the possibility of a unanimous action of both powers has nowhere sunk lower than in Germany itself. The middle states know the situation best, for they are the ones which fan the rivalry of the great powers. Their simple means for doing so is to support every unjust claim of Austria against Prussia. The office of arbitrator between the two powers in peacetime and a plausible excuse in wartime to be able to leave the Confederation in the lurch because of the disunity of Prussia and Austria are the fruits of their policy.

The middle and small states were normally pro-Austrian out of fear of Prussia, Bismarck asserted in 1859; but if Austria became aggressive and Prussia quiescent, they would flock to Prussia's standard. Their policy was "the natural and necessary result of their situation in the Confederation and was not to be expected to change." "We have no means," he concluded, "to come to an enduring and satisfactory arrangement with this policy within the existing constitution of the Confederation."[20]

Bismarck rarely restricted his thinking to negative criticism. Along with the analysis of the defects in the German constitution he developed ideas about reorganization. Nor did he stop merely with a description of what should be introduced in place of the existing structure. As a person concerned with action he considered how the plans would be implemented.

The key to Bismarck's national policy was contained in a letter of criticism of the political program put forth by the Conservative party in 1861. "Our government is liberal in Prussia, but legitimist in foreign policy," he wrote. He proposed that the policy be made not liberal but consistent. Liberal ideas should be used in handling the question of German unity. "In the national sphere," he said, "very modest concessions have been greeted as valuable. One could create quite a conservative national representation and still gain the gratitude of the liberals for it." He thought it possible to achieve a liberal objective with liberal support, to do so under Conservative control and with the preservation of the Conservative political and social structure,

[20] Ibid., pp. 194-95, 198.

making possible the assumption and retention of political power by a Bismarck.[21]

In setting the ultimate objective of German unity, Bismarck did not at this time (1861) go as far along the road toward centralization as the liberals. He had written in 1857 that military, political and commercial authority would be most useful for the Confederation, that "under unified direction the Confederation would accomplish entirely other things in war and peace than at present and in case of war would be really tenable."[22] He was then thinking about the ideal, and he had no intention of subordinating Prussia to such political control. His usual statement omitted the political factor and called for the transfer to a central government solely of military, customs and commercial authority. "We need a tighter consolidation of German military power as much as bread itself," he wrote in September, 1861. "We need a new organization in customs affairs and a number of common institutions in order to protect the material interests against the disadvantages which grow out of the unnatural configuration of the inner German state boundaries."[23] He did not expand his conception of what powers the German government would need until in 1866 and 1867 he actually had to face the issue. One must conclude that his Prussian Conservative standards prevented him from working out an adequate answer to this problem until the crisis, and that the liberals had both a much earlier and a much clearer understanding of it than he had. When the North German Confederation was created in 1867 the character of the central authority bore much more the stamp of the liberals than of Bismarck; but he had the statemanship to accept the additions as useful in achieving the common objective of national unity.

From practical experience Bismarck came to incorporate in his plans the creation of a national parliament to represent the people. The ideal was related in his mind with that of moral conquest in Germany by Prussia and showed extraordinary similarity to the liberals' thinking. Early in 1858 he wrote Prince William in eloquent terms.

> The leading position which Prussia had before 1848 in the Confederation rested not upon the favor of the middle states and the Confederation assembly but upon the fact that Prussia was in the vanguard in all lines of state development, that all that was specifically Prussian was recognized in the other states of the Confederation as model and according to ability was imitated. The precipitancy of this line of development in the revolutionary period and the resulting mistrust aroused in the German

[21] *Ibid.*, pp. 204-05.
[22] *Ibid.*, p. 42.
[23] *Ibid.*, pp. 204-05.

governments have necessarily caused a decided setback to the
advance of Prussian influence. The weakening of the powerful
influence of public opinon since 1848 resulting from the reaction
to that movement and the novelty of Austria's coming forth as
competitor make it difficult at present to regain the ground
which Prussia has lost. Nonetheless, this is the only way to win
the position which Prussia needs for the fulfillment of its state
tasks, and its superior means in this area are in comparison with
Austria and the other German states still significant. The assurance that His Majesty the King of Prussia would still remain
king in his country if the entire standing army were drawn out
of it is shared with Prussia by no other continental state and no
German one. On this fact rests the possibility for developing
public life to satisfy the demands of the present time more nearly than any other states are able to do. The degree of free movement which is permissible without hurting the authority of the
government is much greater in Prussia than in the rest of Germany. Prussia is able to allow its representative body and its
press even with respect to political questions more freedom of
action than before. It knew how to gain and preserve the position of the intellectual leader of Germany before 1848 under an
almost absolute government, and would irrespective of its present constitution be able to do the same at present. For that
end it is only necessary that its domestic conditions be such that
they do not disturb the impression abroad of unified cooperation of all organs and forces of the country and that they actually
further this cooperation. If the present Prussian constitution is
a definitive institution, then the firm unity of the governmental
organs and their harmony with the representative assembly
should reach such a degree that the force of Prussia is not in
part broken by controversies within between mutually hostile
currents. Otherwise Prussia cannot exercise abroad, at least during peace, the predominant moral influence on Germany which
is assured it if its power is not weakened. The royal authority
rests in Prussia upon such a secure basis that the government can
create for itself without danger very effective means of action
toward German conditions by more vigorous activity of the
representative assembly. It is worth noting what an impression
upon entire Germany was recently made by the discussion in the
Saxon parliament of the Confederation policy and the position
of Saxony toward the Confederation. How much more powerful
would the impression have been if a similar discussion had occurred in the Prussian parliament. If Prussia should openly discuss the German policy, its position toward the Confederation,
the difficulties which it has to overcome, the endeavors of its
opponents, perhaps a few sessions of the Prussian Landtag would
suffice to put an end to the presumption of the majority in the
Confederation.[24]

[24] *Ibid.*, pp. 196-98.

Although the picture of Prussian conditions was too idyllic and that of other states, German and non-German, much too black, the urgent advocacy of harmony between the government and the Landtag in Prussia and of full discussion of the German question in the latter as powerful means of winning support among the other Germans reads like a plea by the liberals.

The idea was in keeping with Bismarck's proposal to establish a German national parliament. In each case, in Prussia and in Germany, the people should cooperate in affairs of government, and Bismarck severely condemned the Conservative party's election program of 1861 for its negative attitude toward parliaments. "I do not understand," he wrote in September of that year to a leading Conservative, "why we recoil so prudishly before the idea of popular representation, either in the Confederation or in a customs union parliament. We cannot combat an institution as revolutionary which is legitimately accepted in every German state, which we Conservatives would not like to do without even in Prussia! . . . One could create a conservative national assembly and nonetheless gain thanks from the liberals for it." Bismarck supported the idea of a national parliament as an integral part of the central government in order to establish a unifying force as a counterbalance against "the diverging tendencies of dynastic special policies." He wished the parliament to exercise wide powers so that it could adequately perform its function, and he wished it to represent, not the governments of the separate states, but the German people. In 1863 he explained his reasons:

> Only such a representation will assure Prussia that it makes no sacrifice which does not accrue to the good of entire Germany. No organization of Confederation agencies, however artistically thought out, can eliminate the play and counter-play of dynastic and particularist interests. These must find a counterweight and corrective in the national representation. In an assembly which is chosen for all Germany according to the principle of numbers by direct elections the center of gravity will never be found outside Germany or in any one state which is trying to separate itself from the rest. Therefore Prussia can enter the assembly with assurance. The interests and needs of the Prussian people are basically and inseparably identical with those of the German people. Where this force achieves its real significance Prussia need never have any fear of being drawn into a policy contrary to its own interests—a fear which would be doubly justified if, in addition to having an organization in which the center of gravity would lie outside Prussia, the mutually hostile particular-

istic elements would be on principle the basis for the formation of the popular representative body.[25]

History was to show that Prussian interests did not always coincide with German interests, except by Prussian definition; but that Bismarck was so clearly aware of the need for the people to participate directly in the governance of the future Germany revealed how far he had travelled from his stock Prussianism of a decade earlier.

Bismarck saw in the creation of a German national assembly the advantage for the political training of the people. He had as sharp an eye as the liberals for the depressing effect of particularism upon political understanding, and like them he wished to change it. "Such a representative assembly for entire Germany," he stated, "should with some certainty also bring it about that the deplorable tendency of most German Landtags to devote themselves predominantly to petty controversies with their own government may be beneficially diverted to broader and more generally useful paths, and the insignificant conflicts of the estates give way to a more statesmanlike handling of interests of German scope."[26] Bigness appeared as essential for the development of political talent as for economic expansion. Bismarck and the liberals alike hoped and expected that it would lift politics out of local pettiness to the plane of major issues. They were to find that the handling of problems on a national scale did at times elevate the character of German politics. It gave political life a seriousness and scope which had been present, if at all, only in the larger states. But if one may judge from this remark alone, Bismarck, like the liberals, was much too optimistic. Other statements show that he was aware of that fact and that he was here mainly expressing a hope in the days of the liberal New Era (July, 1861). He was answering one of the constant Conservative arguments against parliamentary life.

The question of how national representation could be created under present circumstances with adequate powers to be effective in achieving unification concerned Bismarck just as it did the liberals. Like them, he thought of developing that kind of assembly in connection with the Zollverein. In writing to the King in 1861 about the forthcoming renewal of the Zollverein he expressed the wish to discontinue that organization in its present form because the veto power of each member prevented any development of commercial legislation. He proposed that a two-thirds majority be given the power to legislate, and he recommended further

[25] *Ibid.*, pp. 201, 205, 207-09.
[26] *Ibid.*, p. 202.

. . . that committees of larger or smaller numbers of members from the parliaments of the individual states come together and seek to harmonize through their discussion and conclusions the differences in opinions of the governments. Such a customs parliament can under circumstances and with clever guidance become the organ for initiating agreements in other spheres, in which German states would be inclined all the more readily to participate if they were always to remain able to withdraw. The first beginnings of customs unification with Darmstadt were scarcely more important than in its way the military convention with Coburg-Gotha and other similarly disposed small states would be. The influence of existing parliamentary bodies offers prospects at the present time of faster progress in national endeavors than thirty years ago, and foreign events can exert a favorable influence. Common military organization should be kept in mind as an ultimate, realizable goal, for which the common income from customs and related taxes would serve as a budget and supplement a common legislation for trade and transportation, all on a terminable treaty basis with the cooperation of a popular representative body chosen out of the Land-tags.[27]

Bismarck recognized the need of having the German people participate in the political unification of their nation. He even spoke of using revolution if it would help to achieve the objective of national unity.[28] The irony of this remark lies in the fact that he actually unified the country in the face of public hostility. To him popular participation was only one of three major instruments for unifying Germany; the other two, diplomacy and war, carried much more weight in his estimation than the nationalist public.

As soon as Bismarck became Minister President in September, 1862, he openly announced to the Budget Commission of the Lower House his standards of action. "Germany does not look to Prussia's liberalism but to its power. Bavaria, Württemberg and Baden may indulge in liberalism; therefore no one would atrribute to them Prussia's role. Prussia must concentrate its power for the favorable moment which already has several times been missed. Prussia's frontiers as set by the Vienna treaties are not favorable to a sound statehood. The great questions of our time will be decided not by speeches and majority decisions—that was the great mistake of 1848 and 1849—but by iron and blood."[29] Bismarck praised the National Verein as having achieved

---

[27] *Ibid.*, pp. 202-03.

[28] *Ibid.*, p. 132.

[29] *Ibid.*, p. 206. This is a summary of his extemporaneous remarks. He had expressed the same belief in August, 1849. *Ibid.*, p. 183.

recognition "because of the justice of its demands"; but he utterly condemned "the chase after the phantom 'popularity' " in Germany, and he poured scorn upon the idea of relying upon the support of the democratic associations in the lesser states.[30]   At the time of the Schleswig-Holstein crisis in December, 1863, he wrote the Prussian diplomat Count von der Goltz as follows:

> If we turn our back now on the great powers and throw our-
> selves in the arms of the policy of the small states, a policy
> caught in the net of the democracy of private societies, the
> monarchy would be in the worst situation within the state and
> toward the outside world of which it is possible to conceive.
> Instead of pushing we should be pushed. We should depend
> upon elements which we do not control and which are neces-
> sarily hostile to us, but to which we should have to surrender
> unconditionally. You believe that in "German public opinion,"
> parliaments, newspapers, and so forth, there is something which
> could help and support us in a policy of union or hegemony.
> I hold that to be a grave mistake, a figment of the imagination.
> Our strength cannot arise out of parliaments and press politics
> but solely out of militarily strong, great power politics, and we
> do not have enough reserve to waste it on a false front and in
> words. . . .

In this letter Bismarck was exaggerating somewhat in order to stress his major point, just as he had overemphasized in his letter to the King the importance of moral conquest. He wished to use all these forces according to need and possibility; but there can be no doubt that diplomacy and war conducted by Prussia as a great power represented to him the main means for accomplishing his objectives. Germany could be unified solely within the framework provided by international power politics, and he referred to the liberals' proposed solution as that of "professors, county judges and small-town chatter-boxes."[31]

Bismarck was willing to use whatever means were at his disposal— the Zollverein, other princes, military might, diplomacy. While hold- ing to his objective, he was a thorough opportunist in selecting his means and in timing his action. He worked out the main lines of that objective, and he was gifted with the ability to learn from the clarify- ing experience of action what those main lines should be. In adhering firmly to his basic policies, he was quite willing to compromise on details, in fact, not merely to compromise but frankly to accept changes that seemed to be sensible.

[30] *Ibid.*, p. 206.
[31] *Ibid.*, pp. 130-31.

The liberals, on the other hand, never had the chance to learn the ways of statesmanship by practical experience in the responsibility of government. Necessarily, they seem dogmatic. Some of them were, but many of them possessed the potential qualities of statesmen. While Bismarck damned the constitution of the Confederation as useless, he played with the idea that the Zollverein might be developed into the organization for a unified Germany. The liberals never had any illusions about either. They recognized that the fundamental issue was political and would ultimately have to be faced on the political plane. They may have overestimated the power of public opinion; but we know today from experience with the attempts to unify Europe that the liberal proposal was far from being foolish. When the liberals lost faith in the willingness of the Prussian ruler to lead in the creation of the new Germany, they advocated the reintroduction of the German constitution of 1849. They had a reasonable, concrete objective and a feasible method of attaining it.

The fundamental divergence between the liberals and Bismarck may be seen most clearly in their respective estimate of the relative importance of internal and foreign affairs. To the liberals with their belief in rationality and peaceful discussion as means for solving problems, internal matters took priority. Germany could be unified by action within the country. In a statement to the Lower House in February, 1866, Bismarck expressed the contrary belief. Deputy Twesten, he said, had surmised that he, Bismarck, used foreign policy only as a means for furthering the domestic struggle against parliamentary claims. He denied the accusation absolutely. "For me foreign affairs are ends in themselves and are superior to the others [that is, internal affairs]. And you," he said to the liberals, "should also think so, for under some future liberal ministry you could very quickly regain in foreign affairs the ground which you may have lost in domestic affairs."[32]

It may be doubted whether Bismarck, pressed to do so in an extensive debate, could have defended the position which he took, in fact whether he even fully believed his own words. Once again he was exaggerating to support his main idea. It is even more doubtful whether he could have maintained the proposition as one of general application. Questions of internal and of foreign affairs are so interconnected that one can hardly gauge exactly the significance of one as over against the other. Certainly in the case of German unification

[32] *Ibid.*, pp. 137-38.

the problem was created not by foreign affairs but by internal develop-ments. Diplomacy responded to this change in German society and fulfilled the popular desire for national unity. While Prussian ad-vantage as a power-state coincided with this popular movement, the latter force initiated the situation in which the former could act. The validity of Bismarck's estimate arises from the fact that a least temporarily and on the surface he made it valid. He did unify Ger-many by way of foreign affairs, diplomacy and war, and in spite of the hostility of the public. He did correctly recognize that at the time Austria's aversion to German unity could be overcome solely by war. He accurately estimated the weakness of the other German states and predicted correctly that once Prussia showed determination, the govern-ments of those states would adjust themselves to the inevitability of German unity under Prussian leadership.[33] He misjudged the value and strength of the internal forces in this work, just as the liberals may have underrated the significance of the international aspect of national unification. The liberals had no concrete and clearly enunciated method to offer for the ultimate ousting of Austria as a German power. They had no force to oppose to it, and unless broken up by nationalism, Austria would not have acquiesced without com-pulsion in the *klein-deutsch* solution. If they erred in the case of Austria, they were more likely correct with respect to France. By their method of unification war with France could probably have been avoided. It is quite thinkable that in time the liberals might have unified the non-Austrian states by peaceful means, and that neither Austria nor France would have dared to interfere. By flouting liberal popular support for so long and so flagrantly, Bismarck had to recover the support of the German people by some dramatic events like the wars against Austria and France and thereby arouse the public to press their particularistic rulers and governments into accepting na-tional unification. Even apart from that fact he had chosen the method of power politics and involved himself in a system which practically assured a war with both countries. In the case of Bismarck and the liberals, internal and international affairs were inextricably inter-connected, and neglect of one needed to be counterbalanced by an ac-centuation of the other. The liberals' weakness—too great a con-centration on the internal factors—was never proved because of lack of opportunity for action; but Bismarck's exaggeration of the role of

[33] *Ibid.,* pp. 192-93.

international diplomacy and war had results which were permanently harmful to German life.

It was unfortunate that Bismarck inherited the constitutional conflict and felt compelled to fight the liberals. He himself regretted the fact,[34] for actually he and the liberals agreed in their fundamental conception of German unity, and each needed the abilities of the other. The King's stubborness had created a situation which prevented Bismarck from utilizing one of the three means of unification which he had recognized. He had to forego popular support and to rely upon diplomacy and war to a much greater extent than he had anticipated. The effects were bad upon him as well, in that he henceforth tended to belittle internal affairs and to look for solutions of these problems in the play of international power politics. Nonetheless, he kept in mind his plan of 1858, and as soon as the Austro-Prussian war was won, he again, and this time successfully, endeavored to associate the people with his work of unification. The German constitution bears the evidence of the cooperation. A figure of less stature might have endeavored to impose a constitution upon Germany which would have excluded popular participation in a representative assembly. Bismarck recognized that national unity made no sense and would have no permanence without the cooperation of the nation.

What did each of the four forces, the King, the liberals, the Conservatives, and Bismarck, know about the plans of the others for national unification? The ideas of the liberals and the Conservatives were well known. These parties depended upon public discussion for the effectiveness of their programs. The King's attitude was also public. Stories of such incidents as the following went the rounds of the liberals and, together with their knowledge of the tame and ineffective course of the current Foreign Minister's German policy, made the liberal public pessimistic about the King's willingness to take any significant measures toward unity. Von Hoverbeck related the incident in a private letter of January, 1862:

> Today at twelve o'clock there took place in the Opera House
> [in Berlin] a concert for the navy. The Berlin choral society
> had brought together 1,500 singers for it. The remaining seats
> in the Opera House with the exception of the first row of boxes
> were fairly well filled; this row, however, was intentionally emp-
> ty, for practically not a single army officer was present. The
> King and Queen were present. Next to the last song was one
> about Old Blücher, "The Armies Remain on the Rhine," and
> could be regarded as a threat to France. The King listened to it

[34] Zechlin, *op. cit.*, p. 324; Parisius, *von Hoverbeck*, II, 102.

with great satisfaction, and then left quickly, *immediately* before the first notes of "The German's Fatherland." But the public here has good sense and knows in its turn how to demonstrate. As soon as the King left the box and the first four notes of "The German's Fatherland" were sung, the audience interrupted the song by energetic applause in the middle of the first line, an unprecedented event. The song was rendered by the 1,500 voices with much love and joy and received stormy applause. About the fact itself there is nothing further to say than *"Our poor country."*[35]

With respect to Bismarck, the liberals knew about his ideas, that he favored Prussia's taking the intitiative for *klein-deutsch* unification, that he wished the German central authority to have power over military and commercial affairs, and that he advocated the creation of a national assembly as part of that government. They were appalled at Bismark's assertions about "blood and iron," and about legality's being that which force makes valid.[36] Such assertions ran utterly counter to their moral sense. They were even more repelled by his behavior in the constitutional conflict and refused to believe that a person could follow a liberal policy in German unification while seeking to destroy, as they thought, the constitution in his own state. As Deputy von Sybel said in the Lower House, January 29, 1863: "How one can expect that one can question the entire legal power of the Prussian parliament and at the same time interest the German people in a German parliament under the same auspices? This is something that goes beyond the limits of my limited understanding as a subject (*beschränkter Untertanenverstand*)."[37] The liberals felt such mistrust of Bismarck that they refused to support him in his program of national unification, a program of the same general content as their own.[38]

The Economic Interest

The *Bremer Handelsblatt* served as a leading organ of expression for liberalism and for national unification. Its editor had close contacts with others of like mind all over Germany. As much as any other, this journal can be considered a spokesman for the Prussian liberals. The personnel worked together in the National Verein, the Congress of German Economists, and the other important associations.

[35] Parisius, *von Hoverbeck*, II, 8.
[36] Rothfels, *op. cit.*, p. 133.
[37] *Adress-Debatte*, p. 228.
[38] On liberals' knowledge of Bismarck's plans, see Zechlin, *op. cit.*, pp. 324-25; Parisius, *von Hoverbeck*, II, 87-88, 102; Heinrich von Poschinger (ed.), *Erinnerungen aus dem Leben von Hans Viktor von Unruh* (Stuttgart, 1895), pp. 207-09, 216-17.

The *Handelsblatt* reported all the economic activities of the time and supported all those making for national unity along liberal principles. The following article, published on July 11, 1857, may be read as the expression of its views as well those of its Prussian colleagues.

Whoever in Germany could write about the economy and the commercial policy without touching politics would make himself extremely beloved in the highest circles and would not be unwelcome even among burghers [the article here used the word to refer to citizens]. The governments would easily give a patent to anyone who knew how to isolate the entire economic area as a contented idyll in which land and people would quietly and obediently carry on their material progress and would bear in their hearts exclusively the political feeling of gratitude toward the high officials, the furtherers of their fortune. Many a good burgher agrees with the boldest national economic liberalism but lets his voice noticeably drop at every approach to the really political aspect. Such views, high and low, prove most clearly that we in Germany are in both respects still in the beginning of our development. Whoever looks at the situation without prejudice and fear will recognize immediately the intimate connection especially in Germany of the national economic with the national political problem, this Alpha and Omega of German politics. The commerce and transportation of a country have in spite of the egoism among individuals a common aspect. They demand one law, one legislation, one defence abroad. This need has been satisfied in all other countries which we may mention, but not in Germany. A common code of commercial law is now slowly struggling to life; a common legislation is a pious wish, and abroad we all enjoy the same right, defencelessness. Now there are people who like, for example, the Geestemünde trade in its Geestemünde particularity as something specifically Hanoverian, and are able to close their eyes to the fact of its undeniable Weser nature. There are others who judge the transit tolls solely by whether their preservation is more advantageous to Stettin or their abolition more favorable to Hamburg. With people of such exceptional gifts and views we have nothing to do. The *Bremer Handelsblatt* has sought to represent the interests of German commerce and still seeks to do so. But we have something to say to and about such people.

The great evil of German disunity is denied by no one, but we have grown accustomed to bear it. To throw it off seems to us too bold a hope. Petty sufferings, on the other hand, anger, excite, make wild. Since they do not burden us continuously, sensitive trade has not yet blunted itself against them. We have recently discussed these daily vexations. We have called attention to a supreme railroad committee, have shaken the transit tolls, have sought with the idea of an economic congress to arouse continuing, all-sided agitation. We may twist and turn as we will: a solution of this and all other related questions is possible only within the realm of national politics. To avoid this area in the discussion of these questions is inconceivable. For where do these needs and demands lead to? To the one demand of impartial justice, unified representation of common interests prior to and above particular ones. That is nothing else than another expression for the demands of national politics.

Four years later, on May 31, 1861, another organ for advancing the views of Prussian liberals and nationalists, the *Wochenschrift des National Vereins,* was assertive and specific about the relation between economics and politics.

We suffer everywhere in the most important nerve for the entire economy, namely, in confidence in our own state power, which is so necessary for all trade and industrial undertakings. We lack the protection and support for enterprise and speculation which develop with an international political position of states which command respect. Instead, we enjoy the doubtful benefit of paternalism, of a system of much governance, which hinders us in the development of our trade and industry.

Capital has no confidence in the stability and duration of a confederation which rests solely upon common dynastic interests and has never done or even wished to do anything beneficial for the material interests of the people. The capitalists therefore seek opportunity for advantageous outlay of money on the stock exchange rather than in national production. Therefore, one has on the average to use much less money in industrial enterprises in Germany than in other industrial states. The German industrialist is also seldom in a position to exploit a favorable situation on the world market, but is always exposed disadvantageously to such situations. The larger capital sum invested in industry is assured of its interest and can more easily save funds because it has the advantages of large-scale operations. The smaller industrial capital must save on wages, on the quality of the raw materials or of the products themselves. The results have become very perceptible in many branches of German industry. The low wages in Germany have driven the good workers abroad, and the poor-quality wares have ruined the market.

The complaints of the *Wochenschrift* represented a refinement upon the more basic ones expressed by the other journal. Both criticisms were justified; those of the *Handelsblatt* were much more frequent. If they were taken care of, the others would be met automatically. Public opinion concentrated upon overcoming institutional deficiencies. The acceptance of a common German economic legal code, the reorganization of the Zollverein to give it body and authority to act, the establishment of common citizenship and of the right of freedom of movement and domicile and occupation, the creation of a unified transportation and communication system, the formation of a German consular service abroad and of organs of power at home able to protect and further German economic interests abroad, the introduction of a uniform system of weights, measures and coinage —these constituted the main economic desires, and all implied the organization of national political unity. As the *Bremer Handelsblatt* had declared, politics and economics were inseparable; the furtherance of economic interests in Germany required political unification.

The intimate relation between liberalism and nationalism was evident in every line of desired reform. The life of the German states, declared the *Bremer Handelsblatt*, was becoming increasingly interdependent.

> It is not possible that Oldenburg and Bremen should for long experience the advantages of free interest rates while Hanover continues to believe the church fathers rather than science. It is not possible for Bavaria and Hanover to preserve guilds, to which Saxony and Württemberg have given the deathblow. For good or evil, Prussia must soon introduce the economic reforms in which Austria and the middle states have taken the lead. And as soon as Prussia raises its foot for this forward march, its freedom of movement, its . . . freedom of occupation will be irresistibly contagious. . . . The economic reform movement in the end conquers reaction, for it attracts the more teachable members of this party and victoriously drives the others off the field.[39]

This line of thinking led the liberals and nationalists to believe that in the economic sphere of life as well as the political, they had the forces of history on their side. It offered a source of great confidence in the outcome.

Of basic importance among the demands for economic reform was the question of freedom of movement throughout Germany. The resolution passed by the Congress of German Economists in 1863 will indicate the nature of the problem. The resolution read in major part as follows:

> 1. Everyone, irrespective of the community, state or nation to which he may belong, shall be permitted to live in any place where he wishes, to carry on any occupation which is permitted, to marry and establish a family, to acquire property in land.
> 2. This right shall not be limited to natives or be dependent upon reciprocity or the payment of immigration tax or upon other burdensome and restricting conditions.

[39] Feb. 23, 1861.

3. The right to domicile does not include automatically the right of citizenship and community membership. Nonetheless, the latter right should be attainable if one has maintained his domicile continuously in a community for three years without becoming a public charge. . . .

5. The right to carry on an occupation is included in that of domicile and may not be made dependent upon the previous acquisition of state or community citizenship.

6. The permission to marry shall depend solely upon the terms of the general civil law, and shall not depend upon the permission of the community of residence or citizenship, or upon a preliminary examination and approval by a state or other police bureau, or upon evidence of a livelihood or upon other burdensome and restricting conditions.

7. The acquisition of state and community citizenship is to be made as easy as possible; if membership in the community also includes legal property requirements, an admission fee corresponding to the latter may be raised.[40]

Nothing is as revealing of the practical import of the resolution as contemporary descriptions of actual conditions. The press constantly supplied evidence of the most condemnatory sort. An article in the *National Zeitung* of October 10, 1863, reproduced the feeling of exasperation as well as any.

When in a great land inhabited by one people the thousands of communities which it contains shut themselves off one against the other, not in respect to material goods and capital but in respect to the most important good and the most valuable capital there is, namely, the movement of human beings; when in this people that has one language, more or less extensive groups of communities are united in states and these states in relation to the movement of persons close their frontiers against one another through new restrictions and seek as far as possible to keep out any immigrant from another group as a "foreigner" or as the ancients called him, a "barbarian": can one wonder that this land and people are disunited and lack the common feeling which is indispensable for national cooperation? If we look at the lands where national feeling and national cooperation have developed, freedom of movement obtains everywhere not merely within the nation but also for entry from other nations; for the foreigners which a people attracts and absorbs serve, so one believes there with justice, to augment economic strength and political significance. In Germany alone there survive from outworn times obsolete conditions where each state and each town encloses itself by a police wall and a swampy communal moat so that no one will think of moving there and increasing the

[40] *Vierteljahrschrift für Volkswirtschaft und Kulturgeschichte* (1863), III, 261-62.

capital, the division of labor and the tax resources. And in these abiding conditions of inner defence from which domestic hostility is bound to follow, we wonder why national unity does not progress! One longs for conventions of delegates, reform of the confederation, Kaiser and Reich; but if we acquired Kaiser and Reich and continued to shut ourselves off one from another, Kaiser and Reich would be just as powerless as before. For without the moral and economic basis of a unified consciousness unified constitutions remain dead forms. We see liberal town councils today jubilantly unfold the black, red and gold flag: and tomorrow they stick their heads together in secret session and discuss long and carefully whether they should allow a Hessian or a Saxon to regard his district as part of the fatherland. Is that a fatherland which turns away from the door its son who does not want to steal or to be given his bread, who wishes to earn his bread by ability and hard work? Is that a fatherland which shuts him up in the village where he was born? Can a people become conscious of its unity when unity is not allowed for the utilization of its forces and the winning of its material existence? Unified government by one army can bring together or break up the nations according to the interests of the ruler. What holds them securely together is one fatherland. So long as we in Germany do not have that one fatherland, unified rule will rest on a weak foundation. If we have one fatherland, political unity will come of itself; for a people which has become interdependent in its material conditions of life cannot be politically divided.

Man has the need of a fatherland. No guild, no magistrate or senate can disprove that fact. And the more railroads and telegraphs we build, the more industry and commerce we carry on, just so much more grows the need for a fatherland. For with the cheapness and ease of transportation, the human being develops. He develops in himself the need for movement; the area which he needs for his activity expands. Man is not a plant, which is rooted to the soil; he is more than an animal, which is distinguished from the plant by its movement. If you degrade him in his own land below the animal to the condition of a plant, which cannot move from the spot where chance sowed it, then he will seek a fatherland abroad which you deny him at home. He will go beyond the Rhine or the Channel or the ocean. These are the best persons, those who have the irresistible urge for a fatherland of free participation. They are the best forces, the most courageous, which move to uncertain lands and most easily separate themselves from the home community. Is that a useful institution which invests valuable capital in the workers only to have it exported without compensation at home, which makes the workers skilled and then drives them out because their skill might lay hands on the old pigtails [the survivals of the Old Regime]?

And as for those who stay at home . . . how much devotion to the old fatherland do you expect from them when in it only a poor local district is open for their endeavors and every other door is closed and barricaded, when from youth they are accustomed to long for the foreign land where uncle and godfather made their fortune, because there a big fatherland in all communities gladly opened up even to the adopted sons, while for those at home every fatherland was taken away by the chaos of irrational legislation . . . ?

We will first of all create for the Germans by freedom of movement the conditions which are most desired, a fatherland. Thereby we shall retain the strength and ability which grow so richly in our soil and shall attract strength and ability from other nations which are willing to work with us for our welfare, honor and power. By freedom of movement we create a common spirit and national feeling, welfare and contentment. And to create this high, national benefit, we need no complicated negotiation between large and small sovereignties; no position of power, great or small, will be endangered; no freedom, no right restricted. We need nothing at all other than that people be reasonable. And whatever government, whatever popular representative assembly first opens its land to full freedom of movement will immediately enjoy the advantage of a rising standard of living. And in the competition among the states that exists in Germany the example of advantage will stimulate imitation. It is a relatively easy task and in relation to the effort the results are infinitely rewarding. Therefore, let everyone work in his circle, in his tribe and in his land, everyone who is honorably concerned over the German problem, whether he be *gross-deutsch* or *klein-deutsch,* that economically speaking, a fatherland be given the Germans!

The editor of the *Bremer Handelsblatt* correctly asserted in 1863 that "the German actually enjoys in England, France, America and other states more rights than in his own fatherland, for as soon as he puts foot upon those countries he can freely settle, freely work, freely acquire land, and without any official difficulty marry as he pleases. Millions of Germans have much more interest in these material rights than in the more ideal political rights."[41]

Equally fundamental appeared to these liberals the issue of freedom of occupation. It was so closely related to that of freedom of movement that the two were usually treated together. "No economic question in Germany is at present so burning and so urgently in need of a speedy solution," stated the *Bremer Handelsblatt,* "as that of freedom of occupation." Bremen, for example, had in 1858 guild restrictions upon shoemaking, but freedom in clothing production; the making of bread was restricted to guilds, but that of cakes was free;

[41] *Ibid.,* p. 84.

beer-brewing was restricted, but the preparation of other spiritous drinks, for example champagne, was free. Offenbach had enjoyed full freedom of occupation since 1819 and had flourished. It had increased two-and-a-half fold in population since then, from 6,000 to 15,000, and had 5,000 factory workers. Many states forbade or restricted the import of furniture in order to protect the local guilds. Among these were Saxony, Altenburg, Dessau, Oldenburg, Bremen and Hanover, but not Prussia. Many of them placed obstacles in the way of the sale of men's clothes for the same reason. The Berlin Merchants' Association objected to these prohibitions, but under the conditions of particularism it could do nothing except protest and agitate for national unity.[42]

The question of freedom of occupation affected far more lines of activity than those of the handworkers. In terms of economics alone the handicrafts could hardly be placed in the same class of importance with, for instance, another line of activity which was equally curbed, the insurance business. Because of the character of this enterprise it suffered greatly from the lack of national economic unity. The strength of an insurance company usually varied with its size. Once it established headquarters in one state, it wished to send agents into other states. Since its business depended upon the number and efficiency of these agents, it needed to open the entire national market for its activity and might suffer irreparable hardship if restricted to one or a few states, no one of which with the possible exception of Prussia was large enough to support it. The meetings of the Congress of German Economists and of the German Chamber of Commerce resounded with the lamentations of insurance executives, whose descriptions of the legal conditions under which their business operated in the various states offered revealing insight into the economic effects of particularism upon a developing capitalistic business.

The report to the Congress of German Economists by a Prussian insurance executive may be used as an example.[43] The insurance business, the author stated, was subject to both public and private law. Since thirty-four sovereign states would as yet allow no such thing as a common code of public law to be introduced, he restricted his remarks to private law aspects. He emphasized that the insurance

[42] *Bremer Handelsblatt*, April 3, 1858; *Der Arbeitgeber* (ed. Max Wirth), Oct. 13, 1858, No. 107, Supplement; *Bremer Handelsblatt*, Sept. 25, 1858, Aug. 20, 1859.
[43] The following details are taken from the report made by Richter of Magdeburg to the Congress of German Economists in September, 1865. The histories of insurance companies are also worth reading.

business depended upon magnitude to fulfill its purpose. The larger the coverage, the greater was the risk spread; and he scoffed at the official insurance companies of some of the small states which had an insurance sum of, for example, from 4.7 million Thalers (Lippe-Schaumburg) to 16 million (Lippe-Detmold). He contrasted these amounts with the lowest, namely, 70 or 80 million, for each of the private insurance corporations, and concluded that in the case of fire insurance the loss on a single major policy for one of the small public companies would use up its premium payments for months. Worse than this petty playing at economic sovereignty, he said, were the obstacles to business. Laws, regulations, administrative whim, all scourged the insurance companies. Prussia had cleared out much of this array of controls but in the other states it remained triumphant. The reporter cited the case of Saxony. After the passage of an insurance law in 1863 the administration had issued a regulation for fire insurance of eighty-three paragraphs, some of them a foot long. Then it ordered the companies to submit their insurance terms to be checked against the regulation. After a year's time even the bureaucrats gave up, said that they could not judge whether the terms were in agreement with the regulation or not, and ordered the companies to include in their contracts a statement to the effect that "in so far as the following general insurance terms do not correspond to the laws and regulations in the Kingdom of Saxony, the legal conditions are to replace them in any insurance contract in Saxony." The companies refused to accept this proposed solution, and in 1865 the dispute was still being negotiated with no prospect of settlement.

In the case of fire insurance, the reporter continued, every state in the Confederation except Schleswig-Holstein and the four free cities, that is, twenty-nine states in all, required official concession for doing business. In many cases other insurance lines were subject to similar restriction. Insurance agents, for example, in many states were not allowed to solicit business. Yet how could an insurance company be expected to have an agent in each village or to rely upon a local peasant to make out policies? In Bavaria, in consequence, the peasants remained unprotected in case of fire, and numerous begging letters were circulated on behalf of peasants who had been burned out. The number became so large that the government, responsible for the ban on soliciting fire insurance business, had instructed its officials to inform the peasants about fire insurance and to advise the latter to take out policies. The reporter remarked that a simpler and more economical method would have been to remove the restrictions on the activity of insurance agents.

Twenty-two states had public monopolies in fire insurance, no one of which was large enough to provide adequate security. Private companies could compete with these, but were subject to numerous administrative restrictions. The reporter was irate over the fact that, depending upon the scope of its activity, a fire insurance company might have to know all the terms of regulations pertaining to its business in each of twenty-nine states, all of them different. First, the company had to obtain the concession to do business in the state; for that purpose it had to pay. Then its concession could be cancelled arbitrarily at any moment for any cause which the government might find. In order to prevent itself from falling into the bad graces of the local government, the bureaucrats as well as the ruler, the company had to be very careful in the selection of its agents. It dared not appoint a person who was politically objectionable to the local authorities. The company and each agent in some states had to give to each government a surety for good behavior, in Schwarzburg-Sondershausen a sum amounting to 1,000 Thaler for each agent. Then came the taxes. Some states demanded half the profits. Some imposed a host of petty taxes, which they would commute for an annual percentage or lump sum. One little state demanded a percentage of the insurance sum so that in case of need it could help those who had not insured their property, a stipulation which particularly angered the reporter. Another petty state wrote the companies that they would have to commute the small state fees for a definite sum or, the threat was implied, their concession would be cancelled. "One could hardly say more elegantly in German bureaucratic style," remarked the reporter, " 'your purse or your life!' "

The state governments claimed that they used the funds obtained from the taxes and other financial imposts upon the insurance companies "for purposes of general welfare." The reporter had investigated the nature of these "purposes" in the state of Hesse-Darmstadt and had found that most of the money went to support the military. Then it became clear to him why the ministers of war usually protested against changing the present system of concessions. The funds squeezed from out-of-state insurance companies run by liberals and nationalists were being devoted to the preservation of absolutism, militarism, and particularism in the middle-sized and small German states. Since most of the big insurance companies had their headquarters in Prussia, the ardent devotion of this branch of business to national unification and to economic freedom is understandable.

The Congress of German Economists summed up the demands for freedom of economic opportunity for the insurance business as follows:

1. The formation of insurance companies is to be dependent upon the approval of the state only to the extent that it is necessary in order to obtain the character of a legal personality.

2. The insurance companies do not need a police permit or a concession to do business in any German state.

3. The requirement of insurance purchasers to use exclusively a state (provincial or communal) or other privileged company is abolished.

4. It is not permissible to grant the state and other privileged companies release from the payment of general fees and burdens levied by law.

5. It is not permissible to impose upon private companies special taxes and burdens; they should be subject only to the general ones.

6. State action with respect to the conduct of the insurance business should be restricted to supervision in the wider sense of the word.

To carry out that program meant a revolution in social structure and in the purpose and character of government, and that was precisely what these liberals and nationalists sought.

The banks had to contend with a situation equally chaotic. During the 1850s many new banks had been established in Prussia and in the other states. Those in the smaller states had almost no clientele for their services within their home territories and were founded for the specific purpose of exploiting the urgent demand for capital in the large states, especially Prussia. These banks put out large amounts of paper money and expected to profit from the business. Understanding their intention, the Prussian government in 1858 prohibited the circulation of non-Prussian bank notes within its territory, to the dismay of the outside banks and to the bitter disappointment of Prussian business men, liberals and nationalists. The Prussian economic leaders, eager for funds to invest in the expanding industrial and transportation systems, accused the government of retarding this development in the name of an antiquated autocratic mercantilism. The prohibition, they declared, made Prussia extremely unpopular in the rest of Germany; it was a source of "genuine pain to every patriot. . . . No measure of recent times has antagonized opinion in Germany against the Prussian government to the same great extent as this one has. . . . It has called forth and will continue to call forth reprisals from other states against Prussia. It is likewise preventing Prussian industry from obtaining money which it urgently needs in the present crisis [1859];

probably 30 millions [Thalers] have been kept from it by this act."[44] To the liberals the act resembled closely the policy of the reactionary Manteuffel government, which a few years earlier had requested the Berlin banks not to participate in the founding of foreign, that is non-Prussian, economic institutions.[45]

Even as careful and thorough a business man as Gustav Mevissen, the leader in the economic development of the Rhineland, roundly condemned the Prussian and other governments for such prohibitions and asked for reform. In a memorandum of 1859 he wrote that this and similar prohibitions in other states violated the purpose of the Zollverein to create a nationwide market and the aim of Prussia to make moral conquests in the rest of German. He urged that the banks be free to issue paper money and that this money be free to circulate in all German states. A clearing house could be established in Berlin, he said, in which the money could be exchanged, and no state would suffer from a flood of extra-state paper. He paid a strong tribute to the good judgment of the bankers, citing the fact that under their guidance the present banks had survived two crises and concluding that they were worthy of trust in the future.[46] The numerous remarks of other private bankers made clear that Mevissen spoke for practically all; with very minor exceptions they recognized the relation between banking prosperity on the one hand and freedom and national unity on the other.

The cry among liberals and nationalists for a common system of weights, measures and coinage could be heard all over Germany. Irrespective of differences over the proposals for unifying the nation politically, those millions of individuals who had dealings with persons in other German states sought the abolition of the current chaos and the introduction of common standards of measurement.

The extent of the confusion may be seen from a contemporary example. On May 11, 1861, the *Bremer Handelsblatt* published a list showing that, exclusive of Holstein and Luxemburg-Limburg, eight different monetary systems were used in Germany. Some states used the Thaler unit, some the Gulden, some the Mark. Stories were told of the difficulties with the coinage systems which a housemaid encountered in purchasing food supplies in the market: she had to be a mathematical expert to make correct change. Problems of bookkeeping for firms were even more forbidding.

[44] *Berliner Börsen Zeitung*, Jan. 7, Feb. 12, 1859.
[45] F. Hardegen and K. Smidt, *H. H. Meier* (1920), p. 130.
[46] Hansen, *op. cit.*, II, 553-54.

The situation was improved by the declaration in 1857 that the one-Thaler coin should be regarded as standard in the Zollverein alongside the double-Thaler coin already used since 1838. Particularly after 1857 the amount minted in this Zollverein currency greatly increased in proportion to that coined in the state currencies. It has been estimated that between 1838 and 1857 a little more than 50 million Thalers were minted in the form of Zollverein coins (the double-Thaler), while 80 million Thalers were struck in the form of South German currency. Between 1857 and 1871, some 229 million Thalers were put out in the Zollverein currency (one- and two-Thaler pieces) and coins struck in the form of territorial currencies amounted to only 6.33 million Thalers.[47] Nonetheless, as late as May, 1870, Ludwig Bamberger described the situation to the Customs Parliament as follows:

> I have here a so-called "bordereau," namely, a table setting forth specifically the types of money which a trader enclosed with a draft to his bankers. The "bordereau" is dated the 19th December 1869. It relates to a sum of 15,834 gulden. I have extracted it from the correspondence of a bank. It contains the coins of which these 15,834 gulden were composed, and in order that you might understand its true meaning, I must add that the draft came from a small town in the province of Rhenish Hessen. The town is small, 3,000 to 4,000 inhabitants, and has but a single inn—not sufficiently attractive to be frequented by strangers. It is a payment composed of receipts from rents, purchase agreements, and from sales of wheat, barley, fruit, and similar products, brought from the various surrounding villages into this small town to be sold through the agency of a merchant. What was thus collected from the pockets of the peasants is as follows: The sum of 15,834 gulden consisted of double talers, crown talers, pieces of 2½ gulden, of 2 gulden, 1 gulden, ½ gulden, ⅓, ⅙ and 1/12 Imperial talers, 5-franc pieces, 2-franc pieces, 1-franc pieces, then we have gold coins such as pistoles, double and single Friedrichsdor, half-sovereigns, Russian Imperials, dollars, Napoleons, Dutch Wilhelmsdor, Austrian and Württemberg ducats, Hessian 10-gulden pieces, and last of all a piece of Danish gold.[48]

To supply comparable examples in weights and measures seems superfluous. Since the situation was as chaotic in this field as in currency, the Congress of German Economists and the German Commercial Association zealously passed resolutions in favor of unity. Nationalism had become a practical problem of persuading the states to accept as the basic units meter, liter, and thaler, and these two

[47] Karl Helfferich, *Money* (New York, 1927), I, 150-51.
[48] *Ibid.*, I, 147-48.

prominent associations took the lead for the liberals and nationalists in pressing the reform.[49]

Particularism manifested itself in one of its most irritating and embarrassing forms in the levying of river and transit tolls. These tolls were historical vestiges, bearable in a predominantly agricultural and localistic society, anathema to an economy of expanding commerce and developing industry. Questions of cost of distribution and ability to compete were intimately involved with those of national pride.

The tolls collected on goods in transit across German territory to other countries were in the main abolished in 1860 by general agreement among the Zollverein members. The states decided that it was more profitable to keep the trade to Russia and Austria, for example, using the Zollverein ports and railways and waterways than it was to see this trade shifted respectively to Russian Baltic and to Adriatic ports. One international transit toll continued to be raised and to evoke severe criticism on the part of those suffering from it. That was the toll imposed by Baden upon goods shipped from German ports to Switzerland. Since the negotiations about it were involved with the other question of the tolls on the Rhine river, the two problems may be treated together.

Attempts had previously been made to lower the tolls on the Rhine and to persuade the riparian states to improve the stream bed. Two states in particular, Hesse and Nassau, had refused to make any concessions. They derived large revenues from the tolls, which they needed in maintaining their armies and paying other government expenses. Since the sums came in regularly, the governments were, to the extent of these funds, independent of financial control by the local legislatures, a fact which enhanced the liberal's wrath.

Baden made its abolition of the transit tolls dependent upon the abolition of the Rhine tolls. The *Bremer Handelsblatt* published (January 28, 1860) the following figures on the amount of revenue which each Rhenish state would lose by the elimination of the river tolls:

		Per 1,000 inhabitants
Prussia	398,200 Francs (approx.)	21.99 Francs
Nassau	176,969	406.10
Hesse	157,600	182.62
Bavaria	6,585	1.42
Baden	5,957	4.46

[49] See the resolutions in 1861 and 1865 of the German Commercial Association in *Bremer Handelsblatt,* May 25, 1861, Sept. 30, 1865.

In view of these figures, the journal commented, one can appreciate why Nassau and Hesse should oppose the complete abolition of the Rhine tolls and Baden should favor it. At the time of this article, Prussia, Nassau and Hesse were willing to lower the tolls by one-sixth if Baden would abolish the transit tolls, but Baden refused.

The *Bremer Handelsblatt* was vigorously hostile to Baden's position, calling it an "un-German particularist policy." "According to the recently published agreement between Baden and the French Eastern Railway," it said, "Baden obligates itself to turn international trade to the French railways. The constantly declining returns from transit tolls show that the low sea-freight rates of the German North Sea ports are unable to provide the German railways with a large amount of work in the transport of raw materials to Switzerland and Austria as long as that unfortunate toll remains."[50] "For the paltry toll income of 400,000 Thalers a year," it stated, "Germany is losing out to France in the transit trade," trade which for Switzerland alone in 1858 amounted to 272 million francs. The paper damned the transit toll as "a betrayal of the most sacred interests of our nation when one thinks that that sum of which Germany each year is made poorer accrues to the same country [France] which threatens the greatest danger to our independence and safety."[51]

Baden's determined stand and especially the development of railroads as competitive means of transportation created conditions which inclined even Hesse and Nassau to consider a substantial reduction of Rhine tolls. The toll income of these states was declining; traffic on the Rhine threatened to cease; the representative assemblies in the two states disliked having their states blamed for this misfortune; the governments showed some willingness to negotiate. Baden invited the riparian states to a conference, where in December, 1860, agreement was reached. The river tolls were substantially reduced and in return Baden agreed to abolish its transit toll.[52] Nonetheless, the agreement did not solve the problem. Four years later the Cologne Chamber of Commerce reported that tolls were still too high and that in consequence the river traffic was decidedly declining. Competition from railroads, it prophesied, would ruin the river traffic unless these tolls were eliminated. "It is one of the blackest spots in the public conditions of Germany," stated the chamber in its annual report for 1864,

[50] *Ibid.*, Jan. 7, 1860.
[51] *Ibid.*, March 10, 17, 1860.
[52] See Rudolf von Delbrück, *Lebenserinnerungen* (Leipzig, 1905), II, 191.

"that our most important stream, which if we did not have it as a gift of nature could not be built for hundreds of millions of Thalers, is headed for disuse and desertion because of these excessive and unjust tolls."[53]

The freeing of the Elbe river from tolls proved to be equally difficult. According to Article 111 of the Treaty of Vienna, both rivers, the Elbe and the Rhine, were to have such tolls as would "encourage commerce and facilitate navigation," and the agreement of the same time with respect to navigation on the Elbe had contained in Article 30 a stipulation that the Elbe Commission should "consider arrangements and measures which according to recent experience could facilitate commerce and shipping."[54] Nonetheless, the riparian states had been unable to agree on any improvement. Austria, Saxony and the other states on the upper Elbe, Hamburg, and especially Prussia had endeavored to persuade the Elbe Commission to reduce tolls, but the three states near the mouth of the river, Hanover, Lauenburg, and Mecklenburg, depended upon the tolls to provide them with a considerable part of their public revenue and up to 1860 had refused to budge. The illegality of their action was disputed or ignored by these three sovereign states, and unlike Hesse and Nassau they also owned the potentially competing railroads to the North Sea ports. Mecklenburg charged a high transit toll on the railroad, and both it and Hanover profited from the freight charges on commodities going to Prussia, Austria, Saxony and elsewhere south and southeast.

The first breach in the tight system of Elbe tolls occurred in 1860 when Great Britain forced Hanover to abolish the Stade toll in return for a single lump payment. The Hanoverian foreign minister, Count Platen, was "deeply aroused" over this act and lamented that "from all sides one is storming Hanover and claiming financial sacrifices."[55] The Chamber of Commerce in Magdeburg, in its annual report for 1861, reacted in a different manner.

> It is depressing and embarrassing for national feeling when one hears of plans to turn to foreign governments with complaints about the Elbe tolls. To be sure, the history of the Stade toll teaches that this way is more practical than that of sending tedious and futile complaints to the native governments. The

---

[53] *Preuss. Handelsarchiv*, 1864, *Jahresberichte*, pp. 524-26.
[54] *Ibid.*, 1859; I, 241.
[55] The formulation is Delbrück's. Delbrück conducted the negotiations for Prussia at the Elbe Conference in 1861. See Delbrück, *op. cit.*, II, 190-95, for the story of the negotiations and the agreement of 1863.

intervention of America gave the impetus to abolishing the Sound tolls; the intervention of England moved Hanover to retreat from its excessive demands in return for regulating the Stade toll and to be satisfied with an indemnity which offered only half of its previous income. If such results are attainable by the intervention of a foreign government with respect to the Stade toll, which is based on an entirely different legal right, why should it not be effective in the case of the Elbe tolls, which contrary to all agreements serve as a financial aid and as a specific means for the Hanover state railways systematically to suppress certain branches of Elbe traffic? If Prussia would decide to proceed energetically in this affair and finally break with the method of fruitless conferences, it would assuredly gain the moral support of all civilized nations and would on at least one occasion show by action its supremacy in Germany and especially toward states which continually place petty obstacles in the way of the free, national and economic development of Prussia and Germany.[56]

The goods transported on the Elbe were divided into seven categories, each of which paid a different toll. The Mecklenburg government had arbitrarily introduced another classification, goods that were qualified for transportation by water and those that were not. The former included bulky commodities like coal on which the toll was not very high. The latter included coffee, tobacco, wine and spiritous drinks, yarns, spices, sugar, rags, zinc and so on, goods which were put in the highest class for tolls and could not have afforded water transportation at all if Austria, Saxony and Prussia had not renounced their share of the toll. These latter three states had to do so, a semi-official writer in the *Preussisches Handelsarchiv* said bitterly (March 11, 1859), in order to keep any traffic on the Elbe. He showed by statistics how great the decline in freight on the river had been between 1845 and 1858 in the two highest toll classes and how large the increase in goods carried by rail.

Goods in the highest toll category	1845	2,489,032 Centners
	1857	131,357
Loss of		2,357,675
Goods in the second toll category	1852	436,504
	1857	162,936
Loss of		273,568

[56] *Preuss. Handelsarchiv*, 1861, *Jahresberichte*, p. 257.

Goods carried on railroad	1851	2,613,000
	1857	7,007,000
Increase of		4,394,000
Amount of these subject to highest two categories of tolls	1853	1,991,000
	1857	2,702,000
Increase of		711,000

Mecklenburg was forcing the higher-priced goods to use the Berlin-Hamburg railroad. The state manifestly derived more from transit tolls and freight charges than it did from river tolls; and in Hanover the state railway administration was even more opposed to reducing the Elbe tolls than the state toll administration.[57] Both states were squeezing all the money possible out of the traffic. Since Mecklenburg was an almost feudal agrarian state it could scarcely be affected by reprisals; and Hanover, although more advanced economically and in every other way, enjoyed about equal immunity. Statistical proof of how one could derive more revenue from an increase in volume through lower toll rates did not seem to interest these states.[58]

In 1861 the pressure upon the three obstructive states, Mecklenburg, Hanover and Lauenburg, became too strong to resist. The German Commercial Association at its meeting in that year passed a strong resolution condemning the Mecklenburg transit toll on the railway and the Elbe tolls, and the agreement on the reduction of the Rhine tolls proved to be the turning point. Since the Elbe remained the only river in Germany heavily burdened by tolls, the offending states had to give in to the pressure of public opinion. At a conference of the Elbe states called in November, 1861, agreement was reached which decidedly lightened the burden. The agreement concentrated the payment of tolls at one place, Wittenberge; it cut the number of the classes of goods from seven to three and greatly reduced the amount of toll to be paid. It reallocated the proceeds from the tolls so that Hanover, Mecklenburg, Lauenburg and Anhalt received half and the other states received half; the others agreed to contribute 132,000 Thalers annually to the four states making the greater sacrifice.[59] Although Hanover and the other obstructionists lamented, they signed.

[57] Delbrück, *op. cit.*, II, 193.
[58] See *Preuss. Handelsarchiv*, 1859; I. 22, 241-44.
[59] Delbrück. *op. cit.*, II, 194-95.

The Elbe agreement was generally approved by the business public,[60] just as the comparable one on the Rhine had been. It did not, however, solve the problem of the transit toll collected by Mecklenburg on the Berlin-Hamburg railway line. This was not eliminated until the latter joined the Zollverein in 1868; and the last of the river tolls succumbed only to the unification of the country in 1870-71.[61]

Problems relating to the German railways were so complicated that the economic interests were divided and often confused in dealing with them. The one which stirred up most wrath was that of the differential freight rates. The seaport towns and developing big industry, especially coal, iron and steel, supported the existing practice of the railways of giving lower rates to traffic between major terminals wide distances apart. They did so on grounds of lower cost achieved by less handling of the goods en route and of the necessity to meet foreign competition. The large inland towns, Breslau, Magdeburg, Cologne and others which had for centuries served as distributing centers, thought that their traditional function was being menaced.[62]

The matter was brought before the German Commercial Association at its first meeting in 1861 and remained on the agenda for the rest of the decade. The conference of 1865 was largely devoted to discussion of it, during which the two sides came to understand each other's position and a third group appeared which tried to mediate. The Commercial Association resolution of that year and again of 1868 actually straddled the issue.

A second question that troubled the business world had to do with the multiplicity of freight rates, "the height and the frequent and sudden changes in freight rates." At the end of 1860 the German railways showed 5,223.5 kilometers of state-owned lines, 1,344.8 kilometers of privately owned lines under state administration and 5,064.4 kilometers of privately owned and administered lines. The criticism applied particularly to the railroads in Prussia, where by the law of 1838 the government had allowed freedom to the roads to set their own charges. Besides seven state companies some sixteen private ones had almost unlimited authority to do so. In recent years the government had recognized its blunder, and had written into the contract for each new railroad company a stipulation for close government control over rates. The fact remained that rates on not merely the Prussian but also the non-Prussian lines were a source of constant

[60] *Der Deutsche Handelstag 1861-1911* (Berlin, 1913), II, 345.
[61] *Ibid.,* II, 345.
[62] See, for example, *Bremer Handelsblatt,* April 13, 1861.

criticism by those who had to pay them. Goods were divided into seven classes for purposes of imposing freight charges; nonetheless, the differences in charges for the same commodity were large, and the major companies had developed agreements on rates among themselves which increased the financial troubles of the sender.[63]

Complaints about inadequate service and lack of locomotives and of freight cars in sufficient numbers and at the proper time were numerous and led to further criticism about the absence of cooperation among the railway companies. The latter, so ran the argument, were extremely reluctant to use cars belonging to other companies and to send cars over other lines even when it was cheaper and faster to do so. The delay and extra cost were at the expense of the customer, not of the railroad. Connections between lines of different companies continued to be poorly developed, with additional cost frequently involved in the transfer of goods from one line to another; and the railroads were haphazard in protecting the freight from loss or damage. New railway lines which were badly needed could not be constructed for years because some small state refused to cooperate. The most notorious case was that of Hanover's holding up the building of the railway from Hamburg to Paris. A private company wished to build the line; but since the Hanoverian government insisted on state ownership of the section within its territory, the German part of the project was blocked, to the utter disgust of the liberals.[64]

Businessmen were divided in their opinion about remedial measures. The liberals opposed government interference in business; but they disliked freight rates which were high and arbitrarily subject to change. The temptation to appeal to the government for help against the railroads was strong. The liberals debated the issues back and forth, some favoring government ownership or control and others opposing it. In its meeting in 1865 the German Commercial Association passed a resolution on the subject which tried to compromise among the conflicting interests and opinions by including all points. It laid down for the railroads the ideal not of making the largest possible profit but of serving the entire economy. It sought to further the standard of competition in an economic field in which monopoly was almost inevitable. It straddled the issue of public ownership or control versus private ownership and the question of differential rates.

---

[63] *Der Deutsche Handelstag 1861-1911*, II, 106.

[64] See report of the negotiations of the 7th Congress of German Economists in 1864 in *Vierteljahrschrift für Volkswirtschaft und Kulturgeschichte* (1864), III, 207-10.

The last part of the resolution was most characteristic, the indication of intention carefully to watch the railway matters on an *ad hoc* basis.[65]

All liberals agreed that, although their principles might have to be compromised in favor of some state control or even of state ownership of railways, national political unification would greatly simplify the problems of transportation. With unification, single states could no longer block essential needs, a common railway system and a common railroad law could be developed. A merchant or industrialist in any state in Germany would then know that he could ship goods anywhere in the nation without having to worry about the policy and practice of this little state or that. While much was being accomplished in this direction even under existing conditions many basic problems remained which could be solved easily and speedily by national unification. If the political question could be settled, the railways constituted the essential means of unification of the economy and society. In the meantime, they pushed the political issue to the fore.

The question of unifying the economic organization of Germany came to be vigorously discussed as a practical possibility in connection with Prussia's negotiation of a commercial treaty with France. The treaty itself was signed in 1862, but negotiations had been under way for several years beforehand and everyone in Germany and Austria knew that they were taking place. The treaty precipitated a crisis in the Zollverein and in the relations between it and Austria, a crisis involving both economics and politics in major proportions. It proved to be the most important event in the efforts for national unity during the years immediately prior to Bismarck's wars; and an analysis of the factors involved throws light upon the question whether the German nation could have been unified without war.

When the Zollverein had last been renewed in 1853, Austria had had sufficient strength to force Prussia to include a clause looking toward Austria's joining that organization. Prussia had subsequently succeeded in preventing the clause from being carried out; but the issue came up again when in the late 1850s discussions for a renewal of the Zollverein began. Although in varying degrees of intensity criticism of the existing organization of the Zollverein arose from all quarters and reached a climax in connection with the publication of the Franco-Prussian commercial treaty. The most thorough and intelligent public analysis occurred at the meeting of the German Com-

[65] The best summary of this discussion is found in *Der Deutsche Handelstag 1861-1911*, II, 106-26.

mercial Association in Munich in 1862, where all sides were fully represented and prepared to defend their position.[66]

Businessmen and statesmen in all the Zollverein states, in Austria and even in some of the other states not belonging to the Zollverein agreed that the customs union was valuable and should be continued. They agreed that commercial relations between the Zollverein states and Austria should be close and should be expanded. They all recognized that the Zollverein needed to be reformed and most of them thought that its tariff rates should be reduced. They differed sharply, however, in their views about the constitution.

The Zollverein was composed of sovereign states, each one able to block by its veto power any proposal for reform. Since the discussions by the delegates to the Zollverein conferences, all of them officials, were held in secret, the public was not informed about the negotiations and was unable to exert pressure upon the governments with respect to specific issues. The customs schedule badly needed to be revised; yet nothing could be done from one date of renewal of the Zollverein to the next, twelve years hence. As critics said, the Zollverein had become an obstacle to reform; an international, certainly an inter-state, diplomatic crisis was required every twelve years to try to bring about urgently needed changes.

The Prussian government had decided to force the issue by negotiating the commercial treaty with France. That treaty called for a sharp reduction in Prussian tariff rates, and in Article 31 it accepted the most-favored-nations clause with respect to all other states. It was understood between Prussia and France that the treaty was expected to be approved by the other Zollverein states. Prussia's strategy in the negotiations had definitely aimed at excluding Austria from future membership in the Zollverein. Prussia wanted no major competitor in that organization.

The reactions of the business world represented at the conference of the German Commercial Association in Munich may be roughly divided into three major groups, the pro-Austrians, the pro-Prussians, and the middle party. Politics and economics could hardly be separated. The pro-Austrians denounced the Franco-Prussian treaty as a violation of the Zollverein agreement of 1853. The new treaty, they said, abolished Austria's favored position with respect to Zollverein trade and relegated that German country to the status of every non-German country. The tariff schedule of the new commercial treaty had been set so low, they bitterly complained, that Austrian industry could not possibly accept it without risking bankruptcy. A large trade between Austria and South Germany in particular had developed under the differential system of 1853, which in case the Franco-Prussian treaty were accepted would have to be modified or reduced. The question of preserving special relations with Austria, declared Hänle of Munich, was for the South Germans one of "life or death."[67]

Spitzer of Neuhaus and others stated that the Austrian market had far more value for Germany than the French. Germany would be unable to compete in the French market with industrial products and would have to export to it raw materials. In Austria, on the other hand, German industry would enjoy a vast market for its manufactured products. South German, Saxon, and even some Silesian industry in Prussia itself was eager to retain the Austrian market. The advocates of this position pleaded for a treaty to be made with Austria first; then one could be negotiated with France.

The opponents of the treaty correctly attributed political motives to Prussia, and showed the anger of the small states at such cavalier treatment. Spitzer asserted that by making the agreement with France Prussia aimed to strengthen its power over the other members of the Zollverein. The delegate Karmarsch from Hanover agreed with him and asked, "Who will guarantee that Prussia will not wish other changes and will sooner or later say, 'Agree to them or we shall push you out the door.' " The issue of sovereignty became involved in the issue of tariff rates and the method of negotiating a tariff agreement. Prussia had anticipated this well known reaction and had discounted it in advance.

The novel aspect at this time was furnished by the attitude of the most powerful industrial association in Austria, that of Vienna, which in October, 1862, after a two-days' session approved in theory the idea of union with the Zollverein but wished the fulfillment postponed to some future time. Vienna industry had no inclination to subject itself to the competition of German industry even to gain political advantage for the country. It was willing to make sacrifices, it said, for the sake of union; but it could not afford to sacrifice so much without undergoing the threat of economic ruin. The advocates of Austria's joining

---

[67] For data on the discussion of the Zollverein see *Verhandlungen des II. deutschen Handelstages zu München, 14-18 Okt. 1862; Der Deutsche Handelstag 1861-1911*, 11; also Eugen Franz, *Der Entscheidungskampf um die wirtschaftspolitische Führung Deutschlands (1856-1867)*, (Munich, 1933), pp. 246 ff.

the Zollverein had lost economic support even in Austria itself. The question had in that state become one merely of politics.[68]

A middle group, including such influential figures as David Hansemann, certainly one of the most prominent economic statesmen in Germany, and H. H. Meier, the head of the Nordeutscher Lloyd in Bremen and one of the ablest economic leaders in North Germany, wished to retain both the Franco-Prussian treaty and the close commercial relations with Austria.[69] This group would have liked to exclude Austria from the application of the most-favored-nations clause. It wished preferential relations with that country, although not at the sacrifice of the Franco-Prussian treaty. While this group recognized the interdependence of the political and economic factors in the conflict, it sought to reduce political hostility by stressing the economic advantages of close cooperation.[70]

The pro-Prussian group took the aggressive. It fully supported the changes that the Prussian government had introduced into the Zollverein. First of all, it asserted that the Austrian market could not compare in value with that of Western Europe which the treaty would open. In Austria, declared one speaker, only about nine million people came into consideration as a market; the others, the non-Germans, were culturally too backward to be able to afford Western goods. In the region of Aachen, declared von Beckerath, one would smile at an assertion of the superior value of the Austrian over the West European market. For Silesia, said Weigel of Breslau, the Franco-Belgian market was far more important than the Austrian.

The entire European transportation system, indeed that of the world, declared Braun, was being changed by the development of railroads. Western Europe was beginning to unite into a free commercial system. Germany had to join this great system, he said, or it would be forced back upon the East European market, which was not so capable of consuming goods, or upon the uncertainty of the overseas market. His views were supported by Michaelis of the *National Zeitung* in Berlin, who stressed the importance of a diversified market as protection against economic crises. The *National Zeitung*, like numerous other North German papers, strongly supported the reduction in tariffs which the Franco-Prussian treaty specified. It advocated free trade not merely for economic but for political reasons. Protective tariffs were regarded as a basic support of autocracy and

---

[68] See *Der Deutsche Handelstag 1861–1911*, II, 361-62.
[69] See Meier's report on the meeting, *Bremer Handelsblatt*, Nov. 1, 1862.
[70] *Bremer Handelsblatt*, Sept. 12, Oct. 14-18, 1862.

particularism; free trade seemed to hold out the assurance of liberalism and nationalism.[71]

Weigel of Breslau staunchly defended the method which Prussia had used to reform the tariff schedule. He admitted that it "tasted like compulsion"; but he argued that the reform could not have been achieved by a general tariff conference. "The times have rendered our institutions out of date. . . . We lack an organization to decide this great and weighty question." Action had to be taken by the leading state, namely Prussia, and the other members would have to accept the results en bloc. There was no other way.

The Austrians rejoined that trade had nothing to do with the nationality question. They sought to justify thereby the inclusion of the non-German as well as the German peoples of the Hapsburg empire in the Zollverein. Weigel of Breslau agreed with them, and added that political sympathy did not incline him to approve the Franco-Prussian treaty but that economic interest did. Political antipathy toward Austria, he continued, did not determine his position: "We have first of all to choose between two customers," and he preferred France.[72] His colleague Braun of Winsen disagreed with him completely on the question of Austrian nationalities. He considered a trade agreement acceptable, but he objected to having as a member of the Zollverein an Austria of "Magyars, Croats, Slovenes, Rumanians, Ruthenians, and so forth" who as a potential majority in the Austrian parliament might gain the right of passing on Zollverein affairs.

The pro-Prussians were even more critical of the political and economic conditions within Austria and said that these rendered any customs union impossible. The instability of the Austrian monetary system, the constitutional troubles, the differences in taxation as seen in the Austrian tobacco monopoly, the differences in organization of customs collection and the slowness and unreliability of the Austrian system—these and other factors turned the *klein-deutsch* group away from any notion of a customs union with that country. Von Beckerath of Crefeld, another of the most distinguished older liberals of Prussia, denied that he and his friends were opponents of Austria; they merely disliked the idea of having that country as a member of the Zollverein. "We recognize," he said, "that the power and greatness of Austria is not alone a European but in an eminent sense a German need, that German Austria must draw strength out of Germany in order to be

[71] *National Zeitung*, Sept. 26. 1863.
[72] *Verhandlungen*, p. 77.

the leading race in Austria. "But," he asked the delegates from Austria, "do you believe that you can derive this strength from a Germany which is restricted in its development, which does not progress in the economic field? Well, the entrance of Austria into the Zollverein would have just these results," for Austria could enter only if the present constitution of the Zollverein with the *liberum veto* should be retained. He objected to Austria's entry for two major reasons: first, that its entry under present circumstances would transfer to the Zollverein the conditions that made the Diet of the Confederation an unworkable body, namely, the presence of two great powers, each with the *liberum veto;* second, that by bringing the non-German peoples of Austria into the Zollverein the right of each nationality to its own free self-determination would be violated. "German customs union and only *German* customs union is what we all wish," said Michaelis.

The German Commercial Association passed by a vote of 138 to 55 a resolution in favor of preserving the independence of the two customs areas, that of the Zollverein and that of Austria, but equally in favor of eliminating customs duties and facilitating commerce between the two areas. The latter half of the resolution may be termed an expression of good intentions and of kind feelings toward Austria. More important was a further resolution urging the reform of the constitution of the Zollverein in accordance with the following principles:

> In the renewal of the Zollverein it should be taken into consideration that the legislative functions of the Zollverein should be transferred jointly to representatives of the governments on the one hand and to those of the people of the union states on the other. Common agreements by majority vote of these two bodies are to be introduced as final law in the entire customs area.
>
> In the composition of these two representative bodies due consideration will be given the size of population of the member states.[73]

[73] The resolution had originally been passed at the meeting in 1861. It was reaffirmed in 1862. See a similar resolution passed by the Congress of German Economists in 1862. *Bremer Handelsblatt*, Sept. 13, 1862. The resolution did not satisfy David Hansemann and his friends, who condemned it as too vague to be of any value. Hansemann and a colleague, Hurtzig, offered to the *Handelstag* an extensive and detailed memorandum on the future constitution of the Zollverein. Hansemann's proposal never carried much weight. The German Commercial Association merely called the attention of the public to it, but did not subject it to any discussion. The *Bremer Handelsblatt* in the issues of Sept. 13 and Nov. 1, 1862, criticized it sharply.

While the liberals and nationalists discussed the reorganization of the Zollverein as a means of furthering German unity, they understood the limitations of this approach. The fact was, as von Beckerath, Michaelis and all the Prussian *klein-deutsch* liberals agreed, that economic unity could be gained only by way of political unity. In their opinion the major weaknesses of the Zollverein were the terminability of the agreement, the *liberum veto* and the one-sided power of state ministries, each of which was not an economic but a political question.[74] While they pressed for strengthening the organization of the Zollverein, they had no illusions about the necessity of an inclusive institutional framework for a unified German nation. "We shall not have this customs union for our advantage and for our prosperous development," said Michaelis, "until we also have a German Reich authority and a German parliament."

That the liberal nationalists were interested most of all in political unification is seen in the fact that after the outburst of conflicting views in 1862 about the constitution of the Zollverein, the subject seems to have lost popular interest. The stir of political life caused by the war of Italian unification, the constitutional controversy in Prussia, and the outbreak of the Danish war turned attention away from economic to political action. Bismarck and the Prussian government were so hated by liberals that the *Bremer Handelsblatt* wrote on December 19, 1863, as follows:

> . . . As long as the Prussian people do not succeed in transferring the administration of the Prussian state into other hands, one does not know whether one should even wish a renewal of the Zollverein treaty at all. For at the price of strengthening the political influence of a Bismarck ministry in the Zollverein the material advantages of a continuing free internal trade are bought too dearly, and not much good is to be expected from the leadership in commercial policy of a ministry which allies itself with the Petersburg and Vienna governments in order to obtain a basis for a foreign policy hostile to the Confederation and to support absolutism in Germany.

When the German Commercial Association met in 1865 it could look back on a number of accomplishments toward which it had aimed three years ago at the crucial meeting in Munich, as well as some major setbacks. The Franco-Prussian commercial treaty had been ratified and come into force; Austria and the Zollverein had reached a new agreement which in no way infringed upon the independence of the

[74] *Bremer Handelsblatt*, Nov. 1, 1862.

latter; the Zollverein was assured of renewal. The German commercial law code, prepared in the late 1850s, had been approved by most of the German states. Nonetheless, the constitution of the Zollverein had not been reformed; the *liberum veto* in that body had not been abolished or a national economic legislative body created. At its meeting in 1865 the German Commercial Association without discussion unanimously approved a declaration which summed up once more the existing grievances. It criticized the slowness in making commercial treaties, regretted the failure to create a unified consular system, condemned the persistence of governmental abuses in dealing with insurance business and transportation facilities, denounced the failure to achieve freedom of occupation, and urged once more the reform of the Zollverein constitution as a prerequisite for achieving the other reforms.

After this outcry the German private economic interests took no further steps toward economic unification of the nation before Bismarck imposed political unity and simultaneously solved the economic problems. The success of Bismarck's policy of blood and iron seemed to discourage them from further efforts comparable in vigor and incisiveness to those of the years 1861 to 1863. Politics won over economics as the decisive factor in gaining the objectives of national unity and the concomitant economic reforms for which the economic leaders had striven.

6 / The Constitution

THE constitution, introduced in 1849-50 into a Prussia which had been governed for several centuries by absolute rulers, was found to be the object of much dispute. It had to be interpreted and adjusted to a society in which major elements looked toward the past for their models, while others judged conditions by a liberal ideal yet to be realized. Differing objectives were set for the development of the constitution according to differing social ideals. On the one side were lined the King and the Conservatives, including Bismarck. They all sought, although in varying degree, to preserve under the regime of constitutional government the royal rights of the past. Since the sovereign had sworn allegiance to the constitution, he tolerated it unwillingly but, according to his view, loyally. He interpreted it in the light of absolutism and the divine right of kings. The Conservatives, including the key Minister of War General von Roon, disliked the constitution intensely and wished to abolish it; but they stood by the King, who they hoped might continue to rule by divine right. To Bismarck the constitution provided a useful means of government under a monarch whose power was not greatly restricted by that document. It should not be allowed to develop into a system where parliament exercised final authority over the other organs of government. Opposed to the royal group were the liberals, who interpreted the constitution as promising free government, responsive to the will of the people and assuring the public a powerful role in the conduct of state affairs. In the absence of a willingness to compromise, these differences of views about the constitution led to a constitutional conflict.

King William believed as much as any of his ancestors in kingship by divine right. He accepted the constitution as a historic fact, and he intended loyally to uphold it; but his mental limitations made it possible for him to reconcile the divine-right theory and constitutional government. The confusion in his thinking is evident from two of his addresses, one entitled "To My People," issued on his becoming King, the second at the ceremony of his coronation in January, 1861.

> With free royal hand he [Frederick William IV] gave the country institutions in the development of which its hopes should be fulfilled. When an unfortunate movement of spirits had shaken all foundations of law [he referred to the Revolution of 1848], my brother knew how to bring the confusion to an end, by a new political creation to renew our unbroken development and to direct its advance into fixed channels [he meant the introduction of the constitution].
>
> I will loyally preserve the high heritage of my ancestors, which with constant care they founded and augmented by their best efforts at the risk of their lives. Proudly I see myself surrounded by such a loyal and brave people, by such a glorious army.
>
> My hand shall watch over the welfare and the right of all in all classes of the population; it shall rule over this rich life, protecting and furthering it. It is not Prussia's mission to live in the enjoyment of its earnings. In the exercise of its spiritual and moral forces, in the seriousness and uprightness of its religious thinking, in the union of obedience and freedom, in the strengthening of its military force lie the conditions of its power. Only in this way is it able to maintain its position among the states of Europe.
>
> I hold firmly to the traditions of my house when I set myself the task of elevating and strengthening the patriotic spirit of my people. I will make firm and develop the right of the state according to its historical significance, and will uphold the institutions which King Frederick William IV called into being. Faithful to the oath with which I assumed the regency, I will protect the constitution and the laws of the kingdom.

At his coronation the King declared: "By the ceremony of coronation in the presence of the members of both Houses of the Landtag and of other witnesses summoned to us from all provinces of our kingdom, we wish to give witness to the hallowed and eternal rights of the throne to which by the grace of God we have been called and to affirm anew the bond strengthened by glorious history between Our House and the people of Prussia."[1]

---

[1] Horst Kohl, *op. cit.*, pp. 18-19, 28.

William promised to hold firmly to the traditions of his house and loyally to abide by the constitution. An intimation of how he might resolve this contradiction lay in the assertion that his brother had granted the constitution "with free royal hand." One might infer that as a free royal gift the constitution might have to agree with the will of the giver, or the latter might change his mind and freely give the country something else. The necessity of concentrating power in the King was strongly emphasized along with that of the continued cultivation of Spartan virtues associated with Prussianism, so that the state could continue to play a major role in international affairs. Power meant to William the political and military power of a monarch by divine right. Prussia dared not run the international risk of weakening itself by introducing parliamentry government, that is, ministerial responsibility to a parliament. The King soon blamed the Lower House for his troubles with his fellow sovereigns in the other German states. "When one sees," he asked, "that I can exercise no command at all in my own house, who will trust me?"[2]

The King regarded the constitution as a means of associating the public in the affairs of government, but he expected it to assure public approval of all measures which he particularly advocated. In case of conflict parliament should acquiesce in the King's will. Liberals noted that in his coronation address he did not mention the constitution or the rights of the people and of their representatives.[3] How little the King esteemed the parliament, especially the Lower House, was evident in many ways. When the Lower House in February, 1861, sent him an address stating its wishes as to legislation, he replied: "I am relying firmly upon the representative assembly's standing by my side in the execution of my aims in the sense of the undiminished preservation of the power of my Crown; this is necessary for the true welfare of the Fatherland. With respect to the questions of domestic and foreign policy which are touched upon in your address, my government has clearly emphasized the points of view which accord with my intentions for it and to which it will adhere. I expect the Lower House to support these by its approval. . . . I know that my people stand at my side in unswerving loyalty in good and bad times."[4] The Lower House should pass the legislation which he approved.

The royal conception of the legislative process was equally simple and clear. When the liberal ministers pressed him in 1861 to initiate

---

[2] Von Bernhardi, *op. cit.*, IV, 127.
[3] Parisius, *von Hoverbeck*, I, 215.
[4] Horst Kohl, *op. cit.*, pp. 24-25.

legislation against his will, he reacted as follows: "His Majesty remarked that he also wished this development of our domestic legislation
[which Minister Count Schwerin had declared once more to be as much
'desired as expected'], but that it is not necessary for certain re-sub-
mitted bills to be accepted without change. The highest officials of
the Crown were called to submit to the soverign their proposed laws;
the Crown has to consider them and in case of disagreement to seek a
compromise and a rapprochement of views. One will and one view
must in the end be decisive and this is the King's. Whoever among
the ministers is unable for reasons of conscience to accept His decision
must resign."[5] The ministers should propose legislation, the King
should decide what should be done; the parliament should perform its
part in making the decisions effective. "A wise reciprocal action of
relaxing and tightening the reins of power," expressed the King's
formula of rule, and he compared the art of ruling with the regulation of the flow of a stream.[6]

When the liberals in the Lower House criticized and opposed the
military reforms, the King began to lose confidence in that body. By
March, 1861, he had come to consider the liberal ministers a failure
and condemned the entire constitutional system. He regarded every
new desire of the liberal ministry, trying to appease the Lower House,
as a new "concession" from him, and he opposed it on the suspicion
that this process would continue forever. "The ambition of these
persons is," he declared in April, "for themselves to rule! . . . The
King shall not rule; they want to rule! . . . But that cannot and dare
not be the case in Prussia." As early as March, he was alarmed at the
rise of the "democrats," a word connoting the worst excesses of 1848;
and he thought that a revolt in Berlin was not impossible. His mistrust and anger were so great that one of the liberal von Sauckens,
who knew William well, described the relations with the King as
"rotten, super-rotten!"[7]

In 1861 the elections took place which shifted the strength in the
Lower House from the Old Liberals to the Progressive party and returned several persons like Waldeck and Schulze-Delitzsch, whose
names were associated in the minds of Conservatives with 1848. They
were "democrats." "Our enemies are very active," said the King in
January, 1862, referring not merely to these few so-called democrats

[5] Von Roon, *op. cit.*, II, 50-51.
[6] *Briefe, Reden und Schriften*, I, 496-97; II, 16, 22.
[7] Von Bernhardi, *op. cit.*, IV, 100-01, 107, 118, 137.

but to liberal opponents in general.[8]   He spoke in public of even criminals being elected,[9] and when von Saucken advised him to open the Landtag in person, William became excited, placed his hand over his heart and declared that he could not personally face people like Waldeck (a former high judicial official and a staunch democrat who had been very active in 1848-49). Von Saucken reminded the King that a ruler stood above parties, and William finally agreed to the request.   When Deputy Behrend, a member of the Progressive party, was invited to a concert at court because of his position as vice-president of the newly convened Lower House and was introduced to the King, the latter asked, "The Vice-president?" Behrend: "At your service, your Majesty." The King: "Aha!" Thereafter, his liberal colleagues threatened to rename Behrend "Aha!"[10]

In the statement of his program of rule made in 1858 the King had spoken about the question of whether and in how far the constitution should be developed. His remarks could have been considered promising only by the most willful optimist. There could be no talk of breaking with the past, he declared. "Only the careful and improving hand shall be applied where something arbitrary or contrary to the needs of the time appears. You all recognize that the welfare of the Crown and of the country is inseparable, that the welfare of both rests on a sound, powerful, conservative basis. To recognize these needs correctly, to weigh them and call them into life, that is the secret of state wisdom, wherein all extremes are to be avoided. Our task will in this respect not be light, for recently a movement has appeared in public life which if partly understandable already shows on the other hand traces of intentionally exaggerated ideas which we must oppose by our calm and legal and energetic action. One must hold true to promises without refusing to improve on them wherever necessary; but one must courageously obstruct that which has not been promised. Above all, I warn against stereotyped statements, such as that the government will let itself be continuously pushed into developing liberal ideas which would in any case advance by themselves."[11]

---

[8] *Ibid.*, 182.

[9] He was referring to Becker, a leader in the Revolution of 1848 who had been unjustly sentenced to several years in prison for his activity then and had served his term. He was a good democratic subject, whose radicalism may be judged by the fact that he subsequently served for many years as Oberbürgermeister of Cologne. Parisius, *von Hoverbeck*, II, 1.

[10] Von Bernhardi, *op. cit.*, IV, 198-99; Parisius, *von Hoverbeck*, II, 6.

[11] Horst Kohl, *op. cit.*, p. 3.

With this condemnation of liberalism and the warning that he would not change fundamentals in the state, the King, at that time Prince Regent, inaugurated his reign. During the next years, he clung resolutely to this statement of principles in spite of pressure from his liberal ministers. Not until early in 1862 were his New Era ministers able to persuade him to agree in general to a few very mild structural reforms, especially ones on ministerial responsibility and local government. Within a few months, however, he was able to dismiss these ministers, whom months ago he had ceased to trust, and to drop the reform proposals. After he became involved in the constitutional conflict with the Lower House, he remained steadfast, a favorite word with him, in the defence of his policies. In October, 1863, he wrote to one of his officials: "I feel the heavy burden of the battle, which God has laid upon us, but I also know that I owe it to my people and to the Crown inherited by me to fight it out with determination. Whatever may come, I shall persist in that which I know to be necessary for the welfare and the independence of the Fatherland. I shall not deviate from the path that I have taken. . . ."[12]

Two ministers were mainly responsible for enabling the King to continue his adamant attitude in the conflict with the liberal Lower House. The one, von Roon, headed the powerful military group which knew no other way of life than that of ultra conservatism; the other, the civilian Bismarck, employed every force—King, Conservatives, military, bureaucracy, even the liberals—to fulfill a selection of ideals of his own choosing which proved acceptable in varying degrees to all of them and preserved the authority of Conservatism in Germany far beyond its useful life.

The Junker von Roon was made Minister of War in 1859, replacing the liberal General von Bonin who was lukewarm toward the Regent's military reform proposals and popular with the liberal public. Von Roon was brought in to put through these reforms; he was accepted by his liberal colleagues as a non-political specialist in office for a specific task. The new minister was gleeful over the fact that his colleagues made no attempt to commit him to their liberal program. He openly stated his ideas of government, writing to his friend Perthes at the time of his appointment as follows:

> I have curtsied after I had frankly declared that I never had any use for the whole constitutional business, but that as a true conservative subject I would bow to the completed deed, that I

---

[12] *Briefe, Reden und Schriften,* II, 73.

shall remain "a fool on my own responsibility" but think that I can nonetheless be a minister-expert if one can use me as I am for that purpose. My assertion seemed to surprise no one; they had apparently expected worse from me.

After expressing his aversion to the kind of life he would have to lead as minister, he continued:

A human being of my kind cannot do other than with God's help tackle the most difficult and dangerous assignments when it is a question, as it is here, of the most important and the highest affairs in a man's life work, namely, the political health of his fatherland. Should a soldier, in cowardly fashion, turn his back on his war lord when the latter calls, "Come and support me"—merely because his lord's other helpers do not please him? Never! That which is called political honor I conceive otherwise, for I am a soldier. . . . According to my conception of political honor, it is my honorable duty to say: "Yes, Lord, I will; but do not wish something which you may at some time perhaps regret. See, I am otherwise than you may think and, in view of your other supporters, you may wish. Think over whether you cannot find a more suitable pillar which would less disturb the harmony of your building." When one has said this and similar things with feeling and frankness and the desire remains unchanged, then in my opinion an honest man has done his duty, and it is extraordinary that one replied to him, "If I had and knew a better man, I should not have chosen you."[13]

In spite of this show of modesty von Roon had eagerly sought to obtain the appointment. He took a keen interest in politics, and from the beginning of his service as minister he actively pursued the political side of his task.[14] It would have been impossible for him to keep out of politics, for the military reform became almost immediately the dominant political issue with the ministry, the Landtag and the public. That von Roon would be on the Conservative side was evident from the first. His close relative, Moritz von Blanckenburg, was a Conservative party leader and his circle of friends belonged to the same tradition. Like the Prince Regent, he had been brought up exclusively in the army. While this training did not necessarily make a person a Conservative, it tended to throw the full weight of the military institutions and traditions on that side, and liberal officers continued to be exceptions.

The Regent immediately trusted von Roon more than anyone else in the ministry, and the latter encouraged him in every way to do so.

[13] Von Roon, *op. cit.*, I, 372-73, 375, 378-80.
[14] *Ibid.*, II, 18-19.

As soon as the new Minister of War took over his position he began to plot how he could oust the liberals in the ministry. With Bismarck and Moritz von Blanckenburg he had long discussions of this problem;[15] for von Roon was determined to bring in Bismarck as minister and to do so required breaking the bond between the King and his liberal advisers. In a letter of June 18, 1861, to his friend Perthes, Roon described his strategy:

> The members of the ministry, except the Kultusminister [Bethmann-Hollweg] and, under certain conditions, myself, wish decidedly not to resign and regard their resignation as ruinous for the state and their loss as irreparable. With the best intentions, that is, in blind devotion to constitutional doctrines, they wish to make the King and the state un-Prussian, and with full sails they continue to steer toward a parliamentary regime.
>
> Since they should and must be eliminated, because their continuation would according to Prussian-conservative views be ruinous for the state, they must be eliminated as soon as possible. "Whoever plays with the devil is accursed," says Wallenstein, and in reference to the present case I should appear to myself to be a fool, a stupid fool, if I did not use today the opportunity to seize the rudder of state from the hands of these men caught in dangerous errors and intentions merely because this could be done more advantageously at a later moment. . . . In my opinion nothing would be worse for Prussia than to succumb to a doctrinaire swindle. It can arise with new strength out of the mud bath of a revolution; in the filth of doctrinaire liberalism it will irretrievably rot.

In the next paragraph of the letter to Perthes, von Roon showed his insight into the personality of the sovereign.

> Do not consider me fanatical. I know my terrain and the persons acting on it; I know with what difficulty decisions are to be reached, particularly when they involve acknowledgement of a previous mistake. [That is, the King would have to admit his blunder in appointing liberals as ministers and in making any concessions to their doctrines.] You will admit that on concrete questions (like the swearing of allegiance at the coronation) decisions are easier than in the discussion of abstract theories.

Von Roon knew that the King's intellectual limitations made any ideological discussion useless as a means of overthrowing the liberals and that one had to concentrate on specific acts, like that of the swearing of allegiance, in which ideas were actually in conflict, even though the King explicitly did not recognize the fact. Von Roon planned to

[15] *Ibid.*, II, 19, 22.

work from one concrete act to another, without ever bringing up questions of principle. Thereby he expected to save the King's face about having to dismiss liberal ministers whom he had appointed and to bring the ruler back to Prussian conservatism without his being aware of his own inconsistency. The letter to Perthes continued:

> Do not regard me as a deceiver. I made my challenge openly but no one dared openly to accept it. [For good reason, since the King supported him wholeheartedly]. But for reasons of wisdom, I have not yet come forth with the declaration, that is, with the formal, clearly and sharply emphasized declaration, "They or I," although it lies implicit in the situation. The gentlemen certainly know that, but they say the opposite as ostensibly as possible.
>
> You see I aim at no so-called "change of system" but only at the repudiation of the *liberal* interpretation of the November program [of 1858]. I entered office with a conservative interpretation of it; I can, will and must hold firmly to it, but I also wish and endeavor to achieve that this interpretation, which is actually that of the King, becomes recognized as official. If this public profession should not protect us against red elections, a result of which I do not yet despair, then let the battle for existence be fought. I am confident that it will end victoriously and will lead to health and recovery, and indeed not by a reactionary recipe but by an honorable, open and *courageous* use of constitutional means. God will not forsake us if we do not forsake Him. The reorganization [of the army] has shown that our supreme person is capable of courageous, decisive and determined rule. Unity of views between the ruler and his ministers strengthens and gives wings to *all* governmental activity; the prevailing disunity has weakened and crippled it. That was unavoidable. Everything depends therefore on the choice of persons! The world belongs to the courageous![16]

Von Roon regarded all liberals, democrats, and communists as belonging in the same category of "reds." He preferred a civil war to a liberal regime. He claimed to have God on his side. He had a plan for changing completely the policies of government without the King's being aware of his royal inconsistency. Von Roon expected a Conservative government to apply in all cases the methods being used in the execution of the military reorganization: Once the King decided on a matter the ministers should carry out his orders with parliamentary approval of just enough of the program for them to go ahead with the whole plan. Then parliament would have to give in or the conflict would be brought to a crisis, and the sooner the

[16] *Ibid.*, II, 22-25.

better. If parliament would not approve the proposals, the ministers should follow the King's orders anyway. A group of courageous ministers was needed, and of the possible candidates Von Roon considered Bismarck the ablest and bravest. With Bismarck in the ministry, so he thought, liberals would not be tolerated, the King would once more be strong and firm, and Prussia would be governed in accordance with its tradition.

Von Roon followed his plan in full. On many questions he sided with the King against all the other ministers, and he made certain that the King knew about his stand. He wished to strengthen his sovereign, to give the latter confidence in pressing his policies. When in February, 1861, the liberal ministers wrung from a very unwilling King consent to introduce bills for the development of the constitution in a liberal sense, for example a bill on ministerial responsibility, von Roon immediately wrote the King a long letter which was a masterpiece in the way it undermined his colleagues and their whole program. Cut to the personality of the ruler, the letter proved as effective as its author could have wished.[17]

Still deeply shaken by the outcome of yesterday's meeting of the ministry, I have been struggling to regain the composure which I recognize as necessary in order to speak to Your Majesty about the present situation with some prospects of success. I dare to do this, I must do this, for Your Majesty chose me as an adviser. But I must also do this because after Your statement of yesterday, I belong to a ministry which has forced Your Majesty to approve a measure which is most decidedly contrary to Your conviction, to Your conscience.

I was deeply hurt thereby, for my Prussian soldier's heart cannot bear the thought that my King and Lord should place another will above His own. But I hope confidently that Your Majesty will clear me of the suspcion of solidarity with those who put pressure upon You.

At the present time it is a question on the one hand of the approval of certain things which the Crown expects from the Landtag [the military organization] and on the other hand of certain concessions which the Lower House expects from the Crown[liberal reforms].

The first-named approvals relate to indispensable needs, the satisfaction of which is urgently demanded by the first of all natural duties, that of self-preservation. The concessions desired in exchange are supposed to complete our constitution, after we have already lived and prospered for a number of years in constitutional conditions without this completion. These concessions are far from having been won by other and great countries.

[17] *Ibid.*, II, 35 ff.

The approvals are absolutely necessary; the concessions are from a certain standpoint merely desirable. The values which are here to be exchanged are therefore unequal.

Nonetheless, it would be conceivable that performance and counter-performance considered from the standpoint of legality might be balanced, that the government is legally committed to make the concessions in question because thereby certain promises in the constitutional document should be fulfilled.

But our constitution was given by the King alone. It is not a contract the immediate fulfillment of which can be unconditionally claimed by the contracting party without further ado. Our Prussian Monarchy is not newly created by constitutional agreement, as for example the former bourgeois kingship [of Louis Philippe in France] or as the Belgian; it is far more one created by our great rulers, one which was not abolished but only modified by the constitution granted by free Royal decision. As a product of the free will of a King of Prussia our constitution . . . will be honestly interpreted and faithfully followed. In accordance therewith, the promises of the constitution are also to be fulfilled, not as contractual obligations which cannot be deferred but much more as a freely assumed obligation for the future, the actual fulfillment of which is dependent upon future free Royal decisions. . . . Mere external considerations of the convictions of others, if they should serve as motives for Royal decisions, would create the worst conditions. In other constitutional states the assertion of the will of a ministry against the King is conceivable, but not in Prussia! For, as its entire history shows, Prussia needs for its salvation an absolutely undivided Royal will which is limited only by itself and by the inborn respect for the law of the family of Hohenzollern.

Von Roon's conservative, military constitutional theory may be translated as advising the King as follows: The monarchy gave the state the constitution out of its own free will; it has to abide by its own freely-given constitution, but it can expand that instrument or otherwise change it freely, and it is subject to no legal or institutional restraints in doing so; there exists and may exist in Prussia no power above or conditioning that of the King, for Prussia's history proves that this state cannot afford to weaken itself by any such limitation. In substance, von Roon told the King that this was his constitution, that he should of course abide by it, but that he could do with it as he pleased. Von Roon's letter continued:

This conception, the only one which preserves the interest of the Crown, offers the greatest security for the continuation of its [the Crown's] undiminished brilliance. It does not exclude further delegation of authority; still less does it designate such as absolutely harmful; but it unconditionally demands that all further delegation of power must in truth be made freely with the deepest conviction. [Von Roon thought correctly that under these conditions no sovereign would ever give up any more power. He also know that the kind of minister serving the King under such a conception of the constitution would not advise him to transfer any of his power to others.] Such a conception is therefore to be held to and represented in all matters by the King's first servants, the ministers. If they are unable to do so, either because they have doctrinaire views about the binding nature of the constitutional promises or because they lack courage to face with assurance the consequences of that conception, then acting like honorable men they will request the King to seek other advisers and representatives of his prerogatives. [In these statements von Roon by implication took care of his liberal colleagues in the ministry; they were doctrinaires and cowards and were clinging to their jobs; they were not men of honor, for otherwise they would have resigned].

If on the other hand, in conflict with his interests and his innermost convictions about that which benefits the country they attempt to move the King to act against his own views, then they act in the interest of expanding the parliamentary power, and Prussia demands a strong individual authority!

And I hope that Your Majesty shares all my conceptions.

But if Your Majesty should ever again have the experience that Your own conscientious convictions are found in opposition to the views of Your first servants, whether about the so-called completion of the constitution or about any other measure of utility, then I beseech Your Majesty with all the respect and feeling of a servant's loyalty of over forty years to remember that Your advisers with all their zeal for their views could not wish, and dare not wish, to bend the will of their Lord and to cause division in His sovereign conscience, a state which would deeply embarrass and burden the advisers themselves.

Von Roon was appearing to be most concerned about the royal conscience, not to let it be torn by inner dissention. He knew that in fundamentals the ruler sided with the Conservatives and wished to retain his absolute power. The general was appealing indirectly to the King's sense of honor to keep his conscience free from doubt and trouble by getting rid of the liberals. At the same time, he blamed not the King but the liberals for the split in the royal conscience and said that they should feel shame for causing it.

Von Roon continued in his letter to the King:

Moreover, pressure is not demanded by the situation. In order to attain the great objectives of the government, over-hasty concessions to parliamentarism would in my modest opinion be the most questionable means of all. The King of Prussia is at this moment still in full possession of his sovereignty and for the well-understood interests of the country must remain so. He

does not lack constitutional means in order to execute his justified will in a legal way. If this is so, why should one seize
means which against the will of Your Majesty limit and stunt
the power of the Crown?

The answer to this question could only be found in the assumption that Your Majesty's advisers regarded the immediate
completion of the constitution according to their own political
convictions as an unavoidable necessity, or without such completion they held their authority in the chamber to be endangered
by their own friends in that body, or without initiative aiming
at that objective they would come into contradiction with their
own parliamentary antecedents. Then it would surely be less a
question of a constitutional than of a ministerial need.

Von Roon accused his liberal colleagues of pressing for reforms, not
because the King wanted these reforms or the country needed them,
but because the ministers needed them in order to hold their positions.
He attributed selfish, petty motives to the liberal ministers and did not
even consider worth mentioning the fact that the Lower House existed
as the representative of the people, that the liberals held an overwhelming majority in that house, and that the country manifestly demanded constitutional reforms. He kept the controversy within the
limited, personal group of the King and a few liberal ministers. The
country needed Hohenzollern absolutism; the desires of the people
as expressed in elections and in the wishes of their representatives in
the Lower House did not even deserve to be mentioned, especially
in a letter to a sovereign eager to be shown a way of saving face while
actually repudiating liberalism and restoring the absolutism of the
Hohenzollern tradition.

Since, moreover, under the assumption that only the introduction of the laws but not their passage, that is, not the completion of the constitution but only the beginnings of that process would be intended or at least only needed to be intended,
one could perhaps regard their [the liberal ministers'] measures
as mere sham battles and devoid of danger, if a large part of the
nation did not become angry over such onsets and regard them
as an injury to the Crown. Your Majesty's Minister of War may
not conceal the fact that such views find repercussions in
that part of the nation which bears Your Majesty's arms and in
which Your Majesty has always found the firmest pillar of Your
throne. Whoever is faithful to Your Majesty can only with
reluctance think of the possibility of this "rocher de bronce"
being undermined.

The King's comment on this last sentence was, "I should not survive
that!"

Von Roon was saying that the army, "a large part of the nation," took affront at these liberal reforms; they should not be accepted, for they would lead to undermining the army, the firmest support of the throne. The army represented the nation, and nothing should occur which would offend it. The Lower House was not even mentioned; it did not represent the nation; it was of no importance in the nation. The army expressed the national interest; that is, the top officers, almost all Conservatives, expressed the national interest. Rarely, if ever, has an argument based on self-interest been advanced more blandly. For the sake of its national defence the nation should subordinate itself to the will of the officer-king and his officer advisers. This ideal was the essence of militarism. Von Roon assured the King that the army would defend him in case of any difficulty with the liberals. Far from opposing the King for not accepting liberal reforms, the general was saying that the army would be seriously alienated if the King did accept these reforms.

> Finally, I have to repeat once more the thought that in contradiction to Your own conscientious convictions, Your Majesty may feel that You must make concessions in order thereby to further the great objectives of Your government. But what if the *quid pro quo* were not forthcoming? Parliamentary majorities have always been unreliable. In view of this fact, would it not be much more advisable to expect beforehand the evidence of love and trust . . . ? If this proof is given, and if Your Majesty's power is thereby strengthened to the necessary degree in internal and in foreign affairs, then Your Majesty can be less hesitating in Your concessions. The strong and rich can be obliging and generous; but as long as power and property are found in a doubtful situation wisdom advises caution and economy.

Let the Landtag first approve the military reforms, von Roon advised his lord; after that act the King could think about granting a *quid pro quo*. Two statements in von Roon's advice could be used time and time again to block any reforms: first, since "parliamentary majorities have always been unreliable," how could an absolute monarch ever trust them by granting reforms at any time; second, what is the "necessary degree" of power "in internal and in foreign affairs" which a state must possess before the absolute ruler dare allow any constitutional concessions to a parliament?

The heart of von Roon as Prussian soldier was instructing the monarch how to be at the same time an absolute sovereign and a constitutional sovereign. He was teaching constitutional law as interpreted by the military, a subject in which he was undoubtedly proficient.

With the most self-righteous thoughts about serving the state, he was showing the King ways of defying the Prussian people. The content of this document fitted the period over fifty years before, when other Prussian army officers had fought to prevent the Steins and the Hardenbergs from putting through constitutional reforms. The document reveals no understanding of the new society in the making, its problems and desires. It does not consider the fact that industrialists and bankers, merchants and railroad magnates, newspaper editors, professors and other professional personnel were becoming numerous, aware of their social and economic significance in the state, and eager to share the power by which their own fate and that of their state was determined. Von Roon's ideal world consisted of an absolute monarch surrounded by conservative nobility and army officers who were in a position to guide the will of the absolute monarch. Everyone else in the state belonged in the general category of "people," second and third class subjects who did not know enough to run the state or even their own affairs.

The King wrote in his own hand on von Roon's letter, "You deserve for your candour my sincerest thanks for all time!" And at numerous places on the margin, he commented, "Agreed" and "Entirely agreed."[18] He withdrew his approval of the reforms for which his liberal ministers, especially Count von Schwerin, had been pressing; but his troubles were not over. A few months later in the same year, 1861, he turned to von Roon again for reassurance against the renewed pressure from the ministers. Von Roon replied in a long letter manifesting the increased strength of his position. He turned from the defensive to the offensive. One of the liberal ministers had

> . . . demanded of Your Majesty to give way to his urging or to dismiss him. Can there be . . . a choice? Your Majesty believes that You cannot dismiss him because the survival of the ministry would thereby be endangered. The disadvantage from it should not be underestimated. But on mature reflection it appears in fact to be tolerable. [It certainly did to him since he had been working for months for this objective.] Your Majesty will by virtue of Your authority appoint other ministers, and if You do not select them from among the leaders of the loudest and most extreme parties, the outcry of the parties will not be worse than it is at present. Your Majesty's pure intentions are known. You wished and wish to govern according to the constitution, but You wished and wish also to rule as a true King of Prussia. In this lies the insufficiency of several of Your present advisers.

[18] *Ibid.*, II, 38-43.

Because You wished to rule constitutionally, You chose men who helped develop the constitutional doctrine in Prussia, whose names therefore had a good repute among their party comrades. But Your Majesty overlooked the fact that they had only the loudest but not at all the most competent voices in the country in their favor, that the consequences of the constitutional doctrine of these men could be harmonized only with the sham-monarchy of Belgium, England, or of Louis Philippe, but not with a genuine Prussian monarchy by the grace of God, with a monarchy in accordance with Your intentions which was rooted in the legal consciousness of Your people. Your Majesty did not wish to break with the past; the legal continuity should be preserved; also an improving hand should be laid upon the traditional. It would not be surprising if these Royal intentions, capable of various meanings, were to be interpreted by everyone according to his own wishes and outlook. In how far an identity of understanding was found between Your Majesty and Your newly chosen advisers remained uncertain from the beginning. When I entered the ministry, I found this lack of clarity; yes, the opposition of opinions and basic views was already plainly marked. Your Majesty had overlooked the fact that the parliamentary antecedents of several of Your advisers imposed party obligations upon them which stood and stand in the most decided opposition to their obligations toward Your Majesty. I often thought that I recognized that Your Majesty's policy would indeed have found the approval of these prejudiced persons if former assertions and party commitments had not made it impossible for them. It was absolutely impossible for them! At the moment in which they had the bona fide wish to follow Your Majesty's political directions, they would have ruined themselves in the eyes of their party; their influence would have been lost; they would have been overwhelmed with insults. They *could* not—and also *would* not do it.

This was von Roon's understanding of political parties. The leaders became such not because the best qualified people chose them but because the loudest shouters favored them; often these leaders would have liked to support the King, but previous public commitments and fear of the party would not allow them. What was the inference? That one could not have absolute monarchy and at the same time a ministry composed of party heads, a view about which von Roon was certainly correct. The further inference to be drawn was that party leaders obtained their position through the aid of the worst elements in the state and were responsible to them, that no respectable and powerful state could possibly be governed by means of a popular representative ministry. The liberals would have had no difficulty in refuting these assertions by citing the example of England; but as long as von Roon was writing for the eyes of the King alone his inferences could not be challenged. One can see why Conservatives preferred the dark of absolutism to the light of representative government: they knew how to intrigue and wield personal influence on a few select individuals; they knew almost nothing about political parties and popular government. These devices were alien to them. Von Roon had a clear eye for the inconsistency of absolutism and party rule, just as Bismarck and subsequent Conservatives had. Von Roon went on:

> That is the situation. It is horrible; it brings the Fatherland to the edge of the abyss. But it should not cause despair.
>
> Your Majesty has two ways out of the confusion of the moment. One is called "giving in," full and complete, unconditional giving in, sacrifice of one's own conscientious conviction, binding the Royal will to the will of the ministers. It leads irrevocably along the path of monarchy by the grace of the people; the special lustre of the Prussian Royal Crown will be extinguished, but in the background will beckon a citizens' crown and Prussia will in the future perhaps compete with Belgium in the material blessings of an unhistorical existence. This would mean a breach with the historical past; the step in *this* direction would be a big one, but it would lead out of the embarrassment of the present on to the smoothest path. All unseasonable friction would cease, the state machine would gain new movement and jubilant approval would not be lacking.

Von Roon failed to mention the fact that the overwhelming numbers of the Prussian people wished, not the extreme form of government here portrayed, but a constitutional monarchy in which they would also have a share in the government. They wished a government responsive to their wishes, one which would keep abreast of the times; they certainly did not desire the alternative which von Roon advocated:

> The other way calls for the assertion of the legally justified Royal will! It loosens the chains of the eagle; the King by the grace of God remains at the head of His people, the center of gravity in the state, ruler in the country, not subjected to ministerial guardianship and parliamentary majorities. There would be no breach with the past, and an improving hand can with wise moderation be applied to the completion of our public life. This way leads at the beginning over a rough path but with all the splendor and all the armed majesty of a glorious battle to the *dominating heights* of life. It is the only way worthy of a Prussian king.

Von Roon was urging his ruler to take steps which would lead to civil war. But it would be a glorious civil war. Just how it would lead "to the *dominating heights* of life" was not any clearer than why "the only way worthy of a Prussian king" was to force his people into a civil war.

> One has attempted to intimidate Your Majesty by the loud cries of the day. The same has occurred in the case of all unfortunate kings of history. Only *because* they believed in ghosts were they frightened and ruined. I beseech our Majesty, do not believe in this cry. Speak *one word* and the phantom will disappear. This word is "change of ministers," not "change of system." You have erred not in your goals but in the tools with which You strive toward that goal. . . . Your Majesty said today that if you dismissed that minister who desired to retire others would follow. I grant this, but I do not recoil from the act. On the contrary, I should thank God on my knees for it if Your Majesty could thereby be free from the chains which now hold captive Your noblest self.

Von Roon assured the King that he did not wish the liberal ministers to be supplanted by leaders of the Conservative party. He wanted no parties represented in the ministry, for "ministers with a parliamentary background are Your Majesty's ruin. Among Your Majesty's officials there are to be found many able persons who are not yet bound to parties. Choose some of these no matter whether they are numbered as members of the Constitutional or of the Conservative party."

This has been the time-honored solution of all absolutists, a government of officials supposedly above parties to execute the king's will and serve the best interests of the land. The system transfers the struggle for power to the entourage of the king, turns it into secret channels, and prevents the public from exercising any control, short of revolution, over their own affairs and from learning about national welfare and about how to achieve it through the only effective means, namely, the participation of all in public life. Von Roon was consistent to the end. The kind of ministry he proposed was the only one suited to the retention of absolutism under a constitution.

The long letter closed with a display of emotion which the writer no doubt felt but which was cleverly calculated to make the deepest impression upon the King.

> How can I justify the boldness of this letter? I answer: With the zeal of a brave soldier who sees his Prince in bonds, of the faithful servant who sees his beloved master on the edge of the abyss. Should one hesitate to break the chains, to spring to the rescue? Certainly not! Even if one were certain to fall. And another thing: today I saw tears in the eyes of my beloved King which filled me with pain and wrath. I had to write Your Majesty what I could not say today because my heart was

in my throat. Believe me, Your Majesty, millions of Your loyal
subjects would feel the same fury and the same pain if they
should be so unfortunate as to know that their faithful King
was in such deep sorrow, in such profound anxiety of conscience.
No one of them would hesitate to offer Your Majesty his life
and blood to free You from the distress which threatens the
country with the heaviest of all losses, with the loss of its King.[19]

The Minister of War was creating imaginary emotional "millions"
of loyal subjects to counterbalance the results of the liberal elections.
This self-styled "brave soldier" and "faithful servant" was springing to
rescue his King from a situation which he was doing his best to make
worse. He had his way, in that the King again refused to sanction the
proposal of bills for developing the constitution, and against the urgent
advice of his liberal ministers he insisted on carrying through his own
autocratic plans for the ceremony of coronation. To his friend Perthes
von Roon wrote in November, 1861:

> The cardinal point of Prussian internal politics is and re-
> mains the military question. Therefore, I cannot, dare not, and
> will not resign now. Nor dare I show myself to be yielding on
> that question. The army, up to this time the sole reliable
> anchor and pillar of our future, should not become confused
> in its self-confidence and in its convictions; otherwise chaos will
> overtake us. To prevent this by preserving the army in its actual
> physical strength and with its inner values is the political part
> of my task. Herein alone I am able to do something with assur-
> ance; therefore I must restrict myself to this. All other dam-
> age which I cannot prevent is not irreparable; but the decay of
> the army would be the ruin of all ordered social relations. God
> give me sound vision, mental alertness, and the will to act.[20]

From the Conservative point of view von Roon was entirely correct
in his estimate. Since the bureaucracy contained many liberals, in an
emergency it could not be trusted. In last analysis the conflict would
have to be decided by force. The attitude of the army would determine
the outcome. If the army were loyal to the King, the latter could act
as he pleased. The army had sworn allegiance, not to the constitution,
but to the King; and von Roon intended it to abide by that oath. Concessions to the Lower House liberals would disgust the army officers,
overwhelmingly Conservative in their politics, and might cause them
to be indifferent toward the outcome of the constitutional conflict.
In their rigid loyalty to the King the officers might be confused about

[19] *Ibid.*, II, pp. 44-49.
[20] *Ibid.*, II, 54-55.

the import of the conflict. Von Roon had to watch the effect of any legislative proposal upon the spirit of the military. He knew that he controlled the decisive force in the controversy, if he could only persuade the King to be adamant and to allow the issues to come to a crisis. He knew that the outcome of this crisis would determine the future character of Prussian society. He was fighting for the preservation of the Old Regime, for rule by the absolute monarch and the nobility. He did not have to be particularly astute to grasp the social significance of the conflict; all the Conservatives and most of the liberals understood it quite early, and all the liberals did so before the conflict ended. Von Roon's historical significance in the crisis arose out of the fact that he spearheaded the Conservative forces in winning back the King to their side and in keeping in safe control the instrument of their power. To von Roon, as to the other Conservatives, and to the liberals, the army problem was not primarily one to determine the power of the state in international affairs, but one to decide the character of Prussian institutions and society.

By the autumn of 1861 von Roon was defending the Conservative party to the King, saying that apart from a few hot-heads it had come to accept the constitution and was ready to preserve and defend it. "Since a reliable and adequate ministerial party does not exist," he wrote the King, "since alliances with the radicals or democrats are out of the question, there remains only the possibility of looking about the Conservative camp for auxiliary troops in order to oppose the expected assault of the revolutionary party." He formulated once more his solution of the situation: "The King cannot resign, the ministry can!"[21] He was preparing the way for the change of ministry and the appointment of Conservatives. Since no liberals of any shade were acceptable, Conservatives alone remained.

The results of the elections in April and May, 1862, turned out worse for the King than before. The liberals were chosen in even larger numbers and the more determined representatives won over the right-wing candidates. Von Roon felt deep scorn for public opinion in any circumstances, and, although he had hoped for at least the election of moderates who might let themselves be pushed and shoved in the Conservative direction, he was not at all disheartened by the results. He had laid plans for a showdown and, writing to Perthes in April, did not believe that the liberals would dare revolt.

[21] *Ibid.*, II, 51-54. See also von Bernhardi, *op. cit.*, III, IV *passim.*

Do you believe that the liberal mass, the vulgar Philistines, love high stakes? I do not believe it. To wish to force the government either to give in or to drown the darling child of the blind monkey-mother "Constitutionalism," perhaps in blood, is a high stake which not even Vincke [an outspoken liberal aristocrat] would risk.[22]

His strategy for handling the new Lower House remained the same as the one he had used on its predecessors.

A vote of no-confidence in the address debate accomplishes nothing; the address will either be accepted or coolly rejected on the basis of the constitutional rights of the King. Or the proposed laws will be rejected. Good. Things remain as they were. Always cold-blooded, urbane manners, rude despatch only in case of pronounced shamelessness, economical in words, no attempt at engaging manners to curry favor; all corrections factual; no quarrels over theories.[23]

In the following month he wrote Perthes, "The stakes are indeed high, *very* high. It is better to bleed to death than to rot away. . . . Prussia must act, make history and finally exchange the role of anvil for that of hammer!" He was reading the history of Strafford and Charles I; but he thought that he had a much better cause than the English ruler. When the Lower House in the autumn rejected by an overwhelming majority the proposal to provide funds for the military reforms and demanded the two-year term of service and the restoration of the former organization of the army, von Roon saw that the crisis had arrived. He had deliberately baited the liberals so as to bring it on;[24] and he was happy. "Nonsense, you win!" he wrote his friend Perthes on September 20, "and if I do no add 'and I must perish,' this is not because I still feel absolutely no desire and no occasion to perish."[25]

What made von Roon so cheerful was the prospect of obtaining for the first time since 1858 a unified ministry supporting the King with initiative, courage, and determination. He had striven since at least 1860 to bring his friend Bismarck into the ministry and had always met with disinclination on the part of his sovereign. He believed that at last the King could find no one else capable of resolving the conflict in an acceptable way. The ruler had tried a mixed ministry of Con-

[22] Von Roon, *op. cit.*, II, 70, 77-78.
[23] *Ibid.*, II, 84.
[24] See von Bernhardi, *op. cit.*, IV, 190-91, 196-97; *Tagesbericht*, Feb. 4, 1862, citing the *Danziger Zeitung*, No. 1150.
[25] Von Roon, *op. cit.*, II, 84, 89, 101, 107.

servatives and liberals and had failed; in 1862 he had tried a cabinet of Conservative ministers not especially active in party affairs and therefore supposedly not committed to a party program and had failed again. He now had reached the point at which he had either to find some person of extraordinary ability to overcome the difficulties or to carry out his frequent threat of abdicating.

The story of the King's conference with Bismarck at Babelsberg in September, 1862, need not be retold. The King undoubtedly mistrusted this Junker and feared that he could not control him. The ruler hated to repudiate his past relations with the right-wing liberals by appointing a person whose name alone indicated the most profound hostility to liberalism and the willingness to use extreme means. The appointment revealed the King's desperate plight. It required the extreme act of the Lower House in rejecting his military reforms to make him willing to entrust his future to this high-handed, brilliantly versatile and determined aristocrat. The King was thinking of the fate of Charles I, as Bismarck was of that of Strafford. Neither was deterred by his thought for both were determined to win.

When Bismarck became Minister President, he had to maintain himself against or between two centers of power, the King and the Lower House of the Landtag. He knew that the King had appointed him to the present position only as an act of despair. He understood also that the Queen had opposed the appointment with all her influence and that she would continue to be hostile. As for the Lower House, he had entered the ministry at the peak, so far, of the conflict between the King and that body, and he had no illusions about the attitude which it would take toward him.

The King proved to be fairly easy to handle. He was so angry at the liberals and so determined to preserve his military reorganization and his royal power that the more ruthlessly Bismarck fought the Lower House while preserving the appearance of constitutionality, the better the King felt. Once Bismarck took up the warfare in earnest against the liberals, the King for the first time since 1860 became cheerful and confident. As we shall see, the gap theory of the constitution pleased him through and through as an interpretation exactly to his liking.

Within a span of five years the King made the transition from aversion to Manteuffel Conservatism to support of mild liberalism to enthusiastic advocacy of a regime much more ruthlessly Conservative than that associated with Manteuffel. His mentality was so limited and his personal belief in his own divine right so strong that he shifted his opinions easily and with a free conscience. When under proper verbal coverage Bismarck flouted the constitution, the King felt him to be entirely justified. When Bismarck used far more coercion in the elections than Manteuffel had done, the King vigorously approved. When Bismarck punished liberal officials, the King found all in order. The shoe was now on the other foot, the King's foot; he did not like the pinching. As a King by grace of God he reacted favorably to any means which flexible minds could make him think constitutional.

The liberals accused Bismarck of exacerbating the conflict with the Lower House in order to hold his ministerial position. The allegation lacked foundation, even though at the time it seemed plausible. Bismarck was so self-confident and so aware of the possibilities of both the internal and the external situation that he actually would have preferred peace with the Lower House, at his price. His offer of co-operation to liberal leaders immediately upon entering the ministry was not bluff. One may doubt his political acumen in conceiving that the liberals would accept; but from another angle it was good politics. If they accepted, they would lose their popular following and would be dependent upon Bismarck. If they refused Bismarck could always assert that he had come into the governmnet as a dove of peace.[26] He had no fear of a solution of the conflict on terms acceptable to both liberals and the King. Under such conditions the latter would have been highly pleased, and Bismarck would have won his favor by a success which no other ministers had been able to achieve.

Bismarck's conceptions of government possessed a quality of realism that was lacking in the views of his Conservative colleagues. He understood something of the complexity of purpose and conditions which government had to serve, and realized that simple, old-fashioned rule by divine right would not satisfy modern needs. He had positive ideas about the structure and functions of government which resembled in part those of liberals and in part those of Conservatives; but he blended them in an original way appropriate to the furtherance of his own power.

Provided the authority of parliament was restricted in favor of the executive, Bismarck regarded the assembly as useful and essential. As early as 1853 he had written to the Prince of Prussia, the future King William I, as follows:

> It is true that the good reputation and the undoubted achievements of the Prussian bureaucracy have led this body to

---

[26] See Zechlin, *op. cit.*, p. 334; von Unruh, *op. cit.*, pp. 220-28.

overestimate itself, to lean to one side, and to endeavor to rule more than is necessary. This disease points to a gap, the filling of which is the task of the representative assembly. The latter provides a counterweight to the presumptuousness of the officials, a correction of their one-sided and impractical theories and a protection against the dangers which arise out of our scholarly educational institutions. In these institutions our officials receive a higher type of education than perhaps in any other state, but this education easily leaves an attitude of skeptical criticism of life which brings disbelief in the field of religion and classical republicanism in the field of politics. If there is added dissatisfaction with the subsequent position, slow advancement and the entire practical results of such a long, tiresome and costly preparation, then one understands how easily our officials can change from servants of the Crown to opponents; for they anticipate an improvement in their own position from changes in the conditions in the country. Against these dangers the Crown and the country find support in the control and counter-activity which are exercised by the representative assembly with respect to the bureaucracy. But to prevent the representative assembly from becoming itself a danger, it should have not a dominant and aggressive character but basically a defensive one.

In 1861 and 1862 Bismarck still believed in the need for a parliamentary assembly, even on the eve of his assuming power as minister; and the fact that he advocated the creation of a popular representative body for Germany and introduced one in the newly unified country in 1867 and 1871 showed that he did not intend to abolish the Prussian Landtag. He meant to use it in realizing his personal, state, and national objectives.[27]

Bismarck's approval of the Landtag as an institution was conditioned by his views on the political ability of the Prussian people and their liberal leaders. He dismissed any notion of a parliamentary government like that in England by citing the absence of a two-party system in Prussia and the lack of an equivalent of the English gentry. The Prussian nobility, he had stated in 1849, had not acquired the qualities of political leadership possessed by the gentry. As for the party system in Prussia, he declared that the liberals were too divided among themselves to be able to govern even if they had the chance. "We are too educated," he asserted in the Budget Commission of the Lower House in September, 1862, "to be able to maintain a constitution, we are too critical; the ability to judge governmental measures, acts of the representative assembly, is too widespread."[28]

[27] Rothfels, *op. cit.*, pp. 343-44, 50, 205.
[28] *Adress-Debatte*, pp. 242-43; Rothfels, *op. cit.*, pp. 25, 32, 206.

In keeping with this conception of parliament Bismarck scorned the liberal deputies. "Even though we are an educated country, doubtless too much so, I am amazed at the political incapacity of our Chambers," he wrote von Roon in July, 1862. "The other parliamentary bodies are certainly no wiser than the flowers of our class system of elections, but they do not have this childish self-confidence with which ours in full nakedness publicly expose their incapacity as a model. How have we Germans acquired the reputation of timid modesty? There is not one of us who does not believe that he understands everything better than all trained specialists from the conduct of war to picking fleas off a dog, whereas in other countries there are many who admit that they understand less than others about many things and remain modest and silent." In a private letter he referred to liberal deputies as "petty,"[29] and during a session of the Lower House he wrote his American friend, John Lothrop Motley:

> I sit again in the House of Phrases and listen to the people talk nonsense. . . . The chatterers can really not govern Prussia; I must oppose them; they have too little wit and too much self-satisfaction, are stupid and audacious. Stupid in a general sense is not the proper expression; the people are individually in part fairly sensible, mostly informed, with standard German university education; but about politics beyond local interests they know as little as we knew as students, yes, even less. In foreign affairs they are, taken individually, mere children; but in all other questions they become childish as soon as they meet in a body—stupid as a mass, understanding as individuals.[30]

Bismarck was addicted to the use of extreme words about opponents, often to statements which went beyond his actual opinion. There can be little doubt, however, that in this instance he expressed his real views.

Evidence was supplied by the strategy which Bismarck evolved for attacking the Lower House. At least as early as 1861 he believed that ultimately "only by a change in our foreign policy can . . . the position of the Crown within the country be freed from the present pressure."[31] In July, 1862, he proposed to von Roon a plan:

> The longer the affair continues, the more the Lower House will sink in public prestige, because it has committed the mistake and will continue to do so of locking its jaws upon trivia,

---

[29] *Ibid.*, pp. 46, 49.

[30] Quoted in Parisius, *von Hoverbeck*, II. 163, from *Politische Briefe Bismarcks* (Berlin, 1889), p. 124.

[31] Rothfels, *op. cit.*, p. 46.

and because it has no speaker who does not augment the boredom of the public. If one can induce them to bite tenaciously into such petty matters as the continuation of the Upper House and begin a conflict about that and delay the settlement of important business, it will be a great good fortune. They will become tired and hope that the government will give out of breath, and the county judges must be alarmed about the cost of substitutes. When they become soft and feel that the country is bored and urgently hope for concessions from the government in order to be freed from their false position, then the time will have come to show them by my appointment that we are far from ready to give up the battle, and that on the contrary we are renewing it with fresh forces. The display of a new battalion in the ministerial order of battle will perhaps make an impression which at present cannot be achieved. Especially if beforehand they are threatened somewhat with phrases about dictation and coup d'état, my old reputation of lighthearted violence will help me, and they will think, "now it begins." Then all those in the center and all half-hearted ones will be inclined to negotiate.[32]

As soon as the country understood the issue, rule by king or rule by parliament, Bismarck believed, it would support the king. Several elections might be necessary before the government obtained a cooperative Lower House, but he did not doubt that ultimately one would be elected. No concessions should be made and no long debates should be held with the liberals, as they would only encourage opposition. "Patient and persistent efforts at understanding," Bismarck wrote, "will alone lead us through the straits between the Scylla of Kurhessian conditions in the country and the Charybdis of parliamentary rule."[33]

The plan of action is most revealing of Bismarck's mental limitations. The imputation to the liberal deputies of low motives, such as fear of material loss, reflected his usual slight esteem for human beings. In his failure to realize that questioning a parliament's budgetary authority would arouse the deputies to action as no other issue would, he showed such lack of understanding of parliamentary government that one can appreciate the liberal deputy Virchow's remark that Bismarck was acquainted with Russia but not England. His plan manifested the jaunty nonchalance of a Junker concocting a scheme to suit his own measure.

Needless to say, the plan did not work. Bismarck's appointment did not discourage the Lower House or make it ripe for compromise.

[32] *Ibid.*, pp. 48-49.
[33] See Zechlin, *op. cit.*, pp. 257-59.

His procedure did not cause the conflict to degenerate into quarrels over details with the result of alienating the public. In fact, the more Bismarck tried his strategy on internal affairs, the more he consolidated the public against him. He was manifestly not equal to many liberal leaders in debate on constitutional issues. The fact was virtually admitted when he replied to Virchow with personal insults, his usual recourse when cornered. He maintained himself in office simply because he had the backing of the King and the military and because the bureaucracy continued to function for him as it had for the liberal ministers, for Manteuffel, and before 1848 for Hohenzollern absolutism. He won out ultimately because he carried through the unification of Germany, an objective so ardently desired by the liberals that in order to attain it they were willing in internal affairs to swallow defeat.

After having served as Minister President for a few weeks Bismarck perceived that the constitution offered many possibilities of employing terror and enticements, and he was already playing with the idea of a coup d'état in case of necessity.[34] In the following July he urged his Minister of Interior to revive the notorious Hinkeldey regime of the Manteuffel period by banning particular individuals from Berlin, especially writers. The further the conflict progressed, the more ruthless Bismarck became. In accordance with his plan of the summer of 1862 he tried to stir the liberals to fight on a series of continually new issues, some of major, some of minor significance, but all useful, he thought, to wear down the endurance of the Lower House and its supporters in the country. The first opportunity presented itself in the action of the House of Lords. When the Lower House rejected the government budget in September, 1862, the House of Lords refused to follow suit and passed instead the government's original budget. Then each side accused the other of unconstitutional action. In November the government tried to mobilize the provincial Landtags against the Lower House, only to find that even they refused to be exploited for that purpose. In September of the next year after many threats the government required officials who served as deputies to pay the cost of their substitutes and withheld the amount from their salaries; since 1848 the costs had been covered out of public funds.[35]

Each side advanced legal arguments in its favor. When the Lower House in January, 1863, voted an address to the King accusing the ministers of unconstitutional acts, Bismarck declared that he would

[34] Zechlin, op. cit., p. 342.
[35] Parisius, von Hoverbeck, II, 107, 128, 178.

not advise the King to accept the document. The Lower House replied that this attitude violated the constitutional right of Prussian subjects to petition their sovereign. Bismarck countered that "there is a limit to what a Prussian monarch can listen to."[36] The liberal majority severely criticized the government for signing a convention with Russia agreeing to assist the latter in suppressing the Polish rebellion. The government accused the majority of infringing upon the King's constitutional right to declare war and make peace and to conduct foreign relations. The liberals were equally furious at the ministry's attempt to prevent the Lower House from expressing its views about an issue so important for the entire state. In May, Minister von Roon lost his temper in the Lower House, whether deliberately or not would be hard to say. He began to make personal remarks about certain deputies and was called to order by the president of the chamber. The minister refused to be called to order. He swore that the authority of the president did not extend to the ministers, that the constitution entitled a minister to speak at any time he wished. He accused the House of endeavoring to impose censorship upon the ministers and of forcing them under parliamentary control. The president of the chamber, with the full support of the liberal majority, asserted that he did have authority as presiding officer to enforce parliamentary rules and that the minister must abide by them. He denied that the constitutional rights of the ministers were involved and countered with the assertion that the constitution gave to the Lower House the right to organize itself and to establish its own rules of conduct. The liberals denounced the ministry for trying to force the Lower House to obey its orders and feared that if the ministers should maintain their claim to be free from any control by the president of the chamber they would wreck the order of business of that body. Each accused the other of violating the constitution, of trying to extend authority over the other.

The ministry regarded the incident as an excellent opportunity to stir up a maximum amount of trouble over a minor affair. It declared that its members would not appear again in the Lower House until the latter had receded from its position. The liberals refused and appealed to the King, who completely vindicated the ministry's most extreme position in a document that possessed all the characteristics of Bismarck's style. When the Lower House in turn declared to the King that it could not work with this ministry, the King utilized the occasion to close the session and send the deputies home. The affair

[36] *Adress-Debatte*, pp. 5-7; Parisius, *von Hoverbeck*, II, 124-25.

suited Bismarck's prescription exactly, a fight over a matter of no great intrinsic consequence which the public would not understand, thus causing general irritation and disgust. This kind of incident would lead, according to Bismarck's strategy, to an alienation of the public from the liberal Lower House and would help prepare conditions for a new election.[37]

The Landtag was closed on May 27, 1863. On the first of June the ministry began a campaign by which it expected to restore order. The statement of program which it published in the official papers offered such a striking example of ministerial hypocrisy that it deserves to be quoted. First came the justification:

> In Prussia it is something unheard of and entirely unnatural for such a division to occur. Among us there exists no opposition between monarchy and popular freedom, between army and citizens, between the authority of the King and genuine progress. Prussia's Kings have always cultivated and furthered progress in all areas of civic right and welfare.

After having denied by fiat the existence of any conflict between Lower House and government, after having denied by implication the occurrence of the Revolution of 1848, after having established harmony among all Prussians, the ministry explained in kindly terms what it proposed to do in order to restore order to a country already in perfect order.

> Therefore it will certainly need only a time of calm, only a soothing of that unnatural excitement in order to revive once more the traditional spirit of loyalty, the old unity between prince and people, in order to return to complete understanding between the government and the people's representation and thereby to a blessed new development of our constitutional life.

Only a slight controversy existed, the ministry soothingly explained, between the ministry and a Lower House which had little or no support in the country and which would once more return to the happy state of constitutional development as soon as the unnatural excitement was overcome.

> This is the meaning and the purpose of the most recent measures. The government will thereby exercise a policy of pacification and reconciliation, not a policy of anger or of despotic passion. It will use the severity, which it has momentarily adopted, only in the spirit of healing, and in legal discipline, not in the spirit of revenge or of reprisal.

[37] See the pertinent documents in *Die Innere Politik*, pp. 184-95; see also Parisius, *von Hoverbeck*, II, 137, 155-59.

When the government succeeds in restoring peace to the spirits and in finally quieting again the conflict of party passions, it hopes that the results will soon show that with the restoration of order, legality, and moderation it has made possible and again assured the further development of our constitutional liberties.[38]

The few liberal deputies were assumed to be trouble makers, rather than the King, who demanded a huge increase in the army budget, or the ministry, which proposed to rule by interpreting the constitution out of existence. The few liberals were to be handled by the King, a wise father who punished his dear children for their own good. The limited intelligence of the subject was to be enabled by a few stern measures to recover its natural equanimity. Then constitutional freedom would be restored, that is, freedom to reorganize the army in a way which the people did not want, freedom to collect taxes and expend money without the consent of the people's representatives, freedom for the King to rule by divine right under a constitution.

How should peace be restored? The government plan of action had already been initiated as soon as Bismarck became Minister President. At that time the Minister of Interior had sent a secret order to Police President von Bernuth:

The present situation makes necessary the duty of the Royal officials to devote special attention to the expressions of public life and to act with decision against punishable deeds which concern public order. Under the guise of constitutional loyalty and in apparent defence of existing fundamental laws, the manifestations contrary to the laws are increasing. There repeatedly occurs in direct or concealed fashion a violation of the respect for His Majesty the King and in the same way the loosening of discipline in the army is being aimed at. Moreover, there exist numerous provocations to hate and despise the institutions of the state with respect to the sovereign power. . . .

The police were ordered especially to watch the political newspapers and to take all legal steps against them. They should keep under close observation all societies, check on all public meetings, and prevent political associations from entering into contact with each other.[39]

On May 27, 1863, the Landtag was closed. On June 1 the government issued a decree curbing freedom of the press. The government recognized that the press law of 1851 did not permit such an act; it also recognized that since 1860 it did not have the power to apply to

[38] *Die Innere Politik*, pp. 206-07.
[39] *Preussisches Geheim Staatsarchiv.* Pr. Br. Rep. 30. Berlin C. Pol. Präsid. Tit. 94, Lit. P. 377, Vol. II.

the press the concessionary authority that it exercised with respect to other business. Nonetheless, it sought and found means to curb the press during the election campaign, and it now exercised its power ruthlessly. In July, 1863, it declared it to be "the urgent and unavoidable duty of the government" to take all steps to calm "the passionate and unnatural excitement which in recent years as a result of party activity has seized hold of all spirits." To that end it proposed to restrict "the exciting and confusing effects of the daily press." It accused the press of having a large share in "undermining all bases of orderly state life, of religion, and morality." It admitted that the Conservative press was unable to stem these attacks, for it lacked the physical resources and did not have the attention of the public. The press law of 1851 gave insufficient justification for curbing the excesses, it said, since the newspapers were expert at including articles the meaning of which was sufficiently clear to their readers without violating the letter of the law. The government changed the basis for legal action against the press by asserting that not individual articles or statements but "the entire attitude of a paper over a longer period of time" should be used in deciding whether a paper should be banned. Press cases should be decided not by the judiciary but by administrative officials. Knowing that journals from other German states also brought the contamination of liberalism into Prussia, the government assumed the power, in spite of the clause in the press law of 1851 prohibiting such an act, to forbid the entry of foreign newspapers which it considered dangerous.

In justification of its action the government referred to Articles 27 and 63 of the constitution. Article 27 guaranteed the freedom of the press and prohibited the introduction of a censorship. It stated that every other restriction of freedom of the press should be imposed only by law. These constitutional clauses did not cause any concern to a government bent on violating them. The ministry maintained that by its decree "the free exchange of opinions which the constitution guarantees will in reality not be restricted. . . . Since the reprehensible excesses of an unrestrained press will be curbed," it declared, "the freedom of the press will be restored to the foundation of morality and self-respect on which alone it can prosper and permanently strengthen itself."[40]

Just how the prohibition of freedom of the press achieved freedom of the press was a riddle which may have been crystal clear to the Con-

---

[40] *Die Innere Politik*, pp. 195-98.

servatives, but to no one else. Article 63 regulated the conditions under which a decree could be promulgated. It read:

> In so far as the chambers are not in session and under the responsibility of the entire ministry, decrees which do not violate the constitution can be promulgated with the power of law only in case the preservation of public safety or the settlement of an unusual emergency makes them urgently necessary. These are to be laid immediately before the chambers for approval at their next session.

The government had dissolved the Lower House before it had issued the decree, for it knew that the House would never approve the measure. Then it called the time "an unusual emergency," although no rebellion or civil war threatened. Nothing was occurring except peaceful electioneering with the liberals severely condemning the government. It was assumed that the government would lay a bill before the new Landtag in the autumn for approval of its action; but in the meantime the government would have used this arbitrary measure, a clear violation of the constitution, to cripple the liberals in the election campaign. The execution of the act was entirely partisan; only liberal and democratic papers suffered, while the Conservative ones indulged in the most vulgar vituperation against the opponents of the government without being molested.

The liberals immediately declared the decree to be unconstitutional. The law faculties of the universities of Göttingen, Heidelberg, and Kiel issued a public statement condemning it as a violation of the law of the land. The Crown Prince publicly dissociated himself from the act.[41] When the Landtag reconvened in November after the new elections, the Lower House immediately condemned the government action and refused to approve a bill to make the press decree legal and permanent. In analyzing the ministry's justification of the decree, Deputy Gneist declared that the ministry regarded as a state of emergency that which in the rest of Europe passed as constitutional government. The embarrassment of the government was never an emergency for the country, he continued, and he condemned the decree as the "most extreme dictatorial measure since the introduction of the constitution." He accused the government of curbing only the liberal press.

> You speak of the falsification of the truth, of the demoralization which the press spreads. Yes, there is such and it continues.

[41] See, among others, Parisius, *von Hoverbeck*, II, 165-66; R. Haym, *Das Leben Max Dunckers* (Berlin, 1891), pp. 298-99.

The hateful falsification of the truth, the malignings, the summons to revolution, to a violation of the constitution, these continue; but they continue in the press which is found in the camp of the Royal government, in the press which dares to call itself the governmental press, in the press which has not been warned a single time by the presidents of the twenty-six regional administrations. There lies the root of the evil in which we find ourselves.

That the government had succeeded in curbing sharply the oppositional press not even the liberals denied. That it had gained its purpose of calming the "unnatural" excitement in the country could not have been maintained even by the government. As the liberal deputy von Carlowitz asserted, "Figures show that even though the press is not entirely silent, it is nonetheless half silent. Still, the people have understood what is to their interest and have re-elected those deputies in whom they have confidence."[42]

Although the Lower House in the autumn made short work of the ministry's bill to legalize the press decree, the government continued to harass and curb the opposition press by administrative measures. Bismarck had no conception of a free press; he regarded the press as an instrument of political power to be used along with the bureaucracy, the army, and all other available means. The conflict for freedom continued.[43]

The decree of June 1 abolishing for the time being the freedom of the press led to another restrictive measure. One of the main forces of the liberals' political support lay in the personnel of the town and city councils. These councils in urban centers in all parts of Prussia frequently discussed the conflict occurring between the government and the Lower House and passed resolutions or sent petitions and deputations to the House or to the King condemning the government's actions and supporting the liberal majority of the House. They were deeply alarmed by the decree of June 1 on the press, and they denounced it as unconstitutional. On June 6 the government therefore took a further step characteristic of its authoritarian regime by forbidding the urban councils to discuss or pass judgment on "affairs of the state constitution, of the Landtag and of general politics." It restricted their deliberations exclusively to local affairs as the only objects legally within their jurisdiction, and it commanded the com-

---

[42] See the debates in the Lower House, Nov. 19, 1863, in the *St. B.*; see also *Aktenstücke zur Neuesten Geschichte Preussens 1863*, Vol. I *(Verwarnungen)*, No. 1—June, July; No. 2—August, September, October (Berlin, 1863).

[43] See *Die Innere Politik*, pp. 248-57.

munal authorities to take all measures "with all decisiveness" necessary to suppress these "illegal endeavors."[44] Moreover, it advised the King not to receive delegations from the town councils seeking to lay their views on state affairs before him.[45] Thereby, the Bismarck government was endeavoring to restrict participation in political life as sharply as possible. It tried to suppress one of the best organized and most vocal centers of liberal opposition and preclude any possibility of real and effective organization by the town councils, representative assemblies in themselves, for resistance to the government.

At the time that it isolated the King from petitions and delegations from liberals, the government encouraged the Conservatives to use the same means for expressing their devotion to the King and his government. The King was eager to receive every such manifestation of loyalty. The aristocrats headed the procession, but handworkers, peasants, and pastors were found who would also participate. The most famous, or notorious, expression of loyalty was sent to the King by peasants of the village of Steingrund in Silesia. The sentiments may be regarded as typical of this kind of governmental support. "We, Your Majesty's loyal subjects, again confront the elections to the Lower House. Since Your Majesty calls, we shall come as good Silesians are used to doing, whether into military battle or into election battle. If it were possible, we should elect no one else than our King and Lord." Since this was not possible, the petitioners asked the King to tell them for whom they should vote; and the petition ended with the promise to vote for those who supported devotedly the King and the government.[46]

Since Bismarck disliked and mistrusted officials, it was to be expected that he would be doubly hostile to a Lower House in which a large percentage of members was bureaucratic. Under the Manteuffel regime the Conservatives had developed the system of using the bureaucracy for purposes of political control. While still Prince of Prussia, the King had objected strongly to coercion of an official to support the Conservatives; but now that his policies and his ministry had become the object of attack, he swung to the other extreme and approved completely Bismarck's efforts to force the officials into political line.[47]

[44] *Die Innere Politik*, pp. 199-200.
[45] See Abg. H., *St. B.*, Nov. 23, 1863; I, 133. See as an example, J. Stein, *Geschichte der Stadt Breslau im 19. Jahrhundert*, pp. 603-04.
[46] Abg. H., *St. B.*, Nov. 11, 1863; I, 14-15.
[47] See *Die Innere Politik*, pp. 149-50.

The government's position with respect to the political attitude of officials was stated by the Minister of Justice and the Minister of Interior in orders to their respective personnel. Each aimed at the same objective, but because of the difference in the nature of their tenure justice officials could not be treated as arbitrarily as administrative officials. The order from the Minister of Interior read as follows:

> The loyal and self-sacrificing devotion of the Royal officials to the Crown is a foundation pillar upon which the Prussian state is gloriously built. The government of His Majesty the King must rely on this unconditioned devotion all the more completely since the introduction of free institutions has assigned to the bureaucracy in the main the task of supporting the constitutional rights of the Throne. For that purpose it is indispensable that throughout the administration unity of spirit and will, decision, and energy appear. The authority of the Royal rule dare not be weakened and shaken in public opinion by conflicts within its organs, and Royal officials may not misuse the prestige which their position gives them for the furtherance of political endeavors which run contrary to the views and the will of the government.[48]

The circular order meant that the government was determined to force the officials not merely to execute state business but to support the government politically. This fact had been frankly explained by Minister of Interior von Eulenburg in the Lower House during the January debate on the address to the throne.

> We do not doubt that all officials are loyal to the constitution. But we have had to note in the events of recent years that the more sharply the political controversies come to the fore, the more must the government muster its means in the same way as individuals who stand at the head of the parties, and it would sin against its duty if it did not attempt to gain victory according to its possibilities and with the use of all its means.
>
> In the Lower House you also call together your members in every serious debate. You recommend discipline. You call attention in all newspapers to the view that individuals must submit to the decisions of the whole, that they have to place restrictions upon themselves in order not to endanger the success of the whole.
>
> Now, Gentlemen, how will you question the right of the government to do that which you claim as a parliamentary assembly; how will you deny that the government cannot possibly rule if it does not assure that unity of thought is evident in the administration and that the power of execution is not broken?

---

[48] *Die Innere Politik*, p. 132; *Adress-Debatte*, p. 22.

Prior to the introduction of our present constitution the constitutional guarantees of the country lay in the laws and in certain institutions among which the bureaucracy also belonged. The officials were at that time, more or less, not merely the bearers of the Royal power, but also those through whom the King and the government ascertained the opinions of the country. Since no great obstacles were to be overcome, one could be more lenient toward political pronouncements of the officials and request the freest expression of opinions from them as something within their duty. Today the voice of the people has been placed in another body; it lies in you, in these Houses; and the official has fundamentally another responsibility. He must stand by the government. It is impossible to allow an official to say: today I am an official and tomorrow a free man, a deputy, then I will be again an official.

I say, an official who actively follows a line which contradicts that of the government, who opposes the government in a noticeably agitational manner—with such an official the government cannot govern. If it must take measures to get rid of him, the action is not to be blamed upon the government but upon the official.

In other countries it is customary that when a change of ministries occurs, so and so many officials are dismissed or have the tact to resign. In our country this does not occur: one even has the impression at times that certain officials demand that in case of their opposition the ministry must retire. Such conditions are untenable, and assuredly times were better when one spoke of Prussian officialdom as distinguished not merely by intelligence but also by tact. Be convinced that we shall handle all personnel questions *sine ira et studio*. It will not occur to us to wish to eliminate an official merely because he does not please us or is uncomfortable for us. We investigate carefully whether his external behavior is in keeping with his position as state official; and if we find the two out of harmony with one another, we shall take steps against him . . . with all the means at our disposal, even though he appears personally to be worthy of respect or is in close personal relations with us. We take no pleasure in such proceedings, but we regard them as our unavoidable duty.[49]

Acting according to plan, the government shifted liberal officials from positions in the Western provinces or from larger towns to the rural areas of the Eastern provinces, those areas of the purest possible Junkerism, areas where the curse of industrialism, a free press, and an active civic and cultural life had not yet fallen. A liberal deputy estimated in 1878 that during the period of conflict the government had

[49] *Adress-Debatte*, pp. 234-35.

disciplined by transfer or dismissal more than a thousand officials, among them twenty deputies of whom nine were judges.[50]

Since many liberal deputies were officials, it was to be expected that they would be well acquainted with their legal rights and would fight the government's policy. Few of them were administrative offcials, because these, being most exposed to government pressure, had kept out of leading political positions. The judiciary supplied most of those deputies from the ranks of the bureaucracy; supposedly secure from governmental chicanery, judges could take an independent stand in politics. Even they had to defend themselves, for the government had its own interpretation of the law on judicial tenure, an interpretation which it concocted to suit its needs.

In the Lower House the deputies subjected the government's policy to thorough denunciation. Deputy Waldeck, a former judge of the highest court, cited the paragraph from the general law on the judiciary by which the Minister of Justice claimed the power to force his subordinates to refrain from actively working for the liberals. The paragraph read as follows:

> Also the private life . . . and the conduct of the ministers and subalterns of the courts must be the object of attention by the presidents. And although it cannot be expected of or permitted to them to interfere in the private and family affairs of the judicial officials subordinate to them, they must nonetheless take care that these officials lead in public an orderly and respectable life, carefully avoid all excesses and baseness, which would arouse anger and offend the public and dishonor the dignity of the office, and in general do or begin nothing whereby the prestige due them and necessary to the exercise of the office is endangered.

Deputy Waldeck stated that the minister found aggressive party activity for the liberals bad, but that for the party supporting the ministry good and worthy. He demanded the same personal rights for justice officials as for anyone else, and among them he included the right to be active in politics. He condemned the minister's order as another violation of the constitution, another attempt to restore absolutism.[51]

Deputy von Vincke brought out the fact that the Minister of Justice was aiming to force the state's attorneys to be Conservative. Since those officials monopolized the power to bring criminal action

---

[50] Parisius, *von Hoverbeck*, II, 104-05, 176; Zechlin, *op. cit.*, pp. 347-51.
[51] *Adress-Debatte*, pp. 22-25.

against an individual, one could imagine to what extent in a police state like Prussia they could be used to hound persons politically active against the government. Deputy von Vincke stated that such a condition had obtained under no previous government, not even under absolutism.[52]

Deputy von Bockum-Dolffs spoke for the administrative officials of whom he himself was one. Countering the Minister of Interior's accusation of their trying to be at one moment an official and at the next a free deputy, he declared: "I will abide by the constitution as a deputy in the same way that I do as official." He accused the government of overstepping its legal rights.[53] His assertion was elaborated by Deputy Lette, who had grown old in bureaucratic service.

> The old legal teachings of Germany which up to the most recent time were assumed to be inviolable bases of German state law hold that an official is in no respect subordinate to his superior or has to resign his position because of his political and religious opinions, but that of course he has to administer his office loyally—the judge loyal in the sense and according to the letter of the laws, the administrative official strictly and loyally following also the instructions from the appropriate higher officials. But . . . how very much apart from these are religious and political convictions, how little the freedom and independence of them is conditioned by the requirement of fulfilling one's official duty can be seen from an article in the constitution the validity of which the Minister of the Interior has questioned with respect to officials, namely, that no one can be made responsible for his vote in the legislative chamber and for his opinions expressed there. According to my understanding the declaration of the minister has gone so far that he demands of the officials that they should as deputies and as officials represent and support identical political and religious views.[54]

The minister had said nothing about religious conformity; that practice of the Manteuffel era had at least not yet been restored. But Deputy Lette correctly interpreted the minister's remarks with respect to politics. This part aroused Deputy Immermann to speak.

> These measures are objectively immoral because if executed they would bring about a complete demoralization and debasement of the official class. In every person, also in every official, there is a moral kernel; and in the person this moral kernel should above all be loyalty to convictions. Shame and disgrace to the person who recognizes something as completely right and

[52] *Ibid.*, p. 181.
[53] *Adress-Debatte*, p. 238.
[54] *Ibid.*, p. 271.

necessary and does not defend it in word and deed; shame and disgrace above all to officials, shame and disgrace to the judge, whose occupation indicates to him that if he has recognized the right he should under no conditions deviate from the recognition of it but should manifest it in actions. . . . It is a vain delusion to speak of a Christian state devoid of legality, and it is a vain delusion to wish to be Christian without first and above all abiding by the law.[55]

The government did not bother to answer the liberal arguments. It merely asserted the contrary opinions and depended upon its power to enforce them. The liberals were correct when they said that the ministers had different moral standards, different constitutional and political principles from them, that they spoke a different language.

The conflict over the political rights of officials illuminated the difficulties which arose out of the newness of the constitutional system. Each side could claim to be in part correct, but each side pushed its claim to an extreme—the government to the extreme of complete political subordination on the part of the deputy-official, the opposition to the extreme of complete political freedom. It did seem paradoxical that a person who in his official capacity was subordinate to a government should upon election as deputy fight that government tooth and nail. Each side was trying to utilize its position to enhance its strength. It must be said, however, that from the standpoint of moral principles the government was sinning by its endeavor to corrupt the freedom of political personality of its officials in order to transform them into instruments for executing political orders. The liberals did not break any comparable moral ideal. The government accused the liberal officials of wrecking orderly government; the officials aptly and justly replied, as Bockum-Dolffs did, that if the government would act constitutionally the public business would be transacted without any difficulty. While each side claimed to be acting in accordance with the constitution, there can be no doubt that the government was violating both the letter and the spirit of that document and that it aimed at victory irrespective of the constitution. It refused to compromise on any but its own terms. It intimated that if the military conflict could be settled all other controversies could be arranged.[56] It did so while employing every constitutional and unconstitutional means at its disposal for crushing the liberal opposition.

[55] *Ibid.*, pp. 273-75.
[56] *Die Innere Politik*, pp. 237-38.

Each side accused the other of a series of violations of the constitution. The liberals declared that evil begets evil, that once the constitution was violated, it would have to be violated again and again in order to defend the first breach. The ministry accused the Lower House of breaking every clause of the constitution[57] which the liberals accused the ministry of violating. The conflict became superficially a matter of name-calling. Actually it involved the fundamentals of government. In late 1862 Bismarck had coolly advised the liberals not to take the conflict so seriously. By the autumn of 1863 he was waging a fight for popular support against the liberals. His plan had called for a process of softening up the opposition, culminating in an appeal to the country in a new election. That election was held in October and November, 1863. To understand it adequately, one must analyze the liberals' interpretation of the constitution and the government's counter-arguments during the critical year of 1863.

"Absolutism, the noble genuine absolutism," wrote the *Königsberg Hartungsche Zeitung* on April 17, 1862, "has the objective of training the people to the point at which it can cease to exist; for at a certain stage of the people's development absolutism becomes impossible. When industry, trade, the arts, and knowledge have advanced so far that they will not endure arbitrary measures, even well-intentioned ones, then in the course of natural development the constitutional state replaces absolutism. We have reached that point." The liberals were striving to make that "course of natural development" a reality.

Irrespective of party affiliation the liberals shared a common conception of the constitution. They expressed loyalty to King and constitution; they wished "a strong monarchy of the Hohenzollerns and the full assertion of the rights guaranteed the people." They requested "a constitutional, just, and liberal government and the development of the constitution in that spirit by organic laws." The only difference between the right-wing liberals, from whose platform the above quotations are taken, and the left-wing Progressive party arose over the fact that the latter demanded more initiative on the part of the Lower House and the liberals in the ministry. "We think," stated the Progressive party in September, 1861, "that the new Lower House must take a forceful initiative and must decidedly use its constitutional powers to assure an independent and vigorous public life alongside a strong government, a progressive development along with order."[58]

---

[57] *Die Innere Politik*, pp. 177-178.
[58] Felix Salomon, *Die Deutschen Parteiprogramme* (Leipzig and Berlin, 1912), I, 75-83, 87-88.

The liberals recognized that they had been living in a state of doubtful, undeveloped constitutionalism. They knew that they owed their re-entry into the government in 1858 to the ruler. "The present liberal conditions of administration," wrote a Berlin correspondent to the *Magdeburger Zeitung*, "the mild practice of the government, etc., should not deceive one about Prussia and its existing legislation, namely, that Prussia is an absolutist state in which there are some exceptions sanctioned by the constitution. Apart from these exceptions there is no state in Europe in which the state has such extensive power as in Prussia."[59]

By early 1861 the Lower House of the Landtag was inclined to push the center of power from the ruler and his ministers to the body of representatives of the population. The Progressive party took the lead in bringing about this shift.

When the editor of the liberal *Königsberg Hartungsche Zeitung* in November, 1861, tallied up the accomplishments of the New Era government, he noted that some reforms had been accomplished in the economic field, that almost nothing had been done for intellectual and spiritual needs, and that

> . . . in the stony and weedy field of constitutional and legal matters even these precarious and doubtful achievements become ever scarcer and more questionable. We manifestly approach in it the main stronghold of the opponents and feel at every step its laming, dominating influence. One cannot entirely deny the good intentions of the ministry and its dependents. . . . But our ministers remain simply "royal servants."[60]

The liberals recognized that the constitution was full of gaps and uncertainties. That document had been preserved after 1848 by a Conservative government, but modified and conditioned in such a way as to satisfy its wishes. A typical method had been to retain a clause with a liberal content but to make its execution dependent upon future legislation. That legislation would then never be passed, and the *status quo ante* would be restored. Another method had been to cancel the liberal clauses by temporary or transitional clauses added at the end of the constitution and never repealed. Loose phraseology had been employed which could be interpreted according to the will of the government, or one clause had not quite agreed with another one and was subject to interpretation by the government. What had proved to be of especial use to the Conservative government

[59] *Tagesbericht*, No. 1, Jan. 2, 1862.
[60] *Königsberg Hartungsche Zeitung*, No. 261.

had been the omission of terms in the constitution to cover certain fundamental issues; thereby wide freedom of action by the dominating authority had been retained.

When the liberals demanded the development of the constitution and the establishment of a state ruled by law, they meant the abolition of the Conservative methods of preserving absolutism and caste and the passage of laws making the constitution actually effective in a liberal sense. They understood that constitutional development required as a minimum the introduction of reforms of provincial, county, and local government and of ministerial responsibility. They knew that these innovations would mean the transfer of political power from the forces of the Old Regime, the absolute monarch and the conservative and military nobility, to those of the developing liberal society of the middle class and its allies in the other social groups. They recognized that a constitutional conflict involved a social conflict and entailed basic institutional changes in Prussia. They regarded these changes as a continuation of the achievements in favor of freedom during the Stein-Hardenberg period, changes called for by the constitution.[61]

The constitutional crisis arose over the fact that while the government demanded military reforms of such a nature as decidedly to strengthen the power of the Conservative nobility and the military, it failed to put through a single major constitutional reform desired by the liberals. The latter found themselves in the quandary of being expected to supply an enormous increase of men and money for strengthening the most reactionary institution in the state while nothing was done in return to release the energy of the people by liberalizing the political institutions. Since absolutism and caste remained in supreme control of those institutions or at least in a position to obstruct change, the liberals perceived no reason why they should strengthen even more the position of their opponents by acquiescing in the military reforms, especially as they would have to bear the cost and provide the manpower. The constitutional conflict broke out in 1862 over this military issue.

The conflict centered on the question of financial power. "The money is in our pockets," asserted the Progressive party in an election appeal of April, 1862, "and the government always needs more money. It cannot obtain new taxes until our representatives approve, and the latter will only approve when they are convinced that the funds will

[61] *Ibid.*, Nov. 7, 1861.

be used for the benefit of the country."[62] What would happen in case the Lower House refused to grant the money requested by the executive for maintaining permanently a military reorganization for which funds had twice before been granted on a temporary basis? As soon as the issue was joined, it drew into question other clauses of the constitution than those about financial power, until it appeared that the entire constitution was at stake. Although practically all liberals refused consistently to admit it in words, the conflict involved the issue of whether the King or parliament should have ultimate authority. Each side phrased the issue in its own terms, and each swore that it was being constitutional and denied the accusations of the other. In reality the liberals were interpreting the constitution in a forward-looking direction, and the King and the Conservatives in a backward-looking way. Each was defending a conception of the constitution which the other refused to recognize.

When Bismarck took office the Lower House had just rejected the government's budget and passed a budget of its own, eliminating the items for the military reorganization. How should the situation be met? The House of Lords immediately rejected the revised budget and approved the original one, and Bismarck's government continued to collect taxes and to expend the public money for the military reforms as well as for all usual purposes—irrespective of the lack of a legal budget. When the liberal majority of the Lower House condemned this action as a violation of the constitution and proposed to appeal against the ministry to the King, Bismarck responded with a brief but complete statement of his interpretation of the constitution. He adopted what was known as the gap theory, first formulated in an article in the semi-official *Stern Zeitung* in the previous summer.[63] He supplemented it with arguments and assertions of power of his own.

Bismarck initiated the defence of his views about the constitution by an attack. He declared that the Lower House was fighting the Crown for supremacy, that it was claiming rights which it did not possess. He formulated the practical significance of its demands as transferring the constitutional rights of the Crown to the majority of the Lower House.

> You clothe this demand in the form of a declaration that the constitution is violated in so far as the Crown and the Upper House do not bow to your will. You direct the accusation of

[62] *Volkszeitung*, April 24, 1862 (Supplement).
[63] *Die Innere Politik*, pp. 26-28.

violation of the constitution against the ministry, not against the Crown whose loyalty to the constitution you place beyond all doubt. . . . You know as well as anyone in Prussia that the ministry acts in Prussia in the name of and on behalf of His Majesty the King, and that in this sense it has executed those acts in which you see a violation of the constitution. You know that in this connection a Prussian ministry has a different position from that of the English. An English ministry, let it call itself what it will, is a parliamentary one, a ministry of the parliamentary majority; but we are ministers of His Majesty the King. I do not reject the separation of the ministers and the Crown, as you have assumed in the address . . . in order to protect the ministry behind the shield of the Crown. We do not need this protection; we stand firmly on the ground of our good rights. I repudiate the separation because by it you conceal the fact that you find yourself not in conflict with the ministry, but in conflict with the Crown for domination over the country.

Article 99 reads, if I remember correctly: all income and expenditure of the state must be estimated each year in advance and brought together in a state budget.

If it followed that "the latter will be fixed annually by the Lower House," then you were entirely correct in your complaints in the address, for the constitution would be violated. But the text of Article 99 continues: The budget will be fixed annually by law. Now, Article 62 states with incontrovertible clarity how a law is passed. It says that for the passage of a law, including a budget law, agreement of the Crown and of both Houses is necessary. That the Upper House is justified in rejecting a budget approved by the Lower House but not acceptable to the Upper is, moreover, emphasized in the article.

Each of these three concurrent rights is in theory unlimited, one as much as the other. If agreement among the three powers is not reached, the constitution is lacking in any stipulation about which one must give in. In earlier discussions one passed over this difficulty with ease; it was assumed according to analogy of other countries, whose constitution and laws, however, are not published in Prussia and have no validity here, that the difficulty could be settled with the two other factors giving in to the Lower House, that if agreement over the budget is not reached between the Crown and the Lower House, the Crown not only submits to the Lower House and dismisses the ministers who do not have the confidence of the Lower House, but in case of disagreement with the Lower House the Crown also forces the Upper House by mass appointments to place itself on the plane of the Lower House. In this way, to be sure, the sovereign and exclusive rule of the Lower House would be established; but such exclusive rule is not constitutional in Prussia. The constitution upholds the balance of the three legislative powers on all questions, also with respect to the budget. None of these powers can force the others to give way. The constitution therefore points to the

way of compromise for an understanding. A statesman of constitutional experience has said that the entire constitutional life
is at every moment a series of compromises. If the compromise
is thwarted in that one of the participating powers wishes to enforce its own views with doctrinaire absolutism, the series of
compromises will be interrupted and in its place will occur conflicts. And since the life of a state cannot remain still, conflicts become questions of power. Whoever has the power in
hand goes ahead with his views, for the life of a state cannot remain still even a moment. You will say that according to this
theory the Crown would be in a position to prevent the passage
of a budget because of any insignificant difference of opinion.
In theory that is indisputable, just as in theory it is also indisputable that the deputies can deny the entire budget, in order
thereby to cause the discharge of the army or the dissolution of
all government agencies. But in practice this does not happen.
Such misuse of the undoubted theoretical right of the Crown has
not occurred in all these fourteen years.

. . . The Prussian monarchy has not yet completed its mission, and is not yet ripe for becoming a purely ornamental
decoration of your constitutional edifice, not yet ripe to be
integrated like a dead part into the mechanism of a parla-
mentary regime.[64]

In these few paragraphs Bismarck analyzed the situation created
when a constitution is introduced into an absolute monarchy. Irrespective of one's view of why it was introduced, whether through
fear of revolution or out of the goodness of the sovereign's heart, the
monarch would almost inevitably refuse to budge when the parliament opposed him on some favorite measure; he would be certain to
find loyal subjects willing to offer constitutional justification for his
stand.

How did the liberals meet the Bismarckian interpretation of the
constitution? Among their leaders in the Lower House the conception of the conflict as a question of power was generally repudiated.
To the enthusiastic applause of his colleagues, Count von Schwerin,
the former liberal Minister of Interior, spoke against Bismarck. He
attributed to the latter the assertions that "power goes before right,"
that "we have the power and therefore we will put through our theory,"
and he repudiated such views with vehemence. The Prussian dynasty,
he asserted, could not in the long run maintain itself on this belief.
Prussia's greatness and honor had depended and would continue to
depend upon action in accord with the opposite view, that "right goes

⁶⁴ *Adress-Debatte*, pp. 58-64.

before power."[65]   The count, like the other liberals, misinterpreted
Bismarck.   The latter had made no such statement; rather, he had
said that when two opposite conceptions of legality came into conflict,
power would decide which one would win.   The liberals objected to
considering the question from the standpoint of power at all; they
believed that they were right and had legality and morality on their
side and that their opponents had neither legal nor moral basis for
their actions.

The liberals steadfastly denied that they were attacking the King
or trying to take away his authority.   They took the position that the
King should be above parties, that he could do no wrong.   They consistently endeavored to exclude the Crown from the discussion.   When
the King on one occasion in 1863 submitted a statement to the Lower
House not countersigned by the ministry, the liberal majority refused
to consider it.   Deputy von Sybel explained the liberal argument as
follows:

> The King can do no wrong.   This old constitutional prin-
> ciple is nothing more than the juridic expression of the natural
> necessity that a hereditary monarch can never intend to injure
> the fatherland.   In his position such an intention would be a
> suicidal denial of himself and his family, for hereditary mon-
> archy has its highest merit in the fact that it has succeeded in
> placing in the service of the fatherland the strongest passions in
> the human breast, egoism and love of family.
>
> Hereditary monarchy would be insanity if it imposed upon
> every successor to the throne the demand that he must be fully
> educated and read in all branches of political science, in all
> complexities of state law.   The expert minister of the King is
> responsible for every error which may be made in this respect,
> even without a written constitution and without a constitutional
> fiction.   To call the attention of the bearer of the Crown, as our
> address has respectfully done, to such mistakes of the govern-
> ment, particularly when they are of a doubtful, dangerous
> nature, that is in the opinion of your commission not to insult
> but to support the Crown.[66]

The ministers should make certain that the Crown, not able or
expected to be omniscient, abided by the law; if the King proposed a
measure which the ministers considered illegal or unconstitutional, the
latter should prevent the King from carrying out his plan or should
resign.   The liberals regarded the practice of ministerial responsibility

[65] *Ibid.*, p. 78.
[66] *Ibid.*, pp. 8-9.

as essential and as actual under either an absolutistic or a constitutional regime; they considered a law to that effect to be an integral part of constitutional government. They accused Bismarck of violating the basic principles about the position of the Crown and of exploiting the Crown for his and his party's own purposes. Deputy Gneist contrasted Bismarck's behavior with that of the liberal ministers of the New Era.

> The former ministers have with piety interposed their own persons in order to protect the person of the King . . . against this situation, in order to prevent the transformation of every controversy of this kind . . . into a personal conflict between the King and his loyal subjects.
>
> The present ministers have encouraged and furthered this kind of controversy in every way. They have started agitation in the country on a literal interpretation of the slogan, "for the King and against the parliament." This is certainly not constitutional. I will add something more which one who has the deepest respect for the dignity of the King can add. You have done the King a disservice by bringing him, the exalted bearer of the crown of Frederick the Great, into such a situation that in our country, as in the Swiss cantons, one votes over whether one is for or against the constitution, and that one counts and weighs by thousands what is for and what is against the King.
>
> That is the worst service which a loyal servant could do for the King.[67]

The liberals, in a speech by Deputy Gneist, ridiculed Bismarck's assertion that his duty was to execute the orders of the King.

> This view of the ministry that the members do not have to contradict when it is a question of law and the constitution, but that they have only to execute the commands of His Majesty . . . this position is not one of parliamentary government. It is one of rule by privy councillors. . . . The party slogan that you have found, "King or Parliament," was not badly thought out by a party leader; but it is too palpably untrue. The real controversy is . . . very clear: it is a question of government by privy councillors or by the constitution.
>
> To express it more plainly; it is a question of the new regiments or of the oath to the constitution.
>
> Today constitutional ministers tell us that the orders of His Majesty must be carried out, and nothing else. Since the ministers will not inform the King what is legal and what is not, the Lower House must do so. It must say most respectfully that His Majesty has high, holy, inviolable, immovable rights by the

grace of God, which God preserves for him for the blessings of his people, but not those rights which the Minister President . . . has proclaimed as the rights of His Majesty. The King has neither inherited nor acquired such rights, neither by the grace of God nor by the constitution of the country.

As long as a right of German rulers has existed it has never been acknowledged that a German ruler personified the law.

No German ruler has ever had the authority from God or anywhere else ultimately to decide according to his personal opinion about the rights of his subjects. No German ruler has ever had the power in case of conflict to order by decree from his privy council what is right and what is wrong.

And what is true of the fundamentals of our constitution is above all true of our military constitution, which of all the basic rights of the Prussian people is that which was most dearly bought.

The Crown has the highest command over the army and the Crown is the highest bearer of the law about the military, but these are not identical.

The law about the army, which is for us the cherished heritage of King Frederick William III and the War of Liberation and which rests upon constitutional laws, may not be changed except by law and except by hearing those who annually provide 40 million Thalers and 60,000 men for this army.

The Crown cannot almost double the size of the standing army by orders in council; it cannot partially disband the Landwehr and partially push it to one side. And to determine where the borderline of a change in the constitution lies is no military question.

The Crown has the right to give laws, and no syllable becomes law in this country without the approval of His Majesty. But the Crown does not have the right by orders in council radically to change the basic institutions of this country which have been purchased more legally and dearly by the blood and money of the people than anything else in the country.

The Crown does not have the right by orders in council to create hundreds and thousands of new officers' positions which are not approved by the representatives of the country as new expenditures, but are rejected.

The Crown does not have the right by orders in council to empower the ministers to expend money for purposes which are not approved by the constitution and by law. The Crown does not have the right by orders in council to allow millions to be spent which are not founded upon law or the constitution but have been produced only by orders in council as new expenditures.

The Crown does not have the right by orders in council to break off the budget negotiations for the current year, to break off the deliberations over the budget law in the current year and to postpone them to a later year. The Crown cannot make good the necessity of a budget by an order in council or protect the ministers against civil and criminal responsibility. . . .[68]

The logic of the liberals seemed impeccable, unless the opponents refused to be impressed. Bismarck and his colleagues simply denied the validity of the liberals' arguments and met assertion of right by assertion of other rights. "We take our oath to the constitution as seriously as you do," declared Bismarck.[69] The King supported the ministry absolutely, denouncing with heat the accusation that it was violating the constitution. To a complaining address from the Lower House, he replied:

> The Lower House has justly denied all doubt about my serious and conscientious will to preserve the constitution of the country, but it has cited orders of my government, issued with my approval, as facts to justify the complaints about violations of the constitution.
> I should not have approved these orders if I had regarded them as unconstitutional, and I must with complete conviction reject the censure of my government as unjustified.[70]

The King refused to be excluded from responsibility for the acts of his government. He rejected absolutely the liberal idea that the Crown could do no wrong, that the Crown was above parties. The King took it for granted that he could and would do no wrong: that went without saying for an absolute monarch by the grace of God. He assumed that he did not take sides in party conflicts. A monarch by divine right never behaved in a partisan manner; he always acted in accord with the best interests of his country. The King did not even understand the liberal position. His whole training and experience prevented him from regarding the liberals' policies as other than an attack on the rights of the Crown.

The problem of the relation between the King and parliament might have been solved by the introduction of ministerial responsibility, but the conditions were far from favorable for the passage of any such law. The King intensely disliked any mention of the possibility. When in 1858 liberals had advocated a law to that effect, the King had replied with the simple statement, "Place your trust in me."[71] By

---

[68] *Ibid.*, pp. 245 ff.

[69] *Ibid.*, p. 63.

[70] *Die Innere Politik*, p. 148. Reply of the King to the Lower House, February, 1863.

[71] On the King's attitude, see Zechlin, *op. cit.*, pp. 171, 190-92, 199, 210-12.

the end of 1861 the liberal ministers had persuaded him to agree to introduce a bill, much against his will; but the content of the proposed measure left no doubt that it would be meaningless. It provided that a minister could be indicted only by a common decision of both Houses. In view of the character of the Upper House, there was no likelihood that under the proposed law a minister would ever be called to account for anything. The liberal *Kölnische Zeitung* commented that the bill sounded almost like ridicule of the repeatedly expressed wishes of the Lower House, and the Freiherr von Hoverbeck labeled it "shameless."[72]

The constitution dealt with the question of ministerial responsibility in two articles. Article 44 stated: "The King's ministers are responsible. In order to be valid all governmental acts of the King require the counter-signature of a minister who thereby assumes the responsibility." The second article, 61, appeared to supplement but actually opened a way to circumventing the earlier clause. "The ministers," it read, "can be impeached by a decision of one House for violation of the constitution, corruption, and treason. The supreme court of the monarchy in united session decides such indictment. Further stipulations concerning cases of responsibility, concerning procedure and penalties will be reserved for a special law."

As long as no law was passed, Article 61 remained null and void. The Conservatives had seen to it that up to 1858 nothing had been done; and when Bismarck took over the presidency of the ministry, he declared that the time was not ripe for introducing a bill on the subject. He definitely rejected a proposal in the Lower House that questions of constitutionality be referred to the courts for decision. As long as disagreement existed over the relative power of the Crown and of the Landtag, he said, he would not allow the controversy to be settled by any court. The issue affected the King too closely for any such delegation of responsibility to be accepted.[73] Bismarck did not intend to impose any curbs upon his power. In the constitution of the German Reich he subsequently restricted the pertinent clause to the same general statement that the Chancellor is responsible, without saying to whom or in what sense.

The liberals were confused over the meaining of the term ministerial responsibility. In the fourth edition of his work on *Preussisches Staats-Recht*, published in 1864, the prominent jurist von Roenne,

---

[72] *Tagesbericht*, No. 21, Jan. 25, 1862, citing *Kölnische Zeitung*, No. 25; Parisius, *von Hoverbeck*, II, 7.

[73] Abg. H., *St. B.*, April 22, 1863, II, 952.

himself a liberal, distinguished among several kinds of ministerial responsibility.

The general usage of language designates with the expression "moral" responsibility the responsibility before public opinion. By "parliamentary" responsibility is meant the ministers' duty to appear in the sessions of the representative assembly to give the necessary information and explanations; it also include responsibility on the part of the ministers for their bad acts of government which do not violate the constitution. The designation "political" responsibility is used in an entirely different sense, for it may refer to (1) responsibility for the purely political mistakes of the ministers, (2) "parliamentary" responsibility in the sense meant above, (3) the responsibility of the ministers toward the sovereign or (4) the general duty of the ministers to withdraw from office as soon as an insoluble divergence arises between their views and those of the representatives of the people. In contrast, the designation "juridical" or "legal" responsibility is always applied to those cases where an impeachment of the ministers on the part of the representatives occurs. These cases differ widely, for among them one includes at one time violations of the constitution and of the law and at another, breach of duty. The expression "constitutional" as well as "special" or "legally punishable" responsibility is at times used as comparable to "juridic" responsibility. The customary so-called "moral" responsibility before the tribunal of public opinion, the effectiveness of which is mainly conditioned by the degree of political freedom and the sound political sense of a people, stands in no relation to the ministerial position but applies to the judgment of this court of decision and reaches every one in the state. In contrast, "parliamentary" responsibility, namely, the duty of the ministers to stand to account to the representatives at any time, to defend their measures and acts before them and altogether to bring into harmony their views with those of the representatives, is of high significance for the life of the state, because in a representative monarchy government and representative assembly can only fulfill their state responsibilities in common by uninterrupted organic reciprocity. This kind of responsibility, however, derives its significance and thereby its actual value first from "legal" responsibility. If the ministers have caused damage to the state or to individual citizens by violations of the civil law, it is self-evident that of itself nothing opposes their being brought before courts like other officials. Likewise there can can be no doubt that they are subordinate to the general criminal law for common crimes or misdemeanors as well as for special breaches of office like all other public officials who are guilty of such punishable acts. The institution of "juridic" or "legal" ministerial responsibility is therefore in no sense based upon the idea that the ministers are responsible to the monarch and his courts for illegal actions which they have committed of their own accord. The purpose of this institution is especially that the ministers can be arraigned by the organs of the people before an independent court in case they contravene the constitution and the laws as organs of government. This special criminal responsibility of the ministers for the observance of the constitution and of the constitutional rights is the most important security for the preservation of the constitutional state of law. Without it the constitution and the constitutional rights of the people would be exposed at any time to the misuse of power by the government, and the sole security would then consist of the good will of the wielder of power. The realization of this responsibility forms, therefore, the keystone of the constitution and the guarantee which vouchsafes all others their stability and real significance. The Prussian constitution also recognized this principle in that it (in Paragraph 61) stipulates "that the ministers can be impeached by a decision of one House for violation of the constitution, corruption, and treason," and "that the supreme court of the monarchy in united sessions decides such impeachment."[74]

Von Roenne's distinction between "political" and "constitutional" responsibility provides the key to the confusion in the liberals' thinking. They were advocating "constitutional" responsibility and were honestly claiming that they were not aiming to infringe upon the authority of the King. They merely wanted means by which to compel the ministers to abide by the constitution. Deputy Gneist called the absence of a law on the subject "the only gap in our constitution"[75] and believed that by filling it the problems of the relation between the legislative and the executive branches of government would be solved. At the same time the liberals insisted upon the ministry's abiding by the decisions of the Lower House. A typical statement was that by Deputy Beseler in the Lower House in April, 1861. "It is . . . a main complaint against the entire institution of ministerial responsibility that it changes the center of gravity in our state life, that it attacks the monarchical principle, that by means of it parliamentarism is established. This accusation can be refuted without difficulty. . . . How can it be against the monarchical principle if the inviolability of the Crown is protected and made possible by the responsibility of the ministers?"[76]

The confusion arose from the fact that the liberals wished to make the Crown inviolable, to elevate it above party strife, to make the ministers responsible for government action, without infringing upon

[74] Von Roenne, *op. cit.*, II, 352-55.
[75] *Adress-Debatte*, p. 257.
[76] Abg. H., *St. B.*, April 27, 1861; II, 943.

the powers of a king who considered himself a monarch by divine right with powers over and above the constitution. They were endeavoring to evolve practical means by which they could exercise the control over the government necessary for implementing policies which the government opposed.

The liberals' understanding of the nature of ministerial responsibility may be gauged from the report of a commission of the Lower House in 1861 on this subject. Practically all liberal political groups agreed on the necessity for such a law, and this commission was established, not to propose a bill itself, but to urge a supposedly liberal ministry, at least one containing liberal ministers, to introduce legislation to this effect. Besides a few Conservatives the commission was composed of some of the most distinguished members of the Constitutional and of the Progressive patries. Of the members, Gneist and Beseler were both professors, the former in particular being an authority on law and jurisprudence and a profound student of English constitutional practice. The report showed an extraordinarily high level of learning and an equally extraordinary inability to reduce the problem to its simplest, most manageable terms. These liberals had not yet comprehended the difference between the procedure appropriate to the assertion of ministerial responsibility on the one hand and a judicial process for handling violations of the constitution on the other. The judicial experience of a number of them was being misapplied in the attempt to solve an essentially political question. Ministerial responsibility cannot be decided on a legal basis of whether or not the ministers have violated the constitution. Such trials are usually long and costly in time, emotions, and money; and pending the decision, what is to happen in the conduct of state affairs? Ministers maintain or lose the confidence of their supporters depending upon the acceptability of their policies and actions. The English example showed how simple the solution of this complicated political problem should and could be.

In the report submitted by the commission of the Lower House in 1861 the opinions were almost as varied as the membership. The Conservatives frankly saw no justification for a law of ministerial responsibility. The time was bad for introducing one; there was already too much political controversy. Other articles of the constitution had not been executed; why should this one be? Since it was called the keystone to the constitution it should be introduced last. Such a law was not needed "because the necessary guarantee against constitutional and legal violations is already found in the King's conscience." The law would create, the Conservatives argued, a dualism and a contradiction in Prussia, for it would make the ministers responsible both to the King and to parliament, and this system would violate the powers of the Crown.

One liberal member of the commission opposed advocating the law at present. Since the ministers were liberal, he argued, such a recommendation would seem like a vote of no-confidence. He and his friends did not regard the matter as urgent. His view coincided in general with that of a colleague who thought that the present system was "not so bad." Article 61 at least prevented the ministers from being regarded merely as the King's personal servants. Nor, said this deputy, did the public demand the law.

Most of the liberals on the commission wished the law introduced. "In the entire civilized world," they argued, "the view is held that a constitutional regime without ministerial responsibility is incomplete. . . ." The principle was not new in Germany, they declared; for in the organization of estates the diets had participated in the making of laws; they had had the power to grant taxes and by way of the right of complaint to control the administration. The Reich courts had also had the authority to try a prince guilty of illegal acts. One liberal member of the commission in denying that ministerial responsibility violated the monarchical principle cited the precedent of England, where ministerial responsibility had obtained under four dynasties. Another denied that it would lead to "parliamentary party government." Another distinguished between juridical and political responsibility of the ministers and said that only the latter meant rule by a majority in parliament. Repudiating any desire for the introduction of political responsibility, he stated that the liberals sought only juridical responsibility, by which the existing legal responsibility of all officials would also be imposed upon the ministers. Another avoided the issue of the particular kind of ministerial responsibility but emphasized that the Landtag must be able to prevent the ministry from performing acts like the increase in the standing army without its approval.

One member of the commission went at some length into a comparison of the English method of ministerial responsibility and the conditions in Prussia. He found the two to be entirely different.

> An English ministry is a parliamentary combination to put through new laws and general measures and to fill certain offices. The current administration is carried on by the officials of the permanent staff according to fixed principles, that is, according to old and new precedents of the courts which since the Middle

Ages have exercised jurisdiction over public law which with us lies in the so-called administrative agencies. Since 1808 in Prussia the decision over controversial limits of police, finance, and military authority, the interpretation of the laws with reference to them, and the decision over all important controversial questions of public law rest ultimately in the hands of the ministers and in ministerial orders. This is for us the center of gravity of the position, while a responsible minister in England has nothing to do with it. The English ministerial responsibility, which is nothing more than the general responsibility of officials, has for centuries assumed that the courts would decide the legality of an administrative act. It enters into question in a supplementary way in the rare cases in which a court decision could not be had or in which a minister refused to be bound thereby. . . . In this subsidiary sense it is the keystone of the constitution. But the guarantee for the legality of administrative action lies in the decisions of the courts, with which the ministerial responsibility has for centuries stood in inseparable connection.

The speaker warned against trying to introduce the one part of responsibility without the other and urged that both be introduced. "Not until the courts for public law again exist in Prussia will ministerial responsibility assume its proper subsidiary position, and then we hope that it will never be put into practice."[77]

Even the expert on the English constitution was not clear about the nature and purpose of ministerial responsibility. He gave too legal an interpretation to that term; he failed to understand the essentially political use of the institution. He and almost all his colleagues made it too intricate. They should have heeded one liberal who comprehended the problem, namely Schulze-Delitzsch. During the debate in the Lower House on the address to the King in January, 1863, he analyzed the question in some detail. Citing the ministry's use of the King's name to cover its own acts, he denounced this practice as a complete violation of the constitution which could not be "greater or cruder." He condemned it as an attack on the Crown itself, for, he argued, "the undisputed basic conditions of every monarchy, unlimited as well as limited, are the hereditary nature of the Crown and the inviolability of the person of the bearer. If you attack one of these you attack the monarchical principle itself." The speaker then discussed the second of these bases.

The entire constitutional system depends upon the fact that one is no longer ruled by the arbitrariness of one person. . . .

[77] Abg. H., *Drucksachen*, 1861, Vol. V, No. 156.

Now with respect to legislation, approval of the budget, ordering of the state household, that is easy. On these matters the people receive by way of their representatives a vote, a formal, real participation, so that nothing can happen without their approval. But there remains the other equally important side of state affairs, the executive. Here you cannot so proceed. A deliberative body cannot interfere in the executive . . .; it would thereby not only work against the necessary unity in administration but would also come into decided opposition to the sovereign rights of the monarch. How is this to be dealt with? . . . The executive must also be limited or the whole constitutional principle is nullified. How does participation in legislation help the people if the bearer of the Crown is entirely free not to observe the laws at all . . .? Of what value is the constitution if at any minute the Crown is free to annul it or encroach upon it? The sole solution which protects the just interests of the people without infringing upon the sovereign's power is the institution of ministerial responsibility. In it we have the necessary restriction upon the prince as executive. He can no longer act alone; he cannot proceed arbitrarily if he cannot find persons who are willing to assume responsibility for the acts. And what do we gain by this order? On the one hand it protects the people; it gives them the guarantee of a constitutional, a legal government. . . . On the other hand it also protects . . . the throne. For it takes the responsibility for all government measures away from the bearer of the Crown. Responsibility is incompatible with inviolability. . . . A constitutional minister may well defend himself by citing his responsibility to the prince whom he serves if measures are demanded of him for which he does not dare to assume responsibility. But no constitutional minister may protect himself by the person and will of the King against the responsibility which he bears toward the country. The Minister President has by his deductions turned this situation upside down and has thereby violated one of his main constitutional duties.[78]

If Schulze-Delitzsch's view had become valid, the ministers would have been responsible not merely in a constitutional but in a political sense. In practice the English system would have resulted. The liberals' protests against the accusation of their infringing upon the King's power would have had to be dropped. The liberals scoffed at the divine right theory of kings; their newspaper loved to quote a statement of 1850 by the historian Dahlmann: "Even if one is filled with belief in the divine enthronement of princes, I should like to see who can prove that the devil has installed the people. If he has

[78] *Adress-Debatte*, pp. 128-29.

not done so, then who has?"[79] Schulze-Delitzsch repeated his assertion of 1848 that absolutism by the grace of God was bankrupt. He added the general view held by liberals that monarchism should not be identified with absolutism; he supported the one but not the other.[80] Almost all his liberal colleagues failed to understand his line of reasoning for curbing absolutism by the simple institution of parliamentary responsibility.

The liberals were not united among themselves in their attitude toward parliamentary government in the English sense. Deputy Gneist declared in 1863 that not even the slightest trace of any such system existed in Germany.[81] In April, 1860, von Forckenbeck denied at an election rally in East Prussia "that the Progressive party has striven for a government by the majority of the Lower House or has wished to infringe upon the rights of the King. . . . Under the entirely different social conditions of Prussia a government by parliamentary majority as in England is neither possible nor desirable for freedom." If anyone could be accused of desiring the rule of a parliamentary majority, he said, it would be the majority in the Upper House, "which had made impossible the former ministry by its consistent rejection of every liberal proposal."[82]

Other liberals took a different view. "Parliamentary," wrote the *Volkszeitung* in January, 1861, "is only a mild translation of the proposition that it is advisable for a government to defer to the voice of the country when it notes that the country has more accurate views of the needs of the time than one would like to force upon it." A year later the same paper declared that granting a constitution had not sufficed to stop revolutionary action, that a constitution was a contract which changed the relation between a prince and his people. "One may think about the question of parliamentary government as one will," the paper said; "in practice the ministers must nonetheless govern in accordance with the will of the parliamentary majority or seek to do so by corrupting it. And the government must be at least as unified as the present popular assembly."[83]

Two of the leading Progressive newspapers, the *Kölnische Zeitung* and the *Königsberg Hartungsche Zeitung* in June, 1862, drew conclusions about the conduct of the controversy which showed realistic

---

[79] *Königsberg Hartungsche Zeitung*, Nov. 3, 1861.
[80] *Volkszeitung*, Feb. 28, 1861.
[81] *Adress-Debatte*, p. 252.
[82] *Königsberg Hartungsche Zeitung*, April 2, 1860; Philippson, *op. cit.*, p. 110.
[83] *Tagesbericht*, Jan. 24, 1861; Jan. 24, 1862.

understanding of the nature of a constitutional conflict. The former stated that "the right of the King to appoint his ministers according to his wish is undoubted, and our representatives can only gradually and indirectly gain influence over it. It can aim to eliminate all illiberal elements in the ministry by rejecting all illiberal measures, even when introduced by liberal ministers."[84] The Königsberg journal was even more explicit. It denied the accuracy of the government's accusation that the Lower House wished to take over the powers of the crown; and it equally denied the validity of the view of the left-wing liberals, Kirschmann and Waldeck, that ultimate authority should be transferred to the Lower House.

> Parliamentary government is not a legal question but a question of power and as such the product of development. No letter of the law can bring it about; only a series of legal battles, of surmounted illusions and disillusions, of long experience, can do so. A series of good, conscientious parliaments which exercise their budget rights unreservedly and self-confidently and which make the feeling of dependence of every government upon its financial control . . . gradually become habitual: that is the only way under our constitution to introduce parliamentary government. There should be added the consequent introduction of self-government in the counties and the communities . . . and therewith the legal elimination of a system of centralized bureaucracy.[85]

"I am convinced," asserted the Catholic party leader Reichensperger, "that in comparison with the importance of the main question, namely the right of the Lower House to approve or to change the budget of expenditures annually, all other questions recede into the background." The liberals agreed fully with this view. They, as well as the Catholic party, denounced the ministry's action with respect to Article 99 as creating constitutional conditions worse than those under absolutism. "It was the law of the Prussian monarchy even prior to 1848," Reichensperger said, "that the Crown could introduce no new taxes and make no loans without the approval of the representatives of the country. That was decided at a time in which there was no representative assembly, a striking proof of how necessary the monarchy regarded it not to stand there with unlimited power." The liberal deputy von Unruh completed the argument about finances by denying that the government had any authority to expend any state money without a legal budget for the year in question.[86]

[84] *Ibid.*, Feb. 4, 1862.
[85] *Königsberg Hartungsche Zeitung*, June 21, 1862.
[86] *Adress-Debatte*, pp. 53, 43, 68; Parisius, *von Hoverbeck*, II, 29.

To the liberals the gap theory not merely violated the constitution; it destroyed the constitution. The mild and cautious right-wing Constitutionalist Deputy von Simson asserted in a commission of the Lower House that "no one in the entire country would be so forsaken by intelligence as to interpret Article 99 in any other sense than that of the majority." Count von Schwerin accused the Bismarckian ministry of "standing the law and the constitution on their head." Deputy Twesten spoke for all in asserting that "the defraying of expenditures in consequence of the failure of the budget law to be passed, solely according to the judgment of the government, could be continued indefinitely until some catastrophe occurred which would put an end to this theory by means of terror, but then probably not the theory alone." Deputy Virchow denounced the ministry's interpretation of the constitution as "the purest arbitrariness." Deputy Schulze-Delitzsch condemned the gap theory as equivalent to abolishing the constitution. If one questioned the budget rights and other rights of the Lower House, he said, one could call in doubt any and every article of the constitution, and one had absolutism. "When one supplements one system by its opposite, when one supplements constitutionalism by absolutism, the possibility of deduction ceases to exist for me." Deputy Gneist declared that Bismarck's extravagant personal views about the constitution had suddenly become the law of the land.[87]

The liberals defended their position by reference to the constitution rather than by the arguments developed in England and the United States of no taxation without representation. During the three-day debate on the address to the King in January, 1863, only one deputy, von Unruh, advanced the general claim that "it lies in the nature of the newer state forms that those who pay the taxes also have the foremost and most important authority to grant them."[88] He did not elaborate upon the thesis; he merely stated it in passing. The liberals assumed that Prussia had developed beyond the point of having to defend first principles. Bismarck's seeming acceptance of the constitution may have deluded them into thinking that first principles of constitutional government were not in question. In the light of history one knows that they should have gone back to the assertion of fundamentals and not have concentrated, as they did, upon legal rights. They assumed that in case of disagreement among the three factors of government a budget would not be forthcoming. When the govern-

---

[87] Parisius, *von Hoverbeck*, II, 144, 106; *Adress-Debatte*, pp. 88, 149, 126-27, 248-49.
[88] *Ibid.*, p. 66.

ment adopted the gap theory and continued to raise and expend money, the liberals had no other line of attack than the defence of a constitution which the government denied was in any danger.

On only one point of general argument did the liberals attack the government's position. They did so rather from the angle of politics and statesmanship than of constitutionality. Bismarck had justified his use of the gap theory on the grounds that "the state must live," that it could not stand still. Deputy Virchow asked:

Is this the sentence of a statesman? Can one approach a representative assembly which is expected to grant money with the thesis, the state must live; therefore you must give the funds? Is this the entire result of our constitutional development that the constitution, that the long struggle for the legal founding of our financial system should finally arrive at the point where one says to the representatives of the country: the state must live, therefore you must say yes to everything? I shall not continue these questions; one could easily arrive at an observation that would touch a statesman too closely. But I believe that we must most decidedly guard against the assertion of views so contrary to written and sworn constitutional rights, views which were drawn from an ancient time when perhaps a lord of the country would justify to subordinate estates this or that conception by saying, "I could not do otherwise, I had to act in this way, you must acquiesce." . . . The state must live and begs its way from day to day. Is any plan at hand? Is there anything of that which held in the old law of the land, namely, that a regular financial administration should exist? Does this correspond in any manner to the wise and well-weighed plans of Frederick William III?[89]

"We find ourselves," stated Deputy Twesten in January, 1863, "in one of the most dangerous crises in the history of the Prussian state."[90] How did the liberals propose to gain victory? They had refused to approve the budget demanded by the government only to find that the latter conducted the public finances without a budget. They believed that they could not compromise on this question without sacrificing all their constitutional rights. They rejected any idea of revolution, and disliked so intensely the proposal to refuse to pay taxes that the populace overwhelmingly continued as usual to provide the Bismarckian ministry with funds. They depended upon the support of public opinion, believing that the King and the government could not hold out against the will of the population. They understood Bis-

[89] *Ibid.*, pp. 141, 149.
[90] *Ibid.*, p. 93.

marck's strategy to provoke them to anger, to exasperate them, to induce them to extreme measures,[91] and they were determined not to let him succeed. The power of liberal ideas and the force of history, they believed, were on their side. Although they knew about the King's hostility to them, his stand on military reform and his support of the gap theory, they appealed to him against the acts of the ministry and sought to win him over by information about what they considered to be the true situation. In spite of the futility of this endeavor, they stated to the King in May, 1863, that they could not work with the present ministry, again in vain. The King and ministers considered the declaration another unconstitutional attempt to infringe upon the rights of the crown.

The difficulty of the liberals' situation may be judged from an exchange of correspondence in May, 1863, between two liberal historians, the Prussian deputy, Professor von Sybel, and the Southwest German professor, Hermann Baumgarten. Von Sybel listed the efforts of the Lower House to overthrow the ministry, all of them legal and verbal; "but," he continued, "we have no means of impeaching the government. It has money and soldiers and an old bureaucracy which is stuffed with reactionary powers. So we frankly possess no material power; we are not and never will be in a position to gain quick results. We strive to preserve moral superiority." Von Sybel feared that any radical measures would alienate the upper bourgeoisie as they had in 1848 and force it into the arms of the reactionaries.

Baumgarten replied with a rousing proposal for action.

> Prussia's future will presumably be bad if its fate remains tied to the views and will of the Hohenzollerns, if the people cannot take affairs into their own hands. One must force narrow-minded and prejudiced persons to be reasonable or emancipate oneself from them entirely. I should prefer the former . . . and in view of experience elsewhere I should not despair of results even in this case. But one must be deadly serious and arouse in the persons in question the very definite feeling that everything is at stake for them if they do not very soon become reasonable. For this purpose the speeches in the Lower House do not appear to be enough. The entire country must bestir itself and very decidedly express its will. It seems to us that up to this time the conflict in Prussia has been conducted too tamely. Persons who scorn the constitution, reason and right as bad boys must be made to tremble. One must arouse in them the lively concern that one of these days they will be killed like mad

---

[91] Some (in Essen and the vicinity) refused to pay taxes. Heyderhoff, *op. cit.*, I, 176; Philippson, *op. cit.*, p. 109; *Adress-Debatte*, pp. 114, 157, 208.

dogs. One must display to them the passionate determination in case the worst happens to use extreme measures. Such a manner of fighting is certainly not according to the taste of civilized man. But it is not a question of our taste; it is a question of what is necessary. If you allow Bismarck only temporarily to make headway, revolution appears to me unavoidable. If Prussia endured such a regime permanently its position in Germany and in Europe would be at an end. The question, thus, is how can one prevent such terrible dangers. Allow just anger to be fully and energetically expressed. Send deputations to Berlin from all towns and counties! Let them come into the palace by the thousands accompanied by the most respected citizens and speak very seriously and firmly. You would do only what the English did in 1770, for example, against the North ministry. It is possible that you will thereby convulse the peace. But on the other side stands the certainty of a fearful revolutionary change or of deep humiliation.

Von Sybel replied with a virtual confession of defeat.

There has often been talk here since December of the plan [of mass deputations] which you propose. I have always advocated it. . . . But the leaders of the Progressive party have up to now been of the opinion that it would be difficult to start people in motion particularly for this purpose; to petition about this man would be most unpopular. And it would be a great defeat if the demonstration turned out to be slight. On the other hand, if it succeeded, the gain would be less than you seem to assume. If forty thousand deputies came on one day they would receive a polite negative answer and would return home. It would be another chapter in agitation and indignation among the people, but I can assure you there is already a surplus of this in Prussia. I cannot very strongly contradict the estimate of the Progressive party. Our wielders of power have long ceased to tremble over addresses and deputations and popular feeling. They know very well how categorically they are condemned by the latter. Their only question is, have we money and reliable soldiers? They tremble before every under-officer who reads the *Volkszeitung,* before every word in Parliament that could attract the soldiers, but before nothing else. They are correct in their judgment. As long as the army hold loyal the people can use no physical force. Their regime will continue until the army declares for the constitution or until it is defeated in a foreign war . . . or it might be that we should have the good fortune like that of the English in 1688 in the Prince of Orange, a split in the leading circles themselves, for example, a declaration of the Crown Prince for the constitution.

Von Sybel cited historical examples to show that a revolution would not succeed without the support of the army. He cited the opinion of better-informed persons than himself to the effect that the present army remained loyal to the Crown. And to clinch his argument of pessimism he said that no one doubted that Bismarck would enthusiastically welcome an attempt at revolt.

During the summer of 1863 the liberals tried to mobilize the public further for demonstrations against the government. A letter from von Sybel to Baumgarten of June 17 described what was being done.

> The state of mind here on the Rhine is excellent. In Bonn the Catholics and the liberals united for a big celebration for the deputies. The students aimed to stage a torch-light parade, and when that was prohibited to stage a party. When that suffered the same fate they sent in yesterday a memorial. In Crefeld, where I was on Saturday, the entire town was in movement. The stores were closed, the Catholics, if possible, even more zealous than the liberals. My speech at Crefeld has been printed as a pamphlet. You will read it in the South German papers. This month we concentrate on addresses and deputations from town councils, electors, and so forth to the King. It is intended to set in motion the chambers of commerce of the monarchy in July. Also the Rhenish notables plan new action, this time addressed to the ministry, somewhat more strongly peppered than the earlier address to the King. In Berlin ephemeral publications are being organized as a partial replacement of the newspapers. In short we do not doubt that we can solve the present problem of keeping public opinion favorable to us and active up to the end of the year. There is nothing else at present to be done unless foreign affairs intervene. You would not find in all Prussia a single person who did not regard steps of open violence as foolishness and a crime, since they would be sure of immediate suppression. What is frequently in the air is the thought of paying no more taxes. But it is clear that for this to be effective the upper bourgeoisie must begin, and for them the matter must still ripen somewhat.[92]

The liberals' anger at Bismarck in 1863 could scarcely have been greater. Deputy Twesten asserted in the Lower House that the government was "in dangerous hands." In a private letter Von Sybel stated the question he had put before the Crefeld notables: "If the French overrun the left bank of the Rhine and plague you with quarterings, war contributions, and so on, but in the House I still vote against a loan or war taxes without a change of ministry: would I receive a vote of no-confidence? The immediate and unanimous answer was: 'A thousandfold vote of no-confidence if under any cir-

---

[92] Heyderhoff, *op. cit.*, I, 147 ff. In June, 1863, von Hoverbeck knew that the King was to blame for the obstinacy of the government. Parisius, *von Hoverbeck*, II, 169. See also Philippson, *op. cit.*, p. 87.

cumstances you approve the smallest sum for this ministry.' " When Bismarck asked the Lower House at the end of the year to approve a loan in connection with the Danish war, the liberals overwhelmingly refused. In March, 1863, von Hoverbeck wrote a friend in East Prussia: "The bitterness here in Berlin and among almost all deputies against this ministry is so intense that I believe it cannot increase. A part of it also falls back upon other responsible personalities."[93]

What made the liberals so angry was their belief that Bismarck could not be trusted, that he would do anything to gain his end, that he had no principles except those of reaction and power. "You [the government] do not understand our language at all," said Deputy Virchow. "You have no conception of the fact that the written constitution really exists, that compromises are not first to be made, that the law does not have first to be made, but that the only question is one of preserving the law." Deputy von Sybel declared that the ministers lived in a different world with entirely different basic beliefs and views from those of the present day. Futher,

> . . . Your political assumption is that the government possesses from the beginning the power to dispose of the life and property of the subjects, that the government is not allowed to do only that which some law expressly forbids, and even that in certain emergencies, naturally defined by it, the government can cancel such prohibitions and take back the authority. Our assumption is the opposite, namely, that a citizen's money belongs first of all to him and not to the government, and that the latter first receives the right to expend it for governmental purposes and for the country when the citizens have through their legal representatives approved these expenditures.

Deputy Gneist openly asserted that "our government has lost the power to distinguish between right and wrong." He summed up the experience of the Lower House with the ministry by stating: "It is not true that we have repulsed the hand of reconciliation. The hand has on the contrary fallen upon us more roughly and insultingly from year to year."[94]

Deputy von Unruh stated the liberals' belief about the future.

> History speaks for our views. . . . The attempt to restore absolutism again in a constitutional state when absolutism could no longer maintain itself has never gone unpunished. Even more dangerous, even more serious, is the attempt to defend ab-

[93] *Adress-Debatte*, p. 93; Heyderhoff, *op. cit.*, I, 156; Parisius, *von Hoverbeck*, II, 209, 140.
[94] *Adress-Debatte*, pp. 142, 215-16, 246, 258.

solutism under the forms of the constitutional state . . . because it is especially dangerous for the dynasty. Sham constitutionalism cannot be preserved. It may last ten years, fifteen years; but under all circumstances it will collapse, and as a rule the dynasty collapses with it.

I boldly assert that not our opponents but we ourselves are the supports of the monarchy . . . in the only form possible in our time and in the future. We shall persist in this endeavor, we and those who come after us, . . . and we shall hope that the monarchical spirit of our people will not be completely eradicated by interpretations, by granting and withdrawing rights. . . .

The struggle may last a long time. We with gray hair may never see the end of it. But we have one positive conviction, and that is, the future belongs to us![95]

[95] *Ibid.*, pp. 77-78. See similar remarks by Twesten and Schulze-Delitzsch. *Ibid.*, pp. 91-92, 122.

II

THE ORGANIZATION AND STRENGTH OF THE PARTICIPANTS

7 / The Public View of Political Parties

T HE political party emerged in response to practical needs. As soon as representative assemblies were created, political life had to receive some kind of organization. The selection of candidates, the conduct of the campaign for election, the preservation of contact between the representative and his constituency, and the orderly conduct of business within the representative assembly required the establishment of facilities for large-scale cooperative action. The work of the state and national assemblies in 1848 and 1849 introduced conditions in which political organizations developed. The parties in Prussia in the early 1860s conformed to the general pattern of organization and purpose set at that period, not out of any sense of imitation but as a practical way of meeting a common problem.

By the time of the elections of 1862 and 1863 in Prussia, the political organizations had scarcely had time in which to assume their ultimate role. They had not as yet become the standard vehicles of popular activity. The number of Prussians who had had actual experience in the politics of modern constitutional government with representative assemblies was not more than a couple of thousand. In so far as local elections had been held they had offered the voting Prussians little precedent for political participation on matters of general state concern. These elections involved local affairs, requiring the exercise of judgment on grounds of practicality, efficiency and personality, but not of principle. Where the elections were held on a class basis, as in the case of those for representatives of the three estates in the county and the provincial assemblies, the class itself afforded an adequate organization for action and performed those functions which in a larger group of heterogeneous social and economic interests would have required the service of a political party.

The Prussian constitution of 1850, like that of the United States over half a century earlier, contained no provision about political parties as such. Parties were not regarded as an essential apparatus of government and were left within the area of private endeavor. Nonetheless, the constitution established the conditions in which parties would develop. In contrast with the county and provincial assemblies, representation in the Lower House of the Landtag rested not upon caste or class distinctions but upon a numerical basis. The change entailed fundamental adjustments in attitudes and ways on the part of the different social groups, not merely of the Conservatives but of the liberals, not merely of the aristocracy but of the middle classes, the industrial workers and the peasantry. Under the system of county representation by estates election campaigns were unnecessary, for every member of the first two estates knew personally every other member, or in case of indirect elections the electors were or became personally acquainted. Voting was confined to social equals. The three-class system for the state forced this personalized, informal, caste procedure to admit new methods. While preserving a degree of inequality, it shifted the basis from legal privilege of caste to economic interest. The inequality of political power under the three-class system did not alter the new facts that almost all adult males had the power to vote and that to win an election a person must be a candidate and seek support in all three voting classes. He might have to organize a campaign and solicit the vote of classes socially below him. The shift from a social to a political basis for elections entailed the introduction of a degree of actual equality in practice and constituted an essential step in the elimination of caste privilege and the development of equal citizenship.

The significance of the shift may be noted in the difficulty with which public leaders of upper-class origin adapted themselves to the process of social change revealed by this requirement. During the period under discussion, not even all liberal and democratic political leaders were free from the traditional inhibition. The Conservatives made only slight concession to the necessity of conforming to the ways of popular elections and continued to rely mainly upon their accustomed means of exerting power. Their aversion to popular political action followed historic practice in the field of government, wherein membership in a political body was considered a personal right resting upon familial privilege. Although in Prussia the individual aristocrat was drilled to consider the welfare of the whole, he expected to attain this end primarily by defending and furthering his own interest on the assumption that the welfare of the leading social group determined the health of the whole society. He did not accept the principle of representation, where the individual regards himself as an expression of the will of many. He objected to subordinating his will and personality to the interests and wishes of the many and to developing qualities appropriate to a de-personalized representative of people with most of whom he had merely a superficial contact. The aristocratic Conservative in a popular representative assembly still thought and acted essentially in accordance with his rejection of the idea of equality. He still adhered to the counter-principles of social and political hierarchy. In his control of the government he enforced the policy that local governmental bodies should not be allowed to show any interest in state or national affairs. They should concern themselves solely with local matters, as befitted the hierarchical, orderly division of government. Thereby, the Conservatives prevented the growth of practical political experience at the level most important for the development of democratic ways; but it is doubtful whether they thought much about this aspect of their policy. They were continuing in the period of constitutional government and popular state elections the division of function of an autocratic age. They were still acting on the assumption of "the limited intelligence of a subject" in state or national affairs and were endeavoring to prevent the development of the political man with all-round interests and personality. They disliked the political party and press as forms of activity beneath their dignity; and even though they had known about English customs, they would have been loath to follow the example of the English Conservatives.[1]

The attitude of the reactionary element among the Prussian Conservatives is strikingly revealed in the will of Count Diedrich von Bacholz of Alme in 1861. The Count charged his heirs to give up none of their feudal rights, judicial, police, hunting, or church, to oppose the wielders of power and "their faithless, partisan, power-hungry officials, . . . to scorn the favor of princes as well as of the mob, in short, without arrogance and conceit, without avarice and without extravagance, to be a true German nobleman, not according to the letter but according to the deed."[2] The Count was fighting both the ab-

---

[1] *Tagesbericht*, No. 19, Jan. 23, 1862.
[2] *Volkszeitung*, Jan. 16, 1862.

solutism of the Eighteenth Century and the liberalism of the Nineteenth. He remained loyal to the feudal ideals of aristocratic independence. He had not discovered the fact that modern political party life had begun; or if he had, his will expressed his utter aversion to it. A social group in which sentiments like these could be seriously expressed scarcely qualified as a supporter and practitioner of popular politics.

The attitude toward politics taken by most Conservative aristocrats lacked the defiant self-sufficiency of Count Diedrich. Most of his peers had acquiesced in the fact of absolute monarchy and had established effective ways of protecting their interests by serving the King at court and taking high positions in the government and the army. Since the identity of interest between monarch and Conservative aristocracy became well established in the first part of the Nineteenth Century, the latter looked to the King and his government for political guidance. After constitutional government, a state representative body, and state elections had been introduced in 1848-50, the Conservatives had continued to rely upon them for maintaining this identity. In accordance with their name the Conservatives wished to preserve the structure of the state and the distribution of power as it existed in the 1850s when they were in control, and a large number longed for the restoration of pre-1848 conditions. They tended to accept the government's program as their program, the government bureaucracy as their political organization. They preferred to avoid the establishment of a political party of their own in order not to encourage political activity and in order not to lower themselves to the level of the liberals and democrats by entering into competition with them. During the period they constantly used their customary means of influencing the government, namely, by way of private conferences with the King, petitions and addresses of loyalty to him, deputations with asseverations of devotion to him and of aversion to liberalism. They worked through the officials at court, the officers in the army, the church leaders, and the high bureaucrats. They practically surrounded the King in his private life and to a large extent in his public activity. Like Minister of War von Roon they believed that "the King must remain consistent; a change of government from Whigs to Tories as in England should not spread among us." Political parties, that is to say, should continue to play a minor role; the power should remain with the King and his conservative officials. After being dismissed from authority, former Minister President von Manteuffel showed his low estimate of the politics of popular representation by remaining silent in the Lower House of the Landtag, to which he belonged, and finally by resigning. He let it be known that he did not regard the assembly elected by the people as the proper place for him to defend his former administration. For him the honor of having been appointed by and made responsible to the King outranked by far the position of representative elected by the people. To justify himself before the other representatives of the public would have lowered his dignity and might have been misinterpreted by the Lower House as an acknowledgment of its enjoying some political significance.[3]

When Prince William assumed the authority of regent for his sick brother, he placed the Conservatives in a difficult and embarrassing dilemma. He dismissed them from most of the ministerial posts, introduced into power his friends, the mildest of mild liberals, and proceeded to support a general line of policy which ran counter to that of the Conservatives. The latter faced the problem of how to be conservative, to be above parties, and at the same time to oppose both the King and the government. While persevering in the use of their time-honored political methods, they could no longer rely upon government initiative in behalf of their political fortunes and had to enter the arena of political action themselves. They had to organize a party, augment their facilities for campaigning for votes, and compete with the liberals and democrats for popular support.[4] The dialectic of political party life and representative government was drawing them into the kind of activity which was contrary to their principles and repulsive to them in practice.

In spite of the embarrassment caused the Conservatives by the New Era, they found a large amount of agreement with the King and his ministers on the role of political parties. The governmental attitude toward parties and their activities became administratively somewhat more lenient under the liberal ministers than before; but the legal control remained the same. The parties had to register with the police; in order to hold a political meeting, they had to receive an official permit. They were treated more severely than non-political private organizations under the laws and ordinances concerning the right of organizing and the right of assembly. The fact that they constituted the means of enabling the people to express their will in government

---

[3] See von Bernhardi, *op. cit.*, III, 310, 323-24, IV, 173; *Tagesbericht*, No. 25, Jan. 30, 1861, No. 7, Jan. 9, 1861.

[4] See as an example *Preussisches Volksblatt*, No. 6, 1861, as given in *Tagesbericht*, No. 6, Jan. 8, 1861.

did not gain for them any special rights. They were placed in the same category with labor organizations, handicraft associations, and all others. The police subjected party activities to the most careful attention. Dossiers accumulated on them in the police files; the administrative officials reported regularly, although not in much detail, on the general state of political opinion. The Conservatives, who had made these laws, were inclined to consider opposition to the ruler and his government as partaking of the nature of mutiny or treason, or at least of subversive activity. They thought that the liberals and democrats wished to shift the center of political power to themselves and to transform the character of Prussian society, a suspicion that manifestly was well founded. Being unable to think in political terms, to accept the facts of changing conditions and the need for political and governmental adjustments to these changes, they could conceive the liberal and democratic action only in the light of the criteria of power. They had no other experience by which to judge it; their thought immediately applied military and police terms and symbols to this new phenomenon, and the experience with the Revolution of 1848 had confirmed them in this suspicious view. When they opposed the King and government, as they had to do between 1858 and 1862, they did not apply this line of thinking to themselves; they considered themselves as merely more royalist than the King, more governmental than the government. They were maneuvering so as to force the King back to their side. Even a king might err.

The liberals and democrats had been and continued to be the driving force behind the institutions and practice of popular politics. They expressed their power in state affairs by means of politics; and while almost none of them recognized the full implication of popular representative institutions for the character of government and of political parties, they at least understood the simple facts of their position. They tried to conceal from themselves the impulsion of this system toward the English type of parliamentary responsibility and toward equal suffrage and increased efficiency in the conduct of politics as an organized profession. Many of them sought to maintain the right to act as leaders with knowledge superior to that of the voters and to decide issues not according to the wishes of their constituency but on the basis of their personal wisdom. Nonetheless, they knew that in the last analysis they served as representatives and that they owed their position to public support. Although a few of the aristocratic right wing of the liberals had close contacts with the King, the vast majority of the liberals and especially the democrats had no such means of exerting influence. The liberals and democrats could have stirred up a flood of petitions and deputations in support of their action in the Landtag; but, as the Berlin correspondent to the *Königsberg Hartungsche Zeitung* wrote in October, 1862, they held it inappropriate to do so. They represented the people and expressed the popular wishes; additional means of expressing these wishes were thought to be unnecessary.[5] Nonetheless, petitions supporting the Lower House were signed and sent to it.

The decision aptly characterized this stage of development of Prussian politics. It agreed with the attitude toward the pursuit of the game shown in the indifference of the Landtag deputies to election statistics. That a Conservative government never published any statistics of political affiliation according to local districts conformed to their general inclination to reduce the significance of politics; but such unconcern is less understandable in the case of a government of liberals. The failure of the Lower House or of the parties to collect and publish the full political statistics indicated the infancy of political life. When the committees of the Lower House in 1862 and 1863 reported on whether the elections had been run according to the law and on whether the members of the House had received a majority of the votes and were entitled to be seated, they frequently did so without supplying any statistics on the vote of the electors for the winners and almost never for the losers. Even less often did they supply figures on the votes cast for the electors. Since elections had only begun to be held in 1848, party organization and policies were in the beginning stage, and the population itself was even less advanced in political thinking and acting than the leaders.

As soon as parliamentary institutions were established the liberals and democrats faced the practical problem of purpose and organization of the political parties. Contrary to their reaction to most lines of activity of the period they hardly indulged in theoretical analyses. The practitioners were concerned with working instruments rather than with definitions. The concept *party* had not yet acquired the connotation of partisanship which the Conservatives later succeeded in imposing upon it in the mind of much of the public. The liberals and democrats would have repudiated any such accusation, for they were seeking to introduce into Prussia and Germany a new way of life, whole and complete within itself even though contrary to conservatism.

---

[5] *Königsberg Hartungsche Zeitung*, Oct. 2, 7, 10, 1862.

They tended to distinguish between a "party" as the inclusive unit expressing the total view of life of the political group and a "fraction" as a group within the party differentiated on points of lesser importance. They showed most concern over the question of functions of the party or fraction.

The liberal *Kölnische Zeitung* published on February 5, 1862, an article condemning parties for wasting time, for exhausting the participants in preliminary discussion, for preventing the few excellent speakers from exercising their talents in the Landtag and exerting public influence. The writer much preferred freedom of action for the deputies to the restrictive influence of parties. If followed, his advice would have led to the destruction of any kind of party organization. It would have crippled liberal and democratic strength in the Landtag by enhancing the tendency toward anarchy. It sounded like the desires of a certain type of German professor, loaded with knowledge, impatient of control by an organization, determined to live up to his reputation as leader. The effects of this kind of political behavior were described by the historian Professor Baumgarten upon a visit to Berlin in the first part of 1862. He said that he could not understand the conditions there. In spite of the wealth of intelligent, active men nothing was being accomplished in politics. They carried on politics, he said, as if it were a learned subject. They thought that an issue was settled if it was thoroughly discussed. They talked too much and did nothing about execution. "A great genius or a powerful tyrant should arise here; but in Berlin such a person would certainly not be great," he concluded; and he saw little hope for Prussia to take the lead in Germany.[6] Although Professor Baumgarten failed to recognize the source of the trouble, he at least did not conclude that more freedom of action by the individual deputy would cure the state of anarchy.

Manifestly writing from personal experience, a Berlin correspondent to the *Königsberg Hartungsche Zeitung* discussed the problem with no clearer understanding of what it involved than that of uninitiated observers. His definition of a party as a number of deputies who met every evening at a certain restaurant for debate revealed the inadequacy of his own criticism. His description of the activity of a party suffered from an exaggerated sense of the need for formal structure and slight comprehension of the value in political work of a

---

[6] Heyderhoff, *op. cit.*, I, 61-62.

highly flexible and adaptable organization. He wished the party to have definite and recognized leaders, probably a useful proposal, but he did not explain that effective leadership would assert itself only in time and that facilities had to be present for enabling the leading personnel to change in accord with changing political situations. He failed to perceive the advantage of the party as an instrument for working out and agreeing upon policies in an informal, non-public way, as a means of saving much official time and at arriving at satisfactory solutions without hasty and unfortunate public commitment.

The means which the correspondent offered for eliminating the "fraction flaws," as he called them, can scarcely be called profound. "The first would be the construction of a decent parliament building, in which the deputies could comfortably satisfy their physical needs; then the transfer of sessions to the evening, for in the evening the human being is fresher and livelier."[7]

Apart from the absence of physical facilities for conducting business, the parties suffered from more fundamental shortcomings. In view of the newness of parliamentary life many deputies were returned who had no previous party affiliation. Their alignment with a party or fraction would not be known before the legislature met, and they might be quite independent of the party at all times.[8] The lack of clarity of the political situation between 1858 and the appointment of Bismarck in 1862 and the difficulty about promulgating definite programs handicapped the formation of parties. As long as the ministry contained both Conservatives and right-wing liberals, many deputies did not know what line to pursue, what policies to support, what attitude to take toward the government. They did not know what should be the bases of political differentiation and party organization.[9]

The advantage of party organization and a measure of party discipline among the elected representatives in the Lower House became slowly apparent to certain leaders and voters. It would be an exaggeration to assert that the recognition extended to a large numer, but the available evidence leads to the conclusion that by 1861 and 1862 the editorial in the *National Zeitung* (January 6, 1861) of Berlin represented a view of growing acceptance. It was a "lamentable illusion," wrote the paper, "to wish to stand above parties. To be a party man

[7] *Königsberg Hartungsche Zeitung*, July 13, 1862.
[8] See *Volkszeitung*, Jan. 15, 1862; *Königsberg Hartungsche Zeitung*, Feb. 2, 1862.
[9] *Ibid.*, Feb. 2, 1862.

means to have connected and, if possible, thoroughly considered ideas about the desirable outcome of state affairs and to unite with fellow citizens for the realization of them. Whoever does not attain this firmness in thinking and acting stands not above but below parties, for everything that happens in state affairs is accomplished over his head."

The newly established Progressive party (1861) took the initiative in trying to create a formal organization with a feeling of party responsibility among the deputy-members. As the youngest of the liberal political groups and certainly as the most ambitious and the most aggressive, this party had a carefully formulated program. It needed the additional power which organization would supply in order to press its policies upon the other liberals and upon the government and especially in order to increase the number of its voting supporters. Although it split into several fractions and was unable to achieve the unity needed, it did elect an executive committee each month of the parliamentary session, and it succeeded in developing a habit of party loyalty. One of its leading members, Freiherr von Hoverbeck, in January, 1862, accepted a party decision which he had opposed. A decade earlier he had asserted his independence of party. Pressure to this effect was being exerted upon the deputies by their constituencies. In December, 1861, Rupp, a candidate in Königsberg for election to the Lower House, was asked in a meeting of electors of the Progressive party whether in case of election he would join a fraction and in how far he would submit to party discipline even when the decision went against his own conviction. Rupp replied that after his experience in 1849 he regarded it as absolutely necessary to join a party and to submit to party decisions. His statement was greeted "with great approval." In the Western part of the state, in Bielefeld, a few weeks later Deputy Schulz had to explain to a political meeting, two-thirds of which consisted of persons from the rural districts, why he had not joined the Progressive party in Berlin after he had been elected on its program. His reply manifested his slight understanding of the value which Rupp had recognized as early as 1849. He had aligned himself with the Bockum-Dolffs fraction because he had found in it old friends; but he had always voted with the Progressive party, and, he said, "that is in the last analysis the main thing." At about the same date, the electors in Aachen were taking steps firmly to remind Deputy Baur that after having declared himself at the time of his candidacy in accord with the program of the Progressive party and having been elected on that basis he should not then have joined the Grabow fraction. They were pressing him to correct his mistake and affiliate with the Progressives.[10]

The efforts of the parties or fractions to preserve enough unity and identity without depriving the individual members of independence led to the formulation among liberals of party rules of order. Those of the Grabow fraction, published in the *Kölnische Zeitung* of January 19, 1862, contained the following points. An executive committee of eleven members should be elected. One should be secretary, another treasurer, the others should preside in turn over the party conferences. Except for the secretary and the treasurer, the membership should be renewed every four weeks, with the right of re-election. The party should meet on the evening before each plenary session of the Lower House. Any member of the party who aimed to introduce a bill or an amendment in the Lower House or to support one introduced by members of another party should inform the party beforehand of his intention. He should not be prevented from following his aim even if the majority of the party had spoken against him. If a member first planned to introduce an amendment during the course of the plenary session, he should notify two members of the party executive committee of his intention. Except on certain matters stated below each member was entitled to vote in the plenary session against the decision of his party, provided he had expressed his intention in the party conference. If he had been absent from the conference or if he planned during the plenary session to vote against the party decision, he had to inform two members of the executive committee of his aim. He had to abide by the party decision on the following points: the despatch of an address to the King, the interpellation of ministers, the introduction of and decision about a proposal for the establishment of investigating committees, the proposal to change or supplement the constitution. To make a party decision binding upon all members required that the members be informed beforehand of the intended action and that at least half of the membership be present at the conference. The measure had to be approved by a two-thirds majority of those present. For special reasons the party might release individual members from this obligation. In order to achieve unity among the party members in case of votes in the plenary sessions about such matters as proposals to adjourn or to close the session, the members should

---

[10] Heyderhoff, *op. cit.*, I, 114; Parisius, *von Hoverbeck*, II, 5; *Königsberg Hartungsche Zeitung*, Dec. 31, 1861; *Volkszeitung*, March 26, 1862; *Tagesbericht*, No. 45, Feb. 22, 1862, on the basis of a report in the *Volkszeitung*, No. 45.

take their cue from the vote of designated members of the executive committee. Whoever was unable to attend a meeting of the party should learn from a member of the executive committee about what had occurred. If a member wished to resign from the party, he should notify the executive committee in writing or should declare orally his intention in a party meeting.

The rules reflected a high degree of bureaucratism. They read like the statement of organization drawn up by persons trained in government administration who were trying to adapt the method and criteria of precise definition of official function to a group of popularly elected representatives. A party run according to these rules would have been neat and orderly. Although party discipline was needed, it seems doubtful whether such formal rules were appropriate. Even the liberal political leaders had not yet learned how flexible a political party has to be in order to achieve efficiency. Such fixed rules seem contrary to the nature of politics and a manifestation of political inexperience. Nor were the rules effective; the parties continued to be run after the fashion of a local social club.[11]

[11] *Wochenschrift des Nationalvereins*, Feb. 7, 1862.

8 / The Election System

THE conflict between the liberals on the one hand and the King and the Conservatives on the other involved the question of representation. Did the Lower House represent the people of Prussia? Since the answer depended in part upon the nature of the election system, it must be analyzed, and for that purpose three problems will be considered—the legal conditions under which the deputies were returned, the public's actual experience with voting, and the nature of the liberals' and the Conservatives' own thinking about the social bases of representation.

The elections were held under the terms of a law which most political leaders, irrespective of party affiliation, considered adequate. Government, Conservatives and liberals, Catholics and Poles were sufficiently content with it not to make a fundamental transformation or even a modification of it a major political issue. After the electoral districts had been fixed by law in 1860 so as to prevent—though not with entire success—further gerrymandering in favor of reactionary candidates, the liberal majority in the Lower House of the Landtag voted to postpone indefinitely any proposals for revision of the election law, and the New Era government either approved of or acquiesced in the decision. The law seemed to be fulfilling its purpose of providing a neutral mechanism for the expression of the will of the politically active public.

The decisive evidence in favor of this view seems to lie in the fact that since its promulgation in 1849 the law had served to return in the first years an overwhelming Conservative majority of deputies and after 1858 a decided liberal majority. Other factors than the nature of the election law were rightly regarded as accounting for the change in political expression, and each side thought at the time that under the terms of the law it could win future elections. In significance political and social issues ranked so far superior to other matters in the struggle between the old Prussianism and the new liberalism that neither major group was much interested in the conditions of representation.

The system of voting used in 1862 and 1863 had been introduced on May 30, 1849, as a means of re-establishing Conservative control over the fading revolution. It had been drafted by the government headed by Count von Manteuffel with the approval of King Frederick William IV. It had first been issued as a royal decree and then legally accepted by the Lower House of the Landtag elected according to its terms.

The Manteuffel government incorporated the basic principles of the election law into the constitution of 1850. They were to be found in Articles 69, 70, 71, and 72, and contained the following provisions: The Lower House should be composed of 350 members. The election districts should be fixed by law. Every Prussian who had completed his twenty-fifth year and had the right to vote in local elections in his community was entitled to vote. Plural voting was not allowed. An elector should be chosen for every 250 people. The voters should be divided into three classes according to the amount of direct state taxes they paid, in such a way that each third had the power to cast one-third of the entire vote. The total amount should be calculated for each community or for each election district in case the latter was composed of several communities.[1] Voting separately, each class should elect one-third of the electors, who could be chosen from any of the three classes. The deputies were chosen by the electors meeting and voting as a body. In those communities which paid the milling and slaughter tax, this sum should be counted in lieu of the direct state tax. The only essential point of the election law not repeated in the constitution was that requiring the open ballot.

By the provisional Article 115 the constitution validated the decree of May 30, 1849, until a new election law, foreseen in Article 72, should have been approved. Since the new election law was never passed, the decree of 1849 remained in force during the entire life of the constitutional monarchy in Prussia.

[1] According to the decree on the execution of the election law of 1849, an election precinct should not contain more than 1,500 people. Abg. H., *St. B.*, 1849, Vol. I, Part 2, pp. xiii-xv.

The origin of the three-class system of voting remains obscure.[2]   It may have been first suggested by David Hansemann, a Rhineland banker, a leader of the liberal bourgeoisie and a minister in the first Prussian revolutionary government of 1848. He was acquainted with the system in the Rhine province, where it had been introduced in the law on community government of 1845. In the local form, in which numbers of voters were relatively few, the election had been direct, whereas for the state elections the law of 1849 required indirect elections. Apart from the use of the secret ballot in the community election as contrasted with the open voting for state elections, the state law may be considered an elaboration of the local decree to fit the needs of voting in a large area with large numbers involved.

The Rhenish bourgeoisie should not be given complete credit for having originated the system of voting in 1849. The idea of inequality underlay the social and political life of the entire Prussian state and was accepted as a reality by almost all liberals as well as by the Conservative vestiges of the Old Regime. The structure of local, county and provincial government expressed much more inequality than even the new Landtag. The three-class system of voting actually marked an advance in the direction of equality over many of the practices in the lower branches of government. The population was accustomed to inequality in political power, including the right to vote, and, whenever it dared or had the opportunity, it protested primarily against extreme manifestations of this inequality. Doubtless the purest example of the age of privilege survived in West Pomerania and the island of Rügen, where the officials of the municipalities selected new colleagues by co-optation; a written code of laws did not exist and the officials reigned like autocrats.[3]   In the villages throughout the state the right to participate in the community meeting depended upon a property qualification, which divided the residents into two groups, one with some political power in the decision on local affairs, and the other in a position of dependence.

The one exception was provided by the law of 1808 associated with the name of Freiherr vom Stein. This law had given the male population of the towns and cities of all the provinces except the Rhineland and Westphalia a basis of voting so liberal and progressive that it had remained a matter of concern to the conservative or reactionary nobility. By this law vom Stein had abolished the associa-

[2] See A. Wolfstieg, "Wer ist der 'Vater' des Dreiklassenwahlrechts in Preussen?" *Preussische Jahrbücher*, CLXIV (1916) , 349-55.
[3] See Abg. H., *St. B.*, 1862, Vol. II, No. 15, pp. 102-03.

tion of the vote in town affairs with property as a personal privilege. He had supplanted this feudal conception by the modern practice of equal manhood suffrage and secret ballot. Although the Prussian government had whittled away certain of the liberal rights of the town decree, many essentials remained intact in 1848 and did not succumb to reaction until 1853. In that year the government had extended the three-class system of voting to town and city elections of the six Eastern provinces and had abolished the secret ballot.

The county assembly (Kreistag) and the provincial Landtag remained in 1862 what they had been prior to the Revolution of 1848. As bulwarks of aristocratic privilege and power and of authoritarian domination, they afforded few opportunities for popular elections. In so far as elections were held, they threw the force of custom on the side of unequal voting power and of discouragement or prohibition of popular participation. The first estate in the county assembly and the first in the provincial assembly, or where in the latter assembly there were four instead of three estates, the first two were restricted almost entirely to the owners of noble land holdings. Certain holdings carried the hereditary right to a seat in the first estate, while the others entitled the owners to vote for representatives to the assembly. In the case of the second estate, representing the towns and cities, the same practice applied. Certain cities possessed the right of direct election of a representative, and the others chose electors who met together to select representatives for the assembly. In either case the power to vote was restricted to the members of the town or city council, and the number of deputies to which they were entitled was far fewer than that of the first estate. The practice in the villages for choosing representatives to the lowest estate was also indirect, resembling that in most of the towns and cities, and was about equally restricted as to representation in the assembly. Balloting in these elections was secret.

A subject of the King in 1862 and 1863 would have found the three-class system of voting, with one exception, entirely within the limit of his experience gained in provincial and lower elections. In the Western provinces he would have been fully acquainted with the division of the voters into three groups according to the amount of taxes they paid. In the other provinces he would have been accustomed to differences in voting strength based on other, but nonetheless real, criteria. In all provinces he would have understood the workings of indirect elections, either from actual participation or from the experience of others. In all provinces he would have lived under the rule of assemblies in which the upper class was legally and traditionally entitled to far more representatives than the lower ones—in the province and in the county, the nobility over the townsmen and the peasants; in the towns and cities, certain burghers over the rest of the burghers; in the villages, certain peasants over the others. With the one exception of elections for municipal officers in towns and cities between 1808 and 1853 in the six Eastern provinces, the pattern of voting was consistently discriminatory. If one uses the popular right to vote as a standard, the election law of 1849 under which the Lower House was elected in 1862 and 1863 marked a substantial improvement on the norm established in the years of pre-revolutionary reaction.

When the government proposed the three-class system of voting in 1849 it had arranged its justification according to the three basic principles of the bill: first, the division of voters into three classes; second, the use of the amount of taxes paid as a criterion for the division of voters into these classes; and third, the open ballot. Critics of the bill and subsequent law necessarily followed the same form; and a comparison of the remarks made about the several terms in 1849-50 and again in the early 1860s may help to illuminate the degree to which Prussian political leaders of this period understood the character and purpose of elections.

In 1849 and 1850 both the government and the liberal deputies disapproved the French system of direct elections based on a high property qualification, and this aversion persisted among liberals in the early 1860s. They had seen a revolution develop out of the system in France in 1848, and had watched Louis Napoleon manipulate it to the advantage of his imperial control since then. They wished an election law which would reflect not merely numbers but the differentiation of social and political forces. They approved the three-class method of voting, and argued in favor of it, to use the government's justification, as follows:

> The forces of the citizens, on whose harmonious cooperation the existence and prosperity of society basically depend, are in part physical or material, in part intellectual and spiritual in character. Among the material ones the ability to pay taxes occupies a preeminent position. It provides the most general measure of individual contribution to the public welfare. It therefore seems reasonable to regulate voting power according to the tax situation. Thereby one tries to abide by the demand of equal duties, equal rights, and one takes into account the fact that a very important right of the deputies, whose election is being considered, concerns the power to levy taxes. Although the

tax yardstick is very unsatisfactory, one can expect from the allocation of votes according to the amount of taxes paid an appropriate result, for conditions are by and large such that among the poorer elements of the population there is usually the greater sum of physical force and among the richer there is usually the greater amount of spiritual and intellectual power, and thereby the importance which one apparently attributes to material property accrues to the benefit actually of the higher intelligence.

It is not necessary to prove further that the amount of property owned is more or less decisive for the interest in the state organs which protect this property.

. . . When one decides on the three-class system, that decision rests not merely upon the fact that it is regarded as the least offensive form of division or that it furthers the formation of parties less than a two-fold division would, but much more upon the experience that as a rule three main classes of the population can everywhere be distinguished by the amount of property they own, and that the members of each class in other relations also usually have most in common with each other. Thus the system is more organic than on first glance it appears to be.

The government rejected the proposal to divide the population for voting purposes according to occupation. The occupational structure, it said, was still too complicated. When a new social structure had developed, it would be possible to allocate political power accordingly; but at present any attempt to do so would arouse far too much opposition.

The government recognized that the proposed election system had many shortcomings. Some arose from the fact that the state did not possess a uniform system of direct taxation. Another lay in the fact that the first class had too few members to be regarded as a genuine election body. These, it thought, could be subsequently corrected.[4]

In its recommendation of the bill to the King, the government added another argument, with an unusual gift of aphasia about the events of the preceding year.

The similarity of interests of the individual classes of the population is not as externally recognizable as it is real, and the measuring of relative importance among them is so difficult that we do not wish to undertake to advise Your Majesty to try to fix it in law. We have therefore held to the simpler external manifestation of this relation, the participation in the payment of taxes. Since only three classes of voters are formed, we have permitted wide leeway to the association of interests and have taken the particular situation in each locality and in each district

[4] Abg. H., *Drucksachen*, 1849 50, Vol. I, No. 40, pp. 3 ff.

into due consideration in that the classes are to be formed in each community or in each voting district composed of several communities according to the amount of taxes paid in that community or district and not according to a tax standard for the entire state.[5]

The government's defence of open voting incorporated all the standard arguments employed then and in subsequent years by those determined upper-class supporters of responsibility and courage in politics. "Since the principle of publicity and oral procedure has come to obtain more and more in the conduct of public affairs in the other branches of state life," the ministry argued, "many esteemed persons have spoken in favor of introducing it in voting as well. . . . It was most unwelcome apparently," the ministry continued, "to those who wished surreptitiously to thwart the main tendency of the principle of voting classes, in that they hoped to win at least the votes of the masses for the false friends of the people." While recognizing that open voting was also subject to impure influence, it regarded this influence as small in comparison with "the cancerous affection which would be able to grow undisturbed under cover of the secret, written procedure." In a free people, the individual must have the courage to express his convictions openly. "In no other way will the parties learn to know, to respect and to understand each other better." Moreover, the government continued, since the poorest classes were the most illiterate, their vote would be known anyway. "Public voting treats all alike and exposes no one to the humiliation of exceptional handling."

Public voting, the ministry stated, would be most effective in uncovering bribery and other irregularities at elections. Public opinion would condemn such practices and the investigation of the election procedures would impair their success. Whoever sought to misuse his influence to prevent others from freely expressing their convictions would be damned by the press. Whoever suffered from voting according to his conviction would receive public support. Open voting, the ministry concluded, would help to establish the constitutional monarchy and "would keep at a distance the destructive play of political passions and intrigues."[6]

In spite of these arguments it is not clear why in 1849 the government advocated the introduction of open voting. By tradition that manner of voting had been associated with revolutionary terror. The

[5] Abg. H., *St. B.*, 1849, Vol. I, No. 2, pp. vii-viii.
[6] *Ibid.*; Abg. H., *Drucksachen*, 1849-50, Vol. I, No. 40.

Jacobins in 1792 had used it to obtain a majority and had threatened to send advocates of the secret ballot to the guillotine. Stein's law on town government of 1808 had introduced the secret ballot; the revision of that law in 1831 had not changed the system; the law of 1845 on Rhenish communal government had used it; even the Rhenish West-phalian Church law of 1836 had done so for the express purpose of assuring a free and honest manifestation of opinion. The provincial and county elections had been held by secret ballot. In fact, open voting was an innovation of the 1850s, first in the Landtag elections and in 1853 in the communal elections. Apparently the government reasoned that it could exert sufficient pressure upon voters in open elections to win their support.[7]

The general acquiescence of both liberals and Conservatives in the election law was manifest at the beginning. The membership of the committee of the Lower House recommending the approval of the bill in 1849 consisted of representatives of both groups. On that commit-tee, the liberals, from diverse parts of Prussia (Kühlwetter, von Beckerath, Count von Schwerin, Simson, von Saucken-Julienfelde, Pfeiffer, and Gessler) outnumbered the Conservatives by seven votes to four.[8] The committee reporter, the Rhenish liberal industrialist von Beckerath, stated to his colleagues in the Lower House that direct elections had much in their favor but that there was much to be said in favor of indirect elections. According to experience, the latter were, he continued in this profound vein, a guarantee for conservative voting (he meant anti-revolutionary voting), which was "very im-portant" at present. He recognized that the recommended system of voting rested on the principle that the state was entitled to decide who should vote, who should form the pillars of government. He admitted that the three-class system of voting was "not entirely the correct one," that it was a "crude instrument," and that property was not an accurate measure of "the highest political right," but, he said, there was still much to be said for it.[9]

These remarks of von Beckerath's are impressive because of the extraordinarily paternalistic authority conceded to the government (*ex post facto* to the representatives of the people) to decide on (1) who should participate in state affairs even to the modest extent of voting, and (2) what should be the conditions of voting. They disclosed the

---

[7] See H. von Gerlach, *Die Geschichte des Preussischen Wahlrechts*, (1908), pp. 34-39.

[8] Abg. H., *St. B.*, Dec. 13, 1849, pp. 1690-91.

[9] *Ibid.*, Oct. 27, 1849, pp. 900-01.

frank approval of material wealth as the basis of political power. If one wished to increase his political influence he should increase his wealth. The advice belongs in the tradition of the continental bourgeoisie, Guizot and Louis Philippe.

From the beginning of the New Era requests for the reform of the election law were made occasionally in the Lower House of the Landtag, always without success. The government even promised in 1859 to introduce a reform bill, but that particular ministry gave way to another before any steps were taken. Count Schwerin, the next Minister of the Interior, had served in 1849 on the Committee of the Lower House which had recommended the approval of the election law; and in 1861 he persisted in his support of the old law. His successor in the same office, von Jagow, refused to agree to any modification of the law on the grounds that the views of the country were divided on the question.[10]

The Lower House voted in April, 1861, in support of a declaration that a new election law was an "urgent need";[11] but in the same declaration it postponed any consideration of this "urgent need," and the available evidence attests to the accuracy of Minister von Jagow's estimate. On the issue of the best method of voting in state elections the liberals could not agree among themselves. When the Progressive party was founded early in 1861, the leaders admitted this dissension publicly in their official program and had to omit any expression of party policy about it. They called the method of voting an open question. A few leaders vigorously advocated the abolition of the present system in favor of universal equal manhood suffrage and the secret ballot. Others, apparently a great majority, opposed this change with equal vigor; and rather than split the new party, the proponents bowed to the fearful ones. Freiherr von Hoverbeck, Krieger, certain leaders from Berlin, a few from Breslau, some from the Rhineland, and Schulze-Delitzsch led the proponents, while Twesten and professors like Theodor Mommsen were absolutely opposed to their views. In general, the Old Liberals and members of the other liberal groups to the right of the Progressive party lined up against the reformers.[12] The arguments deserve analysis as evidence of the state of political

[10] *Ibid.*, Feb. 26, 1859; I, 256. *Ibid.*, April 6, 1861; I, 650 f. *Ibid.*, Aug. 20, 1862; III, 1337.

[11] *Ibid.*, I, 658.

[12] Parisius, *Politische Parteien*, pp. 36-39; Parisius, *von Hoverbeck*, I, 209; von Gerlach, *op. cit.*, pp. 211-14.

thinking at the time among those who sought to align Prussia with the liberal forces of the century.

As early as September, 1849, Maurach, a member of the Upper House, had disapproved the voting law. He had predicted that the law would separate the deputies from the people and had denied that persons not voting or unable to vote were necessarily stupid. "As representatives of the people," he had warned, "we must go along with the entire people. Only then can we win and maintain the bases of our power and influence."[13] In 1861 Schulze-Delitzsch stated to the Lower House the views of a small group of deputies which justify their being ranked among the most clear and honest thinkers and the most thoroughly liberal leaders of the century, irrespective of country. Although he was speaking on the subject of conditions for voting in town and city elections, the ideals which he supported had general application. An election should assure that real interests, he said, were represented. He believed that important social interests exerted their due influence most effectively under a general election law without property qualification. A factory owner, the owner of a large estate, a person of outstanding intelligence would gain a position of influence irrespective of the nature of the election law. He accused the opponents of equal suffrage of confusing unjustified social equality with a thoroughly just political equality. He argued that the three-class system stimulated class antagonism, and that the restriction of voting rights by a property qualification was no improvement. He stood out staunchly for equal and secret suffrage.[14]

The arguments of Maurach and Schulze-Delitzsch might well have been heeded. These leaders realized that the existing election law divided the public into voting groups in such a way as to deprive the liberals of increasing support from the public. They saw that the law encouraged an authoritarian relationship between government and the governed and tended to preserve the ways of life of the Old Regime, that it caught the liberal bourgeoisie in the framework of Conservative rule and prevented it from gaining the popular backing which it needed. They recognized that the defence of the three-class system of voting could not be reconciled with the liberal program of their party.

The liberal opponents of universal equal suffrage feared that this method of election would lead, as Karl Twesten declared, to "the

---

[13] I. Kammer, *St. B.*, Sept. 7, 1849; II, 625.
[14] Abg. H., *St. B.*, 1861; II, 1049-50.

dominance of dilettantism and charlatanism in politics." The occasion for their most vigorous denunciation arose in 1866 and 1867 when the introduction of equal and direct suffrage was being considered for the proposed North German Confederation; but their opinions as expressed then applied equally to the earlier years. "In normal times," Twesten said, "the pressure of the government and in abnormal times of excitement that of radical agitation would produce undesired results and falsify the voice of the people."[15] His colleague, Professor von Sybel, used even more Cassandra-like expressions. To the professor this was a matter of conscience. His historical knowledge showed him that the introduction of direct and equal suffrage marked the beginning of the end of all parliamentary government. He thought that such an election law could be accepted only under ideal conditions, when all men were good, all were socially equal, all had the same measure of intelligence, when the lion lay down with the lamb. While he believed in progress, he thought that mankind had not arrived as yet at the conditions necessary for it. He declared that the right to vote was the right to select the lawmakers, that this was a right to political dominion and should not be considered in the same category with the right to work or travel or associate with others. A person was not born with a right to select legislators; he had to prove that he possessed the ability to do so. Von Sybel preferred indirect elections to direct ones. The latter, he said, especially with a wide suffrage right, stirred up the passions and killed discussion; it meant the death of independent political life and opened the way to every form of influence. It made people think they were equal when they were not. In Prussia two years ago, he declared, there were about 6,000 students and 44,000 pupils in the gymnasiums and other high schools. Using these figures as a basis, he reckoned that there were about a million men in Prussia with education above the most elementary. He thought that the same relations held true with respect to the degree of social independence and property holding. He denied that the common people knew enough to elect an able man to parliament; he associated democracy with Caesarism.[16]

The liberal leaders failed to agree on the issue of secret versus public ballot almost as completely as they did on that of the three-

[15] Abg. H., *St. B.*, Sept. 12, 1866, pp. 335-36.

[16] Norddeutcher Bund, Reichstag, *St. B.*, March 27, 1867, pp. 427-28. See also Robert von Mohl, *Politik*, (Tübingen, 1869), pp. 715-24; and the views of the Polish deputy, von Morawski, in the Prussian Lower House on March 23, 1860.

class system of voting.[17]   More of them seemed to be willing to support secret suffrage than the equal and direct vote; but persons like Count Schwerin preferred open voting on principle, and Deputy Beseler, the liberal professor of law, shared his opinion.   Open voting, he said, corresponded more "to the moral dignity of a free people" and was closer to "the Germanic principle" of "publicity."   Whoever voted for a deputy, he added, should not feel as if he were acting as a private person, but rather as if he were exercising an official public function. Beseler's support of open voting was shared by a leader of the Polish fraction in the House, Doctor Liebelt, who asserted that a voter must have the courage to express his opinions publicly.   The advocates of secret voting included persons as far to the right among the liberals as Freiherr von Vincke.   Both von Vincke and the far-from-liberal Catholic deputy Reichensperger from Geldern, who agreed with his views in this matter, remarked that open voting had not been customary in Prussia before 1849 in any elections.   Von Vincke accused the Polish deputies of preferring the open ballot so that they could be certain of the vote of their Polish constitutencies, and he had no illusions about government pressure on the voters throughout the state in favor of Conservatism.   Reichensperger quoted from the decree of 1836 in which King Frederick William III had ordered the use of the secret ballot in Rhenish-Westphalian church affairs so as to avoid any suggestion of influence upon the voters.[18]

Many liberal deputies offered irrefutable evidence about the feelings of the public on open voting. They cited numerous petitions from their constituencies asking for the introduction of the secret ballot. Deputy Frystatzki declared that ninety per cent of the people favored it, that open voting was hated.   In his district, he said, half the ones eligible did not cast ballots. Everyone said, Frystatzki added, "Why should I go and let myself be ordered to vote for a particular person? I love peace and . . . this open voting opens the door to ambition and selfishness." Deputy Professor Gneist expressed his conviction that three million signatures could be obtained in favor of the secret ballot. Too many voters had had an experience like that described to the Lower House in 1859 by Deputy Mettenmeyer. The Landrat of Stargard County had kept careful record of how each person voted; when a druggist had voted against his wishes, the Landrat and the Conserva-

---

[17] See von Gerlach, *op. cit.,* pp. 34-39.
[18] See the debates in Abg. H., *St. B.,* April 6, 1861; I, 640, 656. *Ibid.,* Feb. 26, 1859; I, 256-58.

tives had seen to it that he immediately lost one-fourth of his business and had tried to deprive him of the rest. One understands why many deputies did not agree with the government official representing the Minister of the Interior, who told the Lower House in 1861 that the introduction of open voting in Prussia was a "sign of progress." Nonetheless, the House never took active steps to replace it by the secret ballot. It always postponed consideration of the question.[19]

The seeming diffidence of the liberal deputies toward reform of the system of voting for state elections did not extend into the area of town and city elections. The forty-five years' experience under the Stein law in the six Eastern provinces, that is, in all but the Rhineland and Westphalia, had won the devotion of the urban population to the practice of equal and secret suffrage, and the towns and cities of these provinces especially sent impressive petitions to the Lower House in favor of the restoration of the former system of voting. A list of those from which the city or town councilmen sent petitions would include urban centers of all sizes, large, small and medium. The councilmen of only two towns, Breslau and Liegnitz, made an exception: they wished to retain the three-class system, but not, at least in the case of the Breslau councilmen, the open voting. In the two Western provinces the sentiment favored the retention of the three-class system; but many townsmen of prominence disapproved it in their petitions, and almost everyone sought the introduction of the secret ballot.

The evils of the three-class system and open voting were condemned in almost identical terms. As typical as any was the statement sent to the Lower House by a group of 226 prominent citizens of Breslau.[20] According to this system, the petitioners declared, out of 6,992 voters some 362 belonged to the first class and had one-third of the voting power; 1,669 belonged to the second class, and 4,961 to the third. Even apart from the inequality and injustice of this division of political power, the petitioners complained, the system introduced social differences based on income into a communal organization, and involved social distinctions in political controversy. A community had many functions, like poor relief, in which all citizens should cooperate; instead of uniting it, the three-class system of voting tended to divide

[19] *Ibid.*, May 6, 1861, p. 1268; Aug. 20, 1862, III, 1333-38; Feb. 26, 1859, I, 255 ff.; May 16, 1861, pp. 1272-73; Feb. 26, 1859, I, 263; March 16, 1860, I, 558; April 6, 1861, I, 657-58.
[20] See Abg. H., *Drucksachen*, 1859, Vol. III, No. 108. 1860, Vol. VI, No. 262. 1861, Vol. V, No. 160. *St. B.*, May 2, 3, 16, 1861; *St. B*,. 1862, Vol. II, No. 15.

the citizen body. An artificial organization of the citizens thereby re-placed a natural one. The petitioners denied that the three-class sys-tem was necessary in order to prevent mass rule and asserted that a small property qualification or intellectual qualification, as in the old town law, would suffice. Too many persons who should be town leaders were now forced to vote in the third class.

The Landtag deputies could not have ignored the flood of petitions even if they had wished to. As soon as the New Era began, the liberal majority of the Lower House appointed a commission to report on the problem, and as early as 1859 the majority of the latter declared that the three-class system was not suitable for town elections. Apart from the arguments used by the petitioners in Breslau, the liberal de-puties cited one convincing piece of evidence, the tremendous decline in voting since the introduction of the new procedure. One example may suffice. In Berlin under the Stein law over seventy per cent of the voters had cast ballots; after the introduction of the three-class system, in 1858 and 1860, not over twenty-six and twenty-five per cent respectively voted in the third class, not over forty-two and fifty per cent in the second class, and not over sixty-three and sixty-five per cent in the first.[21] With each newly elected Landtag, until the fight with Bismarck monopolized attention, a new commission picked up the work of its predecessor and recommended almost the same liberal re-forms for town elections—the secret ballot and equal suffrage with a low property qualification.

The Conservatives manifested much less interest in the manner of voting than the liberals. They disapproved the entire system of govern-ment and society in which popular elections were required and felt no strong devotion to any particular method. Their basic demand about elections was that the Conservatives be kept in power, and their will-ingness within the space of a decade or less to shift their support from the three-class system with open ballot to that of equal manhood suff-rage with secret ballot attested to their persistence in using any means to achieve their end. In 1849 the Conservative theorist, Professor Stahl, a member of the Upper House of the Landtag, could scarcely find adequate phrases for his scorn of universal and equal suffrage. Speaking with the assurance of a constant communicant with the Absolute, he had denounced elections by individual suffrage as "un-bearable tyranny," as mass rule by the propertyless, by those incapable

[21] Ibid., Drucksachen, 1861, Vol. V, No. 160, pp. 15-16; 1859, Vol. III, No. 108, pp. 26-30.

of governing. Like the liberal Professor von Sybel he had regarded the right to vote not as a personal one but as a public duty to be exercised by a competent few.[22] His colleagues had taken a less doctrinaire view and had followed the government by approving the three-class system.

After the elections turned against them, the Conservatives began to lose some of their preference for the three-class system of voting. They now feared that the present method suffered from some serious defects. As early as 1858 Deputy Count Pfeil condemned the use of indirect elections. When elections were bad, he said, they were made much worse by the electors. When the voters inclined left, or right, the electors voted extreme left, or right, and the true voice of Prussia was not heard.[23] The year after the first major defeat of the Conservatives in the election, Deputy von Blanckenburg stated to the Lower House that if the secret ballot had been employed, many members of his party would have won. Speaking in 1861 for the same group, Deputy von Krosigk declared that there was no such thing as free elections, that influence was exerted upon them from either above or below. He and his friends admitted that in case of open elections, it was possible for government officials to influence the voters; but, he said, the secret ballot opened the way to demagoguery and pressure from below. He continued to prefer the open ballot. In the same session of the Lower House his fellow Conservative, Deputy Wagener, the editor of the main Conservative newspaper, the *Kreuzzeitung*, twitted his opponents for preferring the secret ballot. Indeed, he said, "there has never been a constitution resting on the constitutional principle of the majority which lasted longer than a few decades." He accused the liberal proponents of the secret ballot of being inconsistent; they based their political system, he declared, upon the virtues of independent, spartan-like citizens, who did not have the courage to vote openly. Wagener condemned liberal government by elections as built upon " a political falsehood."[24]

> You tear asunder state and society; you recognize no other citizen than Plato's well-known two-legged animal without feathers, whom you abstract from all possible social conditions and endowments, and then you wonder why in every concrete case reality makes itself effective as over against this abstraction.

[22] Herrenhaus, *St., B.*, Sept. 7, 1849; II, 622.
[23] Abg. H., *St. B.*, April 20, 1858; I, 604-05.
[24] *Ibid.*, Feb. 26, 1859; I, 258. May 16, 1861, p. 1271. April 20, 1858; I, 604-05. April 6, 1861; I, 653-54.

Apart from his social position one has no political significance at all; the social and the poltical significance of a man are
identical.

Look at France, Wagener continued, where one had so-called despotism
and the secret ballot, or at America "where one stands at the ballot box
with revolver and dagger." Wagener did not regard the present system
of voting as ideal; but he still preferred it to any other Prussia had had,
because, he said, "even if only in crude form, it does contain the
thought that the political importance of a name should be graded according to its social and political achievement and significance."

As defeat after defeat rolled over the Conservatives in the elections
to the Lower House during the period of constitutional conflict, they
sought some other system of voting to stop the liberal victories. Bismarck offered a solution, not for Prussia, where the election law remained unchanged, but for the proposed North German Confederation.
In 1866 as soon as the Austro-Prussian war ended, he recommended
the introduction of universal, direct and equal manhood suffrage, and
he acquiesced in the use of the secret ballot as a matter of minor importance. Liberals were startled. Several deputies in the Lower
House of the Landtag mistrusted the proposal as an attempt to undermine the influence of their political groups and of the Lower House.
Others, as has already been stated, condemned it on principle in absolute terms. Most of the liberals accepted Bismarck's recommendation with amazement and seemingly without much relish. The hated
Junker had stolen the thunder of the most leftist of the liberals.[25]

So far as Bismarck's intentions were concerned, the liberals' fears
were justified. The Minister President did not aim to strengthen the
liberals or introduce popular government—quite the contrary. As
early as the meeting of the United Landtag in 1847 Bismarck had believed that the lower classes were much more conservative and monarchical in their thinking and feeling than the middle classes and that
especially in the agrarian provinces of old Prussia the property-owners
would be able to control the votes of their workers even under a system of universal suffrage.[26] At the time, he had rejected both this
method of voting and the three-class system, declaring in 1849 that
the Prussian people were politically so immature that elections would
be "a lottery," "a gamble." The experience with elections during the

[25] *Ibid.*, Sept. 11-12, 1866; Norddeutscher Bund *St. B.*, March 28, 1867. Abg. H.,
St. B., Nov. 26, 1873; I, 95-99, 109-113, 118-20.
[26] See G. von Below,. *Das parlamentarische Wahlrecht in Deutschland* (Berlin,
1909), p. 90.

1850s had inclined Bismarck toward a broad popular basis for voting. In 1854 he had opposed curtailing popular participation in the state elections by a high property qualification, for, he had argued, "the classes excluded thereby are better royalists than the rest of the bourgeoisie and upper classes, even apart from the arbitrariness of any property qualification and the damage resulting from endless playing with constitution-making." After watching the same election system return a Conservative majority to the Lower House in the 1850s and a liberal majority in the 1860s, Bismarck stated that whatever the law might be, the elections always expressed the opinions of the time. It is doubtful, however, whether he actually believed his own words; otherwise, he would not have proposed an election law for the North German Confederation which was the reverse of that of Prussia. He expressed his views more frankly in a circular despatch to Prussian ministers abroad in March, 1866, that is, even prior to the defeat of Austria and to the election defeat and split of the Progressive party later in the same year.

> I consider direct elections and general suffrage greater assurance of a conservative attitude than any artificial election law calculated to achieve manufactured majorities. According to our experience, the masses are more honestly interested in preserving state order than the leaders of those classes which would be preferred by the introduction of some property qualification for the right to vote.
>
> I may assert as a conviction based on long experience that the artificial system of indirect and class elections is much more dangerous in that it obstructs contact of the supreme power with the sound elements which form the kernel and the mass of the people.[27]

Bismarck wished to gain popular support for the new North German Confederation by this move. His use of the election law proposed in April, 1849, by the Frankfurt Parliament as the basis for his proposal may be interpreted as a bid for liberal aid in founding the new German Reich. He hoped to be able to control the vote in favor of conservatism by direct and universal suffrage even with secret ballot and to use the support of the lower classes a a means for weakening the liberals. His miscalculation reveals Bismarck's extraordinary lack of understanding of the social and economic forces of his age; but the fact remains that, in so far as one may make a dogmatic statement about so uncertain a subject as politics, he had very little choice. He

---

[27] Quoted in von Gerlach, *op. cit.*, p. 83.

could accept either an election system restricting political power to the liberal bourgeoisie and their supporters, whether by the three-class system or by some high property qualification, or one based on equal and direct suffrage for all male adults. A Conservative, agrarian Junker, even if a Bismarck, had had enough adverse experience with the bourgeoisie; he preferred to try the masses.[28]

The glee of the Conservatives in supporting Bismarck's proposal can be felt even in the dry pages of the parliamentary debates. They now strode confidently behind their leader, and a mere ideological somersault caused them no qualms. They did it quickly and with as much poise as a Prussian Conservative could preserve in such an act. Strosser, an average Conservative deputy, declared in 1866 that equal suffrage had been contrary to the Conservative views up to now, but that if the government favored it he would heartily give it his approval. "Under any election system," he said, "it depends upon the energy and strength of the government whether one attains good election results."[29] A few days later Deputy von Blanckenburg denied that support of direct elections violated Conservative principles. He believed that this kind of election could be trusted more than the indirect method. For example, he said, in a system of indirect elections a deputy like Dr. Jacoby, who had recently said about the Austro-Prussian War, "This war does not redound to Prussia's honor or to Germany's welfare," would be protected by the electors; in a system of direct elections the voters would not tolerate such a representative.[30]

The most perfect somersault was made by the expert in Conservative debate, Deputy Wagener. He disagreed with his political friends that the method of election would not change the outcome. He now favored direct and universal suffrage, and opposed as unjust not merely the three-class system but even a property qualification on voting. In this society of compulsory military service there should be equal suffrage. Indirect elections were and are, he said, the true source and bearer of factious opposition and rule by a clique and did not favor the intelligent bourgeoise. He still preferred open voting, but was willing to follow the government's proposal. Devising a social theory

[28] On Bismarck's views, see Heinrich Herrfahrdt, *Das Problem der berufsständischen Vertretung von der französischen Revolution bis zur Gegenwart* (Stuttgart and Berlin, 1921), pp. 58-61; von Gerlach, *op. cit.;* Abg. H., *St. B.*, Sept. 12, 1866, pp. 307-08, 320; *Protokolle der Deutschen Bundesversammlungen*, April 9, 1866, pp. 102-03. See also the embellished account in Bismarck, *Gedanken und Erinnerungen*, II, 68-70.

[29] Abg. H., *St. B.*, Sept. 11, 1866, p. 286.

[30] *Ibid.*, Sept. 12, 1866, p. 332.

to support the new line, he said that general, direct suffrage was a necessary sign of a certain social and political condition. The old corporative forms which had been the basis of suffrage had decayed and new ones had not yet developed. He hoped that universal suffrage would further this development. He recognized the danger of the new method of voting, but he knew nothing better to offer. He did not believe that a Berlin merchant with a big bank account should have three or ten times as much voting power as a war veteran. The main attraction of general, direct suffrage was that it would affect persons at the most sensitive point: it would affect their social position and force them to defend that position "not by words" but "by positive social and political action." Thereby Wagener thought that social and political power might once again be united, a line of argument which, except for the difference in objective, was remarkably like that of Schulze-Delitzsch.[31]

The core of Wagener's thought about the new election system consisted in his wish that the Conservative party and the government would seize the initiative in the use of it; for, he said, only thereby would they prevent the institution from getting out of control, only then would they make it serve them.[32] The advice was no doubt sound, but the Conservatives had let loose a Frankenstein monster.[33] Bismarck soon found that not even the lower classes followed his dictates. Mass parties turned against him; the people did not always think like Bismarck and the Conservatives. The Conservatives themselves sometimes failed to support him; all the pressure of which the powerful government disposed failed to win docile majorities. At the end of his dominance in 1890, Bismarck was devising means of abolishing the Reichstag, the creation of his own election system.

Subsequently Prussian liberals did not fare well under the retention of the three-class system and open voting of 1849. Within a few years after the German Reich was established the subject of reform of

[31] Norddeutscher Bund, Reichstag, *St. B.*, March 28, 1867, pp. 420-22.
[32] Abg. H., *St. B.*, Sept. 12, 1866, p. 333.
[33] A small group of diehard reactionaries had never reconciled themselves to the existence of elections at all. It should be remembered that this group had broken with Bismarck, who was too modern for it. Deputy von Gerlach expressed its views in September, 1866, as follows: "Every election is a misfortune," but we should not abolish the three-class system of voting, deficient as it was. We should improve it. Universal suffrage was no improvement; it merely presupposed an atomized people. Society should be organic, and the "natural" leaders should dominate, each in his appropriate sphere, the Schulze in the village, and so on. In other words, von Gerlach wished the election system to be built on the castes of the Old Regime. See Abg. H., *St. B.*, Sept. 11, 1866, pp. 299 f.

the election law came up again (1873) in the Lower House of the Landtag. Once more the liberals postponed consideration of the problem.[34] A Catholic deputy accused them of avoiding it out of fear of the loss of their political influence.[35] A left-wing member of the Progressive party had at the time of the Austro-Prussian war privately expressed the same suspicion.[36] The evidence does not bear out this view. Most of the liberals seem rather to have opposed universal and equal suffrage on grounds of both material interest and principle. Bismarck and the national situation pushed them into accepting it for the Reich; but they undoubtedly preferred the vote to be restricted to the upper classes. After a few years the liberals lost their chance to change the system, for with the change in the social and political situation the three-class system returned a steady majority of Conservatives and their allies which could not be ousted until the Revolution of 1918.

Most liberals, even as the Conservatives, accepted social inequality as a fact, and most liberals wished to divide political power in the same way. The two groups, with the exception of some left-wing liberals, were not far apart in their views about an appropriate election law. They faced a common problem—how during a definite movement toward legal equality to change from a type of representation based on estates and caste to one based on classes. The Conservatives sought an election system which would preserve as much of the power of the estates as possible; the liberals sought one which would retain enough authority to prevent revolution and would nonetheless give the bourgeoisie the power safely to reform state and society in their interest. The three-class system afforded a neat compromise. It retained the principle of inequality; it did not apply a yardstick of the ownership of a specific amount of property to all Prussia but rather left the qualifications for voting to the localities in such a way as to retain the existing relationship of economic and to some extent social power in each locality. It based political differentiation upon the relative amount of taxes paid, a patriotic or civic basis on which one could counter any accusation of selfishness. It widened the group of the powerful without destroying the old ruling group and supplied a neutral foundation for a merger. Its importance, however, depended upon the importance of the institution for which elections were held.

[34] Abg. H., St. B., Nov. 26, 1873; I, 118-20.
[35] Von Mallinckrodt, Abg. H., St. B., Nov. 26, 1873; I, 109-10.
[36] L. Dehio, "Die preussische Demokratie und der Kreig von 1866," Forschungen zur Brandenburg-Preussischen Geschichte, XXXIX (1927), 258-59.

The failure of the liberals to develop the Lower House into the dominant institution of government relegated the elections and consequently the election law to a position of lesser significance, and the Reich method of voting deprived it of further prestige.

The Prussian election law of 1849 was significant for the character of the political standards of the people and the leaders. The discussion of it offered insights, confirmed in many other ways, into the level of cultural life of Prussia. Being in vigorous transition from the caste state to the modern state of high social mobility, this society was setting standards and forms for a long future. Apart from a few on the left, the liberals failed to appreciate that fact and to seek a broad popular basis for their ideals. The historians among them led the fight against this reform. The preservation of the three-class system of voting by the liberals offers an example of their shortsightedness and is one of the reasons why they failed to gain authority. The liberals helped to preserve a political system which within a few years became the bulwark of reaction.

The only respect in which the government of the New Era changed the system of voting had to do with the creation of election districts. The constitution called for the fixing of these districts by law (Article 69), but the Manteuffel ministry had conveniently ignored that clause and had arbitrarily changed voting districts by administrative act. Its one standard in doing so had been that of returning a Conservative deputy. Wherever necessary, it had split counties among several election districts; it had joined Germans and Poles in such a way as to assure a victory for the former, or Protestants and Catholics in order to defeat the latter. It had taken into consideration the state of transportation and wherever possible had forced the opposition voters to travel long distances over bad roads. It had frankly stated that it gerrymandered and had assured the Landtag that it would continue to do so. Even some Conservatives became critical of such flagrant corruption.

In 1860 Minister of Interior Count Schwerin introduced an election district law, the first one which the state adopted. After thorough consideration by the Lower House, the bill was somewhat modified and passed. Catholics and Poles, as well as Protestant Germans, warmly endorsed the law. It went to the Upper House, where it again passed with only minor changes. Once the Manteuffel government was eliminated, the Conservatives in that stronghold did not have the moral affrontery to defend the practices of their former leaders.

The new law introduced as fair and just conditions for everyone as were possible. The liberals agreed that a normal voting district should contain two counties but that in some cases one county might be used and in others more than two might be combined. Counties were selected for union on the basis of historic or cultural associations or of practical considerations. Of the latter, two were of essential importance, the presence of good roads and bridges which would enable the voters (the electors) to come together even in bad weather and the existence of a building sufficiently large to hold the voters and the presence of quarters for them and their teams. A county which had road connections with one neighbor but not with another would have to be attached to the former. A county without a building adequate to hold all the voters assembled to cast ballots by voice should be associated with one which had. A church, an inn, a railroad station, were usually selected; but some counties had none of these large enough to contain the voters. Think of keeping seven hundred or eight hundred voters crammed in a church, one deputy exclaimed, while each expressed his vote by voice! The act of voting would continue all day, voters would fill the church and overflow, evening would come and candles would have to be used. Think of the confusion! One can understand why the committee of the Lower House consulted each deputy before recommending the composition of the election districts, and why another deputy, a Catholic who had not been on the committee, urged the House to pass the bill as submitted by the committee and not to tamper with its details.

The only major objection which a few reactionaries in the Upper House made against the law concerned the relation of rural and urban population. The law designated each city of 50,000 population and over a separate election district for the self-evident reason that one deputy was to be elected for every 50,000 people. In the case of towns of lesser size the law merged them into the county along with the rural areas. Some Conservatives wished to keep the two distinct for fear that the town voters would outnumber the rural ones, or that the former would by superior strategy in campaigning win the latter to the side of liberalism. They wanted to keep the rural areas as dormant as possible. Nonetheless, the administrative difficulty of separating town and country in voting was so clearly evident that the criticism was not pressed. The reactionaries could not justify a division for voting between a town and its surrounding region when for every other purpose the two were interdependent.

A few liberals and Conservatives preferred the single county as a basis of representation, arguing that the county formed an organic, historic unit. They were unable, however, to sustain their proposal against criticism. The sponsors of the law used the most recent census, that of 1858, as the basis of arranging districts so as to be numerically just; and they pointed out that if the county were selected great unfairness would result, since many counties lacked the amount of population necessary to merit a deputy. They stressed the value of the larger district as a means of reducing the political prestige of the Landrat and other traditional wielders of power, and of allowing a larger choice of candidates than at present. More persons would then vote, the committee of the Lower House stated, because they would see greater possibility of their votes' being of some weight. In a small district where the distribution of political strength was already known, it said, the persons on the side certain to lose would be inclined not to vote at all.

The law was manifestly intended to reduce the material obstacles, bad transportation and inadequate quarters, and the psychological deterrents to voting. It was intended to encourage the voters by assuring them of fair treatment. It vastly improved upon the Manteuffel system; but it did not altogether stop gerrymandering. Bismarck revived the practice, not in the creation of election districts, for these were fixed by law, but in arranging the boundaries of the voting precincts within the districts. He was not able to accomplish much by these tricks; he hardly needed to do so. He simply ignored the results of the elections.

The liberals made their mistake in not transforming the three-class system of voting into one of equal manhood suffrage. Then the voters might have come to the polls in numbers comparable to those appearing in town elections under the Stein Ordinance of 1808, and the liberals would have had far more popular strength against Bismarck and the King then they were able to muster. The shortsightedness of the liberals was apparent from Deputy Lette's remark that the new districting law was "perhaps more important" than a new election law.[37]

[37] Abg. H., *St. B.*, May 22, 1860; II, 1229. For the discussion in the Landtag of the districting law see, Abg. H., *St. B.*, Feb. 7, 1856; *ibid.*, Jan. 20, March 22-23, 27, May 19, 22, 1860; *St. B.*, 1860, Vol. IV, Nos. 66, 67; Herrenhaus, *St. B.*, 1860, Vol. III, No. 35; Abg. H., *Drucksachen*, 1855-56, Vol. VI, No. 256; Abg. H., *St. B.*, Feb. 7, 1856; *ibid.*, April 20, 1858; Herrenhaus, *St. B.*, May 19, 1860; Abg. H., *St. B.*, Oct. 26, 1849; Abg. H., *Drucksachen*, 1854-55, Vol. V, No. 214; Abg. H., *Drucksachen*, 1855-56, Vol. III, No. 149; Abg. H., *St. B.*, Sept. 12, 1866; Abg H., *St. B.*, 1858, Vol. 11, No. 65.

9 / The Liberal Parties

A T THE TIME of the two elections of 1862 and 1863 the political alignment had reduced the parties and fractions into two major groups, with the Catholic Center party tending to divide, especially in 1863, in the same way. On the one side stood the Conservatives, as rock-ribbed, intolerant and defiant as ever; on the other was to be found an assortment of liberals and democrats, essentially agreed on fundamental objectives, forced by the government's behavior to act in unity, but suffering from a variety of centrifugal tensions which deprived them of the power of fully harmonious and organized cooperation.

The Relations Among the Liberal Parties

In spite of the fact that all liberals advocated an almost identical program, they split easily into fractions for reasons too insignificant for many intelligent and well-informed contemporaries to grasp. During the first two years of the New Era the Constitutional party dominated the liberal movement. Its leaders held ministerial posts, were friends of the ruler, and acted on the political slogan, "Do not press." They were liberals of the older generation, many of them men of the highest aristocratic standing, who disliked speedy action. They appreciated the wide scope of power of the King and were more concerned with the problem of leading the monarch slowly and gently along the road to constitutional government than they were with that of satisfying immediately the public demand for action in that direction. Accustomed to positions of dignified prestige in the local community as in the state, they preferred to act as individuals and disliked party organization, party control or discipline, campaigning for votes, or anything associated with popular politics. They were people who signed only their family name to a public statement, without Christian name, initials, or any designation of position or location. They expected the public to know who they were and to respect them as public leaders of long and mature experience and ripe learning. "Never in my life have I sought the position of representative," declared one of them, Deputy von Vincke of Hagen, in the Lower House in May, 1861; "I have not sent a single statement to my voters. I have never received an address from them expressing confidence or no-confidence. I have forbidden it every time. I believe that, with respect to my voters, I am in a completely independent position."[1]

The caution and slowness of the Constitutional party so thoroughly exasperated many liberals and democrats, both those in the Lower House and those outside, that in 1861 a group of critics came together in Berlin and formed the German Progressive party. "New people must be elected to the Lower House," declared the *Niederrheinische Zeitung* early in that year; and although the new party was formed mainly by East Prussians and developed its main strength in the Eastern and Central provinces, it undoubtedly responded to a statewide desire for action. It did not wish to destroy or weaken the unity among the liberals in the common struggle against the Conservatives; it sought rather to bring together men of all liberal groups, from the right-wing Constitutionals to the leftist democrats, who wished to work vigorously for the execution of the liberal ideals and national unification.[2] The party divided into several fractions, but on the whole it worked as a cohesive group.

In the Western provinces of Westphalia and the Rhineland but also to some extent in the Central provinces, the liberals in the main held together and without much difficulty made the transition from old liberalism to views and policies similar to those of the Progressive party.[3] The two strongest fractions of the liberals of the Western provinces took their names from the deputies who acted as leaders, Grabow whose group formed the right wing and Bockum-Dolffs whose group kept close to the Progressives. By the time of the two elections of 1862 and 1863 the increasingly reactionary deeds of the government

[1] Abg. H., *St. B.*, May 28, 1861; III, 1440.
[2] *Tagesbericht*, No. 50, Feb. 28, 1861; Parisius, *Politische Parteien,* p. 40; *National Zeitung*, Nov. 21, 1861.
[3] In a letter to Baumgarten, March 25, 1862, von Sybel, a Rhenish deputy, wrote that the liberal majority in the Western provinces was "entirely for harmony," and he hoped that the Progressive party would not cause trouble there. Heyderhoff, *op. cit.,* I, 86.

led to the decimation of right-wing liberals in the Lower House and to the actual unity of all liberal groups under the direction of the aggressive and positive leaders, primarily from among the Progressive and the Bockum-Dolffs, or Left-Center, groups. Petty differences gave way before the common need of defending liberalism against its enemies.

The fact that the liberals and democrats could cooperate in the case of practical necessity does not detract from the actuality and importance of the differences among them. The immaturity of the political life, the struggle for power among the parties and fractions, the search for bases of party distinction, the survival of social and political ways of the pre-parliamentary period, as well as the personal and psychological friction to be found in all forms of group activity at all stages kept the liberal groups apart, but conflict over principles and objectives scarcely existed at all. The right-wing liberals mistrusted the democrats and accused them of endeavoring to introduce parliamentary government and full political equality; but the democratic forces never became strong enough to alarm them. Contemporary comment gauged the relations correctly when it explained the differences on other bases than those of ideal or general objectives.

"Our party [the Constitutional] is a pitiful party," said the historian Droysen to von Bernhardi at the end of 1860. "Our party is discrediting itself in the state," lamented at about the same time another liberal who, like Droysen, had been supporting the government of the New Era. A member of the von Saucken family, disgusted with Minister of Interior von Schwerin for leaving all the reactionaires in office, declared that the liberal ministry had helped no one in the state except the Jews. In November of the next year, 1861, Doctor Kosch, the chairman of a political rally called by the Progressive party in Königsberg, declared, according to the *Königsberg Hartungsche Zeitung*,

> Not only the so-called Constitutional party but we also are "constitutional." The name "ministerial party" fits the former more precisely. They, the Constitutionalists, are blood of our blood, but very much less flesh of our flesh. They are so gentle, they are so soft that every raw breeze affects them unpleasantly. The Progressives are of a less sensitive nature; their energy distinguishes them from the others.

A right-wing liberal accurately described his party as "moderate," the Progressives as "agitational." The Progressive party aimed to supply the political energy, stated the *National Zeitung*, which the "learned liberalism" of the Lower House lacked. The left-wing *Volkszeitung* of

Berlin distinguished between the Constitutionals and the democrats in a cruder way. After stating that both wished to establish a legal state and differed at most over the guarantees for it, the paper declared that the democrats vigorously demanded the legal state, whereas the Constitutionals requested it "with apparent submissive loyalty." Or as the same paper declared three days later, the von Vincke form of constitutionalism wished consciously to "swindle the prince out of his former rights," whereas the democratic party stated freely and openly its demands.[4]

The opposition between the two liberal parties varied according to the traditional strength of the Constitutional group. In places like Halle, Magdeburg and Königsberg, where the Constitutionals had occupied the leading role, they disliked the competition of a young, fresh, vigorous group and felt hurt and indignant at the accusation of lack of activity. They had local vested interests and social prestige to protect.[5] Self-conscious about their superior experience and wisdom, they found reasons to object to many of the Progressives' acts. Even if the reasons seemed flimsy in actuality, they revealed that curse of a highly intelligent people learning the ways of practical politics, disagreement over methods and timing. They had to disagree or be swallowed by their more vigorous ally. One member of the party, Deputy Riedel, frankly said in a political meeting in Berlin that he had changed his stand from affirmative to negative on an amendment proposed in the Lower House because in the second instance a younger member, Freiherr von Hoverbeck, had introduced it. "It is not our custom," he said, "to support measures which are taken up by young, inexperienced members of the House."[6] They suffered from personal antagonism toward the Progressives and, wrote Wilhelm Dilthey in May, 1862, from the illusion that they alone were capable of governing.[7] They had great difficulty in swallowing their pride, and only the pressure of the reaction in 1862 induced them to do so.[8] The Con-

[4] Von Bernhardi, *op. cit.*, IV, 75, 71; III, 278-79; *Königsberg Hartungsche Zeitung*, Nov. 20, 1861; *Wochenschrift des Nationalvereins*, April 17, 1863; *Königsberg Hartungsche Zeitung*, Nov. 16, 1861; *National Zeitung*, June 12, 1861; *Tagesbericht*, No. 60, March 12, 1861; *ibid.*, No. 63, March 15, 1861.
[5] See *Volkszeitung*, March 29, 1862, for a despatch from Magdeburg; *ibid.*, April 15, 1862 from Halle; *Königsberg Hartungsche Zeitung*, April 10, 1862.
[6] Despatch from Berlin to the *Königsberg Hartungsche Zeitung*, Nov. 29, 1861.
[7] Heyderhoff, *op. cit.*, I, 89.
[8] See the statements by the Constitutionals in Königsberg in the *Königsberg Hartungsche Zeitung*, Sept. 25, 1861, March 7, 1862. How unfortunate the intransigent attitude seemed to the other liberal groups was made clear in an appeal to

stitutional party paper, the *Stern Zeitung* of Berlin, in April, 1862, blamed the failure on the part of the liberal factions to ally and to dam back the democrats not on "the well-tested leaders but on the younger, uncontrolled combative forces." The paper deplored the coalition which had begun in 1858 between the Constitutionals and the democrats, and accused the latter of having intentionally poisoned the liberal supporters of the Constitutional ministry and turned them into opponents.[9] The Constitutional leaders were looking for a scapegoat for their failure in the government.[10]

Since issues of such gravity for the future of Prussia and Germany were at stake, the Progressives had great difficulty in comprehending the instransigent stand taken by the Constitutionals. Fortunately for the cause of liberalism, the attitude remained confined to groups in a very few places. In towns like Stettin and Breslau the news of the composition of the new Conservative ministry in 1862 led the Constitutionals to drop their plans for a separate election campaign and to join forces with the other party.[11] Already in the preceding year the liberals of all parties had united their strength in the rural areas and in those urban centers where the Conservatives could muster sufficent votes to constitute a threat. The continuation of competition in elections between the Constitutional party and the Progressives was restricted to the larger cities and to those election districts where reactionary influence scarcely existed.[12] Even the fact of their disagreement revealed in those localities the general strength of liberalism.

The Progressive party had advocated unity of action among the liberals from the beginning. When the liberals in the ministry were eliminated in 1862 and the government became composed exclusively of Conservatives, the force of events achieved what the Progressives alone had been unable to do. The four liberal fractions in the Lower House began in March, 1862, to meet together from time to time in a social way.[13] A few weeks later there occurred a final rebellion. The

---

the Constitutionals in April, 1862, by the election committee of the Progressive party in the election district Königsberg-Fischhausen, *ibid.*, April 2, 1862; see also *Kölnische Zeitung*, Oct. 12, 1863.

[9] *Tagesbericht*, No. 57, March 8, 1861.

[10] One Constitutional paper tried to find a social basis to distinguish the party, but the *Königsberg Hartungsche Zeitung* was unable to discover any proof for this view. See Parisius, *Politische Parteien*, p. 61; *Tagesbericht*, No. 66, March 19, 1861; *Königsberg Hartungsche Zeitung*, March 21, May 25, 1862.

[11] See *Volkszeitung*, March 22, 1862, on Stettin; *Kölnische Zeitung*, Sept. 21, Oct. 4, 1863, on Breslau.

[12] See *National Zeitung*, Dec. 11, 1861; *Kölnische Zeitung*, Jan. 13, 1862.

[13] *Kölnische Zeitung*, March 5, 1862.

Grabow fraction, the current right-wing group of liberals, split into two groups over the question of cooperation with the Progressive party. The small minority under the leadership of that most difficult individualist, von Vincke, refused to accept the recommendation of Grabow in favor of cooperation and formed a separate fraction.[14] The actual effect upon the political strength of the liberals was so slight as to be negligible. This kind of jealously was taken care of by the voters, who increasingly returned to the Lower House those persons able to unite with others against the hated government.

Leadership, State and Local

An analysis of state-wide and local leadership should afford insight into the strength of liberalism in the population. The issues at stake between the liberals and the Conservatives involved the basic organization of society, that is, whether it should be that of caste, privilege and absolutism or that of freedom; and social and occupational interests were sufficiently uniform to enable one to gauge the attitude of these groups from the political affiliation of their leaders.

The method of inference must be used with caution, for without additional information it would not suffice to establish the political alignment of the social and occupational groups. It should work best for the industrialists, merchants, and bankers, those who were most aware of the value of liberalism and most eager to open new opportunities. It should be least effective in disclosing the attitude of the aristocracy and the handworkers, the groups that remained closest to the Old Regime. For insight on the politics of these two groups one must know whether they regarded the preservation of the old order as more important than the development of the new opportunities which liberalism would bring, a question more of choice of ideals than of occupational or social interest. In the case of the peasantry one needs to ascertain whether they had heard of the issues, whether they understood them, and whether they had enough freedom to dare to pursue their own interest. If one keeps these limitations in mind, however, information about the social and occupational bases of political leadership should offer useful evidence on the attitude of the various groups in the conflict.

The types of persons selected as deputies did reflect the changing structure of the population. In the two decades of the 1850s and 1860s the rapid development of industrialism in the state added an in-

---

[14] See Parisius, *Politische Parteien,* pp. 54-55, 61; *Kölnische Zeitung,* May 26, 1862; Parisius, *von Hoverbeck,* II, 47-48; von Bernhardi, *op. cit.,* IV, 194-95.

creasingly strong bourgeois element to the old society of the caste-state. The bases for public leadership became diverse. Certain social groups and certain occupations which had supplied public guidance under the regime of agrarianism and absolutism continued that function after a popularly elected parliament had been introduced. At the same time industrialism created the need for new types of public leaders; and by affording many new opportunities for individuals to rise in the social scale it began to provide the personnel for taking on these functions. In many cases the leaders reflected in varying ways and degrees both the Old Regime and the new industrial society; in others they represented one and not the other. The characteristics of a transitional period appeared in the diversity of criteria.

The aristocracy continued to be expected to provide public leaders and did so. Accustomed to dominance in a society without a written constitution and a popularly elected parliament, they had over the members of the other classes the great advantage of traditional prestige and the habit of leadership. Their difficulty lay in the fact that in order to remain leaders they had to sacrifice their legal privileges and caste status and accept the principle of equality before the law. They had to become natural, useful leaders, depending for their position upon ability. While the liberal aristocrats were willing to do so, the Conservatives refused. Whether liberal or Conservative, the aristocrats instinctively disliked seeking popularity and vying for votes, for these actions violated their standards of upper-class personality. Since the competition in politics had not advanced far enough by the 1860s to require much of this kind of political behavior, members of the aristocratic class continued to be accepted and to serve as public leaders in politics while preserving many characteristics of the Old Regime. The unconscious assumption of social superiority toward the mass of voters and the preservation of a certain degree of dignified aloofness rather enhanced their prestige, provided they were willing to accept the principles of liberalism, to associate on a basis of equality with the leaders from the other classes, and to respect the dignity of even the little man. The public liked leaders whom they could respect, on whom they could rely, to whom they could defer. A good family name seemed to assure the necessary guarantee. Lacking experience in politics and not having as yet developed many new leaders in the Landtag's brief existence, the public turned to members of well-known aristocratic families for deputies. While they did not need to be equalitarian in social practice, they were expected not to adhere too rigidly to the aristocratic tendency toward subjectivity in political behavior or toward a highly personal attitude in political affairs. If they did, as in the case of von Vincke, they lost standing and were subject to political defeat. They had to conform to the discipline necessary for political action.

Among the lower classes, the burghers and workers of the towns and cities, the middle-class landowners, and the peasants, position in the social structure had relegated them by tradition to the role of subject or at most of local leader among social equals. They lacked the aristocracy's unselfconscious feeling of superiority in experience and wisdom. In the period under discussion, the urban industrial workers hardly exerted any political influence; they had not yet developed the strength of numbers and organization which a few years later enabled them to become politically impressive. They supplied no political leaders in the Landtag. The peasants were active only in the local elections and did not count as a source of potential state leadership. In contrast with the constitutional assembly in Berlin in 1848, not a single peasant was sent as deputy to the Lower House in the elections of 1862 and 1863, even though these elections were the most liberal of any between 1849 and 1918. The urban burghers and the landowners of middle-class or aristocratic origin supplied the state political leaders for the lower classes and developed the new standards for political leadership and action in an industrial society. The needs of the institution of politics coincided with many of the basic middle-class traits of character. The burghers were accustomed to a rational approach to problems, to compromise and other manifestations of mutual respect, and to action by a group. As contrasted with that of the aristocracy, their strength depended in addition to their intelligence and aggressiveness upon their large numbers and upon their ability to subordinate themselves to and to cooperate for the achievement of a common objective. Having to learn by experiment the ways which politics required of its practitioners, they made mistakes and did not always understand the nature of the new kind of activity; but they supplied the driving and creative force in it, and they had a more abiding interest in its successful development than the liberals among the aristocracy.

The selection of political leaders depended far more upon occupation than it did upon the social class to which one belonged. In a society as bureaucratically organized as that of Prussia, social prestige varied to such a degree with occupation that the two could not usually be distinguished. Certain occupations of the Old Regime which had carried with them the expectation and responsibility of public leadership continued to do so both in areas and among social groups remaining economically largely in the Old Regime and in those being transformed by industrialism. The government official, the lawyer, the professor and school superintendent, the pastor or priest, the owner of large or middle-seized landed estate, the wholesale merchant—these occupations retained their prestige. To them the industrial society added the industrialist, the banker and insurance director, the newspaper editor, and with the increase in scientific knowledge, the physician. Practically all the Landtag deputies of the New Era and the years of the constitutional conflict came from these occupations; many belonged as well to the aristocracy. A person like Schulze-Delitzsch, able to live by being what one may call a professional public leader, stood out as a rarity; even he had begun his career as a county judge. Not yet reached was the stage of development of modern industrial society when politics was a profession, when economic undertakings were large enough to enable certain members to concentrate on public relations and public service and to enter into political life as part of their jobs.

An analysis of the data on the deputies in five Prussian political assemblies between 1848 and 1866 will show the relative prestige of the occupations for public leadership.[15] The landowners and the government officials, especially the justice officials, played the dominant role. Each of the other occupations, the professors, merchants and industrialists, even the retired officials and officers, provided a small number in proportion. Prussia remained, as it had been for two centuries, a state led by landowners and government officials. These two groups merged, for the landowner usually had some official duties. The two groups had served absolutism loyally and diligently and had managed the subjects of the Hohenzollerns in the name of autocracy. They claimed to reflect whatever public opinion existed, to be the guardians of freedom and the exponents of responsible government, that is, of government responsible to them, who in turn would attend to the welfare of the King's other subjects. The majority of them had become liberal in the course of the Nineteenth Century and were by the 1860s assuming the leadership of the King's subjects in a new capacity and in a new way. The bureaucratic leader and the agrarian lord were being returned to the Lower House of the Landtag in popular election to represent the public. The two were adapting themselves to the changed conditions of society and the state; extraordinary as it may seem, they were striving to transform the old state

[15] See Appendix C.

and society in which they had ruled supreme under the King into a new state and society of liberalism and German national unity.

From the beginning of the parliamentary history of the state the Prussians were impressed by the advantage of having government officials serve as deputies. In October, 1849, Deputy Scherer had declared in the Lower House that the officials enjoyed the confidence of the people, as one could see from the large number elected to the Landtag. Their theoretical and practical knowledge, he said, was indispensable for law-making; without their aid the Lower House would often not know how to proceed. Certain officials were especially suited to be deputies, Scherer stated, namely, the administrative and the justice officials, "who through their direct and continuous contact with the people know and understand their needs best. I mention here for example only the Landrats and the justices of the peace."[16] Almost twenty years later, Windthorst, the Catholic leader in the Reichstag of the North German Confederation, expressed an identical opinion. "In the present stage of development of our social and public conditions it is unthinkable," he said, "that all officials could be excluded" from the Reichstag. He estimated that about 190 officials held seats in the present assembly, and he regarded their participation as a healthy sign.[17]

Not all government officials were equally available for election, for some were more dependent upon the ministry than others. Two categories should be distinguished, those in administration and those in justice. The former were subject to disciplinary action by the government; they could be transferred at will, from an interesting position in a town or city like Cologne with varied social and cultural opportunities to some monotonous work in a wretched garrison town in Posen. Or there were those who could be retired on half pay at any time. Whatever their political sentiments, they usually stood in too great dependence on the government to act very often against its will, above all to become deputies and openly to oppose it. If they were Conservatives, they would enjoy official support in the elections of 1862 and 1863; but they could not win enough votes to be returned. Few openly became members of either the Progressive party or the Left-Center party; for apart from the fact that many were restrained by fear of government reprisal, they had largely been retained in office from the Manteuffel period and many were more or less opponents to

---

[16] Abg. H., *St. B.*, Oct. 27, 1849, p. 908.
[17] Norddeutscher Bund, Reichstag. *St. B.*, March 28, 1867, p. 425.

even the mildly liberal government of the New Era.[18] Among these administrative officials, the most likely ones for election as deputy, the Landrats, personified as a rule the characteristics of autocracy and caste which the liberals and democrats sought to abolish. They had had themselves elected to the Lower House during the Manteuffel regime and had constituted the bulwark of that reactionary rule.

Even apart from their usually reactionary views, the administrative officials occupied a position which ill suited them for the role of elected representatives. "If the opposition especially were led by them," wrote Professor Bluntschli in his famous book *Allgemeine Staatsrecht*,[19] "the unity and authority of the governmental body would be damaged; if the ministry tried to support itself by them in the Chamber, the independence of the Chamber would be endangered. In times of vigorous struggle the voters would, therefore, do best as a rule to elect no administrative officials outside the responsible ministers." Deputy Mathis, a member of the Constitutional party, favored making this class of officials ineligible for election as deputies. That the candidates and the voters were aware of this handicap may be seen from an 1861 election appeal in Bielefeld to support the former judge and staunch liberal Waldeck.

> Do not let yourself be mislead by the illusion that an industrialist would better represent your interests or that an administrative official knows more accurately your needs. Think of the many considerations which an administrative official has to think of when it is a question of opposing openly and freely the misdeeds of the bureaucracy, and do not forget how often in the recent past apparently liberal views in these circles have bowed before superior influences. Elect Waldeck.[20]

It would be wrong to conclude that a large percentage of the administrative officials did not favor liberalism. In spite of government pressure to support the Conservatives, many bureaucrats showed independence and courage in openly aligning with the liberals, and a considerable number were elected as deputies. Far from having been drilled effectively in political docility, they seem to have been convinced by the experience under the Manteuffel regime of the necessity of liberalism; and as soon as the government of the New Era relaxed control over their political behavior they emerged as champions of the

[18] Parisius, *von Hoverbeck*, II, 104; *Königsberg Hartungsche Zeitung*, Jan. 11, 1862.

[19] 4th ed. (Munich, 1864), I, 510.

[20] Abg. H., *St. B.*, April 6, 1861; I, 652-53. *National Zeitung*, Jan. 1, 1861.

new ideals. Some of them possessed independent means, for example, Bockum-Dolffs, who was a big landowner and felt secure against any official coercion. Most, however, occupied positions of economic dependence and felt compelled to gauge the degree of their public participation in favor of liberalism by the attitude of the ministry. When the latter allowed such freedom, they worked for the liberal parties; when it called them to account, they grew cautious and outwardly reserved. The number willing to risk official punishment for the sake of principles, however, was so large that one may regard them as the heroes of this conflict.

The justice officials occupied a different position. They enjoyed life tenure and were legally protected against official chicanery. They could act with independence; they had a distinguished tradition of preserving the laws and, whenever it became necessary, of resisting even the royal authority in defence of the law. The story of a judge's defiance of Frederick the Great had become an essential part of Prussian folklore. The reactionary *Berliner Revue* might write in 1862 that this independence of the judiciary had become "a curse for our Fatherland"; but until Bismarck's breach of this tradition in 1864, the Prussian government had on the whole respected the independence of the judges.[21]

Among the judicial officials the county judge stood closest to the masses of the population. In a state which preserved the police authority of the Old Regime the duties of the county judge were necessarily wide. This official became acquainted with conditions in the area of his jurisdiction as no other one did, not even the Landrat. Into his court there came the everyday life, its difficulties, its problems, its hopes, its frustrations. He viewed it as a judge, seeking to act according to the law, and imposing a code of conduct based on general principles of equity. He had to understand the mentality of the people with whom he dealt, those brought before his court, those who formed the society in which they lived. He saw them as they were, and he realized what they needed in order to become better social beings. His intimate knowledge of the law enabled him to perceive how the government worked and to comprehend by experience in what respects the law should be changed for the welfare of the people. He lived and acted for and was responsible to the government and to the people at that crucial point where government and people might

---

[21] *Kölnische Zeitung*, April 29, 1862. See the statement in Parisius, *von Hoverbeck*, I, 194, that the county judge was more independent than an Oberpräsident.

collide. He was able to look in both directions, to know what the one should do and what the other needed. His profession required careful training in abstract thinking, in thinking through and testing general principles by practical application. He had other criteria than the Landrat's standards of administrative utility, caste or class interest, and prejudice. He could not imitate the Landrat and other administrative officials in clearing his mind of some unfair or inhuman act by throwing the responsibility upon the government or upon orders from his administrative superiors; he had another criterion, the law, and another guide, his own conscience. He served as natural leader of the locality, a person whom one could respect and trust, a person thoroughly acquainted with the locality and its needs, known to everyone, and independent of official or of any other kind of pressure. His liberalism reflected the wish to make his knowledge useful. The New Era opened the way to political activity, and he became one of the heroes of the constitutional conflict, fighting in the vanguard especially of the Progressive party.

The county judge as a political leader aroused the severe criticism of some other liberals, particularly those to the right politically and those who prided themselves on their superior wisdom. The Constitutional party leader from Königsberg, von Simson, a judge of a higher court, complained in March, 1861, about the doctrinaire spirit of the county judges, of whom he said there were seventy-two in the Lower House.

> They wish to conduct politics according to the articles of the legal code, and oppose the ministry in everything; whoever has relations with the ministry is an unreliable person to them . . . for in their opinion they were sent here to control the ministry. That is their conception of parliamentary government, and they consider it their duty in all cases to oppose the government. They cannot go calmly to bed at night without the feeling of having attacked the ministry during the day.[22]

Since von Simson supported the mildly liberal government of the New Era, his opinion scarcely partook of that judicious frame of mind appropriate to one of his profession. The county judges understood the mood and wishes of the people far better than this gentlemen did, and they aimed to act as befitted representatives of the people, not as persons trying to humor the ministers, who in turn were trying to humor the ruler. The deputies were learning the ways of politics and making mistakes in methods and procedures; but they were also, as

---

[22] Von Bernhardi, op. cit., IV, 103.

another liberal critic, Professor von Sybel, was soon to discover, defending principles, the bases of a free way of life; and they were doing so tenaciously.

While the presence of such a large percentage of officials in the Lower House caused some complaint from both agrarian and industrial and commercial groups, the criticism did not assume any significance in political relations and party affiliations, and it did not affect the course of events. Except among the Conservatives, the use of politics as a major means of protecting or furthering special economic interests had not begun. The political issues involved the character of fundamental Prussian institutions, whether the country should preserve caste structure, autocracy and mercantilism or become liberal. Until these issues were settled, controversy among the liberals over representation of economic interests could scarcely serve any purpose. Why quarrel over the proportion of occupational representation until one knew what authority, what role in the state the representatives would have?

The criticism is nonetheless of value for understanding the social and occupational background of political activity of the period. In analyzing the composition of the Lower House elected in 1863, a writer in the *Deutsche Vierteljahrschrift* noted that the rural population was under-represented. It constituted two-thirds of the people, he said, but not even one-third of the deputies consisted of landowners. The urban population predominated; but even in this element only some forty deputies actively engaged in business, while the others were government officials, teachers, professors, lawyers, physicians, and so on. The reasoning and reflecting elements in the population predominated, the writer stated, and he deplored the fact that the same persons approved the taxes as deputies and spent the money as officials. Nonetheless, he said, the Lower House was a truly representative body. Although, he concluded, it would be an exaggeration to say that the entire people stood behind the House, a real and significant proportion gave it full support.[23]

While the author of the analysis correctly judged the dominant driving force of the urban elements in the political struggle for a liberal society, the fact that agriculturalists constituted nearly one-third of the Lower House and in number ranked only slightly behind the officials requires explanation. The conditions of their kind of life must have enabled them to assume this active political role. The

[23] *Deutsche Vierteljahrschrift*, 1866, pp. 33-34, 37.

peasantry can be eliminated at once from consideration; it provided no deputies. It lacked the political interest, the training, the self-confidence, and the time to serve as deputy. A peasant felt that he had to concentrate on the cultivation of his piece of land, if he had any; and he was accustomed to leaving state affairs to the upper classes. The large and middle-sized landowners or cultivators of large rented holdings assumed the leadership of the rural population, whether Conservative or liberal, and were elected as deputies to the Landtag. Agriculture made them independent of government and enabled them to decide matters for themselves. The ruler and the bureaucracy could cause them social discomfort and many inconveniences, but could not deprive them of their economic self-sufficiency. The seasonal nature of agiculture enabled them to leave for several months to serve in the Lower House without suffering economic harm. In some cases their holdings were large enough to require the service of a manager, to whom responsibility could be given during their absence in the Land-tag. They were accustomed to political activity and leadership in the county and provincial Landtags; and they felt responsible toward the rest of the population, especially the rural, for the protection and furtherance of common interests. They did not stop at rural affairs, however, but endeavored to concern themselves with the welfare of the state as a whole. They knew a good deal about government from having the responsibility for police and judicial matters in their locality. Since even in the late Eighteenth Century agriculture had begun to assume capitalistic methods, many of these agrarians had characteristics and interests in common with the capitalistic urban population. The community between the two groups had increased in the Nineteenth Century by the rapid turnover of landed property and its purchase by urban families who had turned agrarian.

The industrial and commercial forces of the population showed a low percentage of occupational representation in the Lower House, a percentage which at the time expressed fairly accurately their number but which was out of proportion to their economic role in the state. As far as economic independence was concerned, they could withstand government pressure as well as the agrarians. Nor did the economic leaders suffer from lack of political knowledge and social self-confidence. They had definite objectives in view, summed up in the term liberalism. They were accustomed to participating in town and city affairs, and for several decades they had been taking an increasing interest in state and national matters. As potential political leaders in the state they suffered from one serious handicap. Unlike the upper-class agrarians, they had as a rule to attend constantly to their business.

The dynamics of capitalistic activity were particularly strong in these years of the 1850s and 1860s with the great expansion of industry and commerce, and to seize opportunities these persons had to remain closely at their business. The international crises, the Crimean War, the wars of Italian unification and the American Civil War, enhanced the uncertainty. The businessmen of sufficient prominence to be elected as deputies rarely had time to assume the responsibility.

Even if the leading business personnel had felt free to serve as deputies, they would not have regarded themselves as exponents of special material interests; they would rather have worked for the establishment of legal conditions making possible the development of a liberal state and society. In this society industry and commerce would enjoy the advantages of freedom from the mercantilist state, and the middle classes would share the benefits of social equality and self-government; but these would accrue to everyone in the entire state, and not merely to the industrial and commercial interests. Although in the last part of 1861 the *Berliner Börsen Zeitung*[24] wished that more persons in commerce and industry would serve as deputies, the general attitude of business, expressed in a meeting of the merchants' association in Königsberg in July of that year, was that in view of the seriousness of the times a deputy representing the entire people was needed more than one to look after special business interests. Even at that early date business interests preferred to play an indirect role.[25]

The popularity of the professor as a public leader had declined since 1848. Conditions had changed, and needs and experience had modified the conception of the kind of person to choose as deputy in the Landtag. A long editorial in the *Königsberg Hartungsche Zeitung* of October 30, 1861, described the characteristics of an able representative. He should have sound judgment about the general world situation, especially about the situation of the fatherland and the immediate tasks of legislation. He should possess a general knowledge of state finances and of the productivity of the people. He should have a good, all-round education and a general understanding of Prussian government, but he should not be expected to be acquainted in detail with all the matters with which he would be called upon to deal. He could find plenty of experts to supply him with the special information. He should be firm and dependable in his views and never sacrifice prin-

---

[24] Sept. 27, 30, 1861.
[25] *Ibid.*, July 24, 1861; *Königsberg Hartungsche Zeitung*, Dec. 17, 1861, Jan. 29, 1862. Most of the deputies who took the initiative on economic affairs in the Lower House were newspaper men and officials.

ciples. Of course, he had at times to make concessions on points, but he should do so only for the purpose of furthering the implementation of his fundamental principles. The writer of the editorial had an entirely different kind of person in mind from the all-wise professor, the examiner of the Prussian people, the master of the classroom, the friend of pure ideals, the expert on everything. The writer was working toward a conception of a representative who should not personify what the people should be or do but who should represent what they were and what they specifically wished. The writer lacked the experience necessary to clarify this conception fully, but he showed remarkable improvement over the thinking of 1848. That he stressed the importance of firm defence of principles reflected the actual needs of the situation. The political conflict between liberals and government involved differences of principle of the most fundamental kind. In such a time men of character were far more essential than persons of expert knowledge.

In every period of parliamentary history some individuals personify the qualities which a representative should not have and some others display those which constitute the ideal type. As nearly as it is possible to select any individuals for these roles for the early 1860s one might choose Freiherr von Vincke to illustrate the first and Schulze-Delitzsch the second.

A Westphalian aristocrat and one of the most prominent liberal leaders in the New Era, von Vincke failed as a party or fraction leader. He split the party to which he belonged, and after having had great difficulty in obtaining a seat in 1862, he was defeated in the election in the next year. Stubborn and haughty, he had an exceptional faculty for transforming any minor difference of opinion into a moral issue and a personal affront. Heedless of political effect he was irascible, bold with words, easy in the use of irony and in denunciation, and quick to attack. His liberalism in principle was unquestioned. He had a reputation for being a leader of the people, an aristocrat who understood the peasant and defended the interests of the lower classes. He publicly attacked fellow aristocrats, democrats, or his own colleagues with the fury and the wealth of expression of his extraordinary mind. The National Assembly of 1848, Waldeck, anyone who opposed him received ample attention. He was too proud to ask anyone to vote for him and he refused to report to anyone on his actions as representative. In March, 1861, the *Magdeburger Zeitung* accused him of servility and erratic conduct. One day he praised Garibaldi and the Revolution, and the next day, it said, he put on his uniform of the Order of St. John and appeared at a big political festival as a colleague of the Conservative. A year later after even more experience, the same newspaper drew up a balance sheet on von Vincke as follows. He was a crank who was incapable of being a party leader. If he had lived a hundred years earlier, he would have been a very liberal person. Unfortunately he was born too late. His father had praised the English for having already undermined the system of entail in the Fifteenth Century. Since 1848 the son had been fighting for the preservation of this aristocratic privilege in Prussia. His father believed in and practiced equality, whereas, said the paper, during his entire life the son had struggled unsuccessfully against his own Junker traits.[26]

Von Vincke refused to cooperate with the Progressive party and split his own party over the issue. He was blamed by some for having misled the liberals at the beginning of the New Era into provisionally approving the money for the military reforms and for having thereby caused all the subsequent trouble. When the conflict broke out, so his critics asserted, he withdrew from politics and declared that his duties as guardian of minors were more important than those of Landtag deputy and party leader.[27] As the *Magdeburger Zeitung* said, he remained an aristocrat of the age of caste and privilege, and his retention of the characteristics of that type in the period of political parties, parliaments, and the spreading social forms of liberalism doomed him to political failure.

Heinrich Schulze had had in the course of time the name of his birth place, Delitzsch, added to his name in order to distinguish him from the numerous other Schulzes to be found in Germany. The custom was not uncommon; it was applied to him of necessity as he became famous. His family lacked any mark of distinction; but the social changes occurring in the two middle quarters of the Nineteenth Century offered him opportunities to rise in the world. After studying law he served as county judge and soon became interested in organizing cooperative associations for helping the handworkers to maintain themselves in the developing industrialism. Since participation as a democrat in the Revolution of 1848 ruined any expectation of an official career, he devoted his energy to the cause of the cooperatives and to other forms of non-official public activity. His sympathy for the

lower urban groups and his struggle by means of cooperatives to prevent the handworkers of the lower middle class from succumbing to
industrial competition and becoming proletariat endeared him to both
handworkers and the developing bourgeoisie. The latter hoped that
he had found the solution to this particular social problem and would
overcome the threat of socialism. He wrote numerous articles and
books, edited a journal, and earned a deserved reputation as a brilliant
popular orator. The position which he developed for himself made
him a point of contact between the upper and lower classes, between
capitalism and the handicrafts, between the small town and even the
village on the one hand and the city on the other. He was equally at
ease and equally welcome and respected in the home of a small craftsman, a peasant, a wealthy industrialist, and an able and distinguished
professor. His reputation spread over the state as that of an honorable,
courageous friend of the people.

Schulze-Delitzsch personified the ideals of liberal democracy, and
he understood these ideals in their practical working and in their full
social implications as almost no other Prussian leader did. His
speeches and writings disclosed a mind which had thought through
the democratic principles to their simplest elements. Among the many
confused utterances of this highly verbal generation of liberals his
assertions possessed the clarity and emotional conviction of a man who
appreciated the meaning of his own words. In the early months of
the New Era the contrast between the precision of his views and the
too often theoretical nature of those of his liberal colleagues, even
the ablest and most learned, was striking. As the conflict with Bismarck grew in bitterness the liberals were forced to use Schulze's ideals
as the logical conclusion of their position. They had to go beyond
their own compromising or halfway views to the fundamentals of
their ideal objectives. The fury of the battle with Bismarck and the
sudden collapse of their defence in 1866 prevented them from comprehending the full meaning of their ideological assertions, and many
of them surrendered to *Realpolitik*. With Schulze-Delitzsch these
democratic ideals, more akin to English liberalism than those of other
Germans, had become too firmly embedded in his character for him to
change. The surprising fact was that although his policies and ideals
were far more liberal than those of most of his colleagues he enjoyed
such wide popularity. In November, 1861, the *National Zeitung* of
Berlin declared in an editorial that "today throughout the entire
state from the East Prussian to the French frontier no name is more
popular than that of Schulze-Delitzsch and no one is considered more

indispensable for the Lower House than he is." Needless to say, Freiherr von Vincke did not agree with this estimate.[28]

In discussing the subject of local political leadership among the liberals, one must distinguish among three types of situations, that in a rural community, that in an urban center with wide and diversified economic interests and relations, and that in a town which remained primarily dependent upon the economy of the surrounding rural area. The first type was to be found over most of the state, but particularly in the Central and Eastern provinces. The second type was most numerous in Westphalia and the Rhineland, but included towns and cities like Berlin in other provinces. The third type predominated in the Eastern provinces. The social composition of each entailed essential distinctions in the nature of the political leadership.

Rural life presented natural obstacles to the development of new political organizations and leadership which under existing conditions were almost insurmountable. The scattered distribution of the people and poor transportation facilities made it difficult to hold meetings for political discussion and agitation. Instead of election committees, as among the urban people, the rural communities depended for guidance upon the traditional leaders. In the village the Schulze assumed the new role as an extension of his regular functions, and he carried out the responsibility of close personal rapport with the villagers in the same way as he did his other duties. The class consciousness of the rural population made it difficult for even a liberal landowner of the upper class to join peasants in any kind of equalitarian election committee; neither lord nor peasant would have felt at ease in such an organization, and both would have regarded it as superfluous. The upper classes in the rural areas lacked the diversity of interests and the actual numbers necessary to make a formal committee.

The urban centers offered a situation favorable to the emergence of political leadership. The large numbers of voters, the complexity of interests involved, the habits of discussion, and the availability of instruments and personnel for political action made the conscious selection of leaders necessary and possible. The Constitutional party tended not to encourage the development of new local leadership; but the other liberal parties sought to arouse the initiative of local individuals in all occupational groups, except those like the day laborer

[28] *National Zeitung*, Nov. 22, 1861. See also the enthusiasm of Königsberg liberals for him. *Königsberg Hartungsche Zeitung*, Oct. 27, 1861. Numerous other examples could be given.

and the industrial worker, who still lacked social and political significance.

The best evidence about the personnel of the local leadership can be seen in the membership of the election committees. Except for certain officials subject to direct government pressure, the lists contained the names of the most prominent members of the community. They showed that in spite of the unwillingness of merchants and industrialists as a rule to take the time to serve as Landtag deputies, these groups devoted many hours of service to secure the election of liberals from their district and were actively concerned not merely with municipal affairs but with problems of state and national life. The lists also included the names of numerous officials, judicial, and administrative, and those in such fields as education. They revealed that the dominant influence lay with the economic upper bourgeoisie but that associated with them were the other local middle-class leaders, the newspaper editors, the professors and teachers, the doctors and the lawyers. Although furnishing some personnel for the local committees, the handworkers lacked the power and drive of their wealthy colleagues.

In the Western provinces of the Rhineland and Westphalia the division of function in the economy had progressed sufficiently by the 1860s for the main lines of the society of industrialism to appear. Urban centers had become so plentiful and large that the population of numerous towns no longer depended mainly upon the immediate rural neighborhood for their market and the source of their supplies and income. The expansion of economic interest beyond the locality or immediate region had been accompanied by a growing social differentiation and the establishment of political organizations predominantly or exclusively for the urban population. The rural people assumed a secondary role. They tended to look to the urban centers for guidance and initiative; and while they cooperated with their more aggressive urban compatriots, they did so in the position rather of a follower than of a group of comparable or equal political interest and influence. Industrialists, bankers, insurance directors appeared as political leaders in the locality and province along with the traditional merchants. With increasing industrialization, the professions became specialized and assumed new functions. The lawyer in particular appeared more and more as the exponent of industrial interests, frequently in the capacity of public representative, of secretary or executive head of an organization set up to further certain interests. Government officials assumed much less significance as public leaders than in those provinces where industrialism had not yet broken into the old structure of society. Where an election committee for a province was established, the owners or managers of large landed estates hardly figured at all.

An analysis of the structure of a few election committees will illustrate the political significance of the occupational changes in Westphalia and the Rhineland. The liberal election committee of Dortmund called a meeting of political leaders of the province for the purpose, among others, of discussing the advisability of creating an election committee for the entire province. The meeting, held at Hamm early in November, 1861, approved the proposal and selected a committee composed of five lawyers, two other professional persons, one school director, three justice officials, one former administrative official, one estate-owner, one physician, three merchants, one surveyor, and five industrialists.[29] At about the same time an election committee was created in Mülheim and Siegburg which consisted of one estate-owner, one teacher, one justice official, one physician, three industrialists, and two city councillors. At Düsseldorf, a similar committee contained a more diversified personnel—two painters, one writer, one editor, one director of an institute, one watchmaker, one apothecary, one estate-owner, one innkeeper, one justice official, one director, one retired colonel, four merchants, nine industrialists, two lawyers, two other professional persons, and one with no occupation listed. Others were added later. In Cologne the local committee included three city councillors, one of whom was a prominent textile manufacturer, two justice officials, one gymnastics teacher, one director, one banker, one master tailor, two lawyers, one assessor, one writer, one bookseller, two merchants, and one without a profession listed. Of the membership on all these committees, only four belonged to the nobility—a director, a retired colonel, an industrialist, and an estate-owner.[30]

The campaign in 1863 aroused much more bitterness throughout Prussia than any preceding one and caused the liberals of all shades to unite in opposition to the government. At Halle in September a large liberal committee was organized for the elections. The personnel indicated the occupational spread of the liberal groups. It contained one banker, one brewer, eleven merchants, ten industrialists, two city councillors, three justice officials, one lawyer, two other professional

[29] *National Zeitung*, Nov. 6, 1861.
[30] *National Zeitung*, Nov. 14, 5, 10, 1861. City councillors were in every town usually prominent businessmen or persons closely related to busines.

persons, one confectioner, one bookseller, five professors, one master saddle maker, two millers, one agriculturalist, a master cabinetmaker, five local officials, one mining official, one owner of a printing establishment, one retired official, one landscape gardener, one director, two estate-owners, two owners of noble estates, one rentier, and two for whom no occupation is given. Of this group, one person belonged to the nobility.

For Berlin the urban pattern was revealed clearly in the personnel of the election committees for each of the four electoral districts and substantiates the conclusions drawn with respect to the Western provinces. As the capital of the state, however, Berlin showed a certain distribution of occupational emphasis which was lacking elsewhere. The importance of the capital as a center for news enhanced the political role of the press and of newspaper editors; at the same time it offered opportunities for persons to live by serving private organizations intended for public purposes. Hence the Berlin election committees contained representatives of these two occupations to a greater extent than elsewhere. If in the industrial cities of the West the executive secretary or public relations expert for economic associations was appearing as a type, in Berlin the same kind of person was beginning to find an occupation with a wider variety of associations than economic ones. Berlin also offered a third type of public figure, the retired official who now stayed in public life by means of political activity, the town councillor and other persons who were beginning to make a career of public life.

The membership of the election committees of the Progressives and center or left liberals in Silesian towns and cities varied from that in the Western provinces. It included, relatively speaking, more members of the older occupations, merchants and handicraftsmen, and fewer industrialists. Nonetheless, all the important occupational groups found representation on these committees. The merchant particularly remained the prominent leader. At Görlitz in July, 1861, the election committee contained twenty-three members—one master coppersmith, one agent, one estate-owner, one cloth manufacturer, one engineer, one lawyer, one gold worker, one watchmaker, four town councillors who were usually prominent merchants or industrialists, one merchant, one factory owner, one justice official, one iron merchant, one master carpenter, one Economic Commission Councillor, and four editors. A few months later a committee in Liegnitz numbered three noble estate-owners, a banker, a schoolmaster, and two without occupation given. Two members belonged to the nobility. Of the noble estate-owners one had the rank of Freiherr, another also belonged to the nobility, and the third had the title of lieutenant. For Breslau the committee in April, 1861, contained a lawyer, three merchants, a physician, a non-conformist preacher, and two whose occupation was not listed. By November the membership had changed and consisted of a lawyer, three merchants, an editor, a banker, an accountant, a master furrier, and a bricklayer.[31]

The committees organized in East Prussia expressed the predominant significance of commerce and agriculture, and the interdependence of these two economic activities. Relations between town and country had to be close, for, except in a very few coastal cities, industry had hardly begun to emancipate the towns and cities from major dependence upon the locality. The committees were frequently dominated by rural agrarian leaders instead of townsmen. Government officials constituted the third element of leadership. In the committee for Niederung county in 1861 the relationship is clear —two justice officials, three estate-owners, a lawyer, and one other professional person. Not a single member belonged to the nobility. The committee for the rural counties of Insterburg and Gumbinnen showed a different occupational interest, but the same dominant position of agrarians—a master bricklayer, a merchant, a justice official, a schoolmaster, and six agrarians. The difference between the occupational makeup of the committee for these predominantly rural counties and the one for the electoral district composed of Königsberg and Fischhausen counties grew out of the location of the city of Königsberg in the latter. Commerce and the university received places on the committee which lent it a distinctly urban character. Industrialists were absent from it, while handworkers played a considerable role. The membership of the committee reflected the economy and society of the pre-industrial period. On the committee there served in May, 1862, two town councillors, (one retired), a bank director, six estate-owners, one estate-renter, two professors, a consul (which means that he was also a merchant), a master cabinetmaker, a lawyer, a master shoemaker, four merchants, a master bricklayer, two physicians.[32]

Although not as selective as in the case of the election committees, further evidence about local leadership may be gained from an analysis of the occupational composition of the electors. The membership varied according to the nature of the economy in the same way as did that of the election committees. While it is impossible to differentiate between those who voted liberal and those who voted Conservative, the fact that persons of certain occupations were chosen as electors has some bearing on the question of the occupational distribution of political interest and prestige.

Judging from samples of urban and rural areas in the East, West, and Center of the state, the electors represented the main groups of the voters even more accurately than the committees did. Only those of the lowest income, such as the day laborers in both town and country, were usually lacking. At the election of April, 1862, in one district in the Western provinces, the voters chose among the 460 electors 222 from trade and industry, sixty-four handworkers, twenty-two military, twenty rentiers, seventeen brewers, fourteen advocates, thirteen innkeepers, twelve administrative, judicial, and city officials, nine physicians, five apothecaries, one pastor, one teacher, one writer, and three lawyers. The dominant influence lay with the business representatives; the handicrafts ranked a poor second, and the other occupations showed such a scattered return as to be relatively unimportant.[33] At the Eastern end of the state the counties of Königsberg and Fischhausen chose electors in keeping with the character of the area. Of a total of 704 electors elected in 1862, 402 were re-elected, and 302 were new. The electors were composed of 153 handworkers and tradesmen, 103 merchants, 258 estate-owners, landowners and rentiers, six inn or tavern keepers, thirty-two physicians, apothecaries, writers, booksellers, printers, artists, thirteen agriculturalists, ten apprentices and workers, fifteen teachers, eleven pastors, twenty-two communal officials, eighty-one royal officials and military personnel.[34] In this area where agriculture and commerce predominated, where apart from Königsberg the towns remained small and largely rural in character, one would rightly expect merchants, handworkers, and agrarians to show the largest number of electors. Nonetheless, the size of the group of officials and military personnel is impressive evidence that in this region the old structure of society—merchant, handworker, agrarian, and official and officer—remained in control.

Berlin, as the capital and the largest city in the state, revealed in the occupational spread of its electors the rapid change into industrial

---

[33] Kölnische Zeitung, May 1, 1862.
[34] Königsberg Hartungsche Zeitung, May 4, 1862.

society. Among the electors chosen in 1863 were some 550 merchants, 240 industrialists, seventeen brewers and distillers, three bankers, forty-three listed as city councillors, who were most likely also prominent in the same fields, and 325 handworkers. The last-named figure is undoubtedly misleading, for many handicrafts had already begun to assume capitalistic proportions—the building industry, clothing, furniture, and other industries exploiting the market provided by a large concentrated population—and they must be classed with the industrialists and merchants. The attractiveness of Berlin as a residence accounts for the 125 rentiers and the eleven estate-owners, and 150 officials would not be an excessive number for a city of bureaucrats. That 120 physicians, apothecaries, and assistants in the field of health should have been politically active points to the opportunities in the city for members of these professions and to their characteristic interest in politics at this period, not merely in Prussia but in other countries. When added together, the number of teachers, professors, doctors of philosophy, writers, editors, artists, booksellers, and publishers chosen as electors seems unusually large. They totaled almost 200, a showing that could not be equaled even on a proportionate scale in any other city in the state.[35]

By way of comparison, the electors in the villages and in rural areas in general consisted of peasants, Schulzes and the owners or renters of landed estates. The estate-owners and other agrarians were elected and served along with the representatives of the inferior and more numerous lower class. A teacher, a pastor, or handworker frequently served for the rural community in the same capacity.

Affiliated Organizations

In May, 1860, the Prussian police received a report from one of its secret agents about a discussion among guests in Habel's Restaurant on Unter den Linden, Berlin. The guests had spoken at length about the establishment of ever more political and other Vereins not merely in Berlin but throughout Germany. The agent reported:

> It was said that if the relevant officials do not soon restrict this activity entirely or at least somewhat and particularly do not observe and control it more carefully, Germany will in a few years have another revolution. The present-day youth, especial-

---

[35] See A. M. Hayn, *Die Abgeordneten-Wahl für Berlin am 28. Okt., 1863 mit der Nachwahl im 1. Wahl-Bezirk am 16. Nov., 1863* (Berlin, 1863). Preuss. Geh. Staats-archiv-Dahlem. Pr. Br. Rep. 30, Berlin C. Pol. Präsid. Tit. 94, W. 178.

ly, is being totally corrupted by these associations, for there is an almost incredible rage . . . to become a member of some association. Almost daily, for example, here in Berlin little clubs are being formed under some favored name in beer halls, private residences, even in schools which, although they seem to be harmless, may become dangerous to the state.[36]

The report did not exaggerate the vogue. About a year later (March 21, 1861) a writer to the *Königsberg Hartungsche Zeitung* from the little town of Gumbinnen in East Prussia doubted whether a Schiller Verein could be established there because of the large number of Vereins already in existence. Handworker Verein, Gesang-Verein, National Verein, Charity Verein, Orphan Verein, Credit Verein, Peace Verein, Gustavus Adolphus Verein, Agricultural Verein, Bible Society, Town Club, lodges, and other Vereins already existed. The article spoke of "a certain Verein satiation."

Except for the economic ones, the list contained the names of the typical associations for all Prussia. The New Era produced in every field of activity organizations which strove to spread over all Germany and to supply the popular basis for political unification and liberalism. Within a decade after the Revolution of 1848 the population sought forms for the expression of its wishes which would a second time be effective. It created them in religion, education, politics, cultural and social affairs and economics. In Prussia, although to a varying extent, people from all classes and occupations participated. The towns-people took the lead, but many burgher and aristocratic agrarians with large estates joined the movement, and even handworkers and peasants participated as much as they could. The only groups lacking were the Conservative aristocrats and their followers, numerically a small minority. While most Vereins were unable to exert much influence upon state action, they did express the longing of the popular masses. In the case of certain economic associations, the Prussian and the German Commercial Associations, the Congress of German Economists, the various organizations of mining interests, of iron and steel, and of other special interests, the power controlled by them had to be respected even by the Prussian government.

The new stir and movement in national public life originated in North and Central Germany, that is, in Germany north of the Main. The drive was associated primarily with the expansion of industrial and commercial activity in the 1850s, the establishment of banks, the

[36] Preuss. Geh. Staatsarchiv. Pr. Br. Rep. 30. Berlin C. Pol. Präsid. Tit. 94, Lit. 7, 377, Vol. II.

construction of railroads, and the creation of insurance companies. It was accompanied by a rise in prices, partly the effect of the increased amounts of gold available from California, and was manifested in an outburst of entrepreneurial spirit and optimistic speculation. The new forces were getting well under way when the commercial crisis of 1857 struck them and made clearer than ever before that golden opportunities were at hand if only, in Prussia, the bureaucratic state would drop its social and mercantilist paternalism and grant the private economic interests the freedom to take the initiative. All the demands or objectives of all the associations merged in liberalism and national unity.

The organizations provided essential means by which liberal persons of various classes and occupations could participate actively in public affairs. Membership enabled individuals to work for liberalism and nationalism without having to run the risk of joining a political party. The organizations concentrated on building a liberal society as a necessary foundation for liberal politics. They all opposed common enemies, absolutism and the conservative society of the Old Regime, monarchy by divine right, feudal aristocracy, caste and privilege, and state particularism. As we have seen, the freedom of the individual entailed the rise in importance of each person; with each person free, active, conscious of his own worth, able to take the initiative, the feeling of nationalism would grow, the feeling of the importance of the nation as a brotherhood of intelligent, alert, self-reliant individuals united by the common national bond. The unification of the nation would have to follow from the pressure of these free individuals; the enemies of national unity, the same enemies as those of liberalism, would be compelled to give way.

The close relationship between these organizations and the Prussian political parties or fractions was substantiated at both the highest level of leadership and at the lowest. The prior existence of these non-party organizations made it possible for the political parties and factions of the New Era to build upon them and to become strong quickly. The Progressive party actually grew out of the Prussian units of the National Verein. The name "Progressive," already being used by new political groups in other states, had been sponsored and popularized by the Verein. The addition of the name "German" to the title of the Progressive party in Prussia was suggested by the same source and attested to the growing respectability and prestige of such a revolutionary act.

A few examples from localities in different areas of Prussia will show the value of the organizations to liberal politics. They pertain primarily to the two most active political groups, the Progressive and the Left-Center, but even the Constitutional party members took an active interest in the organizations and, although to a lesser extent, shared the benefits of their work. In the small town of Pillau in the far northeast corner of Prussia the local members of the National Verein met late in July, 1861, and in preparation for the next election to the Lower House agreed to establish a local election committee which by co-optation should expand into a committee for the entire county. Two months later the meeting of the National Verein, after discussing the forthcoming elections, decided to draw up a list of candidates for electors in Pillau.[37]   At Danzig the local members of the National Verein in February, 1861, sent thanks to the forty-two deputies in the Lower House who had voted for the liberal Stavenhagen Amendment.[38] In July of the same year the Danzig conference of the National Verein of the provinces of Prussia, Pomerania and Posen approved almost unanimously the program of the Progressive party and involved itself further in politics by passing, among others, two resolutions,[39] one in favor of electing to the Landtag men who would work for national unity, the other in favor of the complete transformation of the Upper House.   In September the local members of the National Verein in Danzig agreed that it was time to begin activity for the election of deputies to the Lower House, but they thought it advisable to consider the matter in a special meeting called for that purpose.[40]

In Elbing the Economic Congress,[41] instead of the National Verein, played the political role.   Deputy von Forckenbeck reported to the Congress in February, 1861, about the split in the von Vincke fraction in the Lower House.   A year later the Congress concentrated upon the consideration of the matters before the Lower House, became entirely political in its interests, and discussed in some detail the liberal legislation before the Landtag.   It was educating the local population in political affairs.   The next month it laid plans for the campaign for the elections to the Lower House.   As the report of the meeting stated, "We are sufficiently well organized to be able by the activity of our trustworthy associates in the smaller centers to compensate at present for the lack of mass activity."[42]   That is to say, the Economic Congress

[37] *Königsberg Hartungsche Zeitung*, Aug. 2, Sept. 17, 1861.

[38] *Tagesbericht*, No. 46, Feb. 23, 1861, from *Volkszeitung*.

[39] *National Zeitung*, July 30, 1861; *Königsberg Hartungsche Zeitung*, July 28, 1861.

[40] *Ibid.*, Sept. 14, 1861.

[41] This was the regional unit of the Congress of German Economists.

[42] *Tagesbericht*, No. 44, Feb. 21, 1861, based on *Neuer Elbinger Anzeiger*, No. 1679; *Königsberg Hartungsche Zeitung*, Feb. 9, March 18, 1862.

supplied the organization and the contacts for conducting the political campaign. Deputy von Forckenbeck participated in the meeting and delivered a speech defending his and his party colleague's action in the Landtag.

In the counties Osterburg and Stendal in the Altmark, according to an article in the *National Zeitung* of December 11, 1861, the activity of the members of the National Verein had been mainly responsible for breaking the domination of the Conservatives and returning liberal deputies by a large majority. At Halle the local members of the same organization passed a resolution in August, 1861, which manifested the interdependence of the program of the National Verein and of the liberal political movement in Prussia. Goerlitz and Breslau in Silesia were centers of similar endeavor: the National Verein took a vigorous part in politics and campaigned for liberals. In Breslau it included as members persons belonging to the Progressive party and to the Constitutional party; on national affairs, the two could cooperate. At Elberfeld on October 6, 1861, Schulze-Delitzsch spoke to about 800 to 900 members and friends of the National Verein on the relation of the members of that association to the election. He advised against its taking the campaign actively in hand, but he said that participation of its members in the election campaign was "natural and necessary," and he defended the program of the Progressive party as a coalition of democratic and constitutional members of the Lower House. In nearby Dortmund the Navy Committee actually transformed itself in October, 1861, into an election committee with a full-fledged liberal program.[43]

Almost every organization in the towns and cities became a center of politics in support of liberalism. At Magdeburg late in 1861 the Conference of Elder Merchants heard one of its members, a deputy in the Lower House, emphasize how absolutely necessary it was for more merchants, industrialists, and other businessmen to be elected to the Lower House than heretofore; for, he said, the most important business was transacted in committees and more experts in economic affairs were needed.[44]

The town and city councils, composed of elected representatives, and the Bürgervereins extended their activity into politics, not merely

[43] *National Zeitung*, Aug. 22, 1861; *Tagesbericht*, No. 56, March 7, 1861, from *Breslauer Zeitung*, No. 109; *Volkszeitung*, March 19, 1862; *National Zeitung*, Sept. 20, 1861; *Königsberg Hartungsche Zeitung*, Oct. 11, 1861; *National Zeitung*, Oct. 12, 1861.

[44] *Berliner Börsen-Zeitung*, Dec. 5, 1861.

by passing resolutions in support of the Lower House against the King and the government but by furthering the election of trustworthy deputies. The meetings of the councils offered excellent opportunities for discussing election matters and planning the campaign. A few examples may be chosen from many. The council in Unna, a small town in Westphalia, called a meeting of the local citizens in January, 1862, at which it was decided to organize a Bürgerverein for the discussion of political and communal affairs. At Stralsund the local Bürgerverein, which in 1848 had opposed the Revolution and had since then kept free of political discussion, in 1861 changed its policy and its views and by an overwhelming majority became a supporter of the Progressive party. Two of its oldest directors resigned from the Verein in consequence; but the vote in the Verein of 115 to 39 in favor of the Progressive Landtag candidate could not be changed by such an act. At Magdeburg the Bürgerverein invited the two deputies in Berlin to speak to it about the developments in the Landtag.[45]

In Ravensberg the liberals founded a Culture Verein which sought to spread information and enlighten people in all classes of society "in a liberal sense." This type of Verein became popular as a means of educating the public in the new ways of constitutional government, of keeping it informed about state affairs and of having an effective means of exerting influence in a liberal direction. In Breslau in 1861 the leading citizens organized a Verein of Supporters of the Constitution with 111 members. In Dortmund a similar one, called "Progress," was intended to discuss political questions at regular meetings and especially to follow the debates in the Landtag. At Bonn, one took the name of Constitutional Verein.[46]

One of the most effective and widespread centers of political life proved to be the Städtische Ressource, a social club for the middle class, found usually in every town and city. As an organization already in existence, it offered opportunities for the citizens, ostensibly assembled for social purposes, to talk politics, to hear speeches supposedly of a non-political character, and to plan steps in favor of liberalism. The one in Breslau may be used as an example. The police reported

[45] *Tagesbericht*, No. 26, Jan. 31, 1862, citing *Westfälische Zeitung*, No. 26; see also *National Zeitung*, June 3, 1863; J. Stein, *Geschichte der Stadt Breslau im 19. Jahrhundert*, pp. 603-04; *Tagesbericht*, No. 34, Feb. 10, 1862, citing *Kölnische Zeitung*, No. 39; *Tagesbericht*, No. 53, March 4, 1862, *Magdeburger Zeitung*, No. 52.

[46] *Tagesbericht*, No. 20, Jan. 24, 1862, citing *Elberfelder Zeitung*, No. 24; *Polizei-Bericht*, Breslau, Feb. 11, 1861; *Tagesbericht*, No. 22, Jan. 27, 1862, citing *Westfälische Zeitung*, No. 22; *Tagesbericht*, No. 1, Jan. 2, 1862, citing *Kölnische Zeitung*, No. 1.

to the government in March, 1860, that the Städtische Ressource formed, together with the *Morgen Zeitung,* the center of democratic endeavor in Breslau. With 383 members it had recently begun to expand its activities by petitions and addresses. It had passed a resolution in favor of joining the National Verein and sent it to the Landtag deputies from Breslau; it had signed a petition supporting Italian unification, another advocating the abolition of the reactionary school law, another defending the limitation of military service to two years, another for complete freedom of occupation. The next year it organized a political election committee, which entered into combination with the Verein of Supporters of the Constitution to aid the National Verein and to prepare for the elections. In March, 1861, it listened to an address by Pastor Hofferichter in which that worthy divine showed on the basis of history that empires had been hostile to the idea of nationality and that Germany must give up the dream of Charlemagne and create a German kingdom of German people alone.[47]

The Städtische Ressource, on the liberal side in politics, was often the strongest, the oldest, the most respected of local organizations. Its membership included every middle-class citizen of significance in the urban population. The organization was difficult for the police to control. Its respectability and dignity scarcely invited espionage and police raids. If the members discussed political matters and laid political plans, who was to censor or effectively to forbid them? When the leading citizens of an urban community became actively liberal and opposed the government, the latter found it extremely difficult to treat them like communists or the revolutionists of 1848. They were not single radicals or small groups with which the community was out of sympathy; they constituted the responsible, directing intelligence indispensable to the locality and to the state. The government had not found adequate new means of controlling them, and the old means of autocracy and mercantilism no longer sufficed.

About the middle of 1860 the Berlin police received the following report from one of its secret agents: "I recently heard a leader of the democrats say: 'If the reactionary party knew what a power we are developing for ourselves in the gymnastic and singing Vereins, one which can be used against it at any moment, it would not rest until the last of these Vereins was abolished.' . . . And so it is in fact! Every

---

[47] See *Tagesbericht,* Nos. 58, 59, March 9, 11, 1861; *Polizei-Bericht,* Breslau, March 12, Aug. 27, Nov. 5, 19, Dec. 5, 17, 1860; *Zeitungs-Bericht für Juli-August, 1860, März-April, 1861,* Regierungs-Bezirk, Breslau.

newly established Verein (and in all areas, even in the rural ones, there is a veritable mania for founding Gymnastic and Rifle and Fire-Defence Clubs) provides the democrats with new manpower. . . ."[48]

The police agent no doubt reproduced accurately in his report the belief of many Germans. So far as speeches and other forms of verbalization were concerned, the Vereins did participate in the spread of liberalism. They were organized and directed in a liberal way, and by keeping in close touch among themselves and especially with the National Verein, they served as popular channels for the new ideals. While especially devoted to the objective of national unification they had of necessity to be involved in the work of achieving liberalism within Prussia as a requisite change for the other. While not supposed to participate in politics, they could not keep away from that subject, and their work helped to account for the victory of liberal deputies in the Landtag elections. This type of organization had a long history in Germany and was regarded as eminently respectable.

The Berlin police received a secret report about the Main Valley Sängerfest in September, 1859. Although no one of any importance from North Germany was present and the agent noted no unusual occurrences, the police wished to be informed. The number in attendance, 1,200 singers and 20,000 to 25,000 visitors, was unusually high. The singers came from the "educated middle class" and also from the workers, but numerous rural people were also present. In addition to the entertainment those present engaged in "excited political discussion" which concerned itself with one topic, "National Party, reform of the Diet, unity under Prussia's leadership."[49] Two years later, the Festival of North German Singing Societies held in Bielefeld invited Deputy Waldeck to speak. For two hours he addressed the singers on the policies of the Progressive party.[50] The relation between music and politics could hardly be closer. When local admirers wished to pay tribute to a leading Ruhr industrialist active in liberal politics, they serenaded him. The German liberals had found a safe kind of political activity: they sang.

Although it might be supposed that the Rifle Clubs had more importance in politics, in reality they proved to be similar in nature to other such groups, expansive in hopes, strong in words and weak

[48] Preuss. Geh. Staatsarchiv. Pr. Br. Rep. 30 Berlin C. Pol. Präsid. Tit. 94, Lit. T. 102, Vol. II.
[49] Preuss Geh. Staatsarchiv. Pr. Br. Rep. 30. Berlin C. Pol. Präsid. Tit. 94, Lit. D. 335.
[50] Königsberg Hartungsche Zeitung, Aug. 3, 1861.

in deeds. The German Rifle Association, organized in July, 1861, as a means of furthering national unification, declared its purpose to be the fraternity of all German riflemen, the improvement in the art of rifle shooting and the increase in the defensive power of the German people.[51] How important the Rifle Association considered itself may be gathered from the report of its first big festival published in the *Wochenschrift des National Vereins* (No. 119, 1862), an account which the Prussian police thought worthy of preservation.

> One must have experienced the enthusiasm which from the twelfth to the twenty-second of July surged through the free city of Frankfurt. One must have been moved and gripped by that inexpressible mood which for ten full days ruled the meeting place, the rifle range and the festival hall, in order to be able to speak of the significance and expressiveness of this first German federal rifle festival. This was not merely a shooting contest, although the guns were shot a half-million times, nor was it merely a spirited contest, although the prizes of honor, estimated at a value of 150,000 Gulden, most of them ennobled by artistic hands, were worthy of the sweat of a knight. Nor was it merely a festival where tens of thousands and hundreds of thousands banqueted, drank, and celebrated. It was all this together, but it was more; it was a great national act and the consciousness of this national act.
>
> It is not true that the movement for improvement in which we have all worked since 1858 depends on the graciousness of any single person. The fool's fancy that "The Lord has given, the Lord has taken away" is not true. On the contrary, the revival roots in the people; the people themselves have taken affairs in their own hands and to all the other demonstrations of our folk spirit, the Singing Societies, the Gymnastic Vereins, the economic parliaments, they have added the concluding, the crowning movement: the German shooting festival. It befits this demonstration, which signifies the initiative of the people in popular arming and military training, that it should be made in the most ceremonious manner possible. It has been held in this manner, and the nation owes the free city of Frankfurt the heartiest thanks for having preserved the honor of the German people so nobly and for having staged this national act in the worthiest way.

When the guests arrived at the festival they found that a storm had blown down their hall. They set immediately to work in fraternal spirit to rebuild it and within a day or two that historic demonstration of freedom and national unity had been completed. Shooting con-

[51] Preuss. Geh. Staatsarchiv. Pr. Br. Rep. 30. Berlin C. Pol. Präsid. Tit. 94, Lit. S. 1123.

tests and banquets, toasts and speeches followed one another in ecstatic order. Proclaimed Friedheim from Solingen:

> Oh, may the hope soon be fulfilled that our princes all unite to build a great Reich . . . for the use and blessing of our beautiful German fatherland; may they out of free love renounce all sense of sovereignty and have for Germany's greatness only one heart! Then we shall be strong and powerful within and without and can calmly look about us. No enemy will dare to disturb us, to hinder us in our work, for our power is great through love and trust. We would then stand as firmly as the cliff in the sea through our own harmony, which adorns and blesses and strengthens us. Once the goal is reached, the end is good!
>
> Up, believing, loving, hoping, let us rise with a single cry: Long live Germania!

Doctor Lüning, the democratic physician from Rheda, proclaimed, "The day will come . . . when the Prussian eagle, now much curbed and chained, will lift its powerful wings and offering protection and demanding protection will with powerful beat of its wings descend under the black, red, gold banner of the German Reich (unbounded enthusiasm)."[52]

According to its participants, the first German Rifle Festival was a tremendous demonstration by the German people for national unity and for the ways of personal initiative and freedom. The Progressive Election Verein in Breslau had contributed a cup to it, as had many other organizations, and the festival received enthusiastic publicity.[53]

The gymnastic clubs had a half century of patriotic tradition upon which to develop their activity for national unity and individual liberty. Like the other Vereins after 1848 they had subsided into purely local, non-political activity and had first stirred to new life under the stimulation of the National Verein. In the early 1860s the German Gymnastic Verein was founded as an expression of the will to German unity, and the executive board contained personnel identical with that found in the Rifle Association and the National Verein.

The first attempt to unite the gymnastic Vereins occurred at the festival held in 1860 at Coburg. Thirteen hundred gymnasts, as well as numerous visitors, assembled there. The secret police of Saxony reported the number present, the toasts, the songs, even a long

---

[52] Preuss. Geh. Staatsarchiv. Pr. Br. Rep. 30 Berlin C. Pol. Präsid. Tit. 94, S. 1123.

[53] See *Zeitungs-Bericht für Juli-Aug., 1862*, Regierungs-Bezirk, Breslau, Sept. 8, 1862. But what is one to think of the Statutes of the *Schützen-Verein der Handlungs-Gehilfen in Stettin* of 1863 which did not even mention national unity? See Preuss. Geh. Staatsarchiv. Pr. Br. Rep. 30. Berlin C. Pol. Präsid. Tit. 94, Lit. G. 465.

patriotic poem written for the occasion and recited by the author to an enthusiastic audience. The proposal to establish a German Gymnastic Verein did not receive full approval, especially from the South Germans, and the effort had to be postponed. Differences also arose over whether to favor the use of the German colors of 1848, black, red, and gold, and over the question of whether politics should be discussed.[54] The South Germans particularly were disinclined to unite with their northern colleagues. They were not yet attracted by the inspired phrases of a writer in the *Deutsche Turner Zeitung* (1860) to "build a temple" of unity "under which the spiritual and physical welfare of the people will be furthered, a bulwark against which the attempts of foreign conquerors will miserably shatter."

By August of the next year, 1861, the members of the National Verein in Saarbrücken and its vicinity had progressed so far in their enthusiasm for German unity that they approved the proposal to unite the German Gymnastic Vereins and the Rifle Clubs for training persons in the use of a common type of gun, thereby to create a popular army. They wished in this way to prepare for a reduction in the size of the standing army.[55]

The celebration in 1863 of the fiftieth anniversary of the Battle of Leipzig stirred the gymnastic Vereins to new efforts of heroism. The third German Gymnastic Festival was held in Leipzig in August; the closing ceremony described in the *Deutsche Allgemeine Zeitung,* the motto of which was "Truth and Justice, Freedom and Law," conformed to the pattern of action by this type of organization: "a jubilant celebration," a parade of the gymnasts accompanied by singers, a ceremony in the meeting hall introduced by the singing of "Die Wacht am Rhein," the patriotic speech by Professor Treitschke, which was received with "enthusiastic bravos."[56]

More serious business faced the gymnasts toward the close of 1863. The controversy over Schleswig-Holstein was reaching a climax and war was imminent. The executive committee of the German Gymnastic Vereins issued a call to the comrades to prepare themselves for military service by exercise in marching, gymnastics, parading, bayonet work, shooting, and so on, wherever possible under the direction of a

[54] See police report in Preuss. Geh. Staatsarchiv. Pr. Br. Rep. 30. Berlin C. Pol. Präsid. Tit. 94, Lit. T. 102, Vol. II.

[55] *Königsberg Hartungsche Zeitung,* Aug. 1, 1861.

[56] *Deutsche Algemeine Zeitung,* Leipzig, Aug. 7, 1863. The article is to be found in Preuss. Geh. Staatsarchiv. Pr. Br. Rep. 30. Berlin C. Pol. Präsid. Tit. 94, Lit. T. 102, Vol. II.

trained military person. They should join an army to be developed for Schleswig-Holstein and help to save those territories for the beloved German fatherland.[57] Unfortunately the gymnasts did not win the war; the regular troops of the Prussian and Austrian armies performed so well that the aid of the gymnasts, except in so far as they served as regular troops, was not needed.

Like the other Vereins the gymnastic societies denounced caste feelings as contrary to their ideals. Their membership consisted mainly of handworkers and merchants, with few teachers, students, intellectuals and officials. Only one Verein, that in Munich, contained officers; higher officials, pastors, and rural people were lacking in almost all of them. The gymnastic clubs were a thoroughly middle-class affair, a product largely of the small towns emerging from the Old Regime.[58]

The close relation between the gymnastic Vereins and the liberal parties becomes evident from the names of the persons interested in them. The police noted in 1862 that in Breslau the gymnastic Verein "Forward" was directed by Stein, the liberal editor of the *Breslauer Zeitung,* and other leaders of the Progressive party.[59] The invitation to a gymnastic festival for East and West Prussia to be held in Elbing in 1861 was signed by the leading liberals in the area, men like von Forckenbeck and former Burgomaster Philipps. A year later a group of prominent citizens of the same area issued a call for funds for the furtherance of gymnastics. The list of sponsors of the request reads like the roster of the liberal deputies in the Landtag—Bender, von Forckenbeck, von Hoverbeck, von Hennig, Philipps, two von Sauckens, Schubert, Techow, and many others.[60]

Knowing about the close relationship, the government held the Vereins under observation. In this work it kept in touch with the Saxon government and probably with others. From Dresden in May, 1861, it received a secret report that all the Vereins of whatever sort had a secret central executive committee of unknown personnel which received instructions from a revolutionary committee in London led by the fugitive Carl Blind. The Prussian government took this report with a grain of salt, but in the next year, 1862, when the constitutional

[57] *Volkszeitung,* Dec. 12, 1863.
[58] See the article in the *Ergänzungsheft zur Deutschen Turn-Zeitung* (Leipzig, 1860); Preuss. Geh. Staatsarchiv. Pr. Br. Rep. 30. Berlin C. Pol. Präsid. Tit. 94, Lit. T. 102, Vol. II.
[59] *Polizei Bericht,* Breslau, Nov. 3, 1862.
[60] *Königsberg Hartungsche Zeitung,* June 6, 1861, Nov. 7, 1862.

conflict was growing intense, it became somewhat concerned. In August, September, and October, Minister of Interior von Jagow secretly ordered the police department in Berlin, which had jurisdiction over the police of the cities of the state, to learn whether the gymnastic Vereins were training persons with weapons. If this were the case, the matter was to be brought immediately to the attention of the minister, for such practice with guns might lead to revolutionary action. The minister was assured that these Vereins, including the rifle clubs, were harmless.

Toward the end of 1863 Minister of Interior Count von Eulenburg felt it necessary to prohibit the arming of the gymnastic Vereins. From Dresden came a report emphasizing the liberal and democratic political tendencies in the various Vereins and the close connection between them and the National Verein and suggesting that the governments of the various states keep in touch on these matters. Early in 1864 the police report from Dresden admitted upon investigation that there was no danger of the defence and other Vereins being organized for arming and training the population at large in the German states, in fact, that the existing Vereins were not dangerous and that in Saxony the rifle clubs were even regarded as reactionary. The alarm died down.[61]

The statistical evidence which is available supports the judgment of the police. In 1860 only forty-five gymnastic Vereins with a total membership of about 4,300 persons existed in the entire State of Prussia. By March, 1861, the number in Germany as a whole had increased from 224 to 506, and in Prussia from forty-five to 144. Even if the total membership had grown in similar proportion, it would have remained insignificant for any but political purposes.[62]

However harmless as revolutionary threats, the singing, shooting, and gymnastic Vereins helped to popularize the cause of liberalism and national unification. They aided in electing men of these views to the Landtag. They supplied part of the organizational basis of the liberal political parties by reaching particularly the lower income groups of the middle class. They enabled these people to associate with the upper middle class, and they offered channels by which the latter could influence the lower groups in the liberal and national cause. Through these Vereins the timidity and fearfulness of the

[61] *Polizei Vierteljahrbericht,* Dresden, Dec. 1, 1863; Preuss. Geh. Staatsarchiv. Pr. Br. Rep. 30. Berlin C. Pol. Präsid. Tit. 94, Lit. S. 1123, Lit. T. 162, Vol. II.
[62] See *Bremer Handelsblatt,* July 13, 1861.

middle class about participating in politics and having opinions on public affairs could be combatted, the example of the liberal leaders could be made real to them, and a feeling of personal responsibility and the value and possibility of showing some independence of the authoritarian government might be imparted. The beginning practice of social equality in the Vereins would be useful in developing a sense of the political importance of the individual. As policy formulaters, as sources of potential physical power, these Vereins played no role; as channels of liberal and national expression, they proved to be eminently useful.[63]

The cooperatives, guided by members of the Progressive party, especially by those of a democratic leaning, belonged in a similar category. The movement owed its development primarily to Schulze-Delitzsch, who even prior to 1848 had begun to work for the establishment of these associations. He perceived the democratic character of the cooperative and believed that from this cooperation in economic affairs would develop similar ways and habits in politics.

The movement became popular with the upper middle class and the capitalistic bourgeoisie as a means of preserving the middle-class character and affiliation of the handworkers. The cooperative was expected to enable the handworkers to adjust to industrial capitalism while remaining skilled craftsmen. It aimed to prevent them from becoming a proletariat and succumbing to the enticements of socialism or communism, or, almost as bad, from allying with the forces of re-action. The bourgeoisie supported the cooperatives not merely or not even primarily out of self-interest; the threat of radicalism on the left did not appear sufficiently dangerous at this period for them to be thinking mainly of withholding new socialist recruits, and the threat of reaction on the right could be countered by the spread of information about the advantages of liberalism along with positive assistance. The bourgeoisie felt proud of the tradition of the handworkers and sought to maintain it as a valuable factor in the national culture. The work of Schulze-Delitzsch early received the general reputation of being safe, reliable, practical, and patriotic. Liberal thinking did not extend very far into the field of labor economics, for relatively few liberals had had any practical experience with factory industry. The craftsmen were to be preserved by way of cooperatives; the factories were in some unknown way to obtain labor which would remain middle class,

[63] See among many others the estimate in the *Königsberg Hartungsche Zeitung*, Dec. 11, 1861.

perhaps by cooperatives also; a proletariat was not to arise, it was hoped, to alarm the middle class and the bourgeoisie. Just how this happy situation would be achieved was not clear. The social changes involved in the emergence of industrialism had not advanced far enough for problems of middle-class relations with labor to become acute. Schulze-Delitzsch's cooperatives seemed at this stage the solution to the social question; in addition they could help to win support for liberal politics.

The transitional character of the workers' position in society was clearly evident from the proceedings of the German Workers' Convention held at Leipzig, October 23-25, 1864.[64] The meeting showed almost no proletarian character. A personal greeting from the burgomaster inaugurated a conference mainly devoted to the discussion of cooperatives, education, freedom of movement and domicile throughout Germany, and German unification—an agenda scarcely distinguished from that of any middle-class association. The recommendations in favor of social insurance, to enable the worker to accumulate capital for his old age, and in favor of shorter working hours were acceptable in middle-class circles as well. The condemnation of socialism and the subjects for the numerous toasts hardly seemed in keeping with the presence of the future socialist leader, August Bebel, and with his selection as a member of the executive committee. The social problem considered at this meeting remained essentially the condition of the handworker: how could he be preserved as a member of the middle class even when he became a factory worker? The ideas and interests of Schulze-Delitzsch and of liberal economists like Wirth dominated the conference; the presence of Bebel was significant only for the future. The split between the middle class and the proletariat had not yet occurred. Liberalism and democracy rather than socialism expressed the objectives of the workers.

The Lassallean socialist organization proved to be so weak in the early 1860s that it scarcely did more than provide a little work for the police and considerable opportunity for literary polemics between the elegant Lassalle and his democratic or liberal opponents. In Berlin Lassalle had a following of a couple of hundred members. The case of the Berlin cigar workers may illustrate the attitude of skilled workers. The Progressive party had many supporters among the cigar workers. In Berlin the organization of these workers asked Schulze-Delitzsch

---

[64] See the police report in Preuss. Geh. Staatsarchiv. Pr. Br. Rep. 30. Berlin C. Pol. Präsid. Tit. 94, Lit. A. 212.

318 / Prussia 1858-1864

whether it should join the German Cigar Workers' Association. The distinguished democrat replied that although approving the statutes of the Association, he did not like its Lassallean leadership. The cigar workers chose to ignore the advice and in 1866 the members joined the general Verein. Two years later, however, they broke away from it and formed a cooperative. The fact that they chose to associate with the newly established Hirsch-Duncker organization of cooperatives rather than the one guided by Schulze-Delitzsch did not indicate any diminution in the strength of liberal and democratic principles.[65]

The potential significance of the cooperatives for the liberal and democratic parties cannot be gauged from the small number of the Vereins and of their members.[66] Among a social group as nearly homogeneous as the handworkers the example of liberalism offered by even a small organized minority must have attracted others. The same social elements supplied many supporters and members of the gymnastic and the other Vereins; they tended to be the ardent patriots, the proponents of national unification; they upheld the democratic left of the liberal movement.

The emergence of the society of modern industrialism in Prussia could be seen in the increased number and enlarged scope of economic organizations. A few of these gained particular importance for the state and for the entire German nation, while a large number of smaller ones expressed the needs and wishes of regional or local interests. All the organizations were interrelated by personnel and program. They all aligned with the liberal groups and constituted the backbone of liberal strength in the urban population. Although they claimed to be non-political in character and purpose, their programs and policies were primarily concerned with governmental action —the transformation of an absolutistic, mercantilist government into one with a liberal administration guided by liberal economic policies, the achievement of German national economic unity. With respect

[65] Walter Frisch, *Die Organisationsbestrebungen der Arbeiter in der deutschen Tabakindustrie* (Leipzig, 1905), pp. 39-40.
[66] In 1861 in entire Germany there were 364 credit cooperatives with a membership of about 50,000, and in 1864 some 889 with a membership of 135,000. In 1861 there were in addition some 129 raw materials and consumers' cooperatives, but these were less important than the others. In Prussia in 1861 there were 188 credit cooperatives, and in 1865 some 436. Their distribution according to provinces was as follows: Saxony 101, Brandenburg 89, Silesia 85, Prussia 50, Pomerania 44, Rhineland 26, Posen 25, Westphalia 16. The raw materials and consumers' cooperatives were fewer and much less important. Preuss. Geh. Staatsarchiv. Pr. Br. Rep. 30. Berlin C. Pol. Präsid. Tit. 94, Lit. G. 465.

to the first part of the program one economic association might be more aggressive than the other or more inclusive in its objective; but all agreed on fundamentals. The second part, the question of the form and degree of national economic unity, especially of the political implications of economic unity, also caused little dispute. Most Prussians favored a unified Germany under Prussian leadership with Austria excluded, while relatively few demanded a greater-Germany solution with Austria, at least German Austria, included.

The three leading economic associations, the Prussian Commercial Association, the German Commercial Association, and the Congress of German Economists, were established between 1857 and 1861. Of these the Prussian Commercial Association developed out of a conference in Berlin in May, 1858, of the executive committees of the chambers of commerce in Königsberg, Elbing, Danzig, Stettin, Posen, Breslau, Berlin, Magdeburg, Halle, Leipzig, and Cologne, that is, of about half the cities with a population of over 20,000. At the conference the Prussian Minister of Commerce expressed regret that the commercial class did not represent its interests more fully than it did. Acting on his suggestion—another instance of the initiative on the part of the absolutist state—the representatives of the chambers of commerce in the Prussian towns and cities met and organized the Prussian Commercial Association.[67] Thereupon, the *Bremer Handelsblatt*[68] advocated the establishment of a similar body for all Germany, arguing that none of the questions proposed for consideration by the Prussian Commercial Association concerned Prussia alone. In 1861 the larger organization was created.

These two powerful associations were formed at the time when controversy over the future character of Prussia and Germany began to grow acute. The associations met each year, with representatives of the important chambers of commerce present, with committees reporting on their work during the past year, with recommendations being made by the combined force of Prussian and German economic leaders. Wherever controversies arose in the German Association they as a rule pertained only to the tariff question; on problems of the relation between government and business the opinion was usually unanimous. Almost every business representative disliked the vestiges of mercantilism. He wished economic freedom, and he wished the

[67] See *Bremer Handelsblatt*, Aug. 31, 1861, quoting from *Der Jahresbericht der Handelskammer zu Köln für 1860; Der Deutsche Handelstag*, 1861-1911.
[68] Nov. 5, 1859, p. 385.

government to devote more funds and attention to the furtherance of the economy—technical schools, roads, railroads, and the like. In these respects, the decisions of the German Association agreed with those of its Prussian counterpart. On the whole the initiative was taken in the German rather than in the Prussian organization, but the weight of both was thrown on the side of economic liberalism.[69] The objectives were almost identical with those of the Congress of German Economists and the liberal parties in Prussia. The relationship among these organizations was maintained by the bond of common personnel in leading positions in all of them. Representing Prussia in the executive committee of the German Association in 1861, for example, were the well-known liberals Behrend of Danzig, Weigel of Breslau, von Sybel of Düsseldorf (not the historian but a prominent business-man), Classen-Koppelmann of Cologne, and Hansemann of Berlin (whose influence proved to be less than that of some of the others).[70]

Behind the chambers of commerce and the commercial associations were to be found a large number of special business associations. The *Berliner Börsen Zeitung* estimated the number at the beginning of 1861 to be about 400 for all Germany, with 101 of them located in Prussia.[71] The fact that Prussia had the largest number reflected not merely her size but also the vigor of her economy. Highly industrialized Saxony with eighty-three associations had a larger number than Prussia in proportion to the size of her land area, but no other state approached either of them in economic significance. In the Rhineland and West-phalia, according to an estimate in the *Berliner Börsen Zeitung*, January 26, 1861, there existed in addition to some twenty chambers of commerce many other economic organizations. The paper gave the name of nine of them and then had recourse to a double *etcetera*. One had to do with the marketing of coal, another with mining, another with iron and steel, another with the reduction of freight rates on iron, another with projects for canal construction, each concerned with a special interest, each showing the considerable degree of specialization in the industry of this region. In Silesia the Silesian Central Industrial Association was founded at a meeting of 436 persons in Breslau in April, 1862. It represented thirty-seven individual associations with about 5,000 members and also some 130 single persons, among them twenty-three merchants, twenty-two manufacturers, twenty-six officials, thirteen teachers, and some handworkers. Containing as members the

[69] See remark in *Bremer Handelsblatt*, Feb. 10, 1866, p. 48.
[70] *Der Deutsche Handelstag*, I, 18, 23-24.
[71] *Berliner Börsen Zeitung*, Jan. 9, 1861.

leading economic personnel of the province, it resembled the Congress of German Economists rather than the special-interest organizations of the Western provinces; but it functioned in a way and for purposes similar to those of the other economic associations.[72] The business world was feeling the same enthusiasm for entrepreneurial action that stirred the political leaders to form new organizations. This was the founding period, rich in energy, rich in experimentation, unable as yet to gauge the most efficient distribution of strength and the proper organizations.

The economic associations did not assume as active a role in the other provinces as in the three most industrialized ones of Silesia, the Rhineland, and Westphalia. Nevertheless, they existed elsewhere and in cooperation with the chambers of commerce helped to strengthen the liberal forces. Numerous conferences of economic groups were held with the government. A few examples will show the range of interest and the methods and channels used to uphold them. The Zollverein Beet Sugar Verein had members in 1861 serving as deputies in the Lower House of the Prussian Landtag and planned a conference at which these deputies would be present to discuss how to defend the beet-sugar interests. Representatives of the private banks met in Berlin in 1861 to prepare material to submit to the Landtag about their difficulties and needs. The Merchants' Association in Königsberg complained to the government about the tariff on grain and seed. From Magdeburg came lamentations about the tolls on the Elbe. The papers were full of reports of conferences among business interests, often with Lower House deputies present, for the purpose of exercising pressure on the government in favor of liberal reforms.[73]

Throughout the state the well-established, eminently trustworthy men of commercial and industrial property were profoundly concerned with the outcome of the elections, and they saw to it that candidates sympathetic to their views were selected. An instance of the intimate relationship between economic and political liberalism was afforded in the growing industrial town of Düsseldorf. The local members of the Commercial and Industrial Verein for Rhineland and Westphalia met in October, 1861, to discuss the elections to the Lower House of the Landtag. A similar conference was held in Duisburg. The members urged the election of businessmen as electors and as deputies, and several names were proposed as possible candidates for the Lower

---

[72] See *Bremer Handelsblatt*, Nov. 11, 1865, pp. 400-401.

[73] *Berliner Börsen Zeitung*, May 14, Jan. 16, Sept. 30, 1861. This paper was especially active in reporting these meetings.

House, in particular those of the industrialists von Sybel, Hugo Haniel, Gustav Stinnes, and the young Hammacher, who was to make a distinguished career as a professional representative of the Ruhr.[74]

The third of the most important economic associations was created on non-Prussian initiative. In May, 1857, the *Bremer Handelsblatt* published a call for the establishment of a Congress of German Economists. The idea of such an organization seems to have been derived from Belgium. In the preceding year an International Congress for Tariff Reform had been held in Brussels which had led to the founding of an International Committee for Economic Reforms with headquarters in the same city. The North German towns as the greatest commercial centers of the country had been especially interested, and by the middle of 1857 local committees of the Brussels organization had been established in Hamburg, Bremen, Lübeck, Berlin, Cologne, Stettin, Hanover, Heidelberg, Frankfurt a. M. and Mannheim. The International Committee had not interpreted its function narrowly as pertaining solely to tariff problems, but had proposed to deal with all questions that adversely affected international trade. It aimed, according to the *Bremer Handelsblatt*, to further freedom and security in trade and to arouse a feeling of individual responsibility by spreading knowledge of the natural laws of economic activity.[75] The *Bremer Handelsblatt* used this association as a precedent for the one it was proposing: the new organization should be a place where theory and practice went hand in hand and men of knowledge cooperated with men of practice. The *Handelsblatt* thought that the future Congress of German Economists might affiliate with the international committee; but it pointed out that alongside the problems common to other countries Germany had special ones to deal with, the problems of freedom of occupation, movement and domicile, indeed all the problems caused by German disunity. Since Germany had to solve these before it could catch up with the other countries, the Congress was to assist in the achievement of this goal.

The proposal to establish the new association received the enthusiastic support of the liberal newspapers. When the International Welfare Congress met at Frankfurt a. M. in September, 1857, the German delegates used the occasion to call for the establishment of economic Vereins in the larger and smaller towns of Germany either independent of or in conjunction with the existing commercial and industrial or

[74] *Ibid.*, Oct. 25, 1861.
[75] *Bremer Handelsblatt*, June 27, 1857.

agricultural organizations. The associations were to endeavor to spread the knowledge of accurate economic concepts and to arouse active interest in better economic institutions and ways. The Prussians who participated in the proposal and signed the call were President Doctor Lette of Berlin, Professor Schubert of Königsberg, Schulze-Delitzsch, and Doctor S. Neumann of Berlin, all prominent liberals.[76] Together with eighteen others from the other states of Germany, they set up a small provisional committee to pursue the work, and the first German-wide Congress met in Gotha in September, 1858. From then on the organization was well established, with an enthusiastic membership and, from 1862, with even its own journal, the *Vierteljahrschrift für Volkswirtschaft und Kulturgeschichte,* edited by Julius Faucher and Otto Michaelis, two prominent Prussian liberals. It proved from the beginning to be a highly effective organ of liberalism, emphasizing the economic aspects but doing so with the full realization of their political implications.

The first Congress was composed of those persons sufficiently interested to attend. No other conditions were set. One hundred and ten individuals participated; among them were to be found members of all the important occupations in Germany, for example, about forty government officials, three agrarians with large-scale holdings, six handworkers, two manufacturers, ten merchants, eight lawyers, nine editors, three writers, two teachers, four professors, two pastors, four bankers and bank employees, one physician, one apothecary. The number of handworkers may be misleading in that it may have included individuals who while retaining the title of master had transformed their business into a thoroughly capitalistic enterprise. The title of professor was also not very revealing, for of the four one represented the Industrial Society of Weimar, one taught economics and served as editor of a journal, one taught in a technical school, and one was an authority on law. Most significant was the large number of editors and writers, approximately one-fifth of the persons present.

The purpose of the Congress, to unite men of theory and men of practice and to spread enlightenment about economic problems and criteria, was reflected in the membership and became increasingly evident as the work of the Congress developed and the membership expanded. The active participation of Schulze-Delitzsch, Otto Michaelis, Julius Faucher, Prince Smith, Bergius of Breslau, Hübner of Berlin, G. Weiss of Berlin, Wolff of Stettin, and Lette of Berlin assured close cooperation with the Prussian liberal parties, so much so that in 1861 a group of about twenty deputies in the Lower House of the Prussian Landtag, most of them active in the Congress, formed an informal economic committee to further the work of reform along the lines of the proposals of the Congress. The committee contained persons from the various liberal groups, from the right wing across to the left; even when the liberal parties could not agree on other matters, economic problems brought them together.

The Congress encouraged its supporters to organize in local and regional Vereins. Like the National Verein it had on association to respect the strict laws of Prussia, not to mention other states. For this reason as well as for the practical purpose of demonstrating the efficiency of liberalism it preferred to decentralize its operations. Reliance on local initiative encouraged the habits of self-help, individualism, freedom and personal responsibility. Wherever appropriate organizations already existed, it worked together with them. In some areas of Prussia, like the Western provinces and Silesia, it played a role secondary to that of the industrial Vereins, the chambers of commerce, and the specialized economic associations. The economy and society of the Western provinces and to a lesser degree of Silesia had already advanced beyond the stage in which the proposed type of economic Congress could be of much value. In the Central provinces except for Berlin, which as the capital, the largest city in the state, and developing center for industry, commerce, and banking, was already won to liberalism, the work of the Congress was needed, but it failed to be as significant as that in the East. The area in which the Congress led the discussion and formulation of economic policies and furthered the spread of information about them was East and West Prussia. Associations were established in such number that in June, 1861, one was created for the entire region. The invitation to found the Economic Society for East and West Prussia was signed by the prominent liberals of the area, many of them deputies in the Lower House.

The occupational representation in the Economic Society for East and West Prussia included merchants, large-scale agriculturalists, bankers, lawyers, an editor and a professor, but no handworkers. By the end of 1861 the Verein had 520 members, all of whom one can assume belonged to the upper middle class and the liberal land-holding nobility. At its congress held in December in Königsberg about 110 members were present, and the list of speakers again reads like that of the liberal representatives in the Landtag from this area—Röpell, Schubert, Philipps, von Henning-Plonchet, Behrend, John, von Hoverbeck, Papendiek-Liep. Its standing executive committee, Behrend (Danzig), von Forckenbeck (Elbing), von Hoverbeck (Nichelsdorf), A. Philipps (Elbing), and C. Röpell (Danzig), were all prominent leaders of the Progressive party and Landtag deputies;[77] but the participation of persons like Professor Schubert of Königsberg, a leader of the Constitutional party, attested to the full agreement of the liberal political groups on economic problems. With such individuals as leaders, the Economic Society could not have kept out of politics; it acted as a vigorous center of political organization and propaganda and formed an essential support for the liberal parties, especially the Progressives.

The National Verein proved to be one of the most influential of the new associations. It developed in 1859 out of two almost contemporaneous meetings, one in Hanover of North Germans, the other in Eisenach of South and Central Germans. Finding that their programs were similar, the two groups called a further conference at Eisenach for August of that year, at which a statement of policy was promulgated. Germany, it said, should be unified under Prussia's leadership. A national convention should be held for the purpose of drawing up a German constitution. All parties that loved their country, whether democratic or constitutional (it did not even mention Conservatives), should work together for the unification of the nation. One of the members, Metz from Southwest Germany, read an explanatory statement in which he formulated the plan for accomplishing this objective. Local Vereins should be organized and other legal means should be used; a "national progressive party" should be developed.[78] In this way liberals and democrats should win control of the parliaments in each state and force the rulers to work for national unification. Power and freedom were inseparable, a broadsheet of the National Verein stated in 1860; absolutism was unable to unite the people in enthusiastic defence of the country. The new Verein should be the center for all activity aiming at the single objective of a free, united, and self-governing German nation.

Metz's explanation received the general approval of the conference but was not attached to the declaration of policy for tactical reasons: it might have caused difficulty for persons not present to sign the declaration, and the primary objective was to gain open adherents to the basic proposal.[79] Nonetheless, Metz stressed the essential inter-

---

[77] *Königsberg Hartungsche Zeitung,* Dec. 14, Nov. 24, 27, 1861.
[78] *National Zeitung,* Sept. 2, 1860.
[79] *Ibid.,* Sept. 2, 1859.

dependence of national unity and of liberalism and democracy and introduced the significant phrase "progressive party." When new, aggressive political parties were organized in several German states during the next year or two, the founders took this name, for example, the German Progressive party in Prussia. The name indicated the relationship of the party to the national movement and its guide, the National Verein. The intimacy was well known, so much so that the *Neue Preussische Zeitung* early in 1861 described the address to the throne of the Lower House of the Prussian Landtag as a political program in accordance with the principles of the National Verein, and the *Mainzer Journal* stated that in addition to the three usual factors in law-making Prussia now had a fourth, namely, the National Verein.[80] The meetings of local members of the National Verein in Prussia proved to be useful in organizing and campaigning for the Progressive party. They were acting in accord with the plans to elect liberal deputies to the Landtag who would use their official position not merely to introduce liberalism in government and society but also to bring into power a government which would support the National Verein program for national unification.[81] The enthusiasm with which the *Wochenschrift des National Vereins* welcomed the formation of the Progressive party in Prussia was unbounded. "For the first time," it stated, "the ban of particularism in the chamber of one of the larger German states has been broken; for the first time there arises among the representatives of the people a party which declares the German point of view to be foremost, which places the watchword Germany upon its banner."[82]

The National Verein did not align with any one liberal party, not even with the one using the magic words "German Progressive" in its name. It sought to unite all liberals and democrats in its ranks. The Progressive party in Prussia had the same intention; it welcomed liberals and democrats of all shades and hoped to become the sole or the main liberal party on the basis of common devotion to freedom and to national unity. In the local National Vereins the Progressives

[80] *Tagesbericht*, No. 29, Feb. 4, No. 52, March 2, 1861.

[81] See, for example, the statements by Roepell and F. W. Krüger in the meeting of the members of the National Verein in Danzig, September, 1861. *Königsberg Hartungsche Zeitung*, Sept. 14, 1861; *National Zeitung*, Sept. 20, 1861. Also see the story of the predominant success of the National Verein members in the counties of Osterburg and Stendal in 1861 in winning the voters away from the Conservatives, so that instead of a Conservative majority, the counties voted for 237 Progressives out of a total of 332 electors. See *ibid.*, Dec. 11, 1861.

[82] *Volkszeitung*, Feb. 1, 1862.

and the right-wing liberals were almost always able to work together, even though they quarreled over the means to employ.[83]

The close association between the Prussia liberals and democrats and the National Verein became evident from the fact of common personnel in leading positions. At the conference in 1859 founding the National Verein, five Prussians participated, Schulze-Delitzsch, Franz Duncker, the liberal editor of the *Volkszeitung* in Berlin, Julius Frese of Berlin, Victor von Unruh, an industrialist and future liberal deputy, and Franz Zabel, editor of the liberal *National Zeitung* in Berlin.[84] The first executive committee of twelve members included three Prussians, Schulze-Delitzsch, Veit, bookseller and at the time a liberal member of the Lower House of the Landtag, and Victor von Unruh. The next year the guiding committee consisted of twenty-five members, among them the Prussians Doctor Otto Lüning, a liberal physician from Rheda in Westphalia and future deputy in the Lower House; Theodor Müllensiefen, a prominent industrialist at Krengeldanz near Witten and a liberal political as well as economic leader and future deputy; Schulze-Delitzsch; von Unruh; Veit; and Cetto, an estate-owner at Trier and future liberal deputy.[85]

Almost every Prussian attending the conference in Frankfurt a. M. in 1859 when the National Verein was formally established was a well-known Prussian liberal leader. Franz Duncker of the *Volkszeitung*, Zabel of the *National Zeitung*, Streckfuss, H. Rückert of the *Danziger Zeitung*, President Lette, Veit, the physician Doctor G. Weiss, von Unruh, Frese, and City Councillor Duncker of Berlin were all prominent liberals. Schulze-Delitzsch, Cetto, the manufacturer Berger from Witten on the Ruhr, the manufacturer Friedberg of Berlin, Doctor Lüning of Rheda, Dietzel, connected with industry in Cologne, and Consul Müller of Stettin were present, along with a couple of less-known physicians, Stamm and Norman of Berlin, and Assessor Fischel of the same city. Government officials were conspicuously absent. In contrast to the Congress of German Economists the National Verein was not a safe place for the official of a German state to be. The relative number of editors and physicians (three from Prussia) was high;

[83] See, for example, the split among the members of the National Verein in the Lower House over the Kühne amendment to the military bill, *Königsberg Hartungsche Zeitung*, June 6, 1861.
[84] See *National Zeitung*, Sept. 2, 1859.
[85] *Verhandlungen der ersten General-Versammlung des deutschen National Vereins am 3, 4, 5 Sept. 1860* (Coburg, 1860). Preuss. Geh. Staatsarchiv. Pr. Br. Rep. 30. Berlin C. Pol. Präsid. Tit. 94, Lit. D. 335.

but the group included a fairly wide representation of occupations. The Prussian liberal agrarians were to join in force, but they moved more slowly than the urban residents.[86]

The first general conference in 1860 in Coburg attracted about 500 members. The secret report about the meeting to the Berlin police headquarters, contrary to what one might expect, coolly appraised it as of no great consequence. Among those present, it said, were Wilhelm von Humboldt's son, two Württemberg peasants in costume, a large number of lawyers, many editors, and some Jews. Of the fifteen or twenty persons from Berlin no one, it said, was important.[87]

The secret agent misjudged the personnel; at that conference were to be found once more, and in larger number than ever, the liberal leaders of Prussia, especially those who were to form the Progressive party. Over fifty Prussians attended, among them the prominent liberals Brämer of Gumbinnen, Cetto of Trier, Franz Duncker of Berlin, The Lucas, Doctor Lüning, Lawyer Martiny of Kaukehmen in East Prussia, Parisius, Rohland of the province of Saxony, Schulze-Delitzsch, Werner Siemens of Berlin, Steinitz, the future secretary of the Progressive party, Streckfuss, Temme and von Unruh of Berlin, and von Vaerst of Herrendorf near Soldin. The occupations represented included that of bank director, physician, lawyer, merchant, manufacturer, estate-owner and knight's estate-owner, baker, bookseller, teacher, engineer, editor, master mason, and official. Peasants, workers, professors, and pastors were lacking; otherwise the main occupations were fairly represented, especially those independent of government pressure.

At the general conference held in Leipzig in October, 1863, far larger numbers of Prussians participated, but most of the prominent liberal leaders were forced to remain at home because at that time the election campaign for the Lower House was nearing its close. Nonetheless, the number of Prussians present (ca. 175) was three and one-half times as great as in 1860 and the occupational representation was wider in spread. An extraordinary number of handworkers attended, from small towns as well as the cities. All areas of Prussia were represented, but the largest number came from Leipzig, the region nearest to the meeting place. To judge from the size of their delegations, small towns with growing industry like Lückenwalde and Torgau showed particularly active interest.

---

[86] See the list in the National Zeitung, Sept. 19, 1859.

[87] Preuss. Geh. Staatsarchiv. Pr. Br. Rep. 30. Berlin C. Pol. Präsid. Tit. 94, Lit. D. 335.

By the date of the general conference in 1865 the Prussan liberals had become so deeply involved in the fight with Bismarck that less than a dozen appeared. The continuing failure of their struggle to reform Prussia along with the intense hostility to Bismarck and his national policy in the rest of Germany disinclined most liberals from venturing to attend a conference at which they could only make excuses for Prussia and hang their heads.[88]

The plan of operation and the organization of the National Verein were described by Streit, the executive secretary, at the general meeting in 1860 at Coburg. The Verein would seek to use the right of association in the German states to solve the problem of national unification. Streit recognized that this task faced tremendous obstacles, such as the habits of obedience engendered by years of absolutism, the disappointment over the outcome of 1848, the hostility among parties and classes, the organized, well-established power of ultramontane and reactionary forces. Nonetheless, the National Verein aimed to overcome these obstacles by legal means and to spread understanding of the political need for liberalism and national unity. Streit repudiated any revolutionary intentions. The German people lacked the revolutionary spirit found among other people, he said, nor were conditions such that they needed to develop this spirit. He did not know whether the struggle for the Verein's objectives could succeed by legal means, but he added that no one had ever tried thoroughly to employ them. He considered the free press, the right of association and of assembly to be "powerful levers," and since the German people possessed them to such a large extent, he thought that by using them efficiently and tenaciously over a period of years the goal could be reached.

Since the laws of the German states prevented the establishment of branches, the National Verein organized as a single association on a nationwide basis. Each member belonged and paid dues to the national body, not to a local or regional chapter. The high degree of centralized authority had both advantages and disadvantages, but since an alternative was impossible the Verein made the best of the situation. A large executive committee was selected so that there would be actively interested members on it from each part of Germany. In addition, agents were appointed to serve as centers of endeavor in smaller districts. In this way a considerable number of persons would

---

[88] See the list of those in attendance given in the *Verhandlungen* of the conferences, published at Coburg, 1860, 1863, and Frankfurt a M., 1865. Preuss. Geh. Staatsarchiv. Pr. Br. Rep. 30. Berlin C. Pol. Präsid. Tit. 94, Lit. D. 335.

be directly responsible for pushing the work of the Verein and would be aided by and report to the central office. The disadvantage of not having local branches with elected officers and means of arousing enthusiasm might thereby be overcome. The *Wochenschrift* was started in 1860, but without the expectation that it would earn its own way. It should serve the usual purposes of agitation and information and be a rallying point for all members.[89]

The membership in the National Verein never grew very large. According to the business report made to the general conference in October, 1865, the Verein had in the previous year (1864) 303 agents and 17,862 members. In addition, there were sixty-four agents and 3,160 members who were in arrears on their dues. If they were included, the Verein would have had a total of 21,022 members. Of the 17,862 members, 8,355 were found in Prussia. In August, 1861, the *Wochenschrift* showed a normal sale of 5,324 copies. Of these 1,865 were sent through the mail, 206 were forwarded in other ways, and the rest were sold through bookstores. The only separate figures available about Prussia were those for the number sold in bookstores, namely, 864 copies.

The National Verein suffered most from inadequate financial support. At the general conference in 1863 the secretary reported that the Verein had an annual budget of 55,807 Florens. He contrasted this sum with the £50,000 with which the Anti-Corn Law League had begun in England, the £100,000 which it had raised after the initial sum had been exhausted, the two million Guldens which it had spent over a period of fifteen years of agitation. If the English spent such sums for the repeal of the corn laws, he asked, how much more ought the Germans to give for the cause of national unification? A member from Frankfurt a. M. was so concerned over the state of finances that he proposed a three-class system of self-taxation to be introduced for members. His suggestion was rejected.[90]

Neither the urban nor the rural supporters of the objectives of the National Verein, neither its industrial nor its agricultural members, saw fit to contribute large sums to the cause. Although they were

[89] *Flugblätter des deutschen National Vereins.* Hrsg. im Auftrag des Ausschusses vom Geschäftsführer (Coburg, 1860), Vol. I, 3rd printing; *Verhandlungen der ersten General-Versammlung des deutschen National Vereins am 3, 4, 5 Sept. 1860* (Coburg, 1860).
[90] *Verhandlungen der vierten General-Versammlung des deutschen National Vereins, Leipzig am 16 Okt. 1863* (Coburg, 1863). The rate of exchange at the time was approximately twelve Florens to the British pound. The Gulden current throughout Germanic Europe and England, was equivalent to the Floren.

prospering and would greatly benefit from the victory of liberalism and nationalism, they were disinclined to expend their own money. A reporter from Elbing to the *Königsberg Hartungsche Zeitung* (September 8, 1861) explained the lack of response as a result of years of governmental paternalism and absolutism. Unless the state forced them to do so, the people gave little money to public causes.

The Verein aimed throughout to appeal to the upper classes, primarily the middle class and the bourgeoisie. From the towns the influence was to spread among the rural people in the surrounding area.[91] The membership dues were too high for peasants and most handworkers to afford. One of the members, Habicht of Gotha, proposed in 1860 that the Verein publish an inexpensive popular paper for handworkers and peasants, as the *Wochenschrift* itself was intended for the educated upper classes. The handworkers were, he said, easily interested in political ideas and news. It would be more difficult to influence the peasants; but the work of agricultural associations and expanded educational activity were bringing greater mobility in the political views and interests of even this class. The peasant, he continued, read only one paper completely and loved to hear the school master read to him on Sunday out of a popular journal. This paper should be put out by the National Verein. Habicht's speech failed to convince the audience, and no action was taken to implement the proposal.

The National Verein encouraged the local members to gain the support of the masses for the cause, but it did almost nothing to help them. By this approach it would not tamper with the existing social structure, except to undermine privilege. While seeking to abolish legal inequality it would continue to recognize the fact of social inequality. It would uphold the liberal principles of reasonableness and the liberal methods of discussion, compromise and agreement. Like its Prussian counterpart and ally, the Progressive party, it did not express an official view on the subject of equal and universal suffrage. When urged to oppose the general idea of equality, of which suffrage provided one example, von Bennigsen, the head of the National Verein, refused on opportunistic grounds. He feared that such a step would by indirection alarm the propertied classes who might think that after all the National Verein was unwittingly stirring up revolutionary sentiment. The Progressive party in Prussia, he said, suffered from the same dilemma.[92]

[91] See *Wochenschrift des National Vereins*, Jan. 24, 1862, pp. 745-46.
[92] See *Volkszeitung*, May 25, 1862.

It should not be inferred that the National Verein was composed of political and social snobs, unconcerned about the welfare of the masses and even afraid of them. The strategy may have been at fault; the Verein might have fared better than it did if it had stirred up a popular following and sought by means of a popular national assembly to exert mass influence both upon the state governments and directly in favor of the unification of the country. However, the members recalled the failure of this policy in 1848 and wished to avoid a repetition. They disliked revolution in any violent form on grounds of principle. They believed, and they had a reasonable right to believe, that the nation could be unified and made liberal in the way they proposed—by building up liberal and national parties in each state that would take over the governments and then fulfill the dream of unification by agreement. The German nation would be united with the least upset; the foreign enemies, especially France, would not dare to intervene, as they might in case of a revolution; bloodshed and revolutionary action would be avoided; the even course of business would not be interrupted; in fact, everyone would benefit from this kind of action—the middle classes, the peasants, the capitalists, the agrarians, the workers, everyone except the supporters of autocracy and caste, the vestiges of the Old Regime, the bulwarks of particularism and privilege. Local political and social leadership by liberals and democrats would not be supplanted by some far-away, alien group with headquarters in Coburg; the natural sources of leadership and strength as they existed would be encouraged to practice the liberal principles of private initiative and civic responsibility. Liberalism and democracy would lift themselves by their own bootstraps; the people would receive training by practice. The German nation would unify itself; it would not have unity imposed from above to the advantage of authoritarianism and the detriment of liberalism. It would be a model for the world of what to do in politics and society and business, and of how to accomplish ends with most efficiency and economy, with most reasonableness and freedom. This approach was the antithesis of Bismarck's methods and ways.[93]

The social and economic character of the provincial and local leadership of the Verein was in keeping with the intention and strategy. Well-known liberals of the upper classes everywhere controlled the

---

[93] Hermann Oncken, *Rudolf von Bennigsen, ein deutscher liberaler Politiker* (Stuttgart and Leipzig, 1910). I, 359-60; *Wochenschrift des National Vereins*, April 25, 1862, p. 847. The latter warned that the educated classes must keep in close touch with the masses.

local groups. For example, in Breslau, the lawyer Fischer served as agent of the National Verein in 1862. He, the wholesale merchant Molinari, and Moecke, the editor of the *Schlesische Zeitung*, were all active for the National Verein and at the same time served as guiding spirits in the Constitutional party.[94] In the former they cooperated with the leaders of the Progressive party; but according to the police report of 1865, the National Verein never became strong in Breslau.[95] In Tilsit, a teacher and pastor took leading roles; in Fischhausen County, two merchants, an apothecary, and two knights' estate-owners; in Königsberg, Bender, Professor John, Medical Councillor Doctor Möller, City Councillor Stadelmann, Teacher Witt, City Councillor Böhm, City Councillor and Bookseller Bon, Professor of Medicine Jacobson, Merchants F. A. Kadock and H. Welle, Falkson, Johann Jacoby, Theodor, von Facius, Kleeberg, Professor Hänel; in Gumbinnen, Brämer, Frentzel-Perkallen, and Headmaster Marcus; in Danzig, L. Biber, Th. Bischoff, Professor Bobrik, Lievin, F. Rattenburg, H. Rückert, F. Schattler.[96] Leadership in other regions of Prussia was of comparable significance.

The occupational distribution of membership did not necessarily depend upon the degree of exposure to governmental pressure. Government officials, especially those in the administrative positions and therefore susceptible to discipline, tended to keep away from the Verein. The same was true for pastors, the trainers in Christian obedience, the moral preservers of the old order; but some did participate in the meetings and support the Verein in spite of pressure. The teachers were active to an extraordinary degree. National unification meant for them the realization of such an enticing ideal and opened such an opportunity for this sheltered profession to work and even to suffer for a noble cause that many of them joined the Verein and devoted their efforts to it notwithstanding the danger from their dependence upon the government.[97]

The association had the largest number of members and supporters in the cities and towns, where the population was densest, opportunities for organization were most numerous, and the ability to resist government coercion by mutual assistance was greatest. In reporting a banquet held in Berlin in honor of von Bennigsen, the head of the Na-

[94] *Volkszeitung*, March 19, 1862.
[95] *Polizei-Bericht*, Breslau, Nov. 5, 1865.
[96] See the contemporaneous issues of the *Königsberg Hartungsche Zeitung*.
[97] See, for example, *Wochenschrift des National Vereins*, May 17, 1861, March 7, 1862; *Königsberg Hartungsche Zeitung*, Feb. 27, 1861; *Tagesbericht*, Jan. 30, 1861.

tional Verein, the *Vossische Zeitung* (March 13, 1860) analyzed the audience of 500 as follows: it contained some pastors and elderly military personnel, no one from the Upper House, numerous judges and lawyers, few city councillors and even fewer members of the city magistracy, a large number of the most important industrialists and merchants, the overwhelmingly majority of the booksellers, numerous professors and teachers. The analysis agrees in general with that made by the police of meetings of the National Verein in Berlin in December of the same year and in January, 1861. Of the 350 present at each conference, the police found that the overwhelming number belonged to the "better and well-to-do middle class," namely, merchants, doctors of philosophy, writers, lawyers, and so on. Handworkers were few, laborers were entirely absent.[98]

The National Verein for Königsberg and the surrounding region had 294 members in February, 1862, among them 107 merchants, seventy-one estate-owners, thirty-five handworkers, twenty-seven physicians, eighteen teachers and professors, ten brokers, seven officials, and three writers.[99] In the small town of Pillau, nineteen of the most respected businessmen joined the National Verein.[100] In Danzig by the last of September, 1859, a large number of merchants, four or five physicians, several teachers, manufacturers, brokers, rentiers, apothecaries, brewers, bankers, and the editor of the *Danziger Zeitung* had already become members of the Verein.[101]

In other towns, especially the smaller and medium-sized ones in the Eastern and Central provinces, within a few months of the founding of the Verein, the signers of the Eisenach Program included a wide spread of occupations. Particularly significant among these signers in the small towns were the names of many handworkers. In Bromberg participation was active, for the conflict with the local Polish population made the Germans acutely aware of their nationality. Of the upper-class occupations only certain officials were unable to join: Minister von der Heydt would not allow them to do so.[102] In the Western provinces the leadership and the personnel belonged to the same occupations and classes as everywhere in the state, the same ones that supplied the support for the liberal parties.

[98] Preuss. Geh. Staatsarchiv. Pr. Br. Rep. 30. Berlin C. Pol. Präsid. Tit. 94, Lit. D. 335.
[99] *Königsberg Hartungsche Zeitung*, No. 40, Feb. 16, 1862. The breakdown was given by Professor John of the National Verein.
[100] *Königsberg Hartungsche Zeitung*, No. 121, May 28, 1861.
[101] *National Zeitung*, Sept. 23, 1859.
[102] *Wochenschrift des National Vereins*, April 26, May 17, 1861.

One group, the youth and especially the students, which had been traditionally active in liberal and national movements, was discouraged from participating. That the students were interested in the Verein and that many would have signed the Eisenach Program seems certain. The reason for their exclusion was explained very simply in the *Wochensshrift:*[103] the students were too young; this was a man's affair youth inclined toward impetuous action and revolution; the National Verein relied upon calm, persistent moral and intellectual persuasion and parliamentary influence; if youth became members they might involve the Verein in trouble with the police; it was better to deny them official membership and to restrict their participation to being told what the objectives were and what the adults were accomplishing. The National Verein membership should be mature and safe.

The participation of the workers and the peasantry raised difficult problems. Neither could be expected to assume much, if any, initiative in the cause of national unification. Their economic status, their lack of knowledge and the absence among them of a tradition of political action kept them as a whole in a passive position. In many cases, however, peasants actually did officially belong to the National Verein. In the Goldene Aue along the Saale the well-to-do peasants joined in large numbers.[104] The same was true for the peasants of Carwitz, where as early as 1859 some nine joined, of Schlawin and of Notzkow, in each of which in the same year over a dozen became members. One could cite other examples, all taken from the contemporary press. If given the opportunity numerous peasants would have signed the Eisenach program.[105]

The collection of funds for building a Prussian fleet illustrated the way in which the National Verein and its supporters operated. It provided an opportunity for arousing the interest of the various social groups, including the lower classes, in the question of national unification. The movement set a goal understandable by all, the collection of funds with which to build naval vessels for the defence of the German coast and of German commerce—a goal which in its concreteness symbolized the cause and need for German unification. One may assume that if the lower classes with a modest donation supported the plan for building a Prussian fleet or adding ships to it, they were interested in national unification.

[103] *Ibid.,* July 12, 1861.
[104] *Volkszeitung,* July 29, 1862.
[105] See, for example, the *National Zeitung,* Oct. 28, 1859.

Navy Vereins had been popular in 1848 as an expression of the desire for national unification. Dormant during the years of reaction in the 1850s, they had revived with the New Era; and the war of Italian unification, the outbreak of the Civil War in the United States and the threatening trouble with Denmark over Schleswig-Holstein aroused them to vigorous activity. The Navy Vereins collected funds continuously, but in 1861 a campaign was inaugurated to obtain a large sum for a special number of ships. The National Verein took a leading part in the entire matter; usually the members of the local Navy Verein were also local members of the National Verein. The two worked intimately together, even to the extent of the local Navy Verein's sending its collections to the National Verein headquarters for despatch to the Prussian Ministry of Marine. While some Conservatives supported the Navy Vereins, the usual attitude of their colleagues was decidedly negative. They disliked a fleet, commerce, and all that went with them. The stronghold of their power lay in the army, and they wished no competitor to develop.[106] The staunch support of the navy came from the middle and lower classes, the same ones which formed the strength of liberal and democratic parties and the national movement.

The campaign started in Leipzig and Dresden and was immediately taken up by Hamburg and Bremen, not one of them a Prussian town. The Rhineland and Westphalia showed less interest than other parts of Prussia and Germany. They did not feel the same need for naval protection, for they had few overseas interests in trade as yet, and so far as defence was concerned they were most afraid of France. The Prussian areas most active for the fleet for economic reasons were those of the Center and of the East. They traded by sea in grain, textiles, and colonial products, and they felt danger from the superior power of the Danish fleet. Nonetheless, the main force behind the naval collection was not economic but political. As Schulze-Delitzsch said in August, 1861, it was recognized that the couple of hundred thousand Florens collected during the drive would help very little: but, he added, "the question was one of moral aid and of new pressure for Prussia finally to devote itself to the national cause."[107]

The agitation aimed at the creation of a fleet capable of defending the sea coast of Germany not merely in the Baltic but on the North Sea. It was to protect German interests on the high seas as well.

[106] See *Volkszeitung*, Jan. 30, 1862.
[107] *National Zeitung*, Aug. 29, 1861.

Although Prussia had no territory on the North Sea, the sponsors wished it, as the largest state, to assume responsibility for the defence everywhere of the entire German people. The plan called for building a German fleet under Prussian control; it fitted into the *klein-deutsch* solution of the problem of German unity as supported by the National Verein. While some Prussians may have felt that donations for this purpose could not cause anyone to question their loyalty to Prussia and that in making them they were safe from governmental or social reprisals from the Conservatives, the public statements made the issue clear that the donations were for a German fleet under Prussian leadership and responsibility. Donations could hardly be viewed as other than a mark of approval of and desire for national unity in some form and for its concomitant, liberalism.

Danzig, Königsberg and all the Baltic coastal towns and cities in East Prussia were active in the collection of funds. Without danger the burgomaster in each place could and did assume a prominent role. In Königsberg the executive committee of the Navy Verein contained fifteen members, of whom eight were merchants, one a master cabinet maker, one a banker, one a lawyer, one a manufacturer, one the burgomaster, one an estate renter, one of no listed occupation.[108]

In one town a restaurant proprietor placed a large box in a prominent place so that the guests could contribute and obtained "a considerable little sum" for the fleet.[109] At Darkehmen the handworkers donated seventy-five Thalers to the Navy Verein out of their guild treasury. In the Lithuanian rural counties in East Prussia the peasants became enthusiastic about the German fleet and aimed to donate enough funds to make possible the construction of a boat to be named "Mukkit," that is, "Attack."[110] Silesia took an active part. At Breslau the burgomaster, Elwanger, a Conservative, served as head of the Silesian Committee, composed, as it was, of the most prominent citizens.[111] At Görlitz the organization showed that in a popular cause the people knew how to conduct an effective campaign. The committee was composed of eight town officials and twelve members of the town council. The burgomaster called together the members, the officials in charge of district affairs within the town and the representatives of the press and discussed how to make the collection thorough. It was decided to publish a call in the press, to use printed lists of the

[108] *Königsberg Hartungsche Zeitung*, Oct. 22, 1861.
[109] *Tagesbericht*, No. 74, March 28, 1861, citing *Danziger Zeitung*.
[110] *Königsberg Hartungsche Zeitung*, Oct. 2, 1861.
[111] *National Zeitung*, Sept. 15, 1861.

citizens and to have everyone covered by the house-owners. The guilds were to be asked to contribute out of their treasuries. So successful was the effort that on March 8, 1862, the head of the committee for Silesia was able to send 55,100 Thalers to the ministry for the construction of a cannon boat "Silesia."[112] At Berlin the committee was equally active, but the title it chose did not stress the objective of national unification as sharply as elsewhere, even though the purpose was the same. The Berlin group called itself the Committee for Collecting for the Prussian Fleet to Protect Germany. The title used in other areas of the state was clearer—the Committee for the Collection of Funds for the German Fleet under Prussian Leadership. The membership of the Berlin committee, merchants, bankers, officials, editors of newspapers, most of them prominent liberals, manifested the fact that the latter title would have expressed its sentiments more accurately, but the other title was apparently chosen so as not to prevent even Conservatives from contributing. The committee felt so patriotic that it issued an ardently nationalistic appeal for funds even to the workers.[113] The other towns followed suit, and the newspapers reported the exact amount of contribution from each individual. The total sum did not prove to be large, but it expressed the longing for liberalism and national unity of almost every donor, with only the few Conservatives excepted.

The National Verein took an interest in the other popular movements for strengthening German defence comparable to that for the construction of a fleet. Its relations with the gymnastic Vereins and the rifle Vereins were very close. The executive secretary of the National Verein and editor of its paper, Doctor Streit, edited also the official organs of the other associations and was prominent in their central administration. The common membership and interlocking directorate were as characteristic in these cases as in those of the other liberal and national organizations. Within a few months of its founding the National Verein approved at its general conference (September 5, 1860) two resolutions submitted by von Rochau in the name of the executive committee. One advocated military training in the schools as part of the education of all the youth. The other called for the establishment of shooting societies so that young people could be

[112] *Ibid.*, Sept. 27, 1861; J. Stein, *Geschichte der Stadt Breslau im 19. Jahrhundert*, p. 587.
[113] *National Zeitung*, Sept. 11, 1861; *Volkszeitung*, Jan. 18, 1862.

taught the use of arms.[114]   The next year, 1861, at the general conference in Heidelberg the National Verein returned to the same question and passed among others a resolution in favor of the creation of
military societies for training civilians all over Germany.[115]   It stirred
up interest in national unification among all groups and classes, including the workers and peasants, and used the many related associations for this purpose.

The success of the National Verein depended upon the outcome of
the conflict in Prussia between the liberals and the Conservatives.   If
the liberals won, the National Verein would have a strong chance to
achieve its goal.   If they lost the society saw no immediate prospect of
its own success.   It therefore encouraged the liberals in every possible
way.   At local and regional meetings outside Prussia the members
passed resolutions supporting their battling colleagues and denouncing
the Conservatives.   In October, 1863, Chairman von Bennigsen condemned the policy of the Prussian government under Bismarck as
"suicidal blindness," and declared that the conflict in Prussia could
not prevent the Verein from continuing its work.   The political report
of a committee to the general assembly of the Verein at the same time
stated realistically that "the near future of Germany depends upon the
speedy victory of the constitutional party in Prussia."   So it did,
although not in the implied sense, for the constitutional party lost
the battle.[116]

The Press

The Conservative *Preussisches Volksblatt* early in 1861 asked the
question, who supported the present ministry—the mildly liberal ministry of the New Era, which that journal despised.   The journal supplied its own answer: "It does not depend upon the handworkers and
the peasants who together amount to fourteen million souls, pay most
direct and indirect taxes and almost alone provide the entire force
for the Prussian army.   Nor can the ministry depend upon the other
three million.   What does it depend upon?   First of all upon so-called
public opinion.   But who is public opinion?   All the newspapers of

[114] *Verhandlungen der ersten General-Versammlung des deutschen National
Vereins, am 3, 4, 5 Sept. 1860* (Coburg, 1860) .

[115] *National Zeitung,* Aug. 27, 1861.

[116] See resolutions of support from Frankfurt a. M., Braunschweig and Gera,
Darmstadt, Dresden, to cite a few examples, in *Volkszeitung,* Feb. 5, March 22, 26,
28, 1862; see also *Verhandlungen der vierten. General-Versammlung des deutschen
National Vereins, Leipzig am 16 Okt. 1863* (Coburg, 1863).

the Prussian State, mostly edited by Jews, have scarcely 100,000 subscribers, of whom a part do not even belong to the ministerial party! And this enormous 'minority' of 100,000 persons is the solid foundation of the ministry!" The accusation must be investigated. What was the size and significance of the liberal press?

The creation and continued operation of a press may be said to have been in itself an act of liberalism. Respect for ideas, confidence in the efficacy of reason based upon free information, recognition of the value of knowledge, of news, of data on which people could decide issues for themselves bespoke the acceptance of the liberal way of life. The contrast in tone between the Prussian liberal or democratic and the Conservative journals revealed how harshly and crudely the latter adapted itself to the methods of a free press. The Conservative papers could not and would not discuss an issue coolly and reasonably, for a Conservative did not feel reasonable. He damned and blasted and employed bitter irony to bludgeon his point through. He did not respect his opponent; he was convinced that morality sided exclusively with him. The liberal and democratic press set itself a different purpose and gauged its role in a different way. Where the Conservative journals, with lavish use of superlatives, denounced and demanded, claiming a monopoly of wisdom, virtue, and statesmanship, the liberal and democratic press had a more modest conception of its function. Each kind of press reflected the ideals and ways of its form of life. The one dictated to the people on the basis of dogmas and beliefs; the other sought to express the views of the public. The one scorned a public to which it unfortunately had to appeal; the other sought to enlighten and to interpret the mind of that public, which it respected even when it thought the policies and views of certain groups to be wrong.[117] The mild classical liberal of the old school, Rudolph Haym, took this responsibility as editor of a periodical so seriously that he refused to seek election as deputy in the Lower House. He argued that the political views of the public were not entirely reflected in the Lower House and he believed that the press was needed to supplement the work of that body.[118]

Liberalism and democracy implied the union of ideas and practice, popular enlightenment, and appeals for support on the basis of facts and understanding, not merely for the bourgeoisie and middle classes but for all social groups. All the leading papers throughout Prussia

[117] The editor of the *Königsberg Hartungsche Zeitung* wrote on August 6, 1862, "We liberal newspaper men do not make public opinion with our editorials; we only interpret it."

[118] Heyderhoff, *op. cit.*, I, 128-30.

upheld the liberal or democratic principles and supported one or the other liberal political party or fraction. In Berlin, apart from the *Kreuzzeitung,* the organ of the Conservatives, liberalism and democracy had the field of journalism almost to themselves. The *Volkszeitung,* edited and published by Franz Duncker, catered to the democratic elements. The *National Zeitung,* edited by Zabel with the aid of Otto Michaelis, served as the leading organ of the Progressive party. The *Spenersche Zeitung* expressed the views of the right-wing Constitutional party, while the *Berliner Börsen Zeitung* acted as the main vehicle of liberal economic interests. The *Danziger Zeitung,* the *Ostsee Zeitung* in Elbing, the *Königsberg Hartungsche Zeitung,* the *Morgen Zeitung, Schlesische Zeitung* and *Breslauer Zeitung* in Breslau all advocated liberalism in their respective geographic areas of influence. So did the *Magdeburger Zeitung,* the *Kölnische Zeitung,* and the leading newspapers of the Ruhr. In fact, not merely the prominent papers of statewide or regional appeal but almost all those of merely local circulation supported the liberal side. In Gumbinnen the liberal large landowner John Reitenbach, a cousin of Deputy John Frenzel, founded and directed the publication of the *Bürger-und Bauernfreund* for peasants and the lower middle class.[119] The leading members of the Progressive party urged its support. The liberals living in the counties of Stolp, Schlawe, Lauenburg, and Bütow established an *Intelligenzblatt* for their area.[120] At Neurode the democratic *Allgemeine Dorfzeitung,* subsidized for a time by Count Pfeil in Hausdorf, began to appear in the 1850s.[121] Back of the liberal journals financially stood booksellers, publishers, bankers, industrialists, merchants, even big landowners.

Contrary to the Conservative accusation, very few of the owners or editors of the liberal or democratic papers were Jews. Of the Berlin papers, the *Volkszeitung* had two Jewish editors among a large number of gentiles. The other papers were in the hands of Christians. In Breslau, the popular *Morgen Zeitung* was controlled by Jews, and the *Breslauer Zeitung,* owned by Christians, in 1860 came under the editorship of another prominent Jewish liberal, Doctor Stein; the other papers remained under Christian control. Evidence that race or religion affected the editorial policy of the papers is entirely lacking.

[119] *Königsberg Hartungsche Zeitung,* Feb. 27, 1861; Parisius, *von Hoverbeck,* II, 84.
[120] *Volkszeitung,* Jan. 15, 1862.
[121] Klawitter, *Die Zeitung und Zeitschriften Schlesiens von den Anfängen bis zum Jahre 1870,* pp. 6-7.

The editorial standards of a popular newspaper of the time may be judged from a statement in October, 1861, by the editor of the *Tilsiter Zeitung*. In the political section, he wrote, the paper would bring short articles about the events of the day. With respect to the internal and foreign affairs of Germany it would continue to follow a decidedly liberal policy, to further political progress, to spread political education, to write short, intelligible editorials, which aimed "less at gaining adherents to a definite political party than at stirring up the political conscience of the citizens." The journal would report news from the other towns in the province and supply information about trade, shipping, industry, agriculture, and the like. Finally it would provide material for social conversation, the recent news about the theater, concerts, literature, and so forth.[122]

The main newspapers throughout the state utilized the services of many kinds of correspondents. The Landtag deputies frequently wrote long despatches about events in the capital, especially political events, for their local papers. Professors did likewise for various favorite papers. The universities and the popular press were in close contact, for in the case of the leading newspapers the academic and the newspaper personnel came from and appealed to much the same social class. Prominent citizens when travelling, including businessmen, sent back reports, and a growing number of free-lance journalists was available.

An example of the number and geographic spread of correspondents of a prominent paper is had in the case of the non-Prussian *Augsburger Zeitung*. The journal was widely read by intelligent circles throughout Germany and enjoyed the service of a large assortment of writers, probably few if any of them being professional journalists. In 1867, according to a Berlin police report, it had one or more correspondents in each of forty-three towns. Twenty-three of these were in towns in Germany, the largest contingents being in Munich (thirteen), Frankfurt a. M. (eight), and Berlin (six). The others were located in Austria, England, the Ottoman Empire, France, Italy, Switzerland, and Sweden.[123]

Most papers merely took news items from others, either reprinting whole articles with a credit line or condensing the information. The range of information provided in local papers was wide as to topic and geographic coverage. However, the need for better facilities led

[122] *Königsberg Hartungsche Zeitung*, Sept. 27, 1861.
[123] Berlin-Dahlem, Preuss. Geh. Staatsarchiv. Pr. Br. Rep. 30. Berlin C. Pol. Präsid. Tit. 94, S. 129.

to the establishment of the *Berliner Liberale Correspondenz,* the first issue of which appeared in January, 1863. It proposed to serve the local papers which did not have regular correspondents in Berlin. The leaders of the Progressive party agreed to write for it and especially to provide news about affairs in the Landtag and about party conferences and decisions.[124] The degree of success of this service may be estimated in only a rough way. The news appeal of the constitutional conflict in Prussia was so high that an abundance of items was available for an eager public, and the service responded to the demand.

Statistics on the edition of the important papers were frequently published at the time. In December, 1862, the *Magdeburger Zeitung* made the following estimate. The Berlin liberal press paid a tax on a daily edition of about 100,000 copies. In the provinces the liberal press turned out probably 150,000 copies, not including the small local papers. Thus the liberal press printed a total of 250,000 copies each day. By way of contrast, the Conservative Press in Berlin, even when the *Volksblatt* and the *Stern Zeitung* were included, printed probably 15,000 copies. It was much more centralized in Berlin than the liberal papers, for many liberal journals in the provinces competed with those in Berlin, while among the Conservative ones the *Kreuzzeitung* stood alone. The feudal papers in the provinces probably printed 20,000 copies, making at most 40,000 subscribers for Conservative journals. If five readers are reckoned to one subscriber, the liberal press had 1,250,000 readers, the Conservative press 200,000. One should also add the liberal non-Prussian papers or periodicals read in Prussia, for example, the *Gartenlaube,* of which out of an edition of 130,000 copies at least 40,000 were subscribed for in Prussia.[125]

Figures about the size of the edition in Berlin, Breslau, and a few other larger cities tend to support the estimate of the Magdeburg journal. For Berlin these are available for the years 1858 and 1863, as follows:

	1858	*1863*
Neue Preussische Zeitung (*Kreuzzeitung*)	4,000	8,500
Spenersche Zeitung	8,000	4,000
Vossische Zeitung	15,000	13,000
National Zeitung	5,000	8,500
Volkszeitung	9,000	36,000

[124] *National Zeitung,* Jan. 10, 1863.

[125] Article reprinted in *Königsberg Hartungsche Zeitung,* Dec. 2, 1862; *Allgemeine Zeitung* (Augsburg), Oct. 31, 1863.

In Breslau in 1864 the *Schlesische Zeitung* published 7,520 copies daily, the *Breslauer Zeitung* 5,004, the *Provincial Zeitung* 1,800, the *Morgen Zeitung* 12,200, the *Schlesisches Morgenblatt* 4,000. By way of comparison, the *Kölnische Zeitung* printed in 1858 some 14,000 copies. The available figures on the number of out-of-town papers distributed in a particular locality tend to show that readers mainly relied upon regional or local journals, and that those with a state-wide reputation achieved that position not through the spread of their circulation but by enabling the local papers to borrow the important news stories. For example, of the two main local papers in Trier in 1857 one had a circulation of 696, the other of 559. The *Kölnische Zeitung* was subscribed to by 389 persons there, the *Vossische Zeitung* and the *National Zeitung* of Berlin by sixteen and fourteen respectively. Cologne had even fewer subscribers to outside papers; the *Kölnische Zeitung* sufficed for local needs. The same conditions held true in Breslau.[126]

The quality of articles in these liberal and democratic papers compared favorably with that of the best articles in any journal in England or other countries of free institutions. The superior intelligence of the writers, whether professional editors, professors, public personages, businessmen, or lawyers and members of other professions, was manifested in the broad range of interest, the marshalling of evidence, the clarity and succinctness of expression, and the thoroughness of analysis. The reader could rely on finding in each issue a compact article giving facts and expressing a balanced opinion in a cool, reasonable tone. In the liberal press of this period German journalism reached a peak. Facts were not omitted or warped to conform to an editorial policy as they were later under Bismarck and his successors in all but the few best papers like the *Frankfurter Zeitung*. While news and editorials were mixed together, the latter interest had not yet begun to cause violations in the accuracy of reporting. The articles or despatches, written usually by public-minded private citizens, not professional journalists, were intended for persons like the authors, persons of intelligence whose judgment deserved respect; they were not meant to flame the public or to serve a tactical purpose in a political game among professional politicians. The journalism of upper-class liberalism still prevailed; and the liberal papers for the workers, peasants, and lower middle class adopted equally high standards. The Prussian people in the towns and cities were well supplied with objective news

[126] Preuss. Geh. Staatsarchiv Dahlem. Pr. Br. Rep. 30. Berlin C. Pol. Präsid. Tit. 94, Z. 81, 169, P. 383; *Polizei-Bericht*, Breslau, March 4, 1866; *Allgemeine Zeitung*, Oct. 31, 1863.

and with calm, objective analyses of the news. The rural areas were not as yet able to obtain the news service that they needed to keep informed, and the liberals criticized themselves for not taking steps to develop a widespread local press for the agricultural communities. Nonetheless, in some regions big landowners of liberal or democratic views were beginning, with the aid of persons of similar views in the towns or cities of the region, to establish journals for these social groups.

The relatively high cost prevented the lower classes as a rule from being able to afford the newspapers. Many middle-class persons preferred to read them in the public reading rooms, which were found in each large town and city. There all the journals were at the disposal of those paying a small entrance fee, and together with the numerous rental libraries for books they enabled every person to keep informed at a low cost.[127] The estimate of the *Magdeburger Zeitung* that each copy of a newspaper had about five readers may be considered as fairly accurate. The people in both town and country were accustomed to lending their newspapers and journals to others; and since time and speed had not yet become for most of them an essential factor in regulating their lives, they did not object to an issue's being several days old. Reading material was not yet so plentiful that they would pass by a paper or journal merely because it was out of date. They read carefully and conscientiously, and especially the upper middle-class members in town and country tried to arrive at their own conclusions on the basis of the evidence.

One may strongly doubt whether the Conservative government's efforts in 1862 and 1863 to restrict the freedom of the press had any appreciable effect upon the spread of news. The repression certainly failed to change opinion in favor of Conservatism. The fact of government censorship became immediately known far and wide and increased the extent of antagonism to the existing ministry and its policies. The liberal and democratic papers in Berlin had as early as May, 1862, followed the practice of destroying manuscripts as soon as they were used, so that in case the police searched the newspaper offices they would be unable to identify the authors.[128] It may be assumed that other newspapers adopted the same procedure. Under these circumstances the readers acquired the faculty of knowing when

---

[127] Breslau alone had in 1863 some thirteen of these libraries and ninety other localities in the province had 163. *Jahresbericht der Handelskammer in Breslau,* 1863, pp. 95-96.

[128] *Königsberg Hartungsche Zeitung,* May 23, 1863.

and how to read between the lines, and that fact enhanced their antagonism to the kind of regime that forced them to do so. The suppression of the freedom of the press in a society beginning a period of vigorous economic and political development afforded sufficient news in itself to induce the social forces back of this development to oppose an oppressive government.

The Organization for the Elections

When the New Era began, the liberal political parties had had little experience in conducting election campaigns. During the years under discussion the diversity of methods and policies employed not merely by the different parties or fractions but often by individuals or groups within them showed that they were learning the ways of politics by trial and error. The Constitutional party never did develop anything approaching adequate facilities for party activity among the voters; and, setting the example as usual, the Progressive party experimented most and in spite of mistakes achieved the best results.

Each party created a central election committee by having its deputies in the Lower House choose a couple of dozen members from among their number, with considerable power of subsequent co-optation in case of need. The fractions within the Progressive party never became so independent as to establish their own committee, and for the elections of 1862 and 1863 the Left-Center fraction and the Progressive party joined forces under a common committee. The Left-Center, or Bochum-Dolffs, fraction, in fact, never established any kind of permanent organization. The Constitutional party had its own committee, but in the elections of 1862 and 1863 it also declined in the main to compete with the central organization of the other liberal parties and left the responsibility for political action to the local groups. As a rule, for these two elections all the liberal parties and fractions agreed to help each other against the government candidates. Wherever the one liberal group had had a representative in the previous Lower House, all liberals were to support his re-election.[129]

On the whole the central election committees did not rank in practical importance with the local committees. That of the Progressive party drew up a program for the entire state, not as a body of dogma but as a basis for common action on the part of the local election committees. Any local group was free to change the program according

[129] See Parisius, *Politische Parteien*, p. 56; Parisius, *von Hoverbeck*, II, 108; *Kölnische Zeitung*, March 29, 1862.

to its wish, but the central committee expected it to serve as a statement of proposals acceptable to all. The party leaders sought a minimum basis of agreement with maximum freedom for local action and initiative.[130] They were practicing their ideals of responsible government.

The central committee of the Progressive party served as a clearing house for information and advice.[131] The value of this work was recognized. A Berlin correspondent of the *Königsberg Hartungsche Zeitung*, who manifestly had close working contacts with the committee or was even a member of it, declared in an article (July 4, 1861) that

> . . . the main deficiency of our popular representation rests on the isolation of the election districts and the resulting preponderant influence of local authorities. If the proper candidates are lacking, the so-called respected people, the officials and rich landowners, will be victorious; and, since the representation of the rural population is larger than that of the towns, an unfree representation of too conservative a character must arise. This deficiency can only be overcome if the election committee becomes very active and proposes a sufficient number of liberal candidates and sends them to places where prospect for them exists.

The central committee of the Progressives received a number of requests from the local groups for a list of names of reliable and worthy persons whom they might propose as candidates for the Lower House. The localities often lacked the means of transportation and communication which would enable them to keep well informed. They could not know whether their political views agreed with those held elsewhere in the state, and whether the persons for whom they might vote on the basis of merely local knowledge were in harmony with the party as a whole. Recognizing the practical need for the list, the central committee prepared one and in the autumn of 1861 sent it confidentially to the party leaders in the various localities. The list contained names of individuals of the Progressive and of other liberal political groups; for, true to its original intention, the party aimed to unite all shades of liberal and democratic opinion for the purpose of positive action. By the time of the election of 1863 the events of the constitutional conflict had aroused the population so

---

[130] See statement by Virchow, *National Zeitung*, July 17, 1861.
[131] See *National Zeitung*, Nov. 8, 1861; *Königsberg Hartungsche Zeitung*, Oct. 3, 1861.

intensely that central guidance on personnel had become unnecessary.[132]

That the guidance offered by the central committee was welcome appears proven from the large number of places in which the local election committee discussed and approved the program—to mention merely a few, Tilsit, Gumbinnen, and Lötzen in the East, Cologne and Düsseldorf in the West.[133] Whether the advice on the names of worthy candidates gained much attention is less certain. In the urban areas of the East and Center and throughout the Western provinces the advice was not needed, for adequate information already existed about available candidates. The quality of political activity in these regions ranked superior as to knowledge, experience, and supply of current information to that in the rural area of the Central and Eastern provinces.

Throughout the state the party leaders organized election committees on a local basis, or for a county or an election district. The adherents to the party usually did so by vote in an open political meeting. At Pillau, for example, the party instructed its local election committee to co-opt persons known and respected throughout the county and become an organ for the entire county. In November, 1861, the election committees of Cologne and Düsseldorf called a conference of representatives of the local committees of the Rhineland province. Most of the local committees actually sent delegates, especially those of Coblenz, Bonn, Düsseldorf, Trier and Aachen. The meeting decided to form a provincial committee which would continue beyond the election, would work closely with local committees, and would further the political education of the population by party literature and meetings.[134]

The extent of organization in the cities and towns varied according to the degree of enthusiasm of the local leaders. In Berlin, for the election of 1861, the Progressives established a committee in each of the four election districts and usually in the precincts.[135] The election of 1862 was announced so short a time ahead that in the first election district of Berlin the party was unable fully to organize the campaign and had to rely upon the initiative of a leader elected for that task in each precinct to call rallies and maintain contact with the election

[132] See *Kölnische Zeitung*, Nov. 1, 1863.
[133] See *Königsberg Hartungsche Zeitung*, Aug. 6, July 27, Sept. 28, 1861; *National Zeitung*, Nov. 17, 1861.
[134] *National Zeitung*, Nov. 17, 1861.
[135] *Königsberg Hartungsche Zeitung*, Oct. 5, 20, 1861.

committee for the district.[136] It was evident that in the capital the party had established no continuing local organization. At Cologne the city election committee of 120 members of the Progressive party prepared more efficiently for the election of 1862. It divided the city into fifteen sections and arranged for each section to name its own committee with a president.[137] At Elbing the Progressive party in October, 1861, held a meeting of about 300 members to discuss the necessary preparations for the campaign. The chairman of the meeting, Burgomaster Philipps, proposed that a committee of twenty-five persons be selected by secret ballot to draw up the list of electoral candidates. The list, he said, should then be submitted to a subsequent meeting of the party members for discussion and ultimate approval. Another liberal criticized this proposal as not encouraging public participation in political affairs and suggested instead that public meetings be held in each precinct to select candidates and that the central election committee for the district restrict its work to making certain that in these meetings the party performed its duty. The majority of the members, however, found even Philipps' proposal too complicated and asked him to select a committee to recommend candidates. He did so, and about a month later the liberals approved the list by acclamation.[138]

For the election of 1862 the party in Elbing put into practice the more liberal suggestion. Instead of referring the task to a large committee it stirred the voters into action and held small meetings in each precinct for the selection of the electoral candidates. A contemporary observer wrote:

> This independent participation gives the voters a far greater interest in the victory of their candidates. It has the further advantage that in individual precincts associations are formed in these political meetings which plan to come together periodically for social and political conferences and especially during the time of the Landtag sessions will work beneficially for the political development of the members.

The party likewise had agents in the small rural localities around Elbing and helped them to spread information about issues and candidates among the peasants. In this way it expected to overcome the handicap of impassable roads which prevented the rural voters from attending the city rallies.[139]

[136] *Volkszeitung*, April 20, 1862.
[137] *Kölnische Zeitung*, April 10, 1862.
[138] *Königsberg Hartungsche Zeitung*, Oct. 4, Nov. 14, 1861.
[139] *Ibid.*, March 18, April 26, 1862.

The laws caused such difficulty in establishing associations and subjected them to such close supervision that party leaders had tended in 1861 not to create election associations but to be content with the more flexible and less formal institution of the election committee. As the conflict with the government grew in intensity, liberals in certain areas, for example, Königsberg town and county and Dortmund and the surrounding area, established associations (1861 and 1862) for spreading knowledge of the constitution and of politics, so that "in the most remote and the smallest cottage one would find alongside the Bible and an almanac a copy of the constitution."[140] They were a kind of society for adult education in constitutional government and were supported by the most prominent liberals in the region. In numerous places all over the state local leaders created informal groups of electors and even voters to keep in touch with the deputies during the Landtag sessions. Many liberal deputies wished to maintain these close contacts. They sent reports to friends for circulation or wrote articles for the local paper. Whenever possible, as in Berlin, the deputies appeared in person at meetings, spoke and discussed with those present the course of legislation in the Landtag. Voters and electors singly or in groups sent letters or resolutions to their deputies on many subjects.[141] Indeed, the evidence points to the conclusion that in the vast majority of cases the relations between liberal deputies and their constituencies were close all the time. For the election of 1862 the issues were clearly understood by upper classes and numerous members of the handworkers and peasantry. For the election of 1863 the liberals did not even consider it necessary to campaign as vigorously as before.[142] It required little effort to gain votes for the liberals. The fact that the elections were fought over basic principles of society and government, the meaning of which could be dramatized by concrete details, made it relatively easy for the liberals to win the lower classes to their side. A couple of speeches or a pamphlet were usually enough to show the classes, provided they were sufficiently independent to risk antagonizing their Conservative masters, that their advantage lay with the liberals.[143]

---

[140] *Ibid.*, July 10, 1861, May 9, 1862; *Volkszeitung*, Feb. 21, 1862.

[141] See the many examples in the contemporary press.

[142] See *Kölnische Zeitung*, Oct. 20, 1863.

[143] The small amount of money spent on an election points to the same conclusion, that the political propaganda of the liberals was carried on largely through the normal channels of social influence, the press, and personal contacts. The expenditures of the Progressive party election association of Breslau for the election

In a few cities, Breslau for example, the Progressive party even extended its activity to the election of city councillors and through them to the election of the burgomaster.[144] On the whole, however, the liberal political parties kept elections for local offices separate from those for deputies to the Lower House. They still distinguished between issues of what they called a political character, namely, of statewide significance involving principles, and problems of only local import, problems merely of detail. Few of them perceived the advantage for self-government of stimulating political activity at all levels, of associating local with state politics as a means of increasing political interest and providing concrete, practical ties between the two for the benefit of each, of expanding the area of politics as far as possible for purposes of general education in individual political initiative and civic responsibility. Without the close affiliation with local organizations, vigorous in every election, local or state, the organization would not be permanent, the interest would not be all-inclusive and continuous, the liberal deputies in the Landtag would lack the wide institutionalized support which comes from the intimate inter-relatedness of local and state politics. The Conservative government would be able, as it actually was, to prevent wide-spread activity in politics by obstructing the development of a sense of political responsibility in local as well as state affairs. It succeeded in keeping politics at the state level, where they seemed too exalted and offered too few opportunities for the common man, the bulwark of democracy, to participate. An occasional use of the ballot did not afford much opportunity for him to learn about politics; the election of local officials and the deciding of local issues on a party basis would have enhanced his opportunities and would have increased the vested interests in popular government. The action of the Progressive party in Breslau was sound and healthy, but it lacked sufficient imitators.

of 1862 amounted to 1,111 Reichsthalers, 16 silver Groschen, and 3 Pfennig. Of this amount 185 Reichsthalers were used for advertisements and 275 Reichsthalers for printing. See *Polizei-Bericht, Breslau,* July 2, 1862.
[144] *Polizei-Bericht,* Breslau, July 21, Oct. 27, Nov. 24, 1862.

10 / The Conservative Party

THE NUMBER of deputies elected by the Conservatives to the Lower House of the Landtag declined from 181 in 1855, to forty-seven in 1858, to fifteen in 1861, to ten in 1862; it rose to thirty-six in the election of 1863. What kind of party was it that fell from power so completely and so fast?

The Conservatives differentiated themselves sharply from every other political group. Occasionally the members were willing to cooperate with other parties on a local basis, as in Königsberg and Breslau, where in November, 1861, the Conservative committee of the electors proposed cooperation to the election committee of the Constitutional or right-wing liberal party. In Königsberg the offer was refused, but in Breslau the two parties traded support so that in 1861 each elected one deputy.[1] In the Western provinces, the Conservatives actually did establish working relations with conservative Catholic voters. On the whole, however, they defended such reactionary political, economic and social principles that they repelled every other party or fraction. Minister von Roon privately criticized them for refusing to give any support to the government of the New Era because it contained a few right-wing liberals. He thought that they felt the need of adapting themselves to the constitutional system and of aligning with the government, but that personal antagonism between them and the liberal ministers, who had opposed them for over a decade, made rapprochement difficult.[2] It is more than questionable whether the

---

[1] *Königsberg Hartungsche Zeitung*, Dec. 1, 1861; *National Zeitung*, Dec. 11, 1861.
[2] Von Bernhardi, *op. cit.*, IV, 174.

Conservatives ever thought of cooperating with other groups except on their own terms. In politics they were fanatical dogmatists.

Upon Prince William's becoming regent in 1858 the Conservatives found themselves in an embarrassing situation. Many of them had openly opposed the Prince's being given this power, for they knew that he intensely disliked many of the acts of the Conservative Manteuffel government. They considered him far too friendly toward the liberals; and they wished to delay as long as possible his coming to authority and ending their happy regime.

When Prince William dismissed the most objectionable of the ministers in 1858 and appointed right-wing liberals instead, the Conservatives lost their political power. Since the new Minister of the Interior issued a directive to the officials to remain neutral in the Landtag election, the Conservatives lost their party organization. The Prince Regent's somewhat liberal program of government deprived them of a political directive. Their fundamental political problem became that of how they could be Conservative and at the same time loyal to a ruler who was not Conservative. After having become accustomed to receiving what they called a "tip from above," a "Wink von Oben," they were suddenly not receiving it. Deprived of the "tip from above," deprived of their political workers, the bureaucrats, deprived of the royal sanction of their policy and activity, what should they do?

The Conservatives were not accustomed to taking the initiative in political activity. Those in the bureaucracy as well as those in private life had been brought up to receive political orders. Those outside the bureaucracy disliked intensely having to organize political activity and to seek votes. Such work seemed utterly out of keeping with conservatism. They were too comfortable and apathetic as a group to cope with the extraordinary situation of having to fend for their political lives. They understood almost nothing about political propaganda or party organization and instinctively disapproved of any such activity. In a well-ordered state with a sensible, that is, conservative ruler, one did not have to lower oneself to this kind of behavior.

The loss of the election of 1858 did not shake the Conservatives out of their apathy. In fact they seemed so stunned by the appearance of an apparently liberal Hohenzollern ruler that they could not reconcile themselves to the continuation of such an aberration. They worked by way of their contacts at court and in the army and by means of the Conservatives remaining in the ministry to bring the ruler back to their policy. They supplemented these efforts of social persuasion by actions aiming to place the ruler in such a position of difficulty that he would be forced back into their camp. This was a matter of political strategy, and Prince William lent himself admirably to it by his adamant stand in military reform. They also endeavored to develop a political program and organization of their own and on their own responsibility and initiative to regain strength in the Lower House by entering into political party battles. The first and second lines of action have been treated above and need not be reconsidered here; the third deserves some analysis. It should be kept in mind that the Conservatives did not again become a powerful political party until they were able to line up once more behind the government and to use official resources for winning political victories.

The *Neues Preussische Sonntagsblatt,* an offshoot of the *Kreuzzeitung,* wrote in June, 1861, that the Conservatives needed "a firm, integrated organization in which the individuals would willingly sacrifice their favorite personal views and opinions for the sake of the great good for which we fight, and attaching themselves to the larger totality would feel themselves to be important and effective members of the entire party." Although a few Conservative aristocrats were advocating the same proposal, the bourgeois lawyer Wagener had to take the necessary steps for executing it, and one can say without exaggeration that during the next few years he alone organized and led the party.[3]

Through his speeches in the Lower House of the Landtag, of which he was usually a member, and especially through the articles in the *Kreuzzeitung,* which he edited, Wagener called the Conservatives to battle and strove to arouse them to the necessity of organization. He constantly pointed to the example set by the Progressive party and urged his colleagues to learn from their opponents. The elections to the Lower House forthcoming in the autumn of 1861 afforded the occasion for concrete steps to be taken, and by this time the Conservatives received a "tip from above." In the summer of that year the King said to a deputation of Conservatives, "Think about the next elections!"[4]

Early in June, 1861, a group of Conservatives in Berlin formed a small committee to develop an organization. The committee, composed of Count Eberhard zu Stolberg-Wernigerode, von Below-Hohendorf, von Blanckenburg-Kardemin, Baron von Hertefeld and Wagener,

---

[3] Müller, *op. cit.,* pp. 19, 42, 62, 67.
[4] *Ibid.,* p. 20.

sent a confidential letter to all the Conservative men known to it in the provinces. The committee urged them to campaign even where prospects for success were slight. They should cooperate with the handworkers in this activity and should volunteer their services in organizing a Conservative association in each election district to direct and push the campaign. The committee decided against issuing a central election program, since according to experience such a program caused more division than unity. It urged the group in each district to promulgate its own and to make certain that copies of the program were widely distributed.[5]

The committee found an ally in the central election committee of Prussian handworkers. The latter had come into existence by a change of name. With the organization of the Prussian Handworker Congress for the Preservation of the Industry Law, an executive committee had been established to protect the interests of these guild-minded handicraftsmen against the threat of freedom of occupation. The organization defended the law of 1849 by which some of the monopolistic privileges of former days had been restored to the guilds. The members now transformed their executive committee into an election committee, and since the *raison d'être* for the handworker organization conflicted with the essential principles of liberalism the committee had to line up with the Conservatives. It provided the popular aspect to the latters' endeavor.

In September, 1861, the Conservatives, including the handworkers, held a convention in Berlin. The invitation had been a general one throughout the state to all friends "irrespective of class and influence" who were ready to hold firmly together "under the banner of loyalty, justice and morality." It was expected to found at that convention the Prussian Volksverein as a party organization to combat especially the Progressive party and the National Verein. Over a thousand persons attended, nobles, large and small landowners, handworkers, pastors, teachers, intellectuals and workers. The conference was opened by Vice-Superior Master of the Hunt and Second President of the House of Lords Count Eberhard zu Stolberg-Wernigerode, and among the well-known personalities present were retired Presidents von Meding and von Kleist-Retzow, Lieutenant General von Maliscewsky, Major General von Winterfeld, Counts von Wartensleben and von Finckenstein, Barons von Waldow-Reitzenstein and Senfft-Pilsach, Ludwig von Gerlach, Wagener, and the handworker leaders Master Cobbler Panse

[5] *Ibid.*, pp. 23-24.

and Upholsterer Wohlgemuth. The Verein was created amidst an outburst of speeches and started on its indifferently successful career.

"Hundreds and thousands," said the propaganda of the new organization, joined the Prussian Volksverein immediately; within a year the membership numbered about 12,000 to 15,000 persons. Nonetheless, the central election committee of the handworkers refused officially to the join the Verein or to sign the program. Panse declared that the handworkers would cooperate loyally with the Conservatives without accepting the latter's program. He explained his decision on the grounds that the handworkers had to prevent the suspicion from arising that they were merely "instruments of a political party otherwise alien to them." Their chief aim at present, he said, was to elect a few handworkers to the Lower House of the Landtag to protect their interests.

In the course of the next few months it became clear that the handworkers had nothing in common with the Conservatives except the defence of the Industry Law of 1849. While the Prussian Volksverein claimed, with truth, that many handworkers joined the organization, it also knew that many did so unwillingly and that others declined the invitation because of fear of what the *Kreuzzeitung* called the "jeers of the masses." Panse was reported in the liberal newspapers as having said on October 30, 1861, at a public meeting of the Conservatives in Berlin that "all handworkers would decidedly go with the liberal party, if the latter had not written the fatal words 'freedom of occupation' on its banner." The alliance seems not to have been a happy one. Almost at once after the founding of the Volksverein the leaders of the handworkers were complaining that they had no opportunity to discuss matters privately with the central election committee of the Conservatives.[6] The Count This and That, the Lieutenant General, the Vice-Superior Master of the Hunt seem not to have had much interest in the problems of the handworkers. Let the latter make suits and mend shoes and lay stones, and vote Conservative.[7]

The Prussian Volksverein established headquarters in Berlin and selected a central election committee composed characteristically of thirteen nobles and one burgher, the latter being the indispensable Wagener. It set to work so bureaucratically and with such authoritarian zeal, at least in words, that Professor Leo of the University of

---

[6] *Ibid.*, pp. 29-30, 33-34, 40, 42.

[7] There was also complaint that the aristocrats preferred to buy their clothes from elegant stores and not to entrust their business to mere handworkers. See *Tagesbericht*, Feb. 17, 1862.

Halle, one of the party's most prominent and devoted members, complained. In order to counter the criticism that this was a feudal or Junker party, he said, the committee should have included others besides nobles. He urged that the mistake be corrected so that the party would draw those with conservative sympathy but without sufficiently strong convictions to be immune to the attractions of liberalism. He acknowledged that in the existing "war situation of the party" the member should be obligated to pay dues, but he condemned the bureaucratic way in which the committee proposed to assess and collect them. He disliked the committee's complicated and impractical method of conducting correspondence and its failure to establish personal contact with local leaders and to use them as local agents responsible for party affairs in their district. If the committee continued its present methods, he concluded, the Volksverein would soon lose every member in Halle. He urged that the management be vigorously decentralized.[8]

In one respect Professor Leo's criticism was accepted. In December, 1861, the central committee became composed of seven aristocrats and four burghers, Eberhard Count Stolberg-Wernigerode, von Below-Hohendorff, von Blanckenburg-Zimmerhausen, General Count von Finckenstein - Trebichow, Count von Pückler - Ober - Weistritz, von Krause-Schwarzow, Wagener, Baron von Hertefeld-Liebenberg, Burgomaster Strosser, Knight's Estate-Owners Andrae-Roman and Lösch-Ober-Stephansdorf.[9] Of the burghers two were knight's estate-owners and the other two were officials. Burgher businessmen, handworkers and peasants were not included.

The Volksverein scarcely attempted to meet Professor Leo's other major criticism, that the organization was too centralized and bureaucratic. It was unable to develop branch and local Vereins because of the prohibition contained in the law on associations of March 11, 1850, a law which the government, composed at the time of Conservatives, had passed against the liberals. It followed the example of the hated National Verein in creating only one central Verein—the Prussian Volksverein—to which all members belonged. These could meet in local groups as members of the central Verein in Berlin and conduct the necessary business.[10] The county and the mail station were selected as the natural geographic units of activity. Every county could have as many local divisions of the Volksverein as there were

[8] Müller, *op. cit.*, p. 36.
[9] *Ibid.*, p. 55.
[10] *Ibid.*, p. 55.

mail stations. If possible, every rural community with more than twenty members of the Verein should constitute a separate group. The local group should establish direct connection with the leader of the county organization, the county commissioner. It could likewise enter into direct relations with the central agency in Berlin.

The executive committee of the Volksverein recommended certain measures to be taken by the county and local groups. First, the members should be invited to a discussion in order to elect a chairman. The latter should prepare a list of members, attend to the correspondence with the central office in Berlin and keep the local members informed. The members should pay a small fee to cover expenses. The chairman was expressly empowered to collect the fees and disburse the sums for Verein business.

Anyone entitled to vote could become a member of the Verein by signing the program. If any member acted in public in an antimonarchical or in a democratic manner, he should be excluded from the Verein by a decision of the county or the local organization.

The local chairman or the county commissioner had the power to constitute the organization as he saw fit; the form should be appropriate to local or county needs. At the local level it could just as well be a social organization, a loan association or any other. If a Conservative organization already existed which could be used as the local representative of the Volksverein, it should be kept as it was, irrespective of name, with the influential members also being members of the Volksverein. If sufficient members were available in a locality, the group should select an executive committee, which from time to time should hold social gatherings in order to attract new members. During the summer at least one social event should be held, in common with neighboring local groups, with a full display of flags, shields, and other patriotic emblems. The famous events in the country's history should be celebrated with speeches and other forms of commemoration. Above all, discipline should be carefully preserved in the Vereins so that no democratic elements could creep in and gain the upper hand.

All correspondence, printed material, petitions and so forth sent out by the central committee would be individually addressed at the central office to the members in the local division, but in order to save postage they would be sent *in toto* to the county commissioners. The latter should then forward them through the mail. The same system should be used in case of correspondence from persons at the local level to the central committee; it should be sent to the local chairman,

by him to the county commissioner and by him to the central committee. A semi-annual report should be prepared at the local level
about loss and gain of members and sent via the county commissioner
to the central committee.[11]

The pattern used in these instructions was manifestly that of the
organization of the Prussian government. Orders were issued from the
center to be carried out in the provinces. Instructions were written in
detail; a semi-annual report on accomplishments should be made; the
necessary literature for dissemination should be despatched by the
central office; the expenditure on postage stamps should be carefully
watched; a commissioner in the county and a chairman in the community should be selected, as the equivalents of the Landrat, the
burgomaster, the Junker on his estate, the village Schulze, who were
responsible for the local activity; membership should be restricted to
the pure who signed the pledge, and orders were issued to exclude
all persons disloyal to the King or suspected or guilty of being democratic and liberal. The organization reflected the habitual dependence
upon the government. Just how the Volksverein expected to win
popular support with such an organization is not clear. It seemed
scarcely suitable to perform the functions of a political party.

In 1862 Wagener claimed that the Volksverein had 16,755 members
not counting those in East Prussia. It numbered 462 local units
organized in seventy county "commissariats" as follows:[12]

Prussia	12 Commissariats with		56 local groups	
Pomerania	13	"	" 64	" "
Posen	4	"	" 22	" "
Brandenburg	9	"	" 121	" "
Silesia	15	"	" 96	" "
Westphalia	4	"	" 38	" "
Saxony	13	"	" 55	" "
Rhineland	10	"	"	

The Volksverein reached the peak of its strength in December, 1865,
when it claimed to have over 50,000 members of whom 11,145 were in
Berlin, 34,508 in the provinces, and over 9,000 in a specially constituted Verein in Königsberg. These were organized in 534 locals.[13]

The Conservatives lacked a press adequate to express and defend
their views. They despised newspapers too much to be concerned

[11] *Ibid.*, pp. 55-57.
[12] *Ibid.*, pp. 67-68.
[13] *Ibid.*, p. 86.

with establishing and maintaining their own organs. They disliked the stir which the press caused; they were averse to the obligations of continuous intellectual effort which it entailed; they intuitively felt that any public discussion of issues, even by controlled Conservative journals, would arouse public interest and disrupt the traditional acquiescence of the masses in upper-class dominance. They had relied so long upon the government to supply whatever organs seemed necessary for imparting information to a docile public that they were unable to change their attitude quickly and expand their own press to cover the state. As a Silesian Landrat exclaimed in the 1850s, "What governmental newspaper, no matter how small, does not need subsidies to exist!" Even then it was hard to keep the journal alive.[14]

The New Era found the Conservatives unprepared to use any other than the accustomed methods of action. They had only one newspaper of any consequence, the *Kreuzzeitung*, established during the revolutionary years of 1848-49 and edited by the redoutable Wagener. Supplementing it were the *Neues Preussische Sonntagsblatt*, which was actually put out by the former, the *Volksblatt für Stadt und Land*, the *Preussisches Volksblatt*, and the *Berliner Revue*. The organ of the handworkers, the *Deutsche Bürgerzeitung*, may perhaps be added; and the list is exhausted. A considerable number of local papers were founded during the early '60s to assist in the propaganda; a humorous journal was established; a *Preussischer Volks-Vereins-Kalender* was published for popular consumption; Wagener's *Staats-und Gesellschafts-Lexikon* continued to be edited; and a large amount of pamphlets, broadsheets and similar literature was produced. A correspondence bureau was created in Berlin in January, 1862, to supply news four times a week to the provincial and local press about the debates in the Landtag. By March of that year its services were subscribed for by some fifty papers. At the same time an office was opened to provide the provincial and local papers with editorials and long articles at a modest price.

A few Conservatives recognized the weakness of the party press and urged the party to change its habits. One writer deplored the feeling of superiority toward the press on the part of the Conservatives and cited the example of England where the Conservative papers flourished and editors associated on terms of equality with the highest personages. What a contrast with Prussia, he exclaimed. He urged that editors

---

[14] Willy Klawitter, *Die Zeitungen und Zeitschriften Schlesiens von den Anfängen bis zum Jahre 1870 bezw. bis zur Gegenwart* (Breslau, 1930), p. 8.

be accepted in a "fraternal, comradely" way by the party leaders.[15] The central Verein took up the problem and recommended the following procedure for establishing a local paper which, it said, had proved successful. One should not concentrate on obtaining subscribers but should be much more concerned with arousing personal interest in the existence of the paper. To that end one should issue stocks in the paper and sell them in the county at from one to five Thalers each. A competent pastor or teacher should assume the editorship and the stocks should be repaid from the profits. By following this procedure, the central Verein stated, each stockholder would work to secure subscriptions and advertisements and at the same time would as part-owner represent and defend the journal.[16]

In 1862 the Conservatives controlled only thirty-three newspapers in the entire Prussian state. They were beginning to move, however, and local groups of Conservatives were in the process of founding small local papers to fight the liberals. In the Grafschaft Ravensberg appeared the semi-weekly *Konservativer Volks Freund;* in Posen, the *Neue Bromberger Wochenschrift.* In Silesia, after months of delay, the Conservatives succeeded in founding, in October, 1862, the *Provinzial Zeitung für Schlesien* and in beginning to transform the *Breslauer Kreisblatt* and the *Breslauer Polizei—und Fremdenblatt* into political journals. Good Conservatives in Silesia were thereby able to escape the necessity of reading the liberal *Schlesische Zeitung*.[17]

As soon as the Conservatives returned to control of the government, the process of transforming existing government papers into political journals became much simpler. The local papers which the government had created for publishing official information, many of them in the preceding century, were turned into political supporters of Conservatism. The change occurred throughout Prussia and offered a solution in keeping with Conservative standards. The government took the initiative, paid the bills, created nothing new and merely identified itself with Conservatism and employed the resources of the bureaucracy in the fight of Conservatism for survival. How efficiently the bureaucracy set to work may be seen from the police report from Breslau, July 4, 1863.

[15] *Tagesbericht*, No. 19, Jan. 23, 1862.
[16] Müller, *op. cit.*, pp. 43, 58-59.
[17] Parisius, *von Hoverbeck*, II, 109; *Tagesbericht*, No. 1, Jan. 2, 1862, Nos. 12, 16, Jan. 15, 20, 1862; *Zeitungs-Bericht für Mai-Juni, 1861*, Regierungs-Bezirk Breslau, July 8, 1861.

The Breslau county paper has been transformed into a political weekly for the purpose of opposing the demagoguery of the popular democratic little morning papers. A similar change is being prepared here in the city. The Breslau *Polizei-und Fremdenblatt* has already appeared since the first of the month in a larger format and will be organized on a basis similar to that of the *Decker Berniner Fremden-und Anzeigeblatt*. Great efforts will be made to obtain many subscribers for the paper and by many advertisements to make it a necessary directory and guide for strangers and natives. As soon as this is achieved the paper is gradually to be transformed into a local Conservative political journal.

The Prussian Volksverein proved to be a one-man organization. Wagener ran it from the start; the other members of the central executive committee were incompetent in popular political activity and inclined to do nothing. In the provinces the leadership was, if possible and with not over a dozen exceptions, even worse. The Conservatives were apathetic. Accustomed to issuing and to receiving orders, they understood intrigue at court or among a select few of the upper class, but they had neither the inclination nor the ability to cater to the masses for votes. Apart from Wagener and a few others, they could not make speeches; they could not debate; they could not write popular articles or pamphlets; they could not maintain their position in a public argument with the liberals. They soon learned to avoid public debate with their opponents and sought to exclude the latter from their political rallies.[18]

The political ineptitude may be illustrated by the following two stories, one of the city, one of the rural area. On October 30, 1861, the Conservatives held a rally in the first election district in Berlin. The invitation had contained the statement that "Master Cobbler Panse has promised to attend." Captain von Zastrow opened the meeting, and after announcing that Panse had had to go to Danzig he prepared to read the latter's speech. Vigorous objections were voiced by the liberals and democrats in the audience. These visitors used the opportunity to refute and denounce their opponents so completely that, as Colonel von Alvensleben was reported to have said, the Conservatives were "totally and openly defeated," and a liberal took over the conduct of the meeting. At that moment Panse appeared, declared that he was a "shamefully abused sacrificial lamb" of the Conservative party, and denied that he had anything to do with politics. He asserted that the only reason for the handworkers' aligning with the Conserva-

[18] Müller, *op. cit.,* pp. 41-42.

tives was that the liberals advocated the abolition of the law protecting the handicrafts, that otherwise they sided entirely with the liberals. When he spoke in favor of preserving the examination for those wishing to become handworkers, the liberals revealed the fact that he himself had never taken the examination and that far from being a bona fide handworker he owned a store which sold shoes made by others.[19]

The second example of political incompetence occurred at a meeting of Conservative voters in November, 1861, at Cumehnen in Fischhausen county. About twenty-six persons assembled, estate-owners, peasants and handworkers. O. W. Fischer from Königsberg spoke in his usual vein about the imperfection of all mortal acts. Only the eternal laws of God and His will as revealed in the Christian religion, he said, should be held holy. Several members of the Progressive party were present and objected to the assertions. They emphasized that in state affairs one could manage neither with the divine moral law nor with revelations, that one needed definite laws. They led the meeting to their side, leaving only the seven nobles in a determined minority.[20]

Except for the handworkers and to some extent the factory workers, the Conservatives aimed their propaganda not so much at townsmen as at the rural people, the large landowners, the peasantry, the pastors and county school teachers. They also sought to influence the officials, but as long as the government remained neutral in the elections they had slight success. Throughout the years of the New Era and the constitutional conflict they used their economic and social power over dependent persons to the limit. These means were especially recommended by the executive committee of the Volksverein. Even before the latter had been established, the Conservative committee in Berlin had sent out the following advice:

> In the rural districts the estate-owners should endeavor to have everyone subject to their influence cast a ballot. They should use every proper and legally permissible means of influence on their subjects and on those with whom they do business.

The women should also exert their influence. At the time of the election the most respected Conservatives should be present in the room during the act of voting.[21]

[19] *Ibid.*, p. 42.
[20] *Königsberg Hartungsche Zeitung*, Nov. 17, 1861.
[21] Müller, *op. cit.*, pp. 45, 37; Parisius, *Politische Parteien*, pp. 40-41; *National Zeitung*, Aug. 31, 1861.

In 1861 the Conservatives were a little careful about carrying out the recommendations of the central committee. They complained that Minister von Schwerin's election decree on the attitude to be taken by the officials toward the election lacked clarity and decision. They argued that it was not impartial, that it favored the liberals as against the Conservatives. Since it permitted the officials to participate in the activities of the National Verein, for example, it should also allow full freedom to the Landrats and the other administrative officials in behalf of the Volksverein.[22] The reason for their concern was expressed in a letter which Moritz von Blanckenburg, one of their leaders, wrote in December, 1861, to Minister von Roon. "I shall not let my courage fall, but *against* the governmental stream the Conservatives are completely powerless. . . . If the King does not bestir himself, not necessarily now but soon, very soon, these serious democrats will quietly and piecemeal do away with what is left of the monarchy. I have hope in *nothing*, for I do not think anyone has courage."[23]

When in 1862 the Ministry of the Interior was turned over to a Conservative and officials were instructed to use their power to help return a pro-government majority, the Conservatives once more had fighting troops and backing for vigorous deeds. They became bold and optimistic; they had power; they had good speakers; they could attack the enemy, even beard him in his own political rallies, and challenge him to debate, either written or oral. The officials, who had formerly been curbed by Count Schwerin, could, in fact had to, come out on their side. The Conservatives could now march ahead, for they had a leader; their King was once more calling them to battle. The detailed instructions on each step to take in winning the conflict were again in the finest authoritarian, bureaucratic tradition. The future seemed bright for "King and Fatherland."

The full display of Conservative "freedom of elections" occurred in 1863 after Bismarck had become Minister President. In preparation for the elections the Conservatives in Berlin issued a broadsheet entitled "Advice on Conservative Election Agitation in Town and Country."[24] The advice was divided into two sections, that for Berlin and the larger towns and that for the rural areas. The section on the cities came first. In each election district an election leader was to be named who would choose leaders in each precinct; he in turn would select efficient agents to assist him. These persons were to be respon-

[22] Müller, *op. cit.*, pp. 37-38.
[23] Von Roon, *op. cit.*, II, 56-57.
[24] Müller, *op. cit.*, pp. 73-75.

sible for the campaign. They should by writing or by word of mouth get in touch with the known Conservatives in their area and in private discussion gain further assistance and plan the campaign. Not merely prestige and wealth should be decisive in the selection of these agents, but influence, reliability and energy. Each should be assigned certain houses and streets in which he should learn the views of the residents, win over the undecided and stir up the lazy to participate in the election. The election leaders should work especially on the officials to vote the right way.

Servants and workers dependent upon Conservatives should be instructed about the significance of the election and held strictly to account for their vote. They should be allowed the opportunity to attend Conservative rallies without any penalty for lost working time. In case of a large number of servants, the leader should first be won for the Conservative cause. Conservative landlords should place every possible obstacle in the way of agitation by the opponents. They should not permit propaganda by the opponents to be posted on their walls or literature to be distributed on their premises and should immediately notify the Conservative agents of any attempts to do so.

After the agents had found a sufficient number of supporters they should call a meeting to discuss political issues. In that discussion the danger from democracy to the existing social order should be emphasized and voters urged to participate in the election. All should promise verbally and by a shake of the hand to campaign for the Conservatives. The meeting should select the candidates for the role of elector in each precinct for all three classes.

General district meetings should be attended in person in order to keep an eye on the opponents and openly and firmly to combat them. The liberal leaders should be sharply watched and reports should be made to the Conservative district leaders about the activities of these persons. Improper conduct of officials should also be reported. "All persons dependent on the government or bound by material interest and honor" should be kept under close observation. The Conservative pamphlets and broadsheets should be carefully read and used as a source of material for debates with opponents. The accuracy and completeness of the lists of voters should be checked. To cover costs of postage, publications and so on, a silver Groschen should be collected from each member at each party meeting.

For the election itself the names of the candidates should be published under the superscription "Vote for the Monarchical Party Loyal to the King." Election literature should be posted and distributed among the voters. On election day "stalwart and fearless men" should be stationed in front of the voting place and should once more distribute literature to the voters. The candidates should present themselves to the voters of their district, including the opponents, personally or by letter or by a printed address in calm language, and should ask for their support. Above all, one should see to it that at least one reliable member of the Conservative party should be in the election commission so that no unfair act could occur. The names of the candidates should be spoken loudly and firmly and Conservative elector candidates should vote for themselves. Any illegal acts should be quietly witnessed, and if the election favored the opponents, protest should be raised against the legality of the election. All voters should remain in the room until the conclusion of the balloting so that in case another ballot was necessary the Conservatives would not lose votes.

The Conservatives regarded the campaigning in the rural areas as simpler than that in the towns and cities. First of all the Conservative leaders should arrive at an understanding with the pastors, the officials of the local government, and the estate-owners. These should have the duty of explaining the issues to the voters—"the dangers threatening them from the growing proletariat, the parcelling of estates, the expanding bureaucracy, the harm to church and school from separating them, the equalization of proletariat and taxpayers, of propertyless persons and peasants, the representation of rural interests merely by county judges, the increasing predominance of the cities." Each meeting should be opened by prayer and song and three cheers for the King. The sense of military honor and the memory of military exploits should be aroused; the "old Prussian feeling," "national pride" and "the old love for the Royal House of the Hohenzollerns" should be strengthened. "One should make it a duty and an honor, an expression of Prussian loyalty and love, to vote for the King: that is Conservative!"[25]

The central election committee sent to the provinces in 1863 a list of persons whose return to the Lower House should be especially pressed. The list read as follows:[26]

King's Counsel Wagener in Berlin
von Blanckenburg of Zimmerhausen
President von Gerlach in Magdeburg

---

[25] Summarized in Müller, *op. cit.*, pp. 73-75; also in *Kölnische Zeitung*, Oct. 9, 1863.

[26] Printed in *Kölnische Zeitung*, Oct. 10, 1863.

General-Director von Hülsen in Merseburg
Appellate Court Judge von Prittwitz in Breslau
Superior Forest Master von Wedell in Erfurt
von Tettau-Tolks
Burgomaster Strosser in Herford
Privy Administrative Counsellor Elwanger in Breslau
von Nathusius in Königsborn
Professor Glaser in Königsberg
Consistory Director Noldechen in Magdeburg
County Court Director Ebert in Liegnitz
Appellate Court President von Brauchitsch in Stettin
Chamberlain Count von Pückler of Weisteritz
State's Attorney Wendt in Stargard
King's Counsel Hübner in Breslau
Infantry General on Active Service von Brandt in Berlin
Privy Superior Administrative Counsellor von Klützow in Berlin
Superior Administrative Counsellor von Nordenflycht in Minden
Active Privy Counsellor von Olfers in Berlin
Privy Superior Administrative Counsellor Stiebel in Berlin
Guild Supreme Master Neuhaus in Berlin
Retired Major von Blücher in Berlin
von Rathkirch-Track of Panthen (Silesia)
Landrat Prince von Hohenlohe of Lublinitz
Landrat von Seydewitz in Görlitz
Baron von Hertefeldt
Appellate Court President Holzapfel in Ratibor
City Court President Breithaupt in Berlin
Count von Oriolla of Ruchendorf near Reichenbach
Privy Superior Administrative Counsellor von Krocher in Berlin
Retired City Councillor Doctor Woeniger in Berlin
Retired King's Counsel Gerloff in Berlin

The list contained the name of only one with even a title of hand-worker. All the other persons were gentlemen, nobles, officials, officers, pastors, professors, lawyers. Twenty of them belonged to the nobility; the other fourteen were burghers. Such was the social distribution of candidates with which the Conservatives expected to win, if not the election (for they were doubtful about so great success), at least a large number of seats.

In 1862 the number of stories of pressure on little people began to increase. The Conservatives threatened to cease patronizing hotels which allowed the liberals to use rooms for meetings. They withdrew trade from liberal merchants, restaurant owners, handworkers, and anyone else with whom they had business. They brought pressure to bear upon the peasants. When one merchant protested against such treatment, his client, the Duke of Schleswig-Holstein-Sonderburg-Augustenburg zu Primkenau replied, "You demonstrated in favor of the Progressive party; the men of the Progressive party are revolutionary, subversive elements; they are the most dangerous people in the state. If they are re-elected, we have to expect revolution."[27]

The vigor with which the non-official Conservatives followed the advice of the heads of the Volksverein may be seen from two incidents. One concerned industrial workers, the other, the rural people. Herr von Düring, manager of the Saarbrücken Railway and of the Royal Machine Company, instructed his workers to vote against the liberal candidates for the Landtag. The workers refused to follow his counsel, and after the election he dismissed four of them. Believing that he intended to punish all 150 of them by gradual dismissal, the workers announced that they would all quit of their own accord. Nothing more of Herr von Düring's plan was heard.[28]

The rural incident occurred on the estate of Prince von Pless in Upper Silesia and revealed the great amount of power over the peasants possessed by a big landlord, the methods by which the latter was able to use that power, and the extraordinary courage required on the part of the peasants to resist the pressure. The event was fully investigated and discussed in the Lower House of the Landtag, and the facts were well established.

In the regular election a doubtful liberal named Rygulla had been victorious in the sixth Oppeln District. Because of election irregularities, the Lower House had refused to seat him. When a new election was held, Landrat von Seherr-Thoss was returned, only to have the Lower House refuse to seat him pending an investigation. Requested to report on the election, the Landrat Baron von Richthofen did so on the basis of material supplied mainly by Prince von Pless and failed to interview any of the persons protesting to the Lower House against the validity of the election. When a committee of the Lower House investigated the case it disclosed the following facts. Prince von Pless owned the largest estates in the district and had in his hands the economic fate of his numerous subjects and of many others with whom he dealt. He had served on the government commission to conduct the elections along with the Duke of Ratibor, the second largest landowner in the area. The Prince von Pless was involved in controversies with individual peasants and entire communities over the settlement of the former servile economic obligations, and witnesses agreed that the prince's speech to the local peasant leaders given below and the voter's response were acts in this continuing battle.

Schulze Wrobel was present at the prince's speech and later testified under oath before a court as follows:

> I know only the Polish language and since the last election I have been an elector. Shortly before the election of a deputy held on July 23, 1862, at Sorau a messenger from the Prince von Pless brought me . . . an invitation to Pless. I heeded the summons and found at least forty peasant Schulzes or electors gathered in the Princely riding stables where the Princely Recorder Sarganeck received us in person. He invited those present to eat and drink. On the table meat, bread and butter were laid out and two casks of Bavarian beer, each cask being about half a tun. Sarganeck added: when we have become better acquainted we shall discuss something.
>
> After those present had eaten and drunk, Prince von Pless appeared and made a speech to us, his guests, in the German language which Sarganeck translated word for word into Polish. The Prince had papers in front of him on the table. I cannot recall the exact words of the speaker, but I do remember the sense of it. The Prince exhorted us to vote at the next election of a deputy, not again for Rygulla but for Landrat Baron Seherr-Thoss. . . . Recorder Sarganeck actually said, "Whoever does not vote for Baron Seherr will feel it." I do not remember that the expression was used that anyone not voting for the Landrat would be ejected. We replied to the speaker that not all those Schulzes present were electors. Sarganeck then said, "The Schulzes who are not themselves electors should report to the electors of their communities what has been said here and should request them to vote for Baron Seherr; otherwise all will feel it." No more was said, but all of us present knew what this warning referred to, namely, the permission to gather leaves, branches and moss in the Princely forests at low prices for use in our own economy. This proved to be true. I did not let myself be influenced and cast my vote for Rygulla. When I subsequently spoke to the Princely Forester Kleist at Wyrow about buying the forest refuse and moss, he refused me with the statement that I should receive nothing. I know that the community Wilkowy, whose electors Pilch and Spyra voted in Sorau for Baron Seherr, have received moss and forest refuse from the Princely Forester for nothing. Pilch was, as I recall, also at the breakfast.

Another Schulze who had been present at the meeting told several witnesses that if they failed to vote for his candidate, von Seherr, "it is possible that . . . the Prince would not rent land to us any more."

What did the Prince von Pless actually say to the peasants? Fortunately, the prince had kept a copy of his speech. As an example of

an election address by an aristocrat living according to the standards
of the Old Regime it is worthy of preservation.

I have summoned you as the most influential men in the communities in order to speak a serious word to you in this very serious time. You know that I have always lived with you in the
fullest harmony and I can openly testify that I have always been
proud of you, of your devotion to me and my house, of your
trusting love for our King and Lord. When I have been together
with the King and his highest servants I have often mentioned
you with praise. When I speak a serious word of exhortation to
you today I do so in order for this friendly agreement to continue. The matter is simple. Formerly we were always in agreement on our acts; now you have given ear to persons whom I do
not know and also refuse to know, persons who spread calumny
against the intentions of our beloved King and against my intentions, persons who did not even have the courage to put their
names to the communication sent to you. That you have believed this calumny is proved by the way in which you participated in the Landtag election while I was away from you, and
by the way in which you openly regarded as your enemies me
and those upon whom I bestow my trust. There is in this behavior such appalling ignorance of the truth that I must speak
to you some words of clarification. Your welfare goes hand in
hand with mine. I am a landowner as well as you, and since I
am a large landowner, all the disadvantages which strike the
landowner strike me in a greater measure. I have therefore only
one interest—to care for your welfare because your welfare is also
my welfare. That one or the other of you or even an entire community becomes involved in some controversy with one of my
officials or even has a lawsuit, does not pertain to this matter.
After all, this sort of thing occurs among neighbors. Instead of
considering this simple fact you believed the persons who said to
you that I am your opponent. I speak frankly to you and you
be frank to me. Let one of you cite an instance in which I have
intentionally offended one of my peasants, or, if he were in need,
where I have not attempted to help him as much as possible. If
no one can cite such an instance, what right have you to believe
the lies spread against me? Now it is time for the elections
again, and you have the opportunity to show what will be our
relations in the future. I can only assume that if you choose a
different deputy from me you place no confidence in me and do
not wish to live in friendship with me any more. Although I
shall be sorry not to be able to live with you in friendship any
longer, I shall withdraw myself from you, since I shall assume
that you, if you do not vote as I do, do not wish to live with me
in friendship any longer. The results arising from this split
desired by you are of your own making and you will clearly see
that I shall not suffer from them.

Now go in peace! Report to your communities what I have
said to you. I make it your duty to do this at least before the

elections in Sorau on the twenty-third of this month so that the communities cannot subsequently excuse themselves on the grounds of ignorance, and the blame for the disadvantageous results of your neglect will not fall on you. Tell the electors that I expect them to appear at the election and to do their duty toward the King and the state. Once more. It is a question of showing at the election whether you wish friendship or hostility from me. The results of hostility will become apparent. Now vote as you wish.

The effects of the prince's speech were immediately evident in the extent of participation in the election. The electors from a number of communities who had voted for Rygulla failed to appear at all. Fewer electors voted for all candidates than had in the preceding election voted for the winner alone. Such was the manner in which Landrat von Seherr-Thoss was returned.

When the Lower House refused to seat the winner, the Conservative deputy Count Bethusy-Huc argued against the decision. Influence on an election, he said, could be exercised not only from above but from below. Pressure from one's equals, he asserted, was much more effective than that which was wielded from above upon individual votes. Such influence was entirely private in character, and so long as it did not violate the law it should not be considered by the Lower House. The Prince von Pless, he declared, had not overstepped his rights at all; if one considered the moral side of the case one should far more question whether one should annul the election of a deputy receiving the votes of these electors or annul the election of electors so susceptible to the attraction of a breakfast. Human nature could not be changed, he concluded, and so long as it remained what it was one had no guarantee of free elections in a moral sense and should restrict himself to preventing the exercise of illegal influence by state officials.[29]

The story contained all the elements of the lord-peasant relationship in a period of transition. The lord used his manorial power to preserve his authority under a system of parliamentary representation. He blended a nice assertion of friendship with a threat of punishment in case of disobedience. He entertained the peasants in a barn and appeared personally for a few minutes in order to read a warning speech. He glossed over the main source of trouble, the controversy with the peasants over the sum to be paid for the lord's having to re-

[29] See the documents in Abg. H., *St. B.*, Aug. 16, 1862; III, 1228. *Ibid.*, Jan. 31, April 15, 1863; I, 140-43, II, 835-43.

linquish certain properties and rights to them—a part of the process of peasant emancipation. The peasants, who noted the exact measurement of the casks of Bavarian beer, were aware that they furthered their own interests best by voting liberal. While many of them were frightened away from the voting booth or were induced to vote as their lord wished, a great many understood the meaning of the election for peasant interests and defied the lord. Equally illuminating was the Count Bethusy-Huc's confusion of pressure from above and pressure from one's peers. To this good count the latter seemed worse than the former. Just how one could have elections without some influence from one's peers, he did not say. How one could continue to hold elections of any significance when pressure from above could be freely applied, he likewise did not say. He had recourse to the old Conservative argument: man is an evil being and as far as the law allows he must in private life be controlled by his superiors.

The uniformity of Conservative election orders may be seen in the instructions issued to his subjects by Herr von Saldern of Meffersdorf, Lauban county:

> To the Royal Prussian voters of the Manors Meffersdorf, Schwerta and Volkersdorf. His Majesty our most gracious King and Sovereign has commanded that on the twentieth of this month the elections shall occur and has stated that the elections will be *free* only in case those persons are elected who agree with the views and wishes of His Majesty and His ministers. The former deputies of our election district have voted against the will of His Majesty and His ministers. Since I do not wish that those Royal Prussian voters who vote for electors who vote for a deputy in Görlitz on the 28th of this month who opposes the will of His Majesty and His Majesty's ministers should stand henceforth in any kind of business relations with me, I have commanded as follows: those voters who act to the contrary, if they are laborers in the forest or in the economy, be dismissed, and that the same be done to those in the brick-kiln, the peat-bed and the factory for oven and clay wares; that the officials of the forest, the economy, the garden, the mill, the bakery, be given notice; that final accounts be settled with artisans who have worked for the estates or for the other administrative branches, as well as with merchants who have sold them anything; moreover that those who have rented a dwelling or land or a forest be immediately notified that as soon as the contract has expired it will not be renewed. I demand from all the above mentioned voters who stand in any kind of relations to me that they participate in the voting on the twentieth of this month. Whoever fails to supply me personally with a satisfactory explanation for remaining away from the polls will receive the same treatment as those voters who vote for new deputies in opposition to the will

of His Majesty and His ministers. My manager, Inspector Demnitz, is given the commission to supply me with the information according to individual categories from the election lists for Wigandsthal, Meffersdorf, Grenzdorf, Neugersdorf, Strossberg, Bergstrass, Heide, Heller, Ober-und Nieder-Schwerta and Volkersdorf. Since the shortness of time does not permit inspection here of the election lists, Inspector Demnitz will ride to Görlitz for this purpose and have them laid before him by Election Commissioner Landrat von Seydewitz immediately after the election of deputies on the twenty-eighth of this month, in order at the same time to obtain information about the votes of the electors.[30]

The gentleman covered the situation even more thoroughly than the government. He was a model Conservative.

The Conservative method of campaigning in the rural areas was accurately described in an election appeal by the Progressive party in 1862 as follows:

The matter is made more difficult for you [the peasants] than in the towns. You lack the societies in which you can discuss your affairs. You are merely called together when you are to work on roads or pay new taxes or listen to the reading of an order from the Landrat. But when it comes to voting all sorts of instructions are issued to you, and if you do not wish to obey you are threatened with all kinds of real or imaginary terrors. Here comes your Schulze, there the police administrator, here the Landrat decrees, the pastor preaches at you what you should do. The one says the village, the other the county, the third the state, the fourth Christianity, the fifth the Church, and finally even your poor soul itself is in danger if you do not vote as you are told.[31]

The administration of the Administrative District of Breslau explained in 1862 the success of the Progressive party in the election by the fact "that its doctrines are much more attractive for the masses than the drier and much more reserved doctrines of the different Conservative political groups, and that almost all local papers and the larger daily papers with very few exceptions know how to exploit in the cleverest way the very attractive teachings of complete freedom and equality, of self-government, and to further the efforts of the advanced liberal parties." The writer reported complaints from the country that the bonds of discipline were loosening and that all personal authority was beginning to disappear.[32]

---

[30] Reprinted in the *Kölnische Zeitung*, Oct. 25, 1863, from the *Görlitzer Anzeiger*.
[31] See in *Volkszeitung*, April 24, 1862.
[32] Regierungs-Bezirk Breslau, May 8, 1862, *Zeitungs-Bericht für März-April, 1862*.

What were "the drier and more reserved doctrines" which the Conservatives offered? The only fundamental tenet of the Conservatives was expressed by von Kleist-Retzow: "We demand of our people that they select us; then we must take care of them."[33] Since the people were not quite satisfied with this program the Conservatives had to embellish it. In 1861 the Volksverein offered the following points to the electors:

> I. Unity of our German Fatherland, not in the way of the Italian kingdom through blood and fire, but by the unity of its princes and peoples and in firmly holding to authority and law. No repudiation of our Prussian Fatherland and its glorious history; no sinking into the filth of a German republic; no robbery of the Crown and nationality nonsense. II. No breach with the past in inner affairs of our state. No elimination of the Christian foundation and of the historically preserved elements of our constitution. No shifting of the center of emphasis of our European position through weakening the army. No parliamentary regime and no constitutional ministerial responsibility. Personal rule by our King by the grace of God and not of a constitution. Church marriage, Christian schools, Christian authority, no furtherance of the ever-spreading demoralization and disrespect for divine and human order. III. Defence of and respect for honorable work, property, rights and class. No favoring and exclusive rule of money capital. No sacrifice of the handworkers and of landed property in favor of the mistaken teachings and usurious arts of the time. Freedom of participation of subjects in legislation and in the autonomy and self-government of [feudal] corporations and communities. Freedom in the firm preservation of protecting order. No surrender to bureaucratic absolutism and to social serfdom by way of limitless and uncontrolled anarchy and the imitation of the political and social forms which have led France to Caesarism. Development of our constitution in the sense of German freedom, in love and devotion to King and Fatherland.[34]

The program of 1861 had been composed when the Conservatives had lost favor with the King. When early in the next year the King began to return to the fold, the party changed its platform from one of extensive negation to the simple and clear statement of support of the King. In an election appeal of March 19, 1862, a group of party leaders declared: "The campaign cry for which we fight today should be no other than that of the maintenance of the power of the Crown,

[33] Quoted in Dr. Sigmund Neumann, *Die Stufen des Preussischen Konservatismus* (Berlin, 1930), p. 75 note.
[34] Salomon, *op. cit.*, I, 83-84.

the preservation of the full constitutional rights of the monarchy as the highest and decisive authority which, although bound by the rights of the representative assembly in certain respects, should never be subordinate to the will of the majority."[35] The party did not deviate from this platform during the rest of the constitutional conflict. At last its loyalty to the crown was reciprocated by William's loyalty to the Prussian tradition. The party thereby made the strongest appeal of which it was capable to the voters, but still more to the monarchy, the court and the government.

To know the thoughts and proposals of these Conservatives is difficult, for by nature they were disinclined to put their few ideas into words. They much preferred the status quo, and no fuss. Their ablest politician, Wagener, was vocal in the expression of Conservative views; but it is questionable whether his colleagues by and large bothered to follow his lines of reasoning or understood fully his proposals. The more popular type of Conservative thinking may be exemplified from speeches made at local meetings. In September, 1861, in Berlin the members were urged to "acknowledge our Lord Jesus Christ as the Lord and Savior of the world of Hearts" and to see to it that "in addition to continuous prayer for this important affair they should work according to their power in favor of the election of only God-fearing, sensible men as electors and deputies." At Bromberg in October, 1862, von Massenbach cited Psalms 66, Verse 14, to a conference of Conservatives and expressed fear that "divine punishment must soon strike the present world." He could not look into anyone's heart, he said, and did not wish to damn anyone; but the Progressives were "worse than all Frenchmen, for they wish to abolish all religion and even grant all sorts of rights to the Jews." Agreeing with these assertions Pastor Reinhardt added that "the Democrats even wish to mediatize God just as they wish to mediatize the King and everything else."[36]

A few months earlier the *Kreuzzeitung* published an article about the speech which Grabow, liberal deputy and high administrative official, had made in opening the sessions of the Lower House of the Landtag. In the article occurred the passage, "Woe to those who eat the Kings' bread and betray them; woe to those who seek to swindle the hearts of the people away from the King; woe to those whose

---

[35] Müller, *op. cit.*, pp. 125-26.
[36] *Königsberg Hartungsche Zeitung*, Sept. 8, 1861. By "mediatize" the Conservatives meant the subordination of independent Prussia to the position of one state within a unified Germany. *Volkszeitung*, Oct. 25, 1862.

tongues are spears and arrows." About a year later a right-wing liberal aristocrat, von Flottwell, attended a lecture on "Monarchy by Divine Right" given by Ludwig von Gerlach in the Evangelical Verein. The ladies present applauded the speaker's assertion that "even the authority of the slave owner" is "a divine command and a law justified by God's grace."[37]

An appeal by the Conservative election committee in Preussisch-Holland, October, 1863, may be regarded as a classic of provincial Conservative thought and style.

> After secure hands of dead-tired steersmen have guided our ship of state through the storms of the shameful year of 1848 over the roaring waves into the harbor of ordered conditions and noble peace, after the basis of all people's welfare appeared to be made secure among us again, the benefactors of the people unjustly calling themselves Progressives, whose objective is to establish popular rule by the mob and who must therefore always be called by their true name "Democrats," have again raised their Hydra head and undermine by lies, suspicion and distortion the foundations of our new state constitution. Just as they have the precious life of our blessed King [Frederick William IV] on their consciences, so they are now laying hands again on the rights of his Most High Successor who bears his Crown by the grace of God; and since the elections are upon us, a word of warning to all voters appears to be necessary to guard against those false prophets who go in sheep's clothes but are really rapacious wolves. We must once more take up the battle against Beelzebub and his devilish companions; through the sound sense of the folk we must call a halt to this prevailing democratic epidemic and enter in the breach against heathenism and judaism, against mob rule and the murder of our brothers.[38]

At about the same time the distinguished Professor Leo in Halle defined freedom to the full satisfaction of the *Kreuzzeitung* as follows:

> We also wish freedom, that is, the real feeling that wherever the welfare of our Fatherland or the discipline necessary for it does not set natural limits we can develop ourselves without restriction. But we have also had this feeling completely before there was talk of a constitution among us. Under our King, we were actually the most completely free people on the earth even though the liberal slogans did not fit us. We shall feel ourselves most free again when firm discipline and respect for the Royal authority once more are everywhere firmly fixed in our

---

[37] *Volkszeitung*, May 28, 1862; Manfred Laubert, *Edward Flottwell, Ein Abriss seines Lebens* (1919), p. 99.

[38] *Kölnische Zeitung*, Oct. 14, 1863.

hearts. Abstract freedom represented by mechanical means in majorities and the like, we do not need at all. And that to a certain degree we can bear them is the best evidence of how much discipline still sticks everywhere in our hearts . But we can bear it only as long as a powerful monarchy stands in our midst. Whoever imagines that this discipline will remain as soon as sovereignity in Prussia has left the throne and has taken its seat in the majority of the deputies, is in politics a child.[39]

When the Conservatives spoke of their opponents, they chose words and phrases of color without much restraint upon their emotions. Those around Elbing divided the Prussian people into two groups, the "well-disposed rural people" and the "real and incipient criminals and stock-exchange Junkers." In the latter category were put the Progressives. Another favorite phrase applied to the industrialists was "robber knights behind the smoke stacks." In one piece of election literature produced under the auspices of the Volksverein, the author, von Olfers, accused the liberals of robbery. "Whether one sticks his hand in his neighbor's pocket to steal five Thalers or whether he stretches out his hand after the King's Crown, the result is the same, for theft is theft and stealing is stealing." The same author asserted that the liberals aimed to parcel out the land in such small lots that horses could no longer be used in agriculture, that cows would have to be employed, and that finally "our artillery will have to be drawn by oxen and our cavalry ride on goats."[40]

The accusations made by the Conservatives against the liberals, if believed, should have filled the population with shudders. When hard times hit Rosenberg county in 1861, the *Preussisches Volksblatt* blamed modern industrialism, "which plays such a great role in the New Era." An anonymous broadsheet entitled "The German Progressive Party and Its Aims" listed as the ultimate goal of that party "the abolition of property." From Elbing came the report that a Conservative had spread the statement "that if the Progressive party won the election (1862), Prussia would be partitioned within a year; the French would receive one part, the Russians another, and the Jews the third." Antisemitism was cultivated by the Conservatives as a Christian virtue which they accused the liberals of trying to destroy. The following incident in 1858 at a Kreistag in Silesia was typical. With the beginning of the New Era five Jewish owners of noble estates appeared for

[39] *Allgemeine Zeitung*, Oct. 4, 1863.
[40] *Königsberg Hartungsche Zeitung*, Dec. 21, 1861. Deputy von Beughem, Abg. H., St. B., March 18, 1861; I, 519-20. *Augsburg Allgemeine Zeitung*, Oct. 21, 1863.

the first time to participate in the proceedings. Von Haugwitz pro-tested against the participation of the Jews in the corporation of the first estate, and Count Saurma-Jeltisch proposed to pay two Friedrichs d'or out of the county treasury to each Jewish owner of a noble estate who would voluntarily remain away from the Kreistag. When one of the Jews protested, the presiding officer, the Landrat, refused him the floor.[41] The Conservatives specialized in arousing both class hatred and racial hatred.

The liberal ideal of the legal state aroused the Conservatives' scorn. In the Lower House of the Landtag Deputy von Blanckenburg de-clared that "the liberals are either not aware of the fact or do not wish to be aware of it that their principles . . . always lead to . . . half measures and tolerance of both sides, above and below." A Conserva-tive paper declared early in 1861 that "to transform Prussia into a legal state means nothing more than to put Prussia in the hands of a few so that they can exploit the country in their own interest, promul-gate laws which are of use to them, place the taxes on the masses while they use the money for themselves. The legal state of the liberals means plutocracy, oppression of religion, art, knowledge, the working force of the masses." In keeping with this thinking, the *Berliner Revue* declared in April, 1862, that "the independence of the judiciary . . . has become a curse for our country. . . . Freedom of the press is also degraded for egoistic purposes, and in this wise we shall inevitably attain a situation where the survival of the state demands emergency curbs on egoism."[42]

In keeping with their line of belief the Conservatives constantly accused the liberals of revolutionary intentions. In Prussia, they said, the liberals aimed to destroy the constitutional powers of the King and reduce the sovereign to a figure-head. The forthcoming elections in 1862, they stated in an election appeal in March, laid upon them "the sacred duty" of opposing these forces with all their power and energy. Not the Prussian people but their betrayers, they said, in-tended to make the Prussian representative assembly a workshop for a German revolution, to use the constitutional rights of the people as a means of insurrection and anarchy. In 1861 Deputy von Blancken-burg had already warned the liberals that "if you change the power of

[41] *Tagesbericht*, No. 51, March 1, 1861; *Königsberg Hartungsche Zeitung*, April 15, 1861; *Volkszeitung*, April 25, 1862; Müller, *op. cit.*, pp. 40, 70. J. Stein, *op. cit.*, p. 581.
[42] Abg. H., *St. B.*, May 28, 1861; III, 1433. *Tagesbericht*, No. 11, Jan. 14, 1861. *Kölnische Zeitung*, April 29, 1862.

the Prussian monarchy, if you weaken it to the level of a constitutional parliamentary regime, then . . . just as the military reorganization was put through in spite of you, so will the power of the Prussian monarchy also stride over the constitution." As a rule, however, the Conservatives did not speak so bluntly. The more usual formulation was exemplified by that of Wagener, who in 1863 in a meeting of the Prussian Volksverein was reported to have said that only a royal dictatorship would solve the present conflict in Prussia. He explained that he did not mean by dictatorship the abolition of the constitution; on the contrary, the dictatorship should preserve this "sacred constitution" to which the King had sworn and should defend it against the intended overthrow by the Progressive party. The Conservatives had sworn allegiance to the constitution in the sense intended by Frederick William IV: it should be so developed that it would be possible for the King to rule. "According to the constitution the deputies swore allegiance to the King, not the King to the deputies," Wagener stated. If the liberal parties sought to destroy the constitution, he continued, "by seeking to introduce into it the spirit of parliamentary despotism which is entirely alien to it, then the royal dictatorship must counter such actions. . . . We shall always follow the flag of the Hohenzollerns, but never the bell or the hat of the president of the Lower House." Wagener was stating in Conservative constitutional terms what von Blanckenburg had said more frankly: the King's power should be preserved at any cost. The end justified the means.[43]

The Conservative program and methods failed to arouse the voters. In April, 1862, the *Berliner Revue* condemned its party for political ineptitude:

> One does not win battles . . . with army orders alone; and with election decrees, no matter how well meant and resolute they are, one will hardly emerge from the election battle as victor. . . . As matters are at present the election decrees have accomplished nothing but anarchy, a "pleasant anarchy," which is all the more disorganizing and depressing the more courageous and resolute the words sound at the beginning.[44]

The results were evident in the number and personnel of those who won seats in the Lower House. Of the ten who were elected in 1862, five were Landrats, who in order to qualify for this position had to

---

[43] Müller, *op. cit.*, p. 125. Abg. H., *St. B.*, Feb. 5, 1861; I, 69. *Augsburg Allgemeine Zeitung*, Oct. 15, 1863.

[44] Quoted in *Volkszeitung*, April 23, 1862.

own knights' estates; four others were owners of knights' estates; the tenth was a state's attorney. All belonged to the nobility. In the election of 1863 the party returned only two persons, Wagener and von Blanckenburg, whose names had been placed on the preferred list quoted above. The roster of their thirty-six deputies contained twelve Landrats and one former Landrat; twelve other owners of large estates, most of them being knights' estates; one renter of crown land; two lawyers; two ministers of state and one former minister of state; one major; two justice officials; and two administrative officials. Twenty-seven of the deputies were nobles; the other nine were burghers. Apart from the absence of a member of the handicrafts, the delegation represented fairly well the Old Regime.

Unfortunately for genuine conservatism it became tied to the Bismarckian kind of government policy. Possessing almost no popular appeal it had to follow the lead of a government that gave the illusion of moving in its direction. Bismarck carried the Conservatives far beyond the point at which they had wished to stop. The economic reforms in which he acquiesced were liberal rather than Conservative. His objective of national unification coincided with that of the liberals and not the Conservatives; and his methods of unification were in some respects as repugnant to one as to the other. While Ludwig von Gerlach and a few of his friends were utterly opposed to Bismarck's policy of unification, most of the Conservatives followed the Minister President faithfully in the act but not in the interpretation. They loved the military victories and the Prussian conquests, but they hated to see the existing legal structure of Germany violated and so many princes toppled. The Prussian Volksverein wished to be neither Bismarckian nor isolationist, neither German nor national; it sought to be Prussian and to preserve Prussia's power and influence against Austria or anyone else.

Taken in tow by one of its own kind, a Prussian Junker, the "small but powerful party" did not recover from the shock of Bismarck's success until the agrarian troubles of the 1870s brought it vociferously into the public arena once more in defence of its economic interests. Bismarckian unification of the nation along with industrial and commercial expansion left the Conservatism of the 1860s rather behind the times. Nonetheless, Wagener's confident statement in 1863 expressed the assurance that this old-style Conservatism was far from dead:

> We must never disappear from the battleground. Never under any circumstances. For we have to represent not merely human plans! We have claimed and still claim today that in addition we represent eternal truths and eternal principles of

state and society. Let us hold firmly to our principles and our truths in all circumstances, whether the times be good or bad, whether they please human beings or not.[45]

The Conservatives held to them until the Nazis and, in the Eastern part of Germany, the communists delivered their death blow.

---

[45] Müller, *op. cit.*, p. 76.

11 / The Government and the Elections

T HE ROLE of the government in the elections of 1862 and 1863 was determined fundamentally by King William himself. The Conservative ministers were happy to follow his general orders, which agreed entirely with their own desires; and Conservative county officials most responsible for the execution of the orders, the Landrats above all, improved upon them with enthusiasm. In a somewhat tentative and limited way in the election of 1862 and with full force in that of 1863 the government turned partisan and utilized the resources of the powerful bureaucracy to sway the vote in its favor.

King William had been so disgusted at the chicanery and hypocrisy of the Manteuffel ministry under his brother in its handling of elections as well as other matters that on becoming regent in 1858 he had determined to stop such immoral action, as he called it, and permit free elections. As early as April of that year he had stated to von Vincke that the officials would not be allowed to interfere in the next elections as they had in the previous ones.[1] In the autumn of that year Minister of Interior Flottwell issued the first election instruction to the officials under the authority of the Prince Regent. Since the instruction exemplifies the fundamental dilemma of William's attitude, it needs to be summarized. The government placed great value upon the unchanging loyalty, reliability and legality, as well as the political insight, of the deputies, and it was therefore the indispensable duty of the royal officials concerned directly or indirectly with the elections to

---

[1] Von Bernhardi, *op. cit.*, III, 32.

work to the effect that men of these qualities were returned. At the same time the officials should take care not to exert official pressure upon the voters. They should not seek to intimidate the voters by threats of withdrawing certain advantages and rights which the bureaucracy disposed of. They should, however, cooperate with the important private individuals in their particular district to assure the return of reliable deputies. Government officials might run for office, Flottwell stated; but before they did so they should carefully consider whether they would be of more use to the state by becoming deputies or by remaining at their present positions. In case they were elected, he implied that they should support the ministry.[2]

Within a few weeks the minister had to send further instructions to stop the provincial officials from interpreting the decree as meaning that they should assist only one party.[3] The fact that this corrective had to be issued revealed the confusion of the Prince Regent's and the government's position. On the one hand, William wished free elections; on the other, as has been shown, he was determined to preserve intact his authority; on the one hand, he aimed to uphold the constitution and the law; on the other, he opposed "the stereotyped phrase," the "far-fetched ideas" of liberalism; on the one hand, he wished to develop the state on "sound, strong, conservative bases"; on the other he wished his subjects to follow him. In his confused mind he opposed what he called both extremes, the reaction of the 1850s and the radicalism of 1848. He expected to rule in accordance with "truth, legality, and consistency," but he did not know what these terms meant.[4] He wished to govern with the aid of mild and cautious liberals, like Schwerin and Flottwell, and of Conservatives, but not reactionaries, who would follow his line of constitutional absolutism. As soon as he discovered that the majority of the deputies returned by the elections disapproved his theory and practice of rule, he immediately proposed to interfere and to force the public to elect supporters of his conceptions of rule.

Early in 1861 the King aligned himself publicly against the liberals. To the burgomaster of Berlin, a city overwhelmingly liberal, he declared: "I know that a party exists in my country which aims to renew the conditions of the year 1848. What was able to occur then by reason of surprise will not again succeed; one will find me prepared." As

---

[2] Preuss. Geh. Staatsarchiv. Pr. Br. Rep. 30. Berlin C. Pol. Präsid. Tit. 94, Lit. A. 198.

[3] *Ibid.*

[4] Horst Kohl, *op. cit.*, pp. 3-8.

the year continued similar and even more pointed stories began to appear in the press, for example, one about the King's reply to a deputation from Schweidnitz.

> I thank you for the patriotic views which you have expressed to me. . . . Manifest your patriotism and your love for Me and My House in the . . . elections for the House of Representatives. I wish neither reactionaries nor democrats. Elect only such men as deputies who will go hand in hand with me. If that occurs then we shall certainly see each other in friendly manner again.[5]

When new elections were held in the autumn of 1861 the King wished to intervene personally, but was finally persuaded by the Minister of Interior von Schwerin to permit elections "freely and without hindrance." The officials were to vote according to their convictions; but if they disagreed with the government they should manifest reserve. Their sense of duty and honor, stated the minister's decree, would show them the way to harmonize the exercise of their rights as citizens with their duty as officials.[6] Although sense of duty and honor did not lend itself to uniform interpretation, Count Schwerin succeeded in reducing the pressure of officials on voters to an extent that was reached in no other election. To the King the results were tragic: more and more liberals were returned.[7]

Early in 1862 the ministry had to prepare for another election. This time the King believed that he should interfere personally, and in instructions of March 19 he ordered the ministry to use the officials for explaining to the public the King's policies and wishes. Since the liberal resistance to the government's, that is, the King's, program had led to the dissolution of the Lower House and the holding of new elections, it is clear that the King expected the officials not to support the opposition in any way, that he expected them to assure the return of a Lower House favorable to his policies.[8]

By this extraordinary document the King took side definitely against the liberals, even against those mild ones who had been his ministers, and asked his people to support him. He reiterated his program of 1858 and once more identified the welfare and safety of Prussia with the preservation of Hohenzollern power within that state. He

[5] *Tagesbericht*, No. 7, Jan. 9, 1861, citing *Preuss. Volksblatt*, No. 7; *National Zeitung*, Nov. 20, 1861. See also the King's statement to the burgomaster of Brandenburg. *Königsberg Hartungsche Zeitung*, Dec. 24, 1861.

[6] Abg. H., *St. B.*, 1864, Vol. IV, No. 95, p. 605.

[7] See *ibid.*, July 4, 1862; I, 1862.

[8] *Die Innere Politik*, pp. 9-10.

appealed for a better-informed public, with his officials acting as the sources of enlightenment. He distinguished between the liberal deputies and the public as neatly as any Conservative politician would have done, and called upon the awakened and corrected public to vote in support of his ministers. Making the election a personal affair he asked for a vote of confidence in his conduct of government. The document revealed a confusion of absolutism and constitutionalism, expressing again the King's desire and intention to have his own way, to rule absolutistically in accordance with the constitution. The inconsistency of this position was not at all evident to him, for as certain contemporaries saw, he had no idea of how a constitutional government worked. The election therefore became one of the liberals against the King. The liberals tried to deny the fact, as we shall see, but the Conservatives took up the election stand of the King and fought valiantly for it. With monarchy versus parliamentarianism as the issue the makings of a thoroughgoing constitutional conflict were present.

A few days later Minister of Interior von Jagow sent to the officials an order concerning the elections that was in keeping with the King's instructions. While the instructions were given to all officials in all departments, they were particularly directed to those who had charge of the execution of the elections. The officials should make clearly understood "the guiding policies and intentions" of the government and prevent any misunderstanding or falsification of them. They should make it known that the government stood upon the authority of the constitution, and that it was its "absolute duty" to preserve the power of the Crown and to prevent a so-called "parliamentary government" from being established. There should be freedom of voting, but at the same time the officials should unify, organize and assist all groups willing to support the government. They should participate actively in the campaign against the Progressives and other opponents of the government and King and in favor of the loyal elements. The instructions aligned the government and all officials with a few ultraright liberals and especially with the Conservative party.[9]

It is difficult to comprehend how freedom of elections could be preserved when officials were expected to assist the election of candidates of one particular party. Those officials who supported passionately the Conservatives and hated the liberals interpreted the instructions

---

[9] *Ibid.*, pp. 10-12. See the contemporary press for numerous denunciations of this decree, especially those by the universities.

according to their own wishes. When these acts were brought to the minister's attention in the Lower House in July, von Jagow denied that officials had ever been ordered to give up their party preference and follow the views of the government; but, he added, they had been forbidden to participate in hostile agitation. He disclaimed any knowledge of excesses and promised to take steps against "illegal and unjust" acts to influence the elections.[10]

The full program of action was drawn up and placed in operation only after Bismarck became Minister President in the autumn of 1862. His ministry employed every means at its disposal to coerce the public into supporting it. In a state with a powerful bureaucracy, a large army with a militaristic tradition, a dovetailing of administrative and military authority and social position and prestige, a tradition of authoritarian rule, the resources available to the government affected practically every part of Prussian life. The transitional and indefinite character of much of Prussian law enabled the government time after time to interpret the law in its favor. The advantage to the monarchy and to the Conservatives of having kept the terms of the constitution of 1850 as vague as possible was now manifest. Whereas the liberals sought to construe these clauses and the laws derived from them in favor of freedom, the government undid the liberal gains of the New Era by interpreting the clauses and laws in a reactionary sense. Since Bismarck had an extraordinary gift for picking holes in legal documents to his own advantage and was devoid of respect for or fear of any force or any human being that opposed him, the fight against the liberals reached its fullest scope. In the election of 1863 the government mobilized all its resources against the liberals. Every means used up to that time was brought into action and many new ones were added. The work of the Manteuffel ministry was greatly improved upon, and the King heartily endorsed the far more ruthless acts of Bismarck and his colleagues. It made a difference as to whose ox was gored.[11]

The main instrument of the government for influencing the election in its favor continued to be the powerful, numerous and inclusive body of officials under its control. Count Eulenburg aimed to use them to the fullest extent. First the government obtained a statement from the highest court which placed the judiciary on its side in favor of restricting the freedom of officials to vote. Next, the ministry is-

---

[10] Abg. H., *St. B.*, July 4, 1862; I, 460.
[11] *Briefe, Reden und Schriften*, II, 64-65.

sued an order declaring that henceforth any official elected to and serving as deputy in the Lower House must pay the cost of his substitute while away from his official position; the money would be withheld at the treasury. The government refused any longer to cover these costs.[12] Then on September 24 the Minister of Interior instructed officials regarding their behavior in elections.

> Whoever as official has sworn to be loyal and obedient to the King his most gracious Lord is freed from this oath neither as voter nor as representative, and when His Majesty definitely delineates the constitutional way along which his officials must accompany him, they are all obliged to obey, and those whom because of special trust the King's grace has called to positions of political importance are also obliged to support actively the King's government.[13]

By this order every official had to support actively the election of deputies favorable to the government. All pretence of neutrality was tossed aside; all respect for the rights of officials as citizens to vote as they saw fit was rejected. The officials were not permitted to remain inactive; they were required to take a vigorous and public part in securing the election of governmental supporters. The order was definitely based on the view often expressed by Conservatives that with the most powerful machinery in the state at its disposal, namely the bureaucracy, the government ought to win an election easily. It merely needed to apply its legal authority over the officialdom. It would thereby have with one determined act, so the Conservatives argued, an organization for political purposes incomparably more effective than any other in the state. It would possess the financial resources of the state for its political work; it would deprive the liberals of one of their most active and influential groups, namely the many liberal officials, many of whom sat in the Landtag, many more of whom were chosen as electors and cast ballots for liberal candidates, and even more of whom voted for liberal electors. It would destroy one of the main sources of the organization of liberal strength, that derived from the close association of officials. It would take away from the liberals one of the most respected large groups of leaders in local and state affairs which it possessed. The only question was how to force the officials into line and make them work actively for government supporters. Such a thing as an individual's conscience and convictions did not bother these aristocratic Conservatives. An official should have no

[12] *Ministerial-Blatt*, 1863, p. 194.
[13] *Die Innere Politik*, pp. 234-37.

other master than his superior and over him his King, he should have
no other convictions than those which his superiors allowed him to
have. The government plan was inclusive; in the execution of the
plan it attempted to be thorough.

The instructions were sent to all officials in all ministries, in provincial, district, county and local government, in church and education,
in the economy. Only the army was excluded; for this government
wished to keep it out of political controversy.[14] The orders were even
imparted to town and city councillors and to comparable members of
village government, persons chosen by the local voters and not directly
responsible to the state government. Officials had to watch over and
be responsible for the political activity of their subordinates. Count
Eulenburg stated that in case an official faced a problem too difficult
for him to handle, he should report it to the government. The advice
must have had extra point since this government's ability and willingness to utilize the law, legally or illegally, to its own ends was becoming
well known.

Among all the officials to whom the election instructions were sent,
the most important for the government's purpose were the Landrat and
the village Schulze, the latter being subject to the control of the
former. In the cities and towns the government lacked an official with
the authority, will power and political views of the Landrat. It was
always restricted by the greater ability and willingness of the urban
centers to resist pressure than was the case with the scattered rural
population; but its authority to approve the selection of the local
officials and its use of these officials to execute state laws enabled it to
exercise considerable influence, even though not so much as over the
peasants.

The full weight of responsibility for influencing elections fell on
these officials; they were to utilize their prestige as popular local
leaders to gain votes for the pro-government candidates and to ward off
votes for the opposition. They were subject to pressure to participate
actively in their dual capacity, as officials and as local popular leaders.
They could slip easily from one capacity to the other in favor of the
government party. An ideal arrangement was for both Landrat and
Schulze to be elected as electors, who then would vote for the Landrat
as a Conservative candidate for deputy to the Lower House.

The significance of this combination arose from the predominantly
rural character of Prussian life. In 1864 over 13,000,000 out of a total

---

[14] See Abg. H., *St. B.*, 1864, Vol IV, No. 95, pp. 606-07.

population of nearly 19,000,000 lived in the country. The village vote could have won the election for the Conservatives. For example, in Salzwedel County out of a total of 172 electors, 143 were elected by the 186 rural communities. If the Schulze or his two assistants could have been chosen as electors throughout the state and controlled for the Conservatives, the results would have been an overwhelming victory for the government.[15] The Schulze and the villagers felt the full force of government pressure.

The election law of 1849 imposed upon the Landrat and the Schulze certain responsibilities which enhanced their ability to influence the voting. The Landrat or the community official, who except in the largest cities would also be under the authority of the former, drew up the list of voters, listened to and decided upon complaints, divided the voters into the three classes, and fixed the boundaries of the voting precincts. In their capacity as officials the Landrats acted as election commissioners who handled the administrative details of the voting.[16] It will be seen how these duties opened up opportunities for the Landrat to try to affect the outcome of the vote.

A few weeks before the election the government threw the influence of the King publicly into the campaign on its side. The public that read the newspapers and that had contacts with prominent persons already knew how the King felt, for on many occasions he had openly expressed his desires about the outcome of the election. These statements had appeared in print even in the liberal papers. When the Steingrund peasants sent to the King their protestation of ardent loyalty, the latter replied in a letter which became widely known. The essential part read as follows:

> If the community wishes to show loyalty to Me in the election it can do so only by the election of such men as have the firm resolve to support My ministers in the execution of the tasks imposed by Me upon them. A hostile attitude toward My government is not in harmony with loyalty to My Person; for My ministers are called to their positions by My confidence in

[15] Abg. H., *St. B.*, 1864, Vol. IV, No. 95, p. 623.
[16] Count Schwerin had as Minister of Interior forbidden Landrats to serve as election commissioners in case they were candidates in the election. But von Jagow had already repealed the order before Count Eulenburg assumed office. Under the latter, Landrats were encouraged to act in the dual capacity, as Landrat Hoffman in Jüterbogk-Luckenwalde discovered. Upon being selected by the Conservatives to run for deputy to the Lower House, he offered to resign as election commissioner, but his bureaucratic superior refused to agree. The government liked the combination. Abg. H., *St. B.*, Nov. 23, 1863; I, 120-28.

them and have to support Me in the fulfillment of My great and serious duties.[17]

After the election was held and the Landtag convened, the new Lower House appointed a commission to investigate the violations of freedom of election. The evidence brought forth in the Lower House by individual members and by the commission vividly revealed the character of Prussian politics of the period. The role of the government in politics, the political conceptions and behavior of officials, of aristocrats, burghers and peasants, of Conservatives and of liberals, were all disclosed with the authenticity of actual participation. A cross section of Prussian society was offered, a portrait of social relations, of cultural standards and moral values, of the mixture of the Old Regime and of modern, Western ways that characterized Prussia in this period. The evidence from the election of 1863 will be supplemented by a few examples of similar behavior during the preceding two elections, those for 1861 and 1862, when the government tried to exercise some restraint upon its subordinates.

In accordance with the hierachical order of the bureaucracy, one might begin with the presidents and vice-presidents of the provinces. In 1861 President von Kotze of the province of East Prussia and Landrat von Spiess travelled through Mohrungen County and ordered lower officials to warn the population, mostly peasants, against the Progressive party.[18] The next year the superior president in East Prussia sent the following communication to his subordinate officials:

> The Royal officials will be the best organs to explain in the election meetings the aims and goals of the government. For this purpose there should especially be used the meetings of election officers and their deputies for the discussion of the execution of the election regulations.
> It is self-evident that only such men are to be named as election officers and their deputies about whose reliability and conservative views there is absolutely no doubt. . . .[19]

Since the officials toured their districts at government expense, the Conservative party needed almost no party funds. It had the state budget as a party campaign treasury, a sizable war chest which the liberals could not equal. Neither the government nor the Conservatives saw anything wrong about using the taxpayers' money to force them into agreeing with the views of the government. The holdover of absolut-

[17] *Die Innere Politik*, p. 241.
[18] *Königsberg Hartungsche Zeitung*, Nov. 29, 1861.
[19] Abg. H., *St. B.*, July 4, 1862; I, 478-79.

ism was still too strong for these Conservatives to recognize anything incongruous about employing public money to defeat the will of the public. The liberals knew that the procedure was wrong. To them it was one more example of the kind of political behavior which they wished to abolish.[20]

For the election of 1863 Minister Eulenburg's instructions gave the officials a free hand, and the Conservative ones applied all the pressure that their position afforded. Typical were the orders which the police president of Berlin sent to his subordinates, October 6, 1863. He requested his officials not to vote for government opponents and threatened to use the power of the law against those who ignored these instructions. "I expect," he continued, "not only this but also that they will actively work to the best of their ability in behalf of the election of men who are ready to support His Majesty the King and the Royal government."[21]

The presidents of the provincial administration and the police president of Berlin filled intermediate positions. They rarely came into direct contact with the public in the same way that their subordinates did. The official who entered most fully into the rough battle with groups and individuals was the Landrat, and most of the work affecting elections was organized and directed by him. While the evidence showed that a very small number of Landrats refused to execute the government's orders or assumed a passive attitude or at most one of advising without threatening voters, the overwhelming majority of them went into the campaign with crusading fanaticism.

Even in 1861 Count Schwerin as Minister of Interior had been unable to curb all the Landrats from violating the freedom of elections. Thus, Landrat von Brauchitsch had sent a number of copies of the program of the Prussian Volksverein to a Schulze near Danzig with instructions to distribute them and to collect names of persons willing to join the Verein. An evangelical pastor in Guttland had been used for the same purpose. Von Brauchitsch was seeking election to the Lower House as a Conservative, and in writing to electors to ask for their vote he had described the Progressive party's election material as containing "deceptive lies and insinuations of mistrust."[22]

By the time of the election in the next year and with von Jagow as minister, the Landrats began to act as they had longed to do. Accord-

---

[20] *Ibid.*
[21] *Ibid.*, 1864, Vol. IV, No. 95, p. 609.
[22] *Königsberg Hartungsche Zeitung*, Nov. 15, Dec. 11, 1861.

ing to a report from Minden, Landrat von Horst referred in official business to the opponents of the ministry and of the Conservative party as "scoundrels."[23]   Another Landrat declared: "And who are the leaders of the majority in the dissolved Lower House? Democrats of the purest kind, against whom in the end only soldiers have been and will again be effective."   Another one stated his constitutional views as follows:

> To our dear Friends and Comrades of Goldapp County: The deputies should be Royal advisers; the King wishes to hear not only his ministers and officials but also men from other classes. They should help him in the formulation of beneficial laws; they should support him in economical use of the taxes of his subjects; they should report to him when bad conditions obtain in the country and something useful is to be accomplished.

Then the Landrat denounced the Lower House liberals for seeking to usurp the powers of the King, for having accomplished nothing, for having proposed unchristian, godless laws about marriage, the schools, usury and community government. "I could bring before you many other godless and foolish laws that are advocated in the Lower House, but those given above will suffice." He blamed not the King but the liberals for wasting funds; and he denounced the latter as democrats like those of the "shameful year 1848," and warned the public not to vote for them. He said he knew that many wished the King to rule alone and the elections to be abolished; but, he added, the King had ordered them to vote, and they must obey. "Forward into the election," he cried, "with God for King and Fatherland!"

The Landrats called meetings of Schulzes and other officials to instruct them on how they should vote. They frequently prohibited the distribution of campaign literature by the liberal opposition and cautioned all innkeepers to be vigilant against anyone's distributing leaflets, pamphlets and the like without a permit. Since the Conservatives lacked an adequate number of newspapers to spread their views, the Landrats used the official county paper for that purpose. They threatened to cancel the permit of tavern keepers who allowed oppositional meetings to be held in their quarters or literature to be posted or distributed.[24]

The election instruction of Count Eulenburg in 1863 spurred the Landrats on to bolder and more efficient deeds than ever. They could

---

[23] *Ibid.*, June 13, 1862.
[24] Abg. H., *St. B.*, July 4, 1862; I, 464-74, 481-83. *Volkszeitung*, April 23, 1862.

now threaten any recalcitrant officials, they thought, with government approval and aid; and, as it turned out, they interpreted the minister's instruction correctly. Landrat von Gayl in Teltow County ordered the Schulzes to have themselves chosen as electors so that they could vote for candidates for the Lower House selected by their bureaucratic superiors. He threatened them with punishment and dismissal in case of disobedience. The same Landrat ordered teachers to vote Conservative or be dismissed. In Osterburg County Landrat Count von der Schulenburg wrote to the Schulzes on October 15, 1863, "You are immediately to call a community meeting and in it to read aloud the enclosed statement by His Majesty the King to the Steingrund community. . . ." They were to say that those voting against the will of the King would be treated as "enemies of the King." His colleagues in other counties issued similar warnings. Landrat von Lattorff in Gardelegen sent a printed statement to all Schulzes demanding that they actively oppose the election of members of the Progressive party and support those candidates loyal to the government. He threatened disciplinary action against any official who did not follow this order. His colleague, Landrat von Puttkamer in Demmin, acted in the same way. "Whoever . . . votes for the Progressive party is an enemy of the King," he declared, and would be punished. In many cases the Landrat threatened to dismiss Schulzes who voted against the government and to force them to pay the costs of persons appointed in their place. In many others the official was faced with the prospect of having to pay a fine. At Schievelbein the Landrat von der Golz threatened the hereditary Schulzes that in case they disobeyed the King by voting for the Progressive party he would initiate proceedings against them to deprive them of their office and to force them to pay the salary of their successors.[25]

In the towns and cities the official pressure was exerted on big and little, on persons of importance and those made significant to the president and the Conservatives only by their power to vote. In 1862 the president of the administration in Pomerania assembled all the members of the magistracy in Regenswalde and asked them to work for the election of candidates favorable to the government. When one merchant member refused, the president dropped the effort and left. In the next year he would not have been so mild, as a sampling of the evidence showed. Thus, Landrat von Goerten of Saarbrücken County

[25] *Ibid.*, 1864, Vol. IV, No. 95, pp. 620-21, 623. Nov. 11, 1863; I, 22-23. Nov. 13, 1863; I, 45-46. 1864, Vol. IV, No. 95, pp. 614-15, 613-45, 619.

spoke to Burgomaster Schmidborn of Saarbrücken and Burgomaster Karcher of St. Johann as follows: He understoood that they were liberal candidates for election as electors. He announced that he was a Conservative candidate for election as deputy in the neighboring county, and he warned them to vote as the government ordered or they would lose their positions. At Görlitz City Councillor Halberstadt, who served without compensation, was fined twenty Reichsthalers even prior to the election for being a member of the liberal election committee. His appeal to the Ministry of the Interior against the sentence had not been replied to when the new Lower House commission submitted its report on election irregularities. In Brieg a similar instance occurred, with the city councillors being censured rather than fined. Government pressure in Berlin seems not to have been as heavy as elsewhere, but the following report revealed that it was far from being absent.

According to the testimony of Edward Ludwig, a very minor official, the director of his office had called a meeting of his subordinates on October 11 or 12 and said that each could vote as he pleased. A few days later the director called them together again, read the instructions of the Minister of Interior, and declared that any one voting in opposition to the government or not voting at all would be dismissed. Each official was given the name of a person to consult about the candidate for whom he should vote.[26]

Landrat von Koppy thought it necessary to force the Conservative views upon a meeting of liberals at Gross-Mahlendorf called by the retired Cavalry Captain von Reuss of Sonnenberg to select candidates for the position of electors. The sponsors of the meeting had fulfilled all legal requirements necessary to hold it. When it opened under the chairmanship of von Reuss, the Landrat appeared in official uniform accompanied by a gendarme to oversee the meeting. The Landrat, von Koppy, soon asked permission to speak and gave a lecture on the position of the government and the situation of the country. At a convenient point the chairman interrupted him and closed the meeting with cheers for the King. Then von Reuss left, but the Landrat and others remained and the discussion became heated. The Landrat declared to a liberal teacher that he had acted like a cobbler. He denounced the liberal legislation and threatened that if the county voted liberal the government would cut off poor relief and other forms of financial aid. He threatened to suspend two teachers if they voted

---

[26] *Volkszeitung*, April 23, 1862; Abg. H., *St. B.*, 1864, Vol. IV, No. 95, esp. pp. 623, 646-47, 639.

against the government, called von Reuss "a bad official who forgot his duty." and said that if von Reuss voted as before he would be dismissed from the police administration. Of the townsmen he said that their votes, alas, would be again decisive. He blamed the popular meetings held in those centers; the meetings, he said, were mostly composed of loafers who paid no taxes and were only waiting for revolution as in 1848. He declared that when there had been no parliament and the King alone had made the laws, things had been much better than at present.[27]

In its search for votes the government did not neglect a single source. For example, in some areas the renters of public land were very numerous, and they in turn could exercise control over peasants and workers. Even in 1862 in the administrative district of Stralsund the pressure had been applied to them under threat of material loss. In the next year the pressure was increased throughout the state. Renters of public property were everywhere warned to vote for government candidates and were subjected to the usual threats. In Görlitz railway employees and laborers were told by Privy Counsellor Costenoble to vote as the government wished or to lose their positions. Government financial aid in such matters as road building and bridge building was to be given or withheld according to the way a district voted. Rector Marcus, editor of a liberal paper published in Gumbinnen for the country people, the *Bürger-und Bauernfreund,* was warned by the administration that he had to give up the editorship or his concession to conduct a school would be revoked. Doctor Senftleben, a physician, was dismissed from an engagement with an agricultural academy in Waldau because he was a democrat.[28]

The government dominated three institutions which it particularly wished to keep clean of liberalism, the schools, the church, and the army. It proceeded to use the excellent facilities which it had for exerting influence on them. As early as 1861 Landrat von Brauchitsch of Danzig County had written to a teacher requesting him to cease supporting and reading the *Volkszeitung,* accusing the paper of being hostile to the King and to the Christian religion, and saying that it aroused criticism when an official of a Christian church and an educator of the youth set a bad example by supporting such a journal.[29] The following year von Kotze, one of the highest officials in East Prussia,

[27] *Ibid.,* pp. 617-18.
[28] *Ibid.,* p. 613; *Kölnische Zeitung,* Oct. 20, 1863; *Ibid.,* April 17, May 1, 10, 1862; *Volkszeitung,* Dec. 21, 23, 1862; *Kölnische Zeitung,* Nov. 4, 1863.
[29] *Königsberg Hartungsche Zeitung,* Sept. 22, 1861.

spoke to the teachers of West Preussisch-Holland in the presence of Superintendent Erdmann, Pastor Tackmann, Landrat von Schroter and Burgomaster Gisevius:

> It is unfortunately true that the teachers in the towns mostly incline toward the Progressive party; the young teachers cultivate being enthusiastic about liberalism. . . . The inevitable result of democracy (for the Progressive party is nothing else than that) is the republic, and that this leads to inner decay and in the end opens the door to foreign enemies is evident from the old Greek republics and also from the example of North America. . . . The question is whether we have government by the King or by the people. That a parliamentary regime is something very deficient we see from the example of England, where everything is based on bribery. Elections demoralize the people; therefore I am altogether opposed to a system of government with elections, although conditions are not nearly as bad here as in England. . . . At the preceding election the unfortunate principle was established that officials should not be influenced in voting. . . . The democratic interpretation of the official's oath, that an official is committed only for his directly official activity but otherwise may work against the government, is very wrong. The official's oath lays upon him the obligation to be active for the government even outside his office. . . . The press causes an enormous harm; it spews poison among the people and causes the present epidemic movement. Liberalism is nothing but an epidemic. I speak to you in this fashion not only because I have been ordered to do so and as a government official I am obligated to; I do so much more because it is my innermost conviction that I express. Under the previous ministry I dared not so speak. . . .

Then he urged those present to work for the election of Conservatives and to vote Conservative; and he declared that any official unable to support that party should resign. At about the same time School Counsellor Wantrup in Elbing, a notorious reactionary, told an election meeting of his party that the word *Volk* (folk) was derived from *Folgen* (to follow), that therefore the folk had the duty to follow the princes. A liberal commented on this piece of etymological wisdom by asking whether the word *Wantrup* was not derived from *Wahn* (madness) and *Tropf* (a drop).[30]

The campaign of 1863 brought the teachers into the focus of government attention on a wide scale. In Glatz the president of the regional administration said to the director of the gymnasium as well as to the burgomaster, "Either vote for the Conservatives or resign." Hegewalt

---

[30] *Ibid.,* April 30, 1862; *Kölnische Zeitung,* April 17, 1862.

of the regional administration in Stettin threatened to discipline the teachers if they opposed the government. Regional President Naumann in Köslin issued an instruction on October 5, 1863, to about the same effect. The president of the administration at Magdeburg set forth the educational ideal that should be reflected in the election. "You will agree with me," he wrote the teachers, "that it is absolutely incompatible with the duties of a teacher and trainer of the youth, whose sacred duty includes awakening and cultivating in the youth under his care the feelings of piety and respect for the authority of our King and His Government through word and example, to participate in political agitation against the government and to vote against the King's will." Men of higher culture, he said, knew the difference between the government and the Progressive party.[31]

It would be difficult to conceive of further exertions of loyalty and obedience to the Conservative way of life which could have been demanded of the teachers. Every abuse of patriotism in favor of one political and social group in the state, every violation of freedom of instruction, every manifestation of the subservience of education to politics, every kind of violation of the right of the teacher as an individual were exemplified in these instructions.

The Catholic priesthood could hardly be coerced by the government into following the Conservatives, but the Protestant pastors were ordered to toe the line. In numerous cases these pastors shared the government's views with such devotion that they needed no urging. Even in 1861 and 1862, not to go further back, they had fulfilled their traditional function of maintaining civil obedience. In 1862, for example, a bookbinder wished to name his child "Waldeck," manifestly in honor of one of the most vigorous liberal leaders. The pastor refused to baptize the child under that name, and when the father appealed the case to the church consistory in Berlin, the latter upheld the pastor, replying "that in the evangelical church the giving of only those baptismal names is permitted which have been customary among Christians or at least have a deeper meaning and signify nothing objectionable."[32] It was offensive to the church for a child to be named for a liberal. In April of that year a pastor in Rummelsberg County declared in a sermon that "the Lower House . . . which was composed of pardoned persons [that is, former criminals] had the aim to eradicate Christianity in Prussia. . . . Stupid boys wished to make laws." A

[31] Abg. H., *St. B.*, Nov. 23, 1863; I, 132. *Ibid.*, 1864, Vol. IV, No. 95, pp. 610-12.
[32] *Volkszeitung*, Oct. 5, 1862.

pastor in one of the rural election districts near Lyck spoke to the assembled peasants to the same effect. At the opening of the Landtag in May, 1862, the Superior Court Pastor von Hengstenberg surpassed all his colleagues. He preached a sermon to the Landtag which consisted of a denunciation of the liberals. According to a deputy who was present, the pastor said that "many of the deputies have the mark of Cain on them" and accused the liberals of supporting lies. The sermon was delivered in the presence of the King.[33]

General-Superintendent Moll in East Prussia issued an election statement in the same year which should rank with the finest examples of political piety.

> In the name of God the Father, of the Son and of the Holy Ghost. Amen. Dear brothers in Jesus Christ. There is going through our land at present a movement the noise of which is great. Nonetheless, I should not speak to you about it at this time of preparation for Easter if nothing else than the roar of political election excitement were manifest in it. But I hear a roar not merely as of wild water but of the spirits of destruction which entice the excited people to great errors along the way of destruction. I hear with sorrow and shudders the brazen, sarcastic speeches with which godless people in widely-read daily papers deride the pious minds of loyal men who seek the will of God even in state affairs, place their faith in the Lord even in the present confusion, and exhort the Christian dwellers of our country to devoted prayer about the results of the election according to the heart of God. And I mourn deeply for our poor people that it still does not turn away from these evil tongues with abhorrence and revulsion, but that in part it is even eager for such bad food. I hear with concern and with painful astonishment what reception the false teachings of the sovereignty of the people find among the inexperienced, what secret satisfaction the half-concealed, half-open attacks on the monarchy by divine right arouse among those already uncertain in their loyalty. And I cannot rid myself of the thought that those cannot be the true friends of His Majesty the King who take offence that He took his hereditary Crown from God's altar and who cannot forgive Him for not having accepted the German imperial Crown out of the hands of unjustified party leaders and for not having raised it out of the stream of fraternal blood with the point of his sword and set it on His gracious head by force.[34]

The statement continued in the same vein.

[33] *Kölnische Zeitung*, April 8, June 1, 1862; *Königsberg Hartungsche Zeitung*, April 24, 1862.
[34] Abg. H., *St. B.*, July 4, 1862; I, 480.

Since churchmen expressed such views in 1861 and 1862, one can imagine the thoroughgoing participation expected of them in the elections of the next year, and further evidence scarcely needs to be given. Landrat von Lattorff of Gardelegen County instructed the superintendent of the church in October to have the pastors inform the elementary school teachers of their orders to assist in securing the victory of Conservatives in the election. Since the local pastors exerted considerable power over the schools as well as over the populace, the Landrat had chosen one of the most effective means for bringing morality to the aid of political pressure. In another case after the election Pastor Nöthig of the Jakobi Church openly rebuked an elector who had voted liberal. The good pastor did so in church just before the Lord's Supper in front of the entire congregation. When the liberals requested an investigation, the consistory took a month to reply and saw no reason to discipline the pastor.[35]

How many of the leading pastors felt about the political conflict was manifested again in June, 1865, when they signed a petition to the King condemning the Lower House in the name of Jesus Christ for violating the fourth commandment. They declared that hate and confusion reigned in the country to an unbelievable extent and that they found it difficult further to follow the requirement of praying for the Landtag when the latter misbehaved in such an unchristian way. They regarded as "one of the most sacred duties of the clergy to maintain old and young in the congregation in obedience to the ruler," and they warned that the wrath of God would descend upon a people that no longer walked in the ways of humility before not merely its Heavenly but its earthly master.[36]

In 1863 the military were not permitted by the government to participate in politics as much as before for fear of an undermining of discipline. The feelings of many or most officers were clear, however, from the behavior of these men in the previous election. They employed somewhat different phrases and tones from the teachers and pastors but achieved the same effect, and as became men of valor they occasionally used physical force. A favorite technique was for the commanding officer to call the Landwehr soldiers together before election time and deliver a speech to them, of which the following examples will suffice. Herr von Schmeling, Landwehr lieutenant in Heiligenbeil: "Comrades, you will see from the publication given you

[35] *Ibid.*, 1864, Vol. IV, No. 95, pp. 622, 654.
[36] *Spenersche Zeitung*, June 23, 1865.

for whom you are to vote. Nonetheless, I will in short order make your position clear. It is a question of only two things—either the King continues to rule or the Jews. The democrats wish the latter. Dismissed!" In Seehausen Major von Böhn declared to the reserve on March 29, 1862, "The previous elections are a disgrace to Prussian history. They have hardened the heart of the King. . . . This disgrace must be made good; everyone must contribute to doing so. . . . Whoever does not is a scoundrel." At Lautenburg and Rheden the commanding officer said to the Landwehr men, "It would be best if the army took its weapons, went from one end of the state to the other and trampled everything in the mud!" The election at Herford was edified by the commanding officer's marching the soldiers to the voting place, where they voted Conservative in a body. At the previous election the soldier vote had been cast for liberals, and their officer was taking no chance on a repetition of this offence. As the major left the voting place, he met a Landwehr man, the son of a local liberal merchant, and said, "You should be ashamed to vote with the democrats. You have been a soldier!" A battalion commander wrote to a reserve officer "that . . . because of agitation for the democratic Progressive party and thereby the violation of your duties as officer toward the King's Majesty and because of your forsaking the honor of a Royal Prussian officer, a court-of-honor investigation has been initiated against you." In another town two women who received a small sum to help bring up children by their former soldier-husbands found themselves deprived of these sums because their present husbands, ordinary burgers, had voted for the liberals.[37]

The pressure by officials in 1863 continued into the voting place. Deputy von Bernhardi reported in the Lower House on December 3 of that year that where trouble occurred at the elections it was caused by the election commissioners and that in almost every case these were Landrats.[38] Thus, at Warmbrunn the election commissioner Burghard, a librarian in the service of Count Schaffgotsch, made a long pro-Conservative speech to the voters. When one voter complained about it to the Landrat as a violation of the election law, the latter replied that he fully approved of the speech, that the election law forbade dis-

[37] *Augsburger Allgemeine Zeitung*, Oct. 10, 1863; *Königsberg Hartungsche Zeitung*, April 13, 9, 12, 1862; *Kölnische Zeitung*, April 30, 1862; Abg. H., *St. B.*, July 4, 1862, I, 467-68, 474; see *Königsberg Hartungsche Zeitung*, May 27, 1862, for the story of the assault by two army officers with drawn swords upon a defenseless civilian for having voted liberal.

[38] Abg. H., *St. B.*, Dec. 3, 1863; I, 384.

cussion and the voting on resolutions, but that the holding of a serious, patriotic speech just before the act of voting was both legal and commendable.[39]

Serving as election commissioner in the ninth Oppeln district, Landrat Baron von Koppy devised a more effective technique than that of the Schaffgotsch librarian. According to a report given the commission of the Lower House by County Judge Wagener, Estate-Owner Lorentz, and two other liberals of the district, the following incident occurred. The Landrat election commissioner declared at the beginning of the voting that he would allow no discussion. During the balloting the rural voters who did not support the Conservatives had to come directly to the table and at the request of the commissioner repeat the names of their candidates two or three times. Naturally some of them became frightened and on the second balloting a few stayed away or changed their vote. When a Conservative vote was cast the election commissioner could hear the name from any place in the room, no matter how softly spoken or badly enunciated. He allowed the Conservative voters in the room to converse among themselves, to make remarks to the voters, to talk with the voting officials, to look over the records, even to spill a pot of ink over the lists. If a non-Conservative voter made any comment, the commissioner threatened to have him removed by force, and several policemen were stationed outside for that purpose. Such was the moral quality of Conservatism.[40]

The results of the election of 1863 proved to be almost as disappointing to the government and the Conservatives as the previous ones had been. The disgust of Landrat Freiherr von Massenbach, election commissioner in the third election district of Posen, expressed itself in the manner in which he notified one of the winning candidates of his election. "At the elections for the Lower House held today in Birnhaum and Samter Counties," the Landrat wrote Doctor Langerhans, "the majority composed mainly of Poles and Jews chose you as deputy."[41]

The government immediately began to punish the higher officials who had disobeyed its orders; loyal higher officials in turn punished subordinates; and, wherever they could, officials and officers began to take vengeance on civilians who had ignored their dictates. The government's relations to the election contrasted sharply with those

[39] *Ibid.*, 1864, Vol. IV, No. 95, p. 616.
[40] *Ibid.*, Dec. 9, 1863; I, (1864), 357-58.
[41] *Ibid.*, Dec. 3, 1863; I, 303-04.

after the elections in the preceding two years; the behavior surpassed the worst excesses of the Manteuffel regime. Village Schulzes were disciplined right and left. They were personally censured, fined or dismissed from office.[42] Judicial officials suffered treatment similar to that given administrative personnel. Legal defence was in the main ignored. In one way or another the offenders were punished.

One Landrat felt impelled to take direct action against a liberal Schulze in Olbersdorf. In a letter to Deputy Berndt, the Schulze, Robert Kuschel, described the interview, which lasted two and a half hours. The Landrat accused him of having, against orders, violated his oath of loyalty to the King by voting for liberals. He had also been disobedient, the Landrat continued, in that "after leaving the voting place you said to the county messenger Nowack, 'Victory, we have in spite of all put them through,' and you laughed scornfully. You have also been disobedient in that you laughed at the policeman Weniger in the market place and ten steps farther on you clapped two men on the shoulder." During the interview the Schulze stood firmly on his right to vote according to his conception of what was best for the state. The Landrat tried to dictate into the report on three occasions remarks by the Schulze which were not true; and when the latter objected the official became angry, hit him on the chest so hard that he knocked him over. The Schulze became frightened and tried to flee, but the Landrat held the door and shouted for the police. The secretary tried to calm the Landrat, who finally did quiet down enough to finish the interview. At the end the Schulze refused to sign the protocol because he had not been properly treated. The Landrat imposed a fine upon him for misbehavior.[43]

The vengeful hand of the government reached into the lives of persons who had only an indirect connection with it. In Guben the owner of a factory, C. Lehmann, had been elected to the unpaid position of town representative, and Langner, another burgher of the town, to that of town councillor. The administration at Frankfort on the Oder at first confirmed Langner's election, but after the state elections for deputies to the Lower House it refused to confirm the election of either man. The two municipal officials-to-be had voted for liberals. In Frankfort on the Oder, Master Chimney Sweeper Künzel, town councillor, member of the poor commission and of the local liberal committee of long standing, learned after the election the disadvantages of be-

[42] See the evidence in *ibid.*, 1864, Vol. IV, No. 95.
[43] *Ibid.*, Nov. 23, 1863, pp. 133-34.

ing a liberal. The government cancelled his rental of a piece of public land; the government director of the railway and a number of government agencies ceased employing him and gave the work to another master who had voted Conservative. On December 2 Kunzel was apprehended by the police over the question of the size of the area within which he could operate his business. It appeared that the government would reduce the extent of it.[44]

The military participated in the disciplinary action with full loyalty. Upon being called back to active duty an officer who had voted liberal found that his superior had imposed a social boycott upon him. No officer was allowed to associate with him. From Potsdam a number of town officials reported the following action by the military stationed there. Soldiers were forbidden to trade with anyone who had voted liberal or who had failed to vote; and since many merchants depended upon this trade for their livelihood, the prohibition meant their ruin. On the list were two barbers, three bakers, a flour merchant, a butcher, a forage dealer, and a brewer, along with many others. A widow had been told by an official that she would have to move out of a government-owned apartment unless she persuaded her son not to vote for liberals. She had refused and had moved. The military had been given the names of the offending tradesmen by the public officials. One could see why it was useful for Conservatives to hold the position of election commissioners.[45]

When the new Landtag convened in the autumn of 1863, the liberals soon brought up for discussion in the Lower House the whole question of the behavior of the government in the election. The debate focused upon certain fundamental problems of government in the state and revealed clearly once more the issues in the constitutional conflict. What role or function did the ministry have, how much authority resided in the King, what powers did the Landtag possess over the ministry and over the bureaucracy, what rights as voters did the officials have under the constitution, what authority did the government possess over the officials, what part should the government play in an election, in what sense should the articles of the constitution be interpreted? The arguments were concerned primarily about these questions, for all of them were involved in the question of free elections.

The liberals knew that their existence as a political force was at stake and that the sympathetic population expected them to act. In

[44] *Ibid.*, 1864; Vol. IV, No. 95, p. 643.
[45] *Ibid.*, pp. 640-42.

a superb speech in the House, on November 28, Schulze-Delitzsch stated the full significance of the conflict: "We have the duty toward our voters that when they are restricted by the officials in the exercise of their most sacred rights, we must step in and fight for them with all the constitutional means at our disposal. Only thereby will they be encouraged; and if we do nothing, we only cause discouragement throughout the country." This was the old constitutional conflict in a new form. Its meaning was brought home to the people to its fullest extent, he said, for the behavior of the government in the elections showed that the conflict involved the most intimate of all civil rights, the right to vote. Addressing the Conservative deputies, he said:

> You must not feel entirely secure since you actually request the government to support your influence illegally by means of the officials. A genuine aristocracy does not think and act in this way. . . . Such behavior could rather destroy the aristocracy than strengthen it. . . . The gentlemen [the Conservatives] who already have such a favorable position through their important social standing display a testimonial of poverty and show that something must be rotten about their position because they do not trust this legitimate influence and evoke another force for their support, that of illegality. . . .

Schulze-Delitzsch accused the government and the Conservatives of relying on what was low and vulgar in human nature, on venality, as the basis of their system of rule. And he said,

> That is a system which arouses against itself the most terrible hate that one can think of among those whom one forces under control. It is the most awful humiliation, the worst affront, which one commits when one forces a man to admit this before his fellow men. The coerced one thinks of wife and child, of his miserable situation, of hunger and sorrow—but nonetheless he will not be free of the feeling that he appears to all his associates as a wretched person. . . . More than one has come to me in burning shame and with the bitterest complaints.[46]

Deputy Assman was equally bitter:

> Whoever speculates on revolutionary conditions should allow things to continue as they are and not oppose this activity of the Landrats. Like a poisonous fungus bitterness and pessimism are quickly and secretly spreading and are consuming the foundations of our state, while the state craftsmen are concerned only to preserve the outer polish of the ornaments.

[46] *Ibid.*, Nov. 28, 1863, Vol. I, (1864), p. 185.

We face, in fact, a bad calamity for the state. To avoid it exceptional measures are necessary, for these are not merely single excesses of individual officials which lie before us, but everything points to organized pressure.[47]

Freiherr von Vincke, a right-wing liberal of the highest social standing and usually a severe critic of Schulze-Delitzsch, directed terms of equally strong condemnation against the government. He called the government's compulsion on the voters "unheard of" and not in harmony with the moral sense of the people. "Among the simple country folk, who are the most loyal supporters of the Royal House," he said, "there prevails the greatest bitterness. They are deeply angered over the offence against their personal rights." Von Vinke urged the government not to continue along this path. "If the Lower House is dissolved another time or two and such election pressure is again exerted as this time, no one can say what will happen. God defend our Fatherland against that!"[48]

The liberals were especially concerned about the position of officials with respect to the government. Many of them were or had been officials themselves and comprehended the full seriousness of the problem from personal experience. Freiherr von Vincke stated that no one demanded that the government remain silent during an election. It should use all legal means to inform the public about the issues, and the officials should be loyal to their superiors. Nonetheless, the officials must have freedom to follow their own political views. Very many officials who at present were considered loyal had formerly opposed the liberal Hohenzollern-Auerswald ministry, von Vincke added, without finding that attitude one of hostility to the King.[49]

Deputy Wachler, a county judicial official elected on the Progressive ticket and now serving as chairman of the commission of the Lower House investigating the violations of freedom of election, revealed to the Lower House the situation of the bureaucrat from personal experience. Landrat von Knebel-Döberitz of his county had warned all officials, Schulzes and others, against voting for him and his Progressive colleague, Knight's Estate-Owner von Gablenz. As an official he had taken the oath of loyalty to three kings and had served the monarchy for almost forty years; yet the Landrat called him hostile to the government. Wachler emphasized how subversive of official prestige it was when a peasant or a townsman one day received a governmental

[47] *Ibid.,* p. 168.
[48] *Ibid.,* Nov. 13, 1863; I, 47.
[49] *Ibid.,* pp. 53-54.

instruction signed "Wachler" and the next day a statement from the Landrat that Wachler was hostile to the government, "a highly dangerous subject," and should not be supported at the election. If this was the way things were done, Wachler continued, it would be better to abolish the constitution, abolish the Lower House, create a Tax Council and replace the Upper House by a Court Assembly which would be obedient.[50]

Deputy Faucher condemned the government's action for another reason.

> If we had all the Schulzes as electors and only Landrats as deputies, the same administrative officials would serve as popular representatives who should be warned by the popular representatives. Then the government, misled by a sham constitutionalism, would allow itself to commit acts which it would later greatly regret and we would all have to say to ourselves that it would have been better if Prussia had remained an absolutistic state.[51]

Deputy Waldeck, a liberal of 1848, a judge who had withstood government pressure many times, expressed further the dilemma of the official.

> Who is responsible for the present situation, that the constitution is violated, that there is no budget, that expenditures are made for the army organization which the Lower House has reduced? The ministry is responsible. The official took the oath of allegiance to the constitution, and if upon being elected deputy he finds the government violating the constitution, what should be do?

Waldeck blamed the government for putting the official in this dilemma. The liberals gladly approved political agitation by the Conservative party, he said, and claimed for themselves the same right. They disapproved putting the officials in disciplinary investigation because of their vote. One cannot call voting, Waldeck concluded, political agitation.[52]

What should be the relation between the official and the government? The arguments chiefly revolved around this question. Deputy Virchow, the famous professor of medicine, declared that once a person was definitely appointed to an official position and once he was expected to fulfill his duty under all ministries, "you must allow him a

[50] *Ibid.*, pp. 49-50.
[51] *Ibid.*, Nov. 23, 1863; I, 129.
[52] *Ibid.*, Nov. 13, 1863; I, 51-52.

certain neutral area within which he can move freely according to his own conscience. You must normalize precisely his official duties." Without this precise statement of obligations, he said, the Prussian state in its present form could not exist. Virchow considered the constitutional rights of the individual as composing that area which the government should not violate.[53] Count Schwerin, the former Minister of Interior and a friend of the King's, a member of the highest nobility, a liberal of the most moderate kind, condemned the government's treatment of officials as completely as any left-wing democrat. In the Lower House on November 13 he denounced the government for having forced officials to put themselves at the head of "a certain party." This is "the worst thing that could happen to the Prussian state," he said, "for it damages the respect which in a state like Prussia the official must have." As minister, he stated, his rule had been that "as long as an official did his official duty and obeyed his superior, I did not ask about his political views." He had disciplined those who had agitated for any political party, whether liberal or Conservative. The present government should have been "more careful" in its instructions to officials. He feared that if present policies were continued, the country might be split between those who were loyal to the King and those who were not. He stated that no worse service could be done the Landrats than to make them the leaders of a certain political party, for thereby they would lose the general confidence on which their prestige depended. He accused the government of bringing them into this unfortunate position.[54]

Deputy Twesten referred to Paragraph 315 of the code of criminal law in which an official "who abuses his official power to force someone illegally to an act, a sufferance or an omission should be punished by imprisonment of not less than a month's duration." The liberals could not at present initiate such proceedings, he said, because the ministry monopolized the authority to bring suit. But "misdemeanors of this kind are not cancelled for five years, and I think there will later be an opportunity to use this paragraph."[55]

On the Conservative side, the statements were equally blunt and problems were raised which the liberals had not actually handled. Since the Conservatives were few in the House and, with the exception of Deputy Wagener, not particularly vocal, their arguments came forth

[53] *Ibid.*, Nov. 28, 1863; I, 175-76.

[54] *Ibid.*, Nov. 13, 28, 1863; I, 52, 48, 183.

[55] *Ibid.*, Nov. 23, 1863, p. 130. Compare Schwerin's statement to the Lower House, March 23, 1860. *Ibid.*, 1860; II, 605.

mainly as fiats. Deputy von Blanckenburg demanded to know: "When the officials work in their offices as state officials in the name of the government and then in the evening as citizens agitate in clubs against the same government—does not that violate the moral conscience of the people more than when an official is simply forced back into doing his duty?"[56] Deputy Wagener asked the liberals tartly whether the officials were only to be allowed to agitate against the government. He saw no difference between a Conservative Landrat's influencing a peasant and a liberal county judge's behaving in the same way. If the prestige of the one was damaged by such action, the same held true for the other official. He preferred the prohibition of any political agitation on the part of the officials, a view, however, which his Conservative colleagues manifestly did not share.[57]

For the government, Minister of Interior Count Eulenburg, who should have carried the burden of defence, proved at first to be rather tame and somewhat apologetic. He even acknowledged that some officials had gone too far in pressing their subordinates and said that he had given instructions to correct the excesses. Nonetheless, he denied that free elections were possible in a time of political excitement like the present. At every election, he said, influence was exerted; every person was influenced and should be. Where different views existed and the government was convinced that its views were correct, it should use all legal means to influence the public in favor of them. He defended his election decree as constitutional and necessary, for a part of the bureaucracy had been getting out of hand and ignoring its official responsibility to the King. Without obedience such as he had demanded, there could be no orderly administration. He admitted that an independent bureaucracy no longer existed, and he blamed the loss upon the introduction of a representative legislative body. The two were incompatible, he said; to rule as before with an independent bureaucracy was completely out of the question.[58]

Minister President Bismarck knew the weakness of his colleague Eulenburg, and in one brief, frank and cool speech in the Upper House he expressed warm approval of the most extreme action of the Landrats and other officials and of the Conservatives in the recent election:

> You may be certain that the government has not been spoiled
> by an excess of loyal zeal to the extent that when this zeal is

[56] *Ibid.*, Nov. 28, 1863; I, 174.
[57] *Ibid.*, Nov. 13, 1863; I (1864), 51.
[58] *Ibid.*, Nov. 13, 23, 1863; I, 46, 50, 130.

manifested it does not esteem the honorable source of it. The government knows how to distinguish such an excess from the careful reserve which washes its hands in innocence and does not come into the position of seriously asking itself whether the limits which I described are touched or transgressed.[59]

Thereby Bismarck described the actual situation without trying to cover up realities by piety and legalism. He criticized the moderate and fair officials, the ones who had tried to make possible the freedom of election. He calmly disavowed much of what the Minister of Interior said about the elections and reassured his supporters that the government stood behind them.

The sharp difference in interpretation of the constitution between the government and the liberal majority of the Lower House showed itself in details at every point. The one wished to draw the limits to the power of the other as tightly as possible; the other sought to expand its authority as far as it could. An example arose in connection with the investigation of election irregularities. The House appointed a commission to conduct the investigation; and since most of the evidence concerned officials, the commission tried to obtain information directly from lower officials. The government prohibited the latter from supplying any data except that which the ministry was willing to give. The government based its position on the constitution and asserted that by the provision for the separation of powers the legislative branch had no authority to consult private citizens or officials except by way of the executive. The Lower House was inclined in general to accept this view, certainly an extraordinary sign of inexperience on its part; but it believed that while the Lower House itself could not carry out an investigation of the sort proposed a committee of the House could do so. When the government forbade officials to appear before the committee, the House was compelled to acquiesce.[60] The government won again because it had the power. It succeeded for the time being at least in making the House dependent upon the administration for all official investigatory work involving public hearings. It set up another barrier to effective relations between the House and the public.

Constitutional or legal arguments had slight bearing on the conflict. Each side claimed legal authority for its action and views, for each referred to a different article of the constitution or a different

---

[59] Herrenhaus, *St. B.*, Nov. 19, 1863; I, 48.
[60] See the discussion in Abg. H., *St. B.*, 1864, Vol. IV, No. 90, pp. 554-57; No. 95, pp. 625, 56.

law. In the stage of development in which Prussia found itself, the controversy could be resolved only by force; no court or Landtag could do so. The outcome depended upon whether the Lower House or the King and his government had the power to gain its way, and, as has already been seen, Bismarck knew this fact. The liberals brought forth excellent legal arguments, all of which were undoubtedly valid, if one accepted them as valid. So did the Conservatives.[61] The gap theory could be applied to this question as easily as it could to that of the financial authority. The entire issue became one of brute power.

This was a crucial period in the history of the relations of the officials and the government. In the pre-parliamentary era of absolutism, particularly in the Stein-Hardenberg period, the officials had considered themselves in many cases as representatives of the people and had defended law and order against autocracy. Protected by administrative law, they had enjoyed a degree of independence in judgment and action which had enabled them at times to defy and block arbitrary measures. After the introduction of parliamentary institutions they attempted to maintain their attitude of independence, even though conditions had changed. Formerly their opposition to the government had been held within the confines of the ruling group. Little or no public activity or expression of support had been involved. Under a parliamentary regime they extended their claim to independence to the right to engage in political party conflicts and to appeal to the public. Thereby they tended to violate the rules of the closed corporation of the governing group. They undermined discipline by appealing to the public, a new power, against their own superiors. They claimed the right to participate in political party life while preserving the security of tenure of the Old Regime of bureaucratic absolutism. The Conservatives' demand that the officials follow the orders of the absolute monarch was equally inappropriate. Misunderstanding the situation created by the introduction of parliamentary institutions, the government claimed that the officials should be active politically in its favor. Thereby it forced the latter into the position either of losing their rights as citizens to vote according to their conscience or of disobeying their superiors. Although in contrary directions, both liberals and conservatives were claiming more power with respect to the officials than was justified.

The issue was critical because of the high importance of the officials in the political life of the Prussian state. Far more so than in a

---

[61] See the Conservative view of 1856 as formulated by Minister von Westphalen. *Ibid.*, Feb. 8, 1856; I, 354; also Deputy Heise's remarks. *Ibid.*, Feb. 8, 1856; I, 364-65.

country like England, the officials continued to provide much of the political leadership. Recognizing that fact, Bismarck and his colleagues determined to break the political independence of the bureaucrats once and for all. By winning the constitutional conflict they were to succeed in reducing the officials to political silence or to active support of the government. This system was subsequently introduced into the unified Germany and lasted as long as the Second Reich. It offered one more example of how Bismarck and the Conservatives imposed upon a government with parliamentary institutions an autocratic conception of the Old Regime. Their policy provided no solution, but it worked, that is, until eliminated by the same means by which it was introduced—sheer power.

12 / The Elections of 1862 and 1863

I N April-May, 1862, and October-November, 1863, elections were held for the Lower House of the Landtag. Of the 350 deputies to be elected, the results according to party were as follows:

Name of Party	Number of Deputies Elected	
	1862	1863
LIBERAL	284	258
CONSERVATIVE	10[1]	36
CATHOLIC	33	30
POLISH	23	26

In each election the liberals won by an overwhelming majority. Since all the Polish deputies and on most issues the Catholic Center Party opposed the Conservative program, the government enjoyed the support in the Lower House of only a very small band of Conservative faithful.

Statistical data on the party vote in the two elections were not available at the time except in scattered form. No official figures on the results were published; and not even the liberals provided an unofficial tabulation. The government's compilation of the statistics was kept secret, reposing in the Prussian State Archives, where it was discovered by the present author.[2] Although the compilation is not quite complete, it does provide figures for both elections on the vote of the electors for the four major political groups, the liberals, the Con-

---

[1] Deputy Hoffman, a Landrat of Oppeln II, is regarded not as a Conservative but as a member of the Constitutional party.

[2] *Statistics on the Prussian Elections of 1862 and 1863*, edited by Eugene N. Anderson (University of Nebraska Press, 1954).

servatives, the Catholic Center, and the Poles. The statistics analyze the vote by county and by urban and rural categories. They also supply the figures, by party, on the voters' vote in 1863 for each county, for each of the three classes of voters and for the urban and rural population. These data make it possible for the first time to analyze the statistical evidence on the political attitude of the Prussian population in the crucial period of the constitutional conflict. They will be used as the basis for the discussion in this chapter.

The size of the total vote cast was certainly not impressive. In the election of 1863, of 90,790 eligible to vote in Class I in the entire state, only 57 per cent voted; of 202,709 in Class II, 44 per cent voted; of 803,954 in Class III, 27.3 per cent voted; of a total of 1,097,453 eligible voters in all three classes, only 30.9 per cent cast a ballot. The percentages were lowest in the two Western provinces (20.6 for Westphalia and 18.1 for the Rhineland), highest for the province of Posen (53.3 per cent). For the other provinces the figures ranged from 38.9 per cent in the province of Brandenburg to 29 per cent in the province of Silesia. Frequently a candidate for the position of elector won in an election at which fewer than a dozen voters cast a ballot. In the towns the percentage in all classes participating in the election was usually greater than that in the rural districts.

Since the statistics on the popular vote are available for the election of 1863, the number of popular votes necessary to elect a deputy for each party can be calculated. The following table contains the pertinent data:

	Liberal	Conserv- ative	Catholic	Polish
Total popular vote	566,000	327,000	48,000	131,000
Number of popular votes per deputy	2,193	9,083	1,600	5,038
Percentage of total popular vote	52.8	30.5	4.4	12.0
Percentage of total number of deputies	73.4	10.3	8.5	7.4

The Catholics manifestly fared best under the election system, the liberals next best, and the Poles and Conservatives suffered heavily. The party with the smallest popular vote seated proportionally far more deputies than any other party. If one were to judge the election system by the standards of equal, universal suffrage or by a system of proportional representation, one would have to conclude that the Catholics were greatly over-represented, the liberals considerably so, and the Poles and especially the Conservatives were greatly underrepresented.

In the administrative district of Köslin, where the Conservatives won seven out of nine seats, on a proportional basis they did better than the liberals in the same area. Their popular vote was 3,100 per deputy, that of the liberals 5,500 votes. They won about two-thirds of the popular votes and seated 77 per cent of the deputies. The liberals received the rest—one-third of the popular vote and 23 per cent of the deputies. In other administrative districts, like Breslau and Oppeln, where the Conservatives returned several deputies but far fewer than the liberals, they fared well or ill in proportion to the number of deputies they were able to return. The more deputies they elected, the lower the number of Conservative voters per deputy and the narrower the gap between the percentage of popular vote they received and of deputies they elected. In those administrative districts in which they seated no deputies and yet polled a large vote, the disparity was greatest. In the administrative district of Königsberg, for example, the Conservatives polled 20,000 popular votes to 32,000 for the liberals and did not seat a single deputy while the liberals returned sixteen. The system of voting favored the party with concentrated strength in an election district, irrespective of whether or not that party had a large following in all or most parts of the state. The Conservatives formed a large minority throughout the state, but they could muster enough votes in 1863 to win in only twenty-one out of 176 election districts. The results of the three-class system of voting proved to be similar to those obtained under any system based upon the returns from a single election district. A majority won; the minority, no matter how large, was unable to seat a representative. The Conservatives were not under-represented any more than a minority party is in England or the United States. They had a large popular following, and they showed that the Conservative government was not lacking in popular support; but they could not muster enough votes in the crucial places, the election districts, to win very many seats.[3]

Although all parties entered the elections on equal terms, one should exercise great caution in drawing conclusions about the political attitude of the Prussian people from the total vote polled by each party. The three-class system acted as a deterrent to voting, especially in Class III where most eligible voters were to be found. When for the entire state an average of 132 voters in Class III had the same voting power as 19.1 voters in Class II and as 7.1 in Class I, the masses saw little inducement to express their political opinions by balloting. During the decades in the first half of the century when the Stein Municipal Law had allowed equal suffrage in the towns and cities of the Eastern

---

[3] Cf. Dr. J. Jastrow, *Das Dreiklassensystem* (Berlin, 1894), pp. 89-90.

provinces, the public had participated in the local elections to an over-whelming extent. It was to do so again when the Reich election law permitted equal and secret suffrage. The three-class system imposed such a handicap upon popular participation that it would be wrong to gauge the results of the elections by a yardstick which is inappropriate for that system of voting. Since the system did not allow equality of suffrage, one should not attempt to interpret the results by a standard that assumes equality of votes. A basis of judgment must be formed which is in keeping with the nature of the election system—a fact which neither the Conservatives and the liberals at the time nor sub-sequent students of these elections have taken into account. The total figures reveal the political attitude of those who took the trouble to vote, of those who felt so strongly or were under such heavy pressure from other forces that they cast a ballot. The data do not indicate that those failing to vote were either uninterested in politics or were content with the status quo.

The three-class system divided the voters in each election district according to the amount of direct taxes paid. The framers of the election law had assumed that the distribution of rich and poor would be about the same in each locality, an assumption that proved to be false, particularly as modern industrialism spread. In some precincts no individuals were eligible for the first class or even the first and second classes, and a few persons had to be arbitrarily assigned to these categories.[4] In wealthy districts like Berlin the average direct tax paid by a member of the first class was 225.8 Reichsthalers, that of the second class 64.1, and that of the third, 6.38. In Heydekrug County in East Prussia the comparable figures were 20.0, 8.5, and 1.71 Reichs-thalers. For the entire state they were 53.7, 16.9, and 2.55 Reichs-thalers. The amount of taxes paid by individuals within each class varied widely. In Stuhm County in the province of Prussia the amount for voters in the first class ranged from 26 to 1,054 Thalers, in the second class from 9 to 129 Thalers, and in the third class from 2 to 37 Thalers. The greatest disparity in voting power was found in the large towns and the cities, where differences in wealth were most pro-nounced.

In spite of the lack of state-wide uniformity it appears to have been generally true that the system roughly corresponded with the natural divisions of society at the time. In any one district the leaders would usually be found in the first or the first and second classes and the

---

[4] See Abg. H., *St. B.*, May 26, 1862; I, 41 (speech by Deputy Neide).

masses in the third. Regardless of whether one district was industrial and urban and another was agricultural and rural, the three-class system represented grades of comparable social and economic importance within each district. A merchant of some wealth who was in Class III in an urban district would have far more income than persons in Class I in other districts. Nonetheless, in his district he occupied a social and economic position of third class; and an individual of much less wealth in a rural district might enjoy a position of first class. The voters represented definite social and economic interests according to the class in which they were placed. Exceptions occurred mainly in two cases. The first concerned intellectuals, who were frequently or usually leaders but on economic grounds were normally found in Class III. The second concerned two groups: wealthy individuals, some of whom, in certain areas, had to be relegated to Class II or Class III, and others where the extent of economic equality was such that persons for Class I or even Class II had to be chosen arbitrarily.[5]

An adequate standard for judging the results of the three-class system of voting would take into account the fact of comparability of social and economic position in each district, irrespective of the diversity of wealth, occupation, and social background. Instead of adding up total figures on the number of persons voting for each party throughout the state, one should use total figures on the number of counties. The figures for each county should then be broken down according to voting class and according to whether they referred to urban or to rural areas. The vote should be tabulated for each county regardless of whether the party was able to return a deputy. If a party won in a county or in one or more classes or in the urban or rural areas even without being able to carry the election district, that fact should be recorded so that the size of the party's following can be shown. By using this method one is able to compile the following table on the liberals and the Conservatives.[6]

In preparing the table the author has confronted the problem of what to do in case an election district returned members of two parties. In these instances it is impossible to learn the exact vote of each winning party. The official compiler has recorded the vote of only one; that of the other party will vary from it according to class and according to the distribution of the vote between urban and rural areas. Where-

---

[5] Cf. von Gerlach, *op. cit.*, pp. 29-34; R. Böckh, "Statistik der Urwahlen für das preussischen Abgeordnetenhaus vom 19. Nov. 1861," *Zeitschrift der Preuss. Statistischen Bureaus*, 1862, II, 77-121.

[6] A similar table on the Catholic and the Polish vote is given later in this chapter.

The Voters' Vote 1863 by County Showing a Majority by Class

Admin. District	Total No. of Counties	IN FAVOR OF THE LIBERALS												IN FAVOR OF THE CONSERVATIVES											
		Total				Urban				Rural				Total				Urban				Rural			
		I	II	III	Tot'l	I	II	III	Tot'l	I	II	III	Tot'l	I	II	III	Tot'l	I	II	III	Tot'l	I	II	III	Total
Königsberg	20	14	14	11	11	15	14	14	14	9	8	7	7	2	4	5	5	1	1	1	1	6	7	8	8
Gumbinnen	16	15	12	14	15	13	13	13	13	14	11	13	12	1	2	2	2	1	0	1	1	2	5	3	4
Danzig	8	4	2	2	2	5	5	5	3	2	1	1	1	2	2	2	2	0	0	0	0	2	2	2	2
Marienwerder	13	7	7	6	6	9	9	6	7	6	7	6	6	3	3	3	3	2	0	2	0	2	2	3	3
Potsdam	15	12	13	11	12	13	14	15	15	6	11	3	5	3	0	4	4	0	1	3	2	8	3	11	9
City of Berlin	4	4	4	4	4	4	4	4	4					0	0	0	0	0	0	0	0				
Frankfurt	17	14	15	11	13	17	17	17	17	8	8	1	2	1	2	6	4	0	0	0	0	8	8	15	14
Stettin	13	12	10	8	7	13	13	13	13	6	5	4	4	7	3	6	6	0	0	0	0	6	7	8	8
Köslin	10	3	4	0	0	7	6	6	7	2	2	0	0	1	6	10	10	3	4	0	3	8	8	10	10
Stralsund	4	3	3	0	0	4	4	4	4	2	2	1	1	1	1	1	1	0	0	4	0	2	2	3	3
Breslau	24	16	19	6	8	17	20	19	19	12	13	3	5	8	5	15	16	6	3	6	4	11	10	20	18
Oppeln	16	4	4	4	4	5	5	5	5	3	3	3	3	8	8	8	8	6	6	8	6	8	8	8	8
Liegnitz	19	17	17	13	13	19	19	17	19	13	14	6	8	2	2	6	6	6	6	2	6	6	5	13	11
Posen	18	1	1	0	0	4	3	1	1	0	0	0	0	5	5	0	0	5	3	0	0	4	3	1	2
Bromberg	9	4	4	4	4	4	4	4	4	4	4	4	4	2	0	0	0	0	0	0	0	0	0	0	0
Magdeburg	15	13	14	13	13	12	13	13	13	10	12	8	9	2	1	2	2	3	2	2	2	3	2	6	5
Merseburg	17	15	17	14	14	16	16	16	16	13	14	10	12	2	0	3	3	1	0	1	1	3	2	6	4
Erfurt	9	3	4	5	5	6	6	5	5	3	3	3	3	4	3	2	2	0	2	0	0	6	4	4	4
Münster	11	4	4	4	5	6	6	5	5	3	3	3	4	0	0	0	0	0	0	1	0	0	0	0	0
Minden	10	6	5	3	3	9	6	5	5	6	5	1	1	0	2	0	2	0	0	0	0	1	2	4	4
Arnsberg	14	12	12	13	13	12	12	13	13	12	11	12	13	0	0	0	0	0	1	2	0	1	1	1	1
Cologne	11	8	8	7	7	5	6	6	6	7	7	6	6	0	1	1	1	1	0	0	1	0	0	0	0
Düsseldorf	18	15	15	13	13	14	15	13	14	11	11	11	10	2	2	2	2	0	0	2	0	1	2	2	2
Coblenz	12	10	11	11	10	9	9	9	9	10	10	9	10	0	1	2	2	0	0	0	0	2	2	3	2
Aachen	11	8	7	8	8	9	9	6	7	6	4	4	6	1	0	1	1	0	0	0	0	1	0	0	0
Trier	13	13	13	13	13	9	11	11	11	12	12	11	12	0	1	0	0	2	0	0	0	0	1	0	0
Sigmaringen	4	4	4	4	4	4	4	4	4	4	4	4	4	0	0	0	0	0	0	0	0	0	0	0	0
Total	351	241	242	204	210	259	262	245	253	182	185	136	149	56	49	85	79	33	25	30	23	92	86	134	123

ever a Conservative won, the compiler most likely tabulated his vote, for the government was most interested in the size of the vote for its supporters. In those cases where a Catholic and a liberal, or a Pole and a liberal, won, it is usually impossible to tell to which one the recorded vote pertains. In order to learn the maximum strength of the Conservatives the author has for this table regarded as Conservative the vote in the three election districts where a candidate of that party was returned along with a member of another party. The one exception to this rule, Erfurt II, is explained by the fact that the official compiler credited the victory to the Catholics. Where a liberal won along with one or two Catholics (in six election districts) or one or two Poles (in five election districts), the author has included the vote not in the liberal columns but in those of the other winning party. By this method he has manifestly underestimated the strength of the Catholics by the three election districts in which they won along with a Conservative, and he has diminished the liberal showing even more by ignoring in this table their winning vote in eleven election districts comprising twenty-three counties. If the figures on the liberals were increased by the number of these counties, the results would be more nearly correct than those given in the above table. In that case the total figures for the liberals would be:

Total				Urban				Rural			
I	II	III	Total	I	II	III	Total	I	II	III	Total
264	275	227	233	282	285	268	276	205	208	159	172

The tables reveal that in Class I the liberals won over four times as many counties as the Conservatives, in Class II nearly five times as many, in Class III about two and one half times as many. In the urban areas the liberals won eight times as many in Class I and from ten to eleven times as many in Classes II and III and in the total. In the rural districts the liberals won twice as many in Classes I and II and gained a majority in Class III and in the total.

The evidence shows that the overwhelming majority of the voters favored one of the liberal parties. Rural as well as urban population voted for the liberals. Counties that were entirely rural cast as high a percentage of ballots in favor of them as did the urban areas. Although not as a rule in such large numbers, the voters of the Masurian and Lithuanian regions, of a few Polish counties and of many Catholic ones favored the liberals as staunchly as the solidly German Protestant districts. The Conservative strength among the voters was concentrated in very few areas. The party was able to win a majority of the popular votes in one half or more of the counties in only three administrative districts, Breslau, Oppeln, and especially Köslin, though it also did well in Stettin and Liegnitz. If it had not been strong in the third class and among the rural voters, it would not have been so successful even in these five administrative districts, for the liberals or the other parties easily gained a majority of the total vote in the first two classes in three of these (Breslau, Stettin, and Liegnitz) and reduced the Conservative showing in Köslin. The urban voters greatly favored the liberals in every one of these administrative districts.

The liberals were able to win a seat in six election districts along with a member of the Catholic party, and in a few instances the Conservatives and the Catholics returned a deputy from the same district. In five cases a liberal won alongside a Pole; but with the one exception of those in Merseburg II the voters were too well informed to commit the mistake of imagining that a Conservative and a liberal could represent their district with equal accuracy.

The percentage of the voters casting ballots in the counties that went Conservative in 1863 was about the same as that for the liberal counties. The degree of participation varied with the amount of influence of the vote, highest in the first class and lowest in the third, with the second class ranking not far behind the first and well above the third. The percentage of voters participating in the election in 1862 was higher in the great majority of counties and classes than it was in 1863. The Conservatives polled as a rule a much larger vote in the rural areas than in the towns and cities. They showed the greatest strength in the third class and least in the second. They won most of their seats in counties of solidly German population in which Protestantism predominated to an overwhelming extent; but they likewise were able to return deputies from a few counties in Silesia where the population was largely Catholic or both Catholic and Polish. The increase in the number of Conservative deputies from 1862 to 1863 is only explicable by the effectiveness of governmental and social pressure. Wherever the local upper class remained Conservative and the general cultural conditions had scarcely felt the effects of new ideas and of commerce and industry, the population tended to follow traditional ways and to acquiesce in Conservative leadership.

The urban vote did not predominate in the elections. The urban population in Prussia remained as yet a minority, and the percentage of voters casting ballots was not much larger in the towns than in the rural areas. The statistics show that the rural vote alone for the liberals by county and class was much greater than the combined urban and rural vote for the Conservatives. While the urban voters overwhelmingly supported the liberals, the rural population likewise gave them sufficient strength to win by a large majority over their main rival.

The electors' vote reveals a similar disproportion in favor of the liberals. The data contained in the following table are divided into two sections. The upper part contains the results in those counties in which the conflict was fought between liberals and Conservatives or in which a liberal or a Conservative victory under one of the rubrics was manifest. The lower part contains the results in those counties in which a liberal or a Conservative won along with one or two members of another party.[7]

Number of Counties in Which the Majority of Electors Voted Liberal or Conservative

Admin. District	LIBERAL Total 1862	Total 1863	Urban 1862	Urban 1863	Rural 1862	Rural 1863	No. of Counties	CONSERVATIVE Total 1862	Total 1863	Urban 1862	Urban 1863	Rural 1862	Rural 1863
Königsberg	16	13	16	13	13	9	20	0	3	0	1	2	6
Gumbinnen	16	15	15	15	16	15	16	0	1	0	0	0	1
Danzig	4	2	5	4	2	1	8	1	2	0	0	2	2
Marienwerder	9	6	10	9	8	6	13	1	3	0	0	2	3
Berlin	4	4	4	4	0	0	4	0	0	0	0	0	0
Potsdam	14	11	15	15	12	7	15	1	4	0	0	2	7
Frankfurt	17	14	17	17	14	7	17	0	3	0	0	2	9
Stettin	13	9	13	13	9	5	13	0	4	0	0	3	7
Köslin	4	2	9	8	2	0	10	6	8	1	2	8	10
Stralsund	4	3	4	4	2	1	4	0	1	0	0	2	3
Breslau	19	14	21	20	15	9	24	5	10	3	3	8	14
Oppeln	2	3	3	5	2	3	16	2	5	1	5	2	5
Liegnitz	17	14	19	19	15	9	19	2	5	0	0	4	10
Posen	3	1	3	1	2	0	18	1	0	5	4	0	2
Bromberg	4	4	4	4	4	4	9	0	0	0	0	0	0
Magdeburg	15	14	15	15	14	11	15	0	1	0	0	0	3
Merseburg	17	14	17	13	12	13	17	0	1	0	2	4	1
Erfurt	7	4	7	5	7	0	9	0	3	0	2	0	7
Münster	1	1	1	1	1	1	11	0	0	0	0	0	0
Minden	4	5	5	8	3	5	10	1	0	0	0	2	0
Arnsberg	9	12	9	12	8	12	14	1	0	0	0	2	0
Cologne	8	8	6	6	7	7	11	0	0	0	0	0	0
Düsseldorf	13	14	11	14	11	10	18	1	1	1	0	1	2
Coblenz	12	12	10	10	12	12	12	0	0	0	0	0	0
Trier	12	12	10	11	11	11	13	1	4	1	0	1	1
Aachen	6	8	6	10	3	6	11	0	0	0	0	0	0
Sigmaringen	3	4	2	4	3	4	4	1	0	2	0	1	0
Total	253	223	257	260	209	168	351	24	59	14	19	48	93
Königsberg		2		2		2							
Danzig		2		2		2							
Marienwerder	2	2	2	2	2	2							
Oppeln	6	3	9	3	5	3		4	5	1	3	5	5
Posen	2	6	2	5	1	4		0		0		1	
Bromberg	2		2		2								
Merseburg		1		2					1				2
Münster	2	2	2	3	2	2							
Minden	2		2		2								
Arnsberg	3		3		3								
Cologne	2	3	1	3	2	3		1		2		1	
Aachen	3		3		3								
Total	24	21	26	22	22	18		5	6	3	3	7	7
TOTAL	277	244	283	282	231	186		29	65	17	22	55	100

[7] In case of a tie the author credits the victory to the Conservatives. Since the official compiler gave to the Catholics the entire Conservative vote in the administrative district of Aachen in 1863, it is assumed that the same allocation occurred in the election of 1862.

The data indicate the effectiveness of governmental pressure in reducing the size of the liberal electors' vote in 1863, especially in the rural regions. The town voters were better organized and had more means of self-protection against the government than the rural population. The number of counties in which a majority of urban electors favored the liberals remained practically the same in 1863 as in the previous year, whereas in the rural areas it declined by nineteen per cent. For both urban and rural electors the liberal vote declined only twelve per cent from 1862 to 1863. In any case the Conservatives could scarcely derive much consolation from these figures. The electors proved to be much more liberal than the voters.

The disparity in the number of counties in which the voters' vote gave a majority to the liberals and that in which the electors' vote did so arises from the system of indirect elections. In the voters' balloting the majority was established not by adding up the total vote as one sum for the election district but by counting the vote within each class. A party might win a majority of the total vote and still lose a majority of the electors. Usually a victory in two classes meant a majority for the party in the entire district; but it was possible for a narrow margin of victory in two classes to be offset by a large majority in the other class. Thus, in some twenty counties the Conservatives won a majority in two or more classes or in the total vote in the voters' election, but a majority of the electors favored the liberals. In three other counties the reverse occurred; the liberal voters' vote was turned by the electors into a Conservative victory. It was also possible for candidates to be non-committal about their party affiliation during the campaign and after being chosen as electors to cast their ballot for the party they personally preferred. The statistics reveal that a number did so, particularly in the rural areas. Again the liberals profited from the change.

The relative strength of the liberals and the Conservatives can be seen most realistically from a comparison of the total number of elec-

Table I

	1862	1863
Total number of election districts	176	176
Total number of counties	351	351
Number of election districts returning liberal deputies	151	137
Percentage of election districts returning liberal deputies	85.8	77.8
Number of counties in these election districts	300	271
Percentage of counties in these election districts	85.0	77.0
Number of election districts returning Conservative deputies	6	21
Percentage of election districts returning Conservative deputies	3.4	12.0
Number of counties in these election districts	12	41
Percentage of counties in these election districts	3.4	11.6

tion districts and the inclusive counties from which each party elected one or more representatives. The figures given in the table below contain the data on those districts and counties in which the parties were able to win all seats and also on those in which they divided the representation with a second party.

These gross figures may be broken down in order to reveal the geographic concentration of the Conservative following. The following table lists the election districts and the counties in which the party was able to seat one or more deputies.

Table II

Election District	Name of County won in 1862	1863
Danzig I		Elbing
		Marienburg
Marienwerder VIII		Flatow
		Deutsch-Krone
Potsdam VIII		Jüterbogk
Frankfurt V		Sternberg
Stettin V		Naugardt
		Regenwalde
Stettin VI		Greifenberg
		Kammin
Köslin I	Lauenburg	Lauenburg
	Bütow	Bütow
	Stolp	Stolp
Köslin II		Rummelsburg
		Schlawe
Köslin III		Schievelbein
		Dramburg
Köslin V	Belgard	Belgard
	Neustettin	Neustettin
Breslau I	Guhrau	Guhrau
	Steinau	Steinau
	Wohlau	Wohlau
Breslau II		Militsch
		Trebnitz
Breslau III		Wartenberg
		Namslau
		Oels
Oppeln I	Kreuzburg	Kreuzburg
	Rosenberg	Rosenberg
Oppeln IV	Tost-Gleiwitz	Tost-Gleiwitz
Oppeln VI		Pless
		Rybnick
Oppeln VII	Ratibor	Ratibor
Oppeln IX		Neustadt
		Falkenberg
Liegnitz IV		Bunzlau
		Löwenberg
Merseburg II		Schweinitz
		Wittenberg
Erfurt V		Schleusingen
		Ziegenrück

The evidence from the electors' balloting confirms that gained from the analysis of the voters' vote. The Conservatives had most influence in the administrative districts of Köslin, Breslau, and Oppeln and to a less extent of Stettin. In 1862 all ten of their deputies came from the first three of these districts; in 1863 twenty-two out of thirty-five were elected from the three districts and four more were seated from Stettin. Apart from the administrative district of Köslin the liberals returned more deputies from each of these areas than the Conservatives. Liberal political power spread over the entire state; that of the Conservatives was decidedly localized.

Although in 1862 the Catholic Center party and the Polish party each elected over twice as many deputies as the Conservatives, the campaigns of these two parties were much less significant for the fate of Prussia than those of the other antagonists. Their vote will be analyzed here primarily as an aid to estimating the size of the popular hostility to the Conservatives and the government. As we have seen, the Polish party opposed the latter on all counts. Catholic opinion was divided; but by 1863 it almost completely aligned with the liberals against the government. While disliking the program of the liberals for national unity, the Catholic party staunchly participated in the fight against militarism and absolutism and condemned Bismarck as thoroughly as the liberals. What strength did these two minor parties have in the population?

In 1864 the Prussian state contained 5,200,000 adherents to the Catholic church, excluding the two million Poles, in a total population of nineteen million.[8] The Catholic party was able to elect thirty-three deputies in 1862 and thirty in 1863, or one deputy in 1862 to every 157,575 members of the Church. In the case of the Protestants the ratio in that year was one to 41,320. One would infer from these figures that the Catholic party was unable to monopolize the vote of all the adherents to its religion, and the further evidence in the table given below substantiates that view. Even in the predominantly Catholic counties and election districts where the Catholic party won, it was not able to keep all its followers in line. Where Catholics constituted over ninety per cent of the population and a liberal or a Conservative as well as a Catholic party member was elected, one must conclude that Catholics had voted for a liberal or a Conservative. Since, as we have seen, a Catholic won in the same election district with a Conservative in only three cases and with a liberal in six, one must conclude that more Catholic voters preferred liberals than Conservatives.

[8] Meitzen, *op. cit.*, I, 326.

Catholic Party [9]

Admin. District with Election District Number	County	Winner 1862	Winner 1863	Percentage of Pop. that was Catholic 1864	Percentage of Pop. that was Polish 1861	No. of Deputies to be Elected
Königsberg V	Braunsberg	Menzel	P. Marquardt	90.4		
	Heilsberg	Rehaag (by-election)	Austen	93.4		2
Königsberg VIII	Allenstein	Stock	Stock	92.9	73.9	2
	Rössel	Siebert		88.9	20.6	
Oppeln I	Kreuzburg	Funke		26.1	73.0	2
	Rosenberg			85.2	88.0	
Oppeln II	Oppeln	Osterrath	Foitzick	85.7	74.2	2
Oppeln III	Gr.-Strehlitz	Biernacki	Engelbrecht	94.8	88.4	2
	Lublinitz	v. Renard	v. Renard	94.0	89.7	
Oppeln VI	Pless	Wanjura	Jaensch	89.1	88.9	3
	Rybnik	(by-election)	Schnapka	94.5	88.4	
Oppeln VII	Ratibor	Strzybny	Weltzel	96.4	44.6	2
Oppeln VIII	Kosel	Wolff	Wolff	95.6	84.1	3
	Leobschütz	Münzer	Münzer	91.6	2.3	
Oppeln IX	Neustadt	v. Oppersdorf	Mader	91.4	49.4	2
	Falkenberg			70.1	11.1	
Erfurt II	Heiligenstadt	Zehrt	Frantz	92.2		2
	Worbis	Ellering	Ellering	77.6		
Münster II	Steinfurt	Rohden	Rohden	89.3		2
	Ahaus	Ziegler	Steinmann	96.9		
Münster III	Münster City	Froning	Froning	90.8		2
	Münster County	Scheffer-Boichorst	v. Kleinsorgen	97.5		
	Koesfeld			98.4		
Münster IV	Borken	Schultz	Schultz	95.7		2
	Recklinghausen			98.0		
Münster V	Lüdinghausen	Hobbeling	Hobbeling	98.6		2
	Beckum	A. Reichensperger		98.1		
	Warendorf			98.7		
Minden III	Wiedenbrück	Schmidt	Schmidt	76.1		2
	Paderborn	v. Mallinckrodt	Kleinschmidt	95.0		
	Büren			96.8		
Minden IV	Warburg	Evers	Weber	92.0		2
	Höxter		Albers	88.4		
Arnsberg II	Olpe	Bender		96.4		1
	Meschede			95.8		
Arnsberg VII	Lippstadt	Plassmann		89.2		2
	Arnsberg			95.6		
	Brilon			95.8		
Cologne IV	Sieg	Reinhardt	Reinhardt	88.9		3
	Mülheim			91.1		
	Wipperfürth			91.1		
Düsseldorf VI	Rees	Gützloe		66.9		1
Düsseldorf VII	Kleve	Krebs	Krebs	88.6		1
Düsseldorf IX	Geldern	P. Reichensperger	P. Reichensperger	95.1		2
	Kempen	Franoux	Haanen	96.4		
Aachen IV	Geilenkirchen	Blum	Blum	97.6		2
	Heinsberg		Osterrath	97.7		
	Erkelenz			94.5		
Total	48	33	30			

While the table discloses the relation between Catholic religious affiliation and political attitude in those election districts from which a Catholic representative was elected, further evidence is supplied by a study of those predominantly Catholic districts which did not return party members as deputies. The administrative district Breslau con-

[9] Statistics on Poles from *Zeitschrift des Kgl. Preuss. Statistischen Bureaus,* 1871 (Berlin, 1871), pp. 359 ff. Statistics on Catholic percentages taken from Meitzen, *op. cit.,* IV, 200 ff.

tained five counties overwhelmingly Catholic in religion, but it did not return a single deputy of the Catholic party in either election. In the eighth election district, composed of three counties overwhelmingly Catholic in religion, three liberals won, all members of the Progressive party. In the ninth district, composed of two counties also overwhelmingly Catholic in religion, two liberals of the Left-Center party won. In the administrative district of Düsseldorf eleven counties out of seventeen had a majority belonging to the Catholic Church. The table shows how meager was the success of the party in winning seats in that district. In the administrative district of Cologne the party was even less effective. Nine out of eleven counties were overwhelmingly Catholic in religion; yet only one Catholic deputy was returned at either election. The administrative district of Aachen (eleven counties) was almost entirely Catholic in religion. It elected one Catholic party member in 1862 and two in 1863. In the administrative district of Coblenz where nine out of twelve counties were predominantly Catholic (seven of them overwhelmingly so), the party seated no one in either 1862 or 1863. The neighboring administrative district of Trier (fourteen counties) was almost totally Catholic in religion, but did not elect a single Catholic party member in either year; and the same conditions were true for Hohenzollern (four counties). Although the Catholic party depended upon the Church for its support, religious affiliation did not determine party affiliation. It remained for Bismarck's political conduct to align the Catholics almost solidly in one party. The liberals of the period under discussion successfully appealed to Catholic as well as to Protestant voters.

The counties of Catholic faith consistently manifested slight interest in the elections. The percentage of participation was considerably lower in Catholic counties than in neighboring Protestant ones; and in the Rhineland and Westphalia, where Catholicism predominated, the percentages were from twenty to forty points below those in most of the state. In these two provinces the third class of voters excelled in remaining at home on election day. It was common for less than ten per cent to cast ballots; the second class appeared to the extent of twenty to thirty per cent, and the first class, thirty to fifty per cent. The Catholics manifestly found satisfaction for their needs and wishes in some other way than politics. The rural population participated in general less than half as much as the urban.

In the voters' vote for 1863 the results by class and by the urban-rural distinction for the Catholic party were as follows:

Admin. District	No. of Counties	CATHOLIC											
		Total				Urban				Rural			
		I	II	III	Total	I	II	III	Total	I	II	III	Total
Königsberg	20	4	4	4	4	1	2	2	2	4	4	4	4
Oppeln	16	5	5	5	5	5	5	5	5	5	5	5	5
Erfurt	9	2	2	2	2	2	2	2	2	2	2	2	2
Münster	11	7	7	8	6	6	5	7	6	7	7	7	6
Minden	10	3	4	5	5	1	4	5	5	3	3	5	5
Arnsberg	14	2	2	1	1	2	2	1	1	1	2	1	1
Cologne	11	3	3	3	3	3	2	2	3	3	3	3	3
Düsseldorf	18	3	3	3	3	3	3	3	3	3	2	2	2
Aachen	11	3	4	3	3	1	1	4	3	4	6	4	4
Total	120	32	34	34	32	24	26	31	30	32	34	33	32

The results show a greater homogeneity of political views among all three classes, rural and urban, than was the case even among the Poles. The urban voters manifested somewhat less loyalty to the party than the rural inhabitants. They were more exposed to liberal influence than the latter, and with the movement of population into the towns and cities already under way the urban population in Catholic regions was no longer as solidly Catholic as that of the country districts. Nonetheless, wherever the Catholic party showed political strength it usually did so in all three classes, rural and urban alike.

The Polish population in Prussia numbered about two millions in 1864, or 77,000 to each of the twenty-six deputies elected in 1863. It was mainly concentrated in the administrative districts of Danzig, Marienwerder, Posen, Bromberg, Oppeln, and, to a much less extent, Breslau.[10] The political attitude of the Poles in these districts depended upon cultural conditions, especially upon whether a Polish landholding aristocracy or a Polish middle class was present to provide leadership. In the districts of Oppeln and Breslau the Poles lacked direction. They formed the economically dependent and culturally backward mass of the working people and served under German overlords, many of them old established noble houses with vast estates. In these two administrative districts the Polish party did not win a single seat, in spite of the fact that in one election district in A-D[11] Breslau they constituted a majority of the population and in A-D Oppeln they amounted to fifty-eight per cent of the population, with ten out of sixteen counties being seventy-three per cent or more Polish. In these two administrative districts the Poles had to vote for other parties, and each of the other three parties succeeded in winning sufficient

[10] The Poles in Königsberg and Gumbinnen districts were referred to as Masurians and had become too thoroughly incorporated into German life for them to be interested in Polish nationality politics. They are excluded here from consideration.

[11] Administrative District.

support from them to return some deputies. The effective political activity of the Poles was therefore restricted to the administrative districts Danzig, Marienwerder, Posen, and Bromberg, where the presence of Polish leaders in town and country enabled the population to organize for political action.

The following table shows the distribution of Polish political strength:

Polish Party [12]

Admin. District with Election District Number	County	Winner, 1862	Winner, 1863	Percentage of Pop. that was Polish, 1861	No. of Deputies to be Elected
Danzig III	Neustadt	v. Olszewski	v. Bolewski	42.1	2
	Karthaus	v. Thokarski	v. Thokarski	63.8	
Danzig IV	Berent		Wagener	52.1	2
	Stargard			49.1	
Marienwerder III	Löbau	Bartoszkiewicz	v. Sulerczycki	79.2	1
Marienwerder IV	Strassburg		v. Lyskowski	63.8	1
	Konitz	Dekowski	Dekowski	54.3	2
Marienwerder VII	Schlochau			13.0	
Posen II	Posen County	v. Chlapowski	v. Chlapowski	75.4	2
	Obornik	v. Plater	v. Lubienski	52.3	
Posen III	Samter	v. Lubienski	Motty	59.8	2
	Birnbaum			22.1	
Posen IV	Meseritz		Gawrecky	11.2	2
	Bomst			37.0	
Posen V	Buk	v. Cieszkowski	v. Cieszkowski	56.6	2
	Kosten	A. v. Zoltowski	A. v. Zoltowski	76.9	
Posen VI	Fraustadt	Respondek	Respondek	22.6	3
	Kröben	v. Prusinowski	v. Stablewski	58.9	
		v. Stablewski			
Posen VII	Schrimm	v. Bentowski	v. Potulicki	73.7	
	Schroda	v. Dzialynski	v. Zychlinski	79.8	3
	Wreschen	v. Guttry	v. Guttry	87.9	
Posen VIII	Pleschen	v. Niegolewski	v. Niegolewski	79.6	2
	Krotoschin	M. v. Zoltowski	M. v. Zoltowski	65.7	
Posen IX	Adelnau	v. Morawski	Szumann	82.0	2
	Schildberg	Pilaski	Pilaski	80.9	
Bromberg III	Schubin		Wagner	53.8	2
	Inowraclaw	Kantak	Kantak	65.2	
Bromberg IV	Mogilno	Libelt	Libelt	69.9	
	Gnesen	v. Janiszewski	v. Janiszewski	76.9	3
	Wongrowiec	v. Koszutski	Danielewski	72.4	
Total	30	23	26		

In A-D Danzig the Poles were numerous in four counties, which with proper respect for justice the liberal election districting law of 1860 had organized into two election districts. Karthaus (63.8 per cent Polish) and Neustadt (42.1 per cent Polish) formed election district III and returned two Polish deputies in the elections of both 1862 and 1863. Stargard (49.1 per cent Polish) and Berent (52.1 per cent Polish) did not contain quite enough Poles to assure victory. When

---

[12] Statistics on the Polish population are taken from "Versuch einer Statistik der Nationalitäten im Preussischen Staate für das Jahr 1867. *Zeitschrift des Kgl. Preus. Statistischen Bureaus,* 1871 (Berlin, 1871), pp. 359 ff.

the Germans all held together, as they did in 1862, they were able to win both seats for that election district (IV).[13] When they became somewhat negligent and the percentage of those casting ballots declined, as was the case in Berent in 1863, the Germans lost one seat to the Polish party.

The situation in A-D Marienwerder resembled that in Danzig. The Poles made up a substantial majority of the population in the two counties (Löbau, 79.2 per cent Polish, and Strassburg, 63.8 per cent Polish), each of which formed an election district. The party won in Löbau in both elections, but it failed in Strassburg in 1862. In election district VII, containing the counties Konitz (54.3 per cent Polish) and Schlochau (13 per cent Polish) the party was able to return one deputy out of two at each of the elections. In some four other counties in Marienwerder (Stuhm, Thorn, Kulm, and Schwetz) the Poles formed between forty per cent and fifty per cent of the population but failed to return a single deputy from them in either election.

Five counties in A-D Bromberg had a majority of Polish inhabitants. Organized into two election districts (III and IV) the Poles won four out of five seats in 1862 and made a clean sweep in the next year. In four other counties where the population was from twenty per cent to thirty-five per cent Polish, they were unable to gain a single place.

The Poles constituted 58.9 per cent of the population in A-D Posen. They had a majority of seventy-five per cent or more in eight counties and one of fifty-five to sixty-nine per cent in five others. In only five counties did they amount to forty per cent or less of the inhabitants. The vote went along straight nationality lines. In the election districts where they had a large majority (II, V, VII, VIII, and IX) the Poles voted overwhelmingly for their own candidates and won every seat in each election. In election districts III, IV, and VI the Polish population formed a large minority. Two of these districts were composed of a county with a Polish majority and one with a large German majority. The Poles were unable to win more than one seat at either election in any of the three districts. The Germans gained the other place. In election district I the Polish people were clearly outnumbered and each time lost to a German.

In the voters' balloting in 1863, the Polish party won in election districts comprising thirty counties. A analysis by class of the total vote and of the urban and rural vote reveals the following results:

---

[13] *Kölnische Zeitung*, May 10, 1862.

Admin. District	No. of Counties	POLISH											
		Total				Urban				Rural			
		I	II	III	Total	I	II	III	Total	I	II	III	Total
Danzig	8	3	4	4	4	1	1	3	2	3	4	4	4
Marienwerder	13	4	4	4	4	4	4	4	4	4	4	4	4
Posen	18	11	13	15	15	6	8	14	14	12	13	16	15
Bromberg	9	5	5	5	5	5	5	5	5	5	5	5	5
Total		23	26	28	28	16	18	26	25	24	26	29	28

Although not to the same extent, the Polish party was strong in the urban centers as well as in the rural areas. It was almost as powerful in the second class as in the third, and its showing in the first class was not far behind that in the second, particularly in the country. These results can be explained on the grounds that wherever it is able to win at all, a party representing a culturally backward national minority should make a good showing in all three classes. The party should be, as it was, relatively weakest in the first class where the influence of the Germans should be greatest, and strongest in the third class, where numerically speaking the Poles should predominate. The Germans and some Poles formed the upper, wealthy social groups in these areas, but the Poles made up the mass of the population. While Polish numbers in the third class were unable to win an election, with leadership and voting aid from upper-class Poles in one or both the other voting classes, they could and did win.

An analysis of the statistics for the elections of 1862 and 1863 reveals that in those election districts in which the Poles won, the voters in all three classes, urban and rural, participated in the balloting consistently to a greater extent than the Germans did in districts of purely German nationality. Government pressure in 1863 did not succeed in reducing appreciably the Polish participation in any class. In those districts where the Poles won, the percentage was highest in Class I—in the large majority of counties between sixty per cent and eighty-four per cent; it was almost as high in Class II; and it was some ten to twenty points lower in Class III. Few solidly German counties could show such a record.

The interpretation of the election results varied according to the interests, the wishes, and the party affiliation of the individual. To the liberals the evidence seemed so overwhelming that they scarcely bothered to argue the magnitude of their victory. They took it for granted that the country supported them. Deputy von Unruh acknowledged in the Lower House that the liberals had won with the support of a majority in the first and second classes and that the participation of the third class in the election had been small. He defied the government, however, to change the election law so as to induce the third class to vote in larger number than at present. "The present election law has not developed out of our principles," he said, "and we have nothing against changing it so that the homeopathic share for the third class is made the proper amount."[14] In every case the liberals maintained that they represented at least the educated and propertied groups in the population, but they also declared that they spoke for the vast majority of the others. They claimed the support of both the voters and the non-voters and challenged the government to submit the issues to another election.

The King never could understand why the public acclaimed him so enthusiastically and at the same time elected his enemies to the Landtag. It lay beyond his comprehension that a monarch with powers actually limited by the constitution could also be popular, and that his popularity rested upon his reputation for being loyal to that document. He was deeply touched by the deputations of loyal peasants and pastors led by a local Junker which the Conservative party organized and sent to court. They typified the Prussian folk as he wished them to be, and he was readily convinced that these few thousand carefully controlled groups represented the country far better than the liberal Lower House.[15]

Of the two ministers, von Roon and Bismarck, the former asserted to the Lower House quite frankly that he regarded the development of the system of political parties since 1848 as a "great misfortune." He claimed that many very respectable and honorable persons were not interested in political parties; they belonged, he said, to "the party of order, the peace-loving party," the party undisturbed by political problems and tasks. They were loyal to the King, his government and the constitution, he said, and did not vote because of the terror employed by the liberals. If the government could stir them to vote, it would have an "overwhelming majority" of supporters in the Landtag; in the absence of this overt support, von Roon inferred, the government would continue to act on the assumption that this majority did favor it over the liberals.[16]

Bismarck denied the basis of representation. How do you know, he asked the Lower House, that the population supports you? According to the constitution, he continued, both houses represent the entire people. The fact that the Lower House was composed of elected repre-

[14] *Adress-Debatte*, pp. 264-65; *Kölnische Zeitung*, May 9, 1862.
[15] See Zechlin, *op. cit.*, p. 207; *Die Innere Politik*, pp. 128-31, 149.
[16] *Adress-Debatte*, pp. 159-60.

sentatives gave it, according to the constitution, no higher right than the House of Lords. Furthermore, he said, only a small percentage of the population was sufficiently interested to vote for the liberals. It was doubtful whether this small percentage actually followed the House's activity with full understanding and knew where this activity was leading the country. In June, 1865, he asserted to the Lower House:

> Most voters scarcely bother to form a personal opinion whether or not an army can exist with one less year of service, whether the state can get along with somewhat less or more taxes. At any rate they would be glad if it were possible. If an educated gentleman superior to them in insight and a Royal official in addition comes forth as election candidate and says to them: they deceive you dreadfully on that matter; an excellent army is possible with two years of military service; the state can exist with much less taxes; you are overburdened— then the people would agree and say: the gentleman speaks sensibly, our vote costs us nothing, let us try it. If what he says succeeds, then well and good; if he cannot do it, he will come again and say: it has not yet succeeded, but you must have the two years' service. The confidence of the people in the King is so great that they say to themselves: the King would not permit them to ruin the country or put it in debt. As a result of former traditions the people underestimate the significance of the constitution. I am convinced that the confidence which they place in the wisdom of the King will not cause them disappointment.[17]

Leaving no loophole for the validity of statistical evidence, Bismarck asserted that numbers of votes or signatures of loyalty addresses had "no great value," for "we live not under the regime of general suffrage but under the rule of the King and the laws." "You do not feel and think like the Prussian people," he said to the Lower House liberals in January, 1864. "If the Prussian people felt like you, one would simply have to say that the Prussian state had lived beyond its term, and the time had come in which it must give way to another historical creation. But we have not yet come so far!"[18] Bismarck expressed the belief of his Conservative colleagues and of the King that on crucial issues votes must be not counted but weighed. In his view the King and a handful of Conservatives were right; everyone else was wrong.

[17] Rothfels, *op. cit.*, pp. 278-79.
[18] *Adress-Debatte*, pp. 260-61; Rothfels, *op. cit.*, pp. 26, 209-10.

13 / Prussia — Conservative or Liberal?

DURING the years of the New Era and the constitutional conflict was the Prussian population Conservative or liberal, or was it indifferent to the entire conflict? The data analyzed in the preceding chapters have been taken from a variety of aspects of Prussian life and should enable certain conclusions to be drawn. Consideration of the issues, of the organization of political groups and of the actions taken by the government, by the Conservatives and by the liberal parties leads to the view that the Prussian people overwhelmingly opposed the preservation of the vestiges of the Old Regime and desired reform.

The most telling evidence was supplied by the government itself, particularly in 1863. The ministry and King used every possible form of pressure to insure an election in favor of the Conservatives. They requested the people actively and positively to vote for those candidates who supported the government. When the voters remained about as hostile to Conservatism as before and the percentage of nonvoters as large, the government claimed that the election results were relatively insignificant and that the non-voters were satisfied with the existing order of affairs. The inconsistency of ministerial action and ministerial words could hardly have been greater. With all the power of coercion at its disposal the government was unable to secure the active political support of the people.

The statistics show that a vast majority of those casting ballots favored the liberals; but what about those who failed to go to the polls? Does the fact that the non-voters did not actively support the government indicate that they opposed the existing regime and favored liberalism? In view of the size of this element of the population one must find ways to provide an answer. One possible way of doing so is to consider the nature of the issues at stake in the election. These were of state-wide significance; they dealt with general problems of the character of government, national and local, the abolition of privilege, the limitation of military burdens and of public financial costs, and the unification of the German nation. Everyone, irrespective of geographic area or social and economic position, was to be more or less affected by the outcome of these issues. The problems concerned general ideals and did not appeal to the politics of special interests. They dealt with the character of the total culture: should it be liberal or should it be that of the society of the Old Regime? From the politics of those active in public affairs and voting one should be able to draw some inferences about the attitude of the non-voting members of the groups in Prussian society with similar interests.

The validity of the method of inference is subject to two major conditions, the extent of understanding of the issues and the amount of compulsion which the government and the Conservatives were able to exert on the people. Not all the areas of economic and social stagnation voted Conservative: many of them turned liberal because, through various means, usually the presence of a few liberal leaders in the area, the population had learned to judge the status quo by liberal ideals. Even in districts subject to intense governmental and Junker coercion liberal ideas and hopes were able to withstand the pressure.

Subject to the conditions stated above, a significant basis for an over-all analysis of political attitude may be had in the social classes— nobility, bourgeoisie and middle class, and peasantry (the proletariat was still too small and too lacking in class consciousness to count) — and in the occupations. Of less importance were religion and nationality. Some, but far from all, Catholics voted with the Catholic party. Most Poles, the only large national minority, supported candidates of their own nationality and a program for the ultimate restoration of an independent Poland.

In all parts of the state some nobles chose liberalism. Most of those doing so resided in East Prussia and in the two Western provinces, and the fewest in Pomerania, Brandenburg, and Silesia. The economic interests of the liberal nobility and of the Conservative nobility were usually similar. As a rule, the latter were found in agriculture, with some having industrial interests as well, but the liberal nobility in East Prussia was likewise interested almost entirely in agriculture and in small industries, like distilleries, for processing some of its products.

In the Western provinces and in Silesia, especially Upper Silesia, certain nobles were becoming heavily involved in mining and the iron and steel industry. Some belonged to families recently ennobled, while others traced their aristocratic lineage to earlier centuries. An accurate statistical estimate cannot be given. Contemporaries, both middle-class and aristocratic, regarded the nobility as predominantly Conservative; but one cannot infer that the conflict between Conservatism and liberalism altogether expressed a struggle between the noble and the middle classes. Even apart from the presence of many liberal nobles in the Lower House, many others actively supported liberalism in their own districts. Nor were they confined to the most moderate wing; nobles were found in each liberal party. A few examples of liberal aristocrats may suffice: in Silesia, Count Henckel von Donnersmarck, Prince Hatzfeldt, Count Dohna of Katzenau, Count York, Count Conrad Dyhrn, Prince Carl Schönaich-Carolath; in Nieder-und Ober Barnim Baron von Eckardstein and Count von Hacke. In East Prussia they were too numerous to name, but the von Saucken family may be cited as an example.[1]

The bourgeoisie and middle class accepted almost entirely the liberal ideals. Wherever industrialism had developed, one could expect liberalism to keep pace with it; and commerce on other than a purely local scale meant usually the support of the same point of view. Iron and steel, textiles, banking, railroads, wholesale commerce, construction—these and many lesser economic enterprises meant as a rule that the participants voted liberal. Irrespective of geographic location, these interests normally wished change in the direction of freedom and national unity. One is entitled to agree with the liberals that the owners of movable property belonged to their side. Whereas the land owners were divided in their affiliation, some being liberal, especially those of middle-class origin, and others being Conservative, in the case of industrialists and merchants only the rare exceptions were Conservative. Although any copy of a contemporary newspaper near election time will provide all the evidence one can wish, a few examples may be chosen. In late autumn, 1862, about a hundred merchants and industrialists in the Rhineland and Westphalia signed a petition to the King to dismiss the Bismarck ministry. It was estimated that the signers represented a taxed wealth of 300,000,000

[1] *Kölnische Zeitung,* April 19, 1862; von Bernhardi, *op. cit.,* III, 62, 66; *National Zeitung,* Oct. 27, 1863; *Königsberg Hartungsche Zeitung,* May 27, 1862; von Bernhardi, *op. cit.,* III, 45-46, 69-73; *Polizei-Bericht, Breslau,* Nov. 6, 1863; *National Zeitung,* Nov. 24, 1861; Parisius, *von Hoverbeck,* II, 65.

Thalers. In April, 1863, a hundred iron industrialists of the Rhineland and Westphalia sent a message of full support to the Lower House. In Memel, Görlitz, Halle, Breslau, in every town and city, the local merchants, bankers, and industrialists supported the liberals.[2]

The handworkers were divided in their political affiliation. In Breslau, for example, the police reported that they voted for the Progressive party, and from the list of electors in Königsberg returned in April, 1862, it is evident that that party found many loyal supporters among them.[3] Three master bakers, fifteen master cabinetmakers, a worker in leather, a master tailor, two master masons, seven master cobblers were selected alongside seventy merchants, nine factory-owners, sixteen doctors of philosophy, and a sprinkling of nearly every occupation in the city. In Minden the handicraftsmen voted in 1862 almost without exception for liberals.[4] The smaller towns and the rural areas, however, remained strongholds of guild sentiment, and insofar as they were politically active, the handicraftsmen usually voted Conservative.[5] Many persons who called themselves handicraftsmen had become capitalistic entrepreneurs employing other craftsmen as wage-earners. Since the guilds had been disintegrating for at least half a century, it would be impossible on the basis of present evidence to state who was a bona fide craftsman and who had risen economically into the bourgeoisie or declined into the status of factory worker or day laborer. It is nonetheless clear from the newspaper reports that the extent to which the handworkers voted liberal depended upon the degree of their understanding of the value of freedom of occupation and of their courage in facing a new type of economic life.

Equally complicated was the political attitude of the peasantry. The peasant's political behavior was decided by the degree of his understanding of the issues and the extent of his economic independence. The peasants who owned their land were most likely to be liberal. The rural laborers usually followed the politics of their master, who, if a Conservative, marched them to the voting place and observed how they voted. In many areas the peasant population was indifferent from sheer ignorance. The *Volkszeitung* published a story from the province of Posen about a local pastor's having persuaded the peasants

[2] "Der Preussische Landtag von 1863," *Deutsche Vierteljahrschrift* (Stuttgart, 1863), No. 3, p. 124; *National Zeitung*, April 1, 1863; *Königsberg Hartungsche Zeitung*, Dec. 29, 1861.

[3] *Polizei-Bericht*, Breslau, May 31, 1862; *Königsberg Hartungsche Zeitung*, April 29, 1862.

[4] *Kölnische Zeitung*, April 30, 1862.

[5] See *Königsberg Hartungsche Zeitung*, Sept. 19, Oct. 24, 1861.

of a village to subscribe to the *Preussiches Volksblatt,* a Conservative paper, only to learn subsequently that the postman by mistake had subscribed instead for the *Volkszeitung,* a Progressive paper. The peasants expressed themselves as very content with this journal and proceeded to vote liberal. In some districts the peasants even belonged to the National Verein.[6] That they were capable of acting in their own interest when adequately informed and encouraged was attested to by the Conservative political leader, Moritz von Blanckenburg, who wrote to Minister von Roon after the election of 1861 as follows:

> The outcome of the elections in Pomerania was decided by the peasants, who, excited by county judges and Jews, take an attitude most decidedly against us. They were persuaded that we were against the King! They believed this all the more easily because the administration here often went against us. Then one dangled before them the prospect of a new law on county government by which they would have the majority and would be able to throw off all communal burdens. The meetings were everywhere stormy; they scarcely listened to me, they were so entranced![7]

Von Blanckenburg's realistic estimate was confirmed by a writer in *Die Zeit* at the time of the election of 1862. The peasantry, the latter stated, knew that the interests of the King were not identical with those of the nobility. Except for a tiny minority the peasantry had learned to distinguish between royalty and Junkerism and was ready to defend its interests even against the former. It understood, he continued, that the liberal reform of county government had nothing to do with the rights of the crown, that this reform was in harmony with the size of the contributions, especially in the form of taxes, made to the state. He concluded that the feudal party had already lost the natural basis of its power, the agreement of views between itself and the peasantry, and he was very hopeful about the prospects of reform.[8]

Even though the writer in *Die Zeit* was too optimistic, by and large the peasant frequently showed as much independence of spirit about voting against the wishes of the authorities as any townsman. Even

---

[6] See *Königsberg Hartungsche Zeitung,* Nov. 27, 1861; *Kölnische Zeitung,* May 2, 1862; *Königsberg Hartungsche Zeitung,* May 2, 1862; Regierungs-Bezirk, Breslau, *Zeitungs-Bericht für Jan.-Febr., 1861; Tagesbericht,* No. 42, Feb. 19, 1861, citing *Volkszeitung,* No. 41; *Volkszeitung,* April 11, 1862.

[7] Von Roon, *op. cit.,* II, 55-56.

[8] *Kölnische Zeitung,* April 26, 1862.

at the risk of losing their positions, many Schulzes voted liberal.[9] The encouragement of a liberal large landowner or the proximity to a town from which liberal ideas could spread was enough to win them to the liberal party. Nonetheless, the land population of the lower class suffered most from cultural backwardness and was least inclined of any of the social groups to participate in the elections. Its indifference in large part accounted for the small vote in the third class. It tended under pressure not to vote at all; or, as one Schulze did, it signed a petition supporting the Lower House and another supporting the King.[10] That its interests lay with liberalism and that if informed and freely allowed to, it would have voted liberal seem beyond question.

Apart from the higher personnel, the Landrats and certain categories that were kept under strong government observation, government officials supported the liberal parties to such an extent that the Conservatives became furious and the Bismarck government determined to regain political control of them. The justice officials, being more independent of the government than the ones in the administrative branches, participated most aggressively in the liberal cause; but the great majority of officials in all lines of service was actively or passively liberal. Many preferred to be passive because of the ruthless policies of control applied by the Bismarck government.

The teachers and professors aligned themselves in the main with the officials and businessmen. The university professors enjoyed sufficient independence by virtue of their tenure to act openly in support of the liberal parties. The teachers, especially in the villages, were like the peasants subject to discipline and pressure; but many instances are known of their open defiance of the injunctions of their Conservative superiors. Although as in the case of the other occupational groups the teaching profession showed many Conservative members, a notorious example being the anti-Semitic, vituperative and vulgar Wantrup of Elbing, this profession as a whole sided definitely with liberalism. Accustomed to thinking and acting in terms of

[9] See Parisius' statement in Abg. H., *St. B.*, Nov. 11, 1863; I, 22-23. *Ibid.*, 1864, Vol. IV, No. 95, pp. 619-21. *Kölnische Zeitung*, April 30, 1862; and all issues of newspapers at election time.

[10] *Königsberg Hartungsche Zeitung*, Nov. 15, 1862. See also the story of the village of Steingrund. Fifteen members of the community had signed the petition of loyalty to the King referred to above. At the election in 1863 out of ninety-six who were eligible only fourteen actually voted. Of these fourteen, seven were for and seven were against the Conservatives. See Abg. H., *St. B.*, Nov. 28, 1863; I, 199-200.

ideals, it felt most at home in the camp of those who looked toward the future.[11]

Religious affiliation played an important role in influencing the political action of Catholics and Jews but not of Protestants. The Catholics with political interests usually voted for their own Catholic Center party, although especially in the election of 1863 many of them, including members of the regular clergy, transferred their vote from right-wing Catholic candidates to liberals. The Jews, a minority group still suffering from social and some legal restrictions, were consistently liberal; but the Mennonites around Elbing voted in 1863 for Conservatives. Both liberals and Conservatives were found among the Protestants, with the pastors being predominantly Conservative and active in support of that party.[12]

Even the military personnel was divided in its affiliation. Officers and soldiers stood under such rigid control that few were able to do other than follow government orders; but occasional reports appeared in the press of soldiers and officers voting liberal. Especially reserve officers tended to do so, to the anger of the regular army officers; and retired officers, many of whom had left the army at an early date in order to go into the civilian pursuits of agriculture and business, frequently voted liberal. The fact that Major General von Syburg in Berlin and Lieutenant Colonel von Stosch, chief of the general staff in Posen, voted liberal, that the non-commissioned officers in 1861 were instructed to vote for Minister of War von Roon and cast their ballots instead for the liberal Kühne, that the leaders in Gumbinnen in support of the re-election of two liberal deputies were almost all military and officials—this kind of evidence shows that the army itself contained at all levels personnel of liberal views.[13]

By way of summary, the contemporary analysis of votes by occupation in a few areas may be given. A correspondent from Swinemünde to the *Königsberg Hartungsche Zeitung* (May 16, 1862) reported the following distribution of the votes in the election of that year. "For the Conservative candidate voted all noble estate-owners, all pastors,

---

[11] The evidence may be found in the contemporary press, especially at election time. One example may be offered. The *Ostpreussische Zeitung*, a Conservative paper of Königsberg, published in November, 1863, a list of 131 royal officials and teachers in Königsberg who voted for the Progressive party. See *Kölnische Zeitung*, Nov. 7, 1863.

[12] See the evidence in the contemporary press.

[13] Von Bernhardi, *op. cit.*, IV, 16, 166; *Königsberg Hartungsche Zeitung*, Nov. 16, 1861; *Augsburg Allgemeine Zeitung*, Oct. 25, 1863; *Kölnische Zeitung*, April 30, 1862.

all military, all country school teachers, a number of inspectors, royal and noble foresters, a few so-called petty rural persons, and very few peasants. For the candidates of the liberal party voted all judges and attorneys, all merchants and factory-owners, all Jews, almost all middle-class large land owners and peasant owners, almost all handworkers, hotel and restaurant proprietors, town officials, in general the electors of the towns with scarcely any exception." For the election of 1861 it was reported to the same paper (April 2, 1862) that the distribution of votes among the three parties, Progressive, Constitutional, and Conservative, in the town district of Danzig was 30:3:7, and in the rural district 14:4:20. The towns were notoriously liberal. Practically every one with a population above 20,000 voted in opposition to the government.[14] One Conservative deputy in the Landtag as early as March, 1861, felt called upon to question the assertion that only the liberals represented the towns. He claimed that all four towns in his district cast a majority for him.[15] The small number of the towns in his district reveals why they did: they were scarcely to be distinguished from the rural areas around them. In the rural communities of the West Havelland district the vote in 1861 went two-thirds for liberals and one-third for Conservatives.[16]

What explanations were offered for the small participation in the elections? First of all, the left-wing liberals who favored universal manhood suffrage blamed the three-class system of voting. It scarcely seemed worthwhile to cast a ballot in the third class. The open ballot kept many away, especially those who might suffer material hardship as a result of revealing their political affiliation. Concern for earning a living prevented others from taking a day off to vote. The long distance to the polling place discouraged many. Where political agitation had not penetrated, the population tended to remain indifferent to politics, especially in rural areas. Some employers would not release their workers to vote, and some peasants, particularly the landless rural workers, when ordered by their lord to vote Conservative, preferred not to vote at all rather than to go against their liberal views. In certain areas the liberals felt so sure of victory that they failed to be very active and lost some votes. Since the representative system was new many had not yet become accustomed to voting; they preferred to continue their pre-1848 political habits. All in all, under

[14] *Volkszeitung,* May 2, 1862.
[15] Abg. H., *St. B.,* March 8, 1861; I, 419.
[16] See *Königsberg Hartungsche Zeitung,* Nov. 23, 1861.

the circumstances the great extent of the participation in the elections is surprising.[17]

The evidence, in sum, substantiates the following conclusions: that the urban population, irrespective of occupation, was overwhelmingly liberal and hostile to the government, that the rural people were more Conservative but that, irrespective of whether they voted or did not vote, they were largely hostile to the government; that the relatively small percentage of those actually casting a ballot does not detract from the facts that the vast majority of the Prussian population who understood the situation actively opposed the government and supported reform, and that the vast majority of the others would have done so if they had understood their own stake in the conflict. Whether Protestant or Catholic, rural or urban, Prussia was actually or potentially—and to an overwhelming extent—in favor of liberal reform within the country. The people usually split along religious lines on the question of national unity; but except for a handful of supporters of the Old Regime they wished liberal reforms and were unanimously opposed to the Conservative government.

The liberals and the general public were much more able to comprehend issues than they were to know how to implement policies. They lacked experience in self-government and were timid about taking steps which might lead to the use of physical force by either side. The fact that the Prussian people did not take up arms and rebel or refuse to pay taxes in no way implies approval of government action. The population expected that time would help in solving these problems and did not think that extreme measures against the handful of leaders which had the instruments of physical coercion at its disposal would assist in introducing reforms.

The liberals made their mistake in failing to be thoroughly liberal. They remained bound by a class prejudice of superiority over the masses and did not perceive the possibility of the peaceful organization of the population against the government. They missed opportunities during the New Era for developing popular support which could be used in an emergency. A new election law based on equal and universal manhood suffrage and the secret ballot was indispensable in order to provide the masses with an incentive to become politically active. An election under such conditions would have enabled the

---

[17] See *Königsberg Hartungsche Zeitung*, Nov. 23, Dec. 12, 1861; July 5, 1862; *Volkszeitung*, May 8, 1862; *National Zeitung*, Nov. 26, 1861; *Zeitungs-Bericht für Okt.-Nov. 1861*; Regierungs-Bezirk, Aachen, Dec. 6, 1861; *Augsburg Allgemeine Zeitung*, Oct. 22, 1863; *Kölnische Zeitung*, Oct. 30, Nov. 3, 1863.

opposition to supply convincing evidence to the King and the Conservatives about the extent of the latter's unpopularity. As long as the class system of voting persisted, as long as public organizations, like political parties, the National Verein, and many others, remained instruments largely of a middle-class élite, the liberals lacked open mass support, and the Conservatives could deny that the general public disapproved of the existing order of things. In this situation the only evidence capable of convincing the Conservatives of their widespread unpopularity would have had to be that of physical action, something to which the liberals and the masses were averse. When the crisis struck them, the liberals were unprepared. They had no resources beyond those of the New Era to throw into the fray. The King and the Conservative government controlled all the instruments of organized political power in the state. With a loyal army and with a bureaucracy shaped and trained during nearly two centuries of absolutism, they possessed the means for continuing to govern in spite of verbal resistance.

The outcome of the constitutional conflict lies beyond the scope of this work; but the historical significance of the events must be indicated. Although the struggle dragged on for another two and a half years, a disinterested observer must have concluded at the beginning of 1864 that the liberals were defeated. They had no plan and no means of winning against the government. Bismarck continued in power; the administrative apparatus functioned as usual; the people paid their taxes; the government expended the public money; the soldiers remained loyal; and as a crowning act the hated ministry successfully participated in the war against Denmark. The denunciation of all these deeds by the liberals handicapped the hated government very little and failed utterly to block or even to delay its actions. The march of industrialism continued vigorously, and the people were more prosperous than they had ever been. The liberals were so successful in their private economy that they eased the government's road to victory with mounting tax returns. Although Bismarck knew too little economics to be aware of the fact, he enjoyed the blessing of coming to power during an upswing of the business cycle. He was not merely powerful, he was fortunate.

The liberals did not surrender until Bismarck won the Austro-Prussian War and set about unifying Germany in the *klein-deutsch* sense. They had held out during two wars, in itself an almost unparalleled achievement; but when the second war gained one of their major objectives, German unity, they succumbed along with the

Austrians. The liberals had opposed the King, the military reforms and Bismarck partly because they had feared a repetition of the defeat of 1806. They had not believed that an unreformed, increasingly militaristic Prussia could muster the resources and arouse the patriotic spirit necessary to protect itself. They saw their moral and political assumptions being wrecked, and they came to believe in the superior efficiency of *Realpolitik*.

The solution to the Prussian and German conflicts which Bismarck imposed had facets that affected the Hohenzollern King, the Conservatives, and the liberals, each in a different way. The ruler preserved as much absolutism as one could possibly command under a free constitution. The King remained in Prussia a sovereign by the grace of God, and in the German Reich his authority was scarcely less impressive. Bismarck retained the military reorganization, and by his use of the army in three wars of national unification he assured in the German Reich the popular as well as the legal continuation of Prussian militarism. For the King and the Conservatives he succeeded in keeping the social and political system of the Old Regime in local government and imparted to a declining agrarian nobility a new political vigor which kept that group in authority for two generations. With respect to the constitution he made the gap theory valid and kept it as an ultimate sanction for a government that remained to a large degree irresponsible. He transferred the legal position of the ministry in Prussia to the chancellorship in the Reich. In each case the government, declared nominally responsible in law, actually wielded authority out of harmony with the fact of constitutionality. To the liberals Bismarck gave national unity and a considerable amount of free economic legislation, although not all that they wished. The King on the whole was satisfied with the results. Many Conservatives disliked intensely German unification and the liberal economic legislation. The liberals remained disgruntled with the vestiges of absolutism and caste. The remarkable fact was, however, that this political master, Bismarck, made it impossible for any one of these forces fundamentally to change the system which he proposed to introduce. Bismarck had won not merely over the liberals but in different respects over the Conservatives and the King as well.

The political and moral effects of the victory of *Realpolitik* were scarcely felt by the King and the Conservatives. The ruler and his Conservative supporters believed in power politics and practiced them in internal as well as international affairs. They continued as they always had to pursue *Interessenpolitik* under the guise of moral principles. Bismarck's victory meant the dominance of these methods in Germany in an age in which Western peoples were seeking to introduce universal principles of liberal conduct.

In the case of the liberals the success of *Realpolitik* destroyed the moral foundations of their beliefs. Wrong had proved to be effective; right had failed. Most of them swung to the side of Bismarck and joined the host of his adorers. The irreconcilable ones were doomed to continue a life of frustration. Until the end of the Second Reich in 1918 the pro-Bismarck liberals could not be depended upon to support a principle in a crisis; the anti-Bismarck ones could talk little but principles. Deprived of the opportunity to learn responsibility in government and faced with the reality of living in an anti-liberal society, the latter continued to defend generalities. Germany became a country largely of doctrinaires and believers in *Machtpolitik* à la Bismarck.

Did Bismarck settle the constitutional conflict in Prussia? The answer can only be that he did not, that he glossed it over by nationalism and by success in international relations. He solved none of the crucial internal social and political problems; he only postponed a settlement. The evidence for this conclusion is found in the fact that within less than three generations the Bismarckian Reich was destroyed, the Junker Conservatives were ruined, and the Hohenzollerns had lost their throne. The predictions of the liberals during the Constitutional conflict have proved to be basically accurate. In the case of Germany, history has substantiated the belief in the validity of moral principles in public life.

APPENDIX A

Population Increase, 1849-1861, in Twenty Leading Prussian Cities*

Name of City	No. of Population 1849	1861	Percentage Increase 1849-1861
Berlin	423,902	547,571	29.17
Breslau	110,702	145,589	31.51
Cologne	94,789	120,568	28.95
Königsberg	75,240	94,579	25.70
Magdeburg	70,488	86,301	22.43
Danzig	63,917	82,765	29.48
Aachen	50,533	59,941	18.61
Stettin	47,202	64,431	36.50
Posen	44,963	51,232	13.94
Potsdam	39,864	41,824	4.91
Elberfeld	38,663	56,307	45.63
Krefeld	36,134	50,584	39.99
Barmen	35,989	49,787	38.33
Halle	33,848	42,976	26.96
Erfurt	32,224	37,012	14.85
Frankfurt	29,969	36,557	21.98
Düsseldorf	26.463	41.292	56.03
Coblenz	25,318	28,525	12.66
Münster	24,664	27,332	10.81
Elbing	21,637	25,539	18.03

* Zeitschrift des Kgl. Preussischen Statistischen Bureaus, 1863, pp. 236-39.

APPENDIX B

Distribution of Railroad Mileage, 1862*

Administrative District	Miles of Railroads	Miles per sq. Mile of Area	Miles per 1000 Population
Königsberg	21.3	0.05	0.02
Gumbinnen	12.6	0.04	0.01
Danzig	16.9	0.11	0.03
Marienwerder	10.2	0.03	0.01
Posen	26.1	0.08	0.02
Bromberg	30.2	0.14	0.05
Potsdam	58.1	0.15	0.03
Frankfurt	49.3	0.14	0.05
Stettin	23.5	0.09	0.03
Köslin	13.6	0.05	0.02
Stralsund	......	......	......
Breslau	42.6	0.17	0.03
Liegnitz	37.5	0.15	0.03
Oppeln	73.5	0.30	0.06
Magdeburg	46.8	0.22	0.06
Merseburg	46.4	0.24	0.05
Erfurt	01.3	0.02	......
Münster	19.4	0.14	0.04
Minden	22.9	0.23	0.04
Arnsberg	52.7	0.37	0.07
Cologne	22.5	0.31	0.03
Düsseldorf	52.7	0.52	0.04
Coblenz	29.7	0.27	0.05
Trier	21.8	0.16	0.04
Aachen	13.7	0.18	0.02
Total	745.5	0.14	0.04

* Zeitschritf des Kgl. Preussischen Statistischen Bureaus (1863), pp. 213-14. A mile was reckoned as 7,532.5 meters.

APPENDIX C

Data on the Deputies in Five Prussian Political Assemblies*

Occupational Groups	Prussian Nat. Assembly, 1848 Deputies (398)	Lower House of Landtag			
		I 1849 (350)	IV 1855 (350)	VI 1862 (348)	IX 1866 (347)
Agrarians	77-19.3%	61-17.4%	78-22.3%	82-23.6%	83-23.9%
Merchants, industrialists	30- 7.5%	24- 6.9%	15- 4.3%	25- 7.2%	28- 8.1%
Officials, excluding justice and teachers	38- 9.5%	56-16.0%	118-33.7%	45-12.9%	71-20.5%
Justice officials	78-19.6%	73-20.9%	56-16.0%	93-26.7%	54-15.6%
Retired officials and officers	1-0.25%	7- 2.0%	18- 5.1%	17- 4.9%	25- 7.2%
Officers	....	3- 0.9%	9- 2.6%	1- 0.3%	1- 0.3%
Community and corporation officials	27- 6.8%	25- 7.1%	14- 4.0%	9- 2.6%	20- 5.8%
Teachers and intellectuals	23- 5.8%	25- 7.1%	2- 0.6%	13- 3.7%	10- 2.9%
Protestant clergy	22- 5.5%	11- 3.1%	4- 1.1%	8- 2.3%	2- 0.6%
Catholic clergy	28- 7.0%	17- 4.9%	17- 4.9%	14- 4.0%	2- 0.6%
Lawyers	17- 4.3%	19- 5.4%	6- 1.7%	14- 4.0%	12- 3.5%
Private officials	2- 0.5%	....	....	....	2- 0.6%
Physicians	15- 3.8%	10- 2.9%	2- 0.6%	6- 1.7%	9- 2.6%
Writers and journalists	....	1- 0.3%	....	3- 0.9%	4- 1.2%
Rentiers	1-0.25%	....	4- 1.1%	5- 1.4%	7- 2.0%
Handworkers, laborers, employees	22- 5.5%	....	....	3- 0.9%	....
Others	6- 1.5%	8- 2.3%	1- 0.3%	....	1- 0.3%
No occupation or indefinite occup.	11- 2.8%	10- 2.9%	6- 1.7%	10- 2.9%	16- 4.6%

* The first figure gives the actual number of deputies, the second, the percentage of the total representation. Gertrud Beushausen, *Zur Strukturanalyse parlamentarischen Repräsentation in Deutschand vor der Gründung des Norddeutchen Bundes* (Hamburg Dissertation 1926) pp. 88-89. Beushausen adds that the number of middle and lower officials was very small.